GEORG SIMMEL

and Avant-Garde Sociology

GEORG SIMMEL

and Avant-Garde Sociology

The Birth of Modernity, 1880-1920

RALPH M. LECK

an imprint of Prometheus Books
59 John Glenn Drive, Amherst, New York 14228-2197

Published 2000 by Humanity Books, an imprint of Prometheus Books

Inquiries should be addressed to
Humanity Books
59 John Glenn Drive
Amherst, New York 14228–2197
VOICE: 716–691–0133, ext. 207
FAX: 716–564–2711

04 03 02 01 00   5 4 3 2 1

Library of Congress Cataloging-in-Publication Data

Leck, Ralph M.
Georg Simmel and avant-garde sociology : the birth of modernity, 1880-1920 / Ralph M. Leck.
p. cm.
Includes bibliographical references and index.
ISBN 1–57392–867–4 (paper : alk. paper)
1. Counterculture. 2. Simmel, Georg, 1858-1918. 3. Sociology—Germany—History. 4. Sociology—Philosophy—History. I. Title.

HM647 .L43 2000
306'.1—dc21
00-040921
CIP

Printed in the United States of America on acid-free paper

To

N.A.R.

CONTENTS

GEORG SIMMEL

2. PHILOSOPHICAL SOCIOLOGY: NIETZSCHE, COMPASSION, AND THE CAPITALIST SOUL 63

3. AN AVANT-GARDE SOCIOLOGY OF WOMEN: SIMMEL, MARIE LUISE ENCKENDORFF, AND MARIANNE WEBER 131

4. A GREAT WAR OF SPIRITUAL DECISIONS: SIMMEL AND THE IDEAS OF 1914 167

ACKNOWLEDGMENTS

THE POLITICAL AND THEORETICAL QUESTIONS THAT ANIMATED THE WRITING OF THIS text precede my interest in Georg Simmel. They derive from my interest in Walter Benjamin and European modernism. These interests were initially kindled by George Cotkin. His influence and support are a substrate of this text. I also express my deep appreciation to Mark Poster. His scholarly and pedagogical interests in existential socialism, gender theory, and antifoundational critical theory frame my interpretation of Simmel.

This study is also greatly indebted to Robert Moeller with whom I studied German historiography and European gender history. In the absence of his tutelage, I would have never found my way to the rich historiography of Wilhelmine culture. Guidance and encouragement also came from Lynn Mally whose mentorship through the historiography of European cultural history was invaluable to this study. The mentorship of Harold Mah was also important to my development as an intellectual historian. To Jean-François Lyotard I owe my limited knowledge of Kantian philosophy. His interpretation of Kant in *The Differénd* and his seminar "An Aesthetic of the Present" contributed immensely to my understanding of Simmel's neo-Kantian sociology. Many thanks go as well to Marjorie Beale for her critical reading of the text.

Special thanks go to my parents, Robert D. Leck and Shirley Wood Leck. Their unfailing support, patience, and loving guidance helped to maintain my spirits. Research and writing are so often a long solitary enterprise that can only be sustained via communal encouragement. Very often my energies were recharged by the fellowship of Bill Billingsley, Casey Candaele, Kyle Courdeleone, Anthony Dawahare, Helen Fehervary, Ed Slack, Andy Spencer, Christa Walter, and Alex Zukas.

I thank the Department of History and School of Humanities at the University of California, Irvine, for their financial support. A tremendous debt of gratitude is owed to Margaret Ying, librarian at Rose-Hulman Institute of Technology and the staff of the Interlibrary Loan Division of Indiana State University. Scores of rare and invaluable texts were located as a consequence of her indefatigable bibliographic energies.

I received a research scholarship from the Friedrich-Ebert-Stiftung. Professor Bernd Witte, my FES mentor in Germany, provided sound advice and encouragement. Without the financial support of the Friedrich-Ebert-Stiftung and the guidance of Professor Witte, the research for this manuscript could not have been completed. I express my appreciation to David Bathrick for permission to reprint "Simmel's Afterlife: Tropic Politics and the Culture of War" from *New German Critique* 75 (fall 1998).

The most daunting task faced by English-language scholars of Simmel is translation. Very often I faced what seemed to be intractable conceptual and grammatical difficulties. Continually, I turned to the expertise of Dr. Ann Rider. If any of my quotes exceed a mere literal translation and attain readability, then Ann is responsible. I and Simmel must take the blame for convolution.

INTRODUCTION

SIMMEL'S LEGACY

MORE THAN ANY OTHER THINKER IN TWENTIETH-CENTURY GERMAN INTELLECTUAL history, Georg Simmel is central to understanding German modernism. His intellectual imprint was vast and varied. He founded the modern discipline of sociology and was the animating force for a German sociology of aesthetics. Simmel's philosophy was a major contribution to European existential thought, and it was largely through his pedagogy and publications that Nietzsche's preeminence was articulated to a new generation of Wilhelmine intellectuals. In the seminal anthology of European existentialism, Walter Kaufmann recognized Nietzsche as a founding figure of existentialism.[1] Simmel was not included in this canon. By placing Simmel within the narrative of existential thought, this text seeks not only to revise Kaufmann but to offer a new perspective on Simmel, his legacy, and his place in European intellectual history. For example, Simmel's conception of culture was incorporated into the early Expressionist movement prior to the Great War. One scholar of this expressionistic generation has referred to the movement's genre as "Existence Literature" because so many of its leading intellectuals drew on the existential philosophies of Nietzsche and Kierkegaard.[2] To date, however, the immense contribution of Simmel's conception of culture to the Expressionists' philosophy of existence has gone unnoticed.

Simmel was, above all else, a Promethean iconoclast. What made his thought so powerful and appealing to the expressionistic generation was its combination of modernist aesthetics, antibourgeois sexuality, and anticapitalist philosophy. Consequently, his critical penchant drew a variety of radical students to his seminars at Berlin University. His unequaled cultural stature derived from the fact that he was the closest approximation of an academic activist to be found in Wilhelmine Germany. In fact, it was one of his students who not only coined the modern term activism, but also founded the modernist movement known as *Aktivismus* during the First World War. Simmel's political and cultural influences, however, extend much further. His thought, like a liberal scattering of yeast, gave rise to some of the most nourishing intellectual breads of twentieth-century German cultural history. It was a significant intellectual fulcrum of twentieth-century Western Marxism, an intellectual well-spring for literary Expressionism, and a major influence on the feminist and the homosexual rights movements in Germany. The most compelling reason for reading Simmel and integrating him into the canon of German intellectual history is that German modernism is inconceivable without him.

MODERNITY AND MODERNISM: A METACULTURAL CONTEXT

The central focus of this study, then, is Simmel's enormous contribution to the analysis and production of European modernism. In order to allude to the broader implications of Simmel's influence, one must begin by posing two simple, if perplexing, questions: what is modernism, and how does it differ from modernity? For historians, modernity typically refers to social and economic processes whose origins date to the Commercial Revolution: international trade, the unprecedented growth in the scale and number of urban centers, and the rationalization of the market and production facilitated by the increasing power of the state. The eighteenth century is typically identified as the origin of the modern era. Despite the imprecision of narrative eras, identification of the eighteenth century as the origin of modernity is more or less justified because it was then that two liberal revolutions emerged: the American and French Revolutions as the origin of political liberalism, and the Industrial Revolution as the emergence of economic liberalism, particularly in England.

These broad strokes, however, do not provide a sound definition of the modernity that Simmel experienced and analyzed. Such a definition might best be proffered by distinguishing modernity from modernism. This distinction can be given content by examining the difference between the French Revolution and the Russian Revolutions on the one hand, and the Enlightenment and Nietzsche on the other. First, a hundred years after the French Revolution there was in central Europe (as a result of rapid industrialization on the Continent) a self-conscious and well-organized industrial working class without which the Russian and German Revolutions would not have taken place. The organizational and theoretical sophistication of an industrial working-class politics did not exist in the late eighteenth and early nineteenth centuries. By the turn of the twentieth century, its core on the Continent was the German Social Democrats who were by 1905 not only the largest party in Wilhelmine Germany but also the largest socialist party in the world. In light of the savage pace of German industrialization, the socialist vision was a powerful moral critique of both economic liberalism and aristocratic illiberalism, namely, of Kaiser capitalism and the culture of money. Suffice it to say, the cultural politics of Simmel and his students, no less than those of the German and Russian monarchies, operated in a cultural force field that could not avoid reference to organized socialism and socialist morality, even if that reference was merely polemical. Thus, on the Continent, the presence of a large, organized, industrial proletariat offering an ethical and economic alternative to capitalism distinguishes modernity from modernism.

Secondly, just as the French Revolution was a hundred years removed from a well-organized union of industrial workers, the Enlightenment, as cultural modernity, was well removed from the epistemological ground of European modernism. The Enlightenment was substantially influenced by the scientific cult of reason and by the volumes of travel narratives resulting from exploration. Voltaire's *Candide*, Diderot's "Supplement to Bourgainville's *Voyage*," and Rousseau's noble savage were examples of "otherness" serving as a basis of critique: the critique of the existing theological episteme and its political correlatives as well as a critique of the assumed superiority of urban civilization. The Enlightenment and European modernism are not, then, distinct in their proclivity toward social critique. There is a critical spirit in both. But this identity belies a deeper difference that is perhaps best denoted as the difference between Enlightenment humanism and antihumanist modernism. To refer to modernism as antihumanist is not to make a claim about its disposition toward humanity. Many intellectuals, upon hearing a discussion or affirmation of antihumanism, assume wrongly that this is an affirmation of anti-*humaneness*. This is in part justified because the central proponent of a critique of Enlightenment humanism, Nietzsche, espoused misogyny, antisocialism, and a brutal defense of self-interest. Nonetheless, any assumed systematic correlation of antihumanism and inhumanity, as this study will show, is untenable.

The distinction between Enlightenment humanism and antihumanist modernism is not a social or political distinction, although it has important social and political implications; it is cultural and philosophical. For the major thinkers of the Enlightenment there was a philosophical terre firma: natural law and natural rights. For European modernists, there was, in the wake of Nietzsche, no such thing as a self-evident and universal Truth. Modernism was characterized by an aesthetic self-consciousness intent on the construction of a new morality, and here the notion of "aesthetics" is a way of life, a means of (re)creating oneself, as opposed to a reference to the realm of the arts. Truth and value are literally understood to derive from the self or, in the case of Nietzschean socialists like Georges Batailles, social-self creation. Life itself was an aesthetic and existential process of creation wherein there is no recourse to epistemological reification, be it theological or Enlightened. Historicized morality (good versus bad) replaced ontologized morality (Good versus Evil). In the language of poststructuralism, Nietzschean philosophy was antifoundational, namely, opposed to theological and scientific claims of absolute Truth. With Nietzsche, Enlightened terre firma thus gave way to a cultural and historical quick sand in which one must wallow for life. To reject that quick sand by struggling for solid ground ensured spiritual death through a descent into cultural decadence, i.e., recourse to fatuous claims to absolute Truth. What cannot be stressed strongly enough is the impact of Nietzsche's philosophical antihumanism on Simmel and his intellectual progeny. This, more than any other cultural characteristic, delineated their modernism from the Enlightened culture of modernity.

BETWEEN NIETZSCHE AND MARX

Opposition to bourgeois cultural and economic values (if not always in the form of industrial socialism) and Nietzschean philosophy were the two major ingredients of Simmelian modernism. This study contributes to an understanding of how these forces coalesced, in a multitude of ways, in the countercultural politics of Simmel and his disciples. In the context of Wilhelmine Germany, this coalescence is described in this study as *Geist-Politik*, or spiritual politics. The spiritual politics of the Simmel circle occupied a cultural space between Nietzsche and Marx. Unlike Nietzsche, Simmel and his disciples were sympathetic toward the socialist critique of capitalism, while maintaining the aristocratic ethical self-conception of Nietzsche. The aristocratic radicalism of the Simmel circle preceded, in the realm of Wilhelmine cultural politics, the political elitism of the Activist League and the Communist Party, groups that emerged from the culture of war. Unlike Marx and Lenin, however, the critique of bourgeois culture found in the Simmel circle often was carried out through spiritual discourses. Simmel and his disciples conceived of themselves as a spiritual elite; theirs was a politics of spiritual intellect.

Although the neologism *Geist-Politik* is dealt with in detail later, its significance for the organization of this study is worth noting here as well. The Nietzschean critique of Christian morality and the socialist critique of liberal ethics were hyphenated in Simmel's critique of bourgeois culture.

We witness this legacy in two cultural groups; the first group was most influenced by the Nietzschean Simmel, and chapters 3 and 5 chronicle the contribution of Simmel's Nietzschean pedagogy to a new politics of gender emerging from the Expressionist movement. A second group of disciples, discussed in chapter 6, were less influenced by Simmel's Nietzschean critique of bourgeois sexuality than by his ethical and aesthetic repudiation of capitalism. By systematically demonstrating the relationship of these groups to Simmel, this book will show that no one was more central to the matrix of German modernism, the birth of a sexual counterculture, and the construction of an antibourgeois ethics than Georg Simmel.

As an allusion to the neo-Kantian revival of the Wilhelmine period, one could say Simmel was the a priori of German modernism, namely, a figure who, more than any other, makes the inconceivable diversity, complexity, and undecidability of German modernism conceivable. But it is not simply as an ideal type that Simmel can be seen as the a priori of German modernism. I alluded before to the fact that his thought was the centrifugal axis and pedagogical origin of numerous modernist trajectories. Through his student, Kurt Hiller (chapter 5), Simmel's theory of culture became the philosophical basis of Germany's greatest modernist movement: Expressionism. It was also in the person of Hiller that Simmel's thought would serve as the framework for a major assault on laws prohibiting homosexuality. Moreover, Hiller's political dispositions are particularly useful for highlighting the political ambiguity of Simmel's legacy: a combination of anticapitalist egalitarianism and cultural elitism.

Besides contributing to the movement for homosexual rights, Simmel's philosophy influenced Helene Stöcker, who drew upon his theories of sexuality in founding one of the most significant feminist organizations of the Wilhelmine period. But the spectrum of his cultural influence extends still further. It includes the history of Western Marxism as well (chapter 6). Simmel was the primary intellectual mentor to Ernst Bloch and Georg Lukács, and, thus, his cultural originality is vital for understanding the origins of Marxist critical theory. Other left-wing modernists, such as Siegfried Kracauer, Karl Mannheim, and Walter Benjamin also attended Simmel's seminars and were profoundly influenced by his thought. Finally, Simmel's thought (particularly his theories of differentiation and his philosophical sociology with its emphasis on the problems of representation) points in the direction of poststructural thought. A rereading of Simmel, then, will not only enrich our understanding of European modernism and German intellectual history; it will refine our understanding of contemporary antifoundational thought as well.

THE HISTORIOGRAPHICAL CONTEXT: PROFILES OF SIMMEL

By investigating the discourse of spirit (*Geist*) and soul (*Seele*) in the work of Simmel and his countercultural progeny, this study charts a particular constellation of German cultural history. The distinctive cartography of this cultural history can best be brought to relief through an analysis of the historiographical terrain of Simmel scholarship. What follows is a categorical interpretation of his reception that does not seek to be a definitive bibliography. For the sake of brevity, the primary focus will be monographs.

By far the most common in his historiography is a profile of Simmel as a sociologist. A representative textual correlative of the sociological Simmel would include the following texts: N. J. Spykman's *The Social Theory of Georg Simmel* (1964), Lewis Coser's *Georg Simmel* (1965), Herbert Becher's *Georg Simmel: Die Grundlagen seiner Soziologie* (1971), Donald Levine's *Simmel and Parsons: Two Approaches to the Study of Society* (1980), Sibylle Hübner-Funk's *Georg Simmels Konzeption von Gesellschaft* (1982), David Frisby's *Georg Simmel* (1984), and Harry Liebersohn's *Fate and Utopia in German Sociology, 1870–1923* (1988). The primary textual matrix of interpretation for all of these works includes canonical sociologists such as Max Weber, Émile Durkheim, and Talcott Parsons. Given the number of fine studies focussing on the sociological Simmel, this study avoids a replication of this matrix of interpretation. Additionally, these studies typically undervalue the significance of Nietzschean philosophy to Simmel's sociological project.

A second historiographical bracketing of Simmel's legacy is his profile as an existential philosopher or philosopher of life (*Lebensphilosoph*). Rudolph Weingartner's *Culture and Experience: The Philosophy of Georg Simmel* (1962) is perhaps the best English language text. It suffers, however, from a narrow focus on Simmel's *Lebensanschauung*, a text published in the year of his passing, 1918. Horst Müller's *Lebensphilosophie und Religion bei Georg Simmel* (1960) and Peter-Otto Ullrich's *Immanent Transzendenz: Georg Simmels Entwurf einer nach-christlichen Religionsphilosoph* (1981) foreshadow this study's emphasis on Simmel as a post-Christian existential philosopher.

The best examination of the Kantian inflection and neo-Kantian context of Simmel's philosophy is found in Max Frischeisen-Köhler's essay "Georg Simmel" which appeared in the Wilhelmine journal, *Kantstudien*, in 1919 and subsequently as a book. This study argues that Simmel transposed Kant's philosophy into the realm of critical and sociological thought. This transposition is evidenced by Simmel's life-long attentiveness to the productive necessity of interpretive form. Three texts highlight the concept of form in Simmel's philosophy and sociology: A. M. Bevers' *Dynamik der Formen bei Georg Simmel*, Rudolph Weingartner's "Form and Content in Simmel's Philosophy of Life," and Mari Steinhoff's "Die Form als soziologische Grundkategorie bei Georg Simmel."[3]

The most recent and still emerging interpretation of Simmel is as a poststructuralist and postmodernist thinker. In his *Literary Methods and Sociological Theory: Case Studies of Simmel and Weber* (1988), Bryan Green reads Simmel's *Philosophy of Money* as an example of deconstructionist theory. In their *Postmodern(ized) Simmel* (1993), Deena and Michael Weinstein similarly seek to establish Simmel as a postmodernist and deconstructionist. These conflations of Simmel and poststructuralism are highly problematic. Ironically, in the name of interpretive difference, they convert similarity into identity. Simmel's uniqueness, his existential theory as a potential resistance to poststructuralism, and the particularity of his theoretical/political positionality is reduced to a mere emblem of contemporary philosophical fashion. These works do serve an important purpose, however. They point to Simmel's relevance to contemporary theoretical and political debates, and, indeed, this study argues for the comparability of Simmel and Jean-François Lyotard's Kantian critical theory. Simmel, nonetheless, must remain a point of critical comparison to, and not simply an affirmation of, poststructuralism. This historical monograph aspires to be a point of departure for just such an important dialogue.

There are two interpretations of Simmel against which this study is positioned. The first, Simmel as a tragic thinker, is by far the most significant because it encompasses much of the sociological and philosophical literature. The list of scholars who interpret Simmel as a tragic thinker is so inclusive that this interpretation lends itself to the title of hegemony more than any other: Andrew Arato, Paul Brienes, Michael Löwy, David Frisby, Jürgen Habermas, Michael Holzman, Gertrud Kantorowicz, Michael Landmann, Georg Lukács, Regina Mahlman, Hartmut Scheible, Ernst Troeltsch, and Rudolph Weingartner.[4] The reason for the pervasiveness of this interpretation is that it constitutes a partial truth. Stated differently, it is one potential interpretation of Simmel's thought. However, in attempting to assess Simmel's cultural influence, this study asserts that the tragic interpretation of Simmel's thought makes sense only after 1914. Prior to the Great War, his philosophy and sociology were largely existential, promising the possibility of personal freedom in and against monetary culture.

The second and far less prevalent interpretation of Simmel against which this study is positioned is the perception of Simmel as a "romantic anticapitalist."[5] While integrating Simmel into his conception of romantic anticapitalism, Löwy wrote:

> Nietzsche sharply diverged from the romantic current and brought a new

> dimension to the "German ideology." . . . Suffice it to say that when romantic anticapitalism developed in certain literary and academic circles at the turn of the century, it often passed through the ideological mediation of Nietzsche's thought.[6]

This passage constitutes a strange intellectual sleight of hand. With one hand, Löwy deftly presents Nietzsche as a challenge to his own rounded interpretation of romantic anticapitalism. With the other hand, he glosses over this cultural difference by suggesting that romantic anticapitalists often passed through Nietzsche's antiromantic thought and remained romantic. It is here emphatically maintained that Simmel was a Nietzschean anticapitalist who possessed none of the romantic longing for a precapitalist community (*Gemeinschaft*) that one finds archetypically in Ferdinand Tönnies' *Society and Community*. There is no longing for a golden age—be it ancient Greece or Catholic medieval Europe—present in Simmel's work. In contrast to romantic anticapitalists, Simmel embraced, if critically, the liberatory potential of the capitalist money economy. His prescription for a moral refinement of the liberatory potential of monetary culture followed not from a nostalgia for the past but from a Nietzschean anticapitalism heralding the creation of a new society and social soul. Simmel, essentially, was a modernist, not a romantic antimodernist. For instance, while many romantic critics of modernity relied on pastoral imagery, he was fascinated with and intellectually enveloped by urban culture. It is worth noting, moreover, that Simmel became a great inspiration to the first movement of German lyric, Expressionism, which rejected romantic pastoral lyric and engaged images of the city. Simmel's legacy, then, does not belong within the narrative history of romantic anticapitalism. He is a modernist both in his Nietzschean sensibility and his embrace of the social potential of an urban, industrial, international, monetary economy.

Two additional elements distinguish this study from most others. First, this monograph demonstrates Simmel's tremendous impact on the history of sexual politics. This is unquestionably the most unknown aspect of his cultural legacy. Secondly, this study will be the first to focus on Simmel's impact on politics and aesthetics during his lifetime. Frisby, perhaps the preeminent Simmel scholar, has remarked that Simmel's influence was greatest in the realm of aesthetics. Proof of this influence is to be found in Frisby's own *Fragments of Modernity: Theories of Modernity in the Works of Simmel, Kracauer, and Benjamin*, which focuses almost entirely on Simmel's posthumous legacy. In contrast to Frisby, the historical scope of this work frames Simmel's influence during his lifetime. Moreover, in the interest of avoiding replication, this study focuses on intellectuals other than Kracauer and Benjamin.

Finally, it is worth noting that Frisby's interpretation of Simmel contains interpretive threads that are strangely absent in much of the English language historiography of the so-called sociological Simmel; Frisby stresses Simmel's relationship to socialism and the history of socialist aesthetics. Frisby's placement of Simmel within the narrative history of German socialist aesthetics is also fundamental to this study. However, in contrast to Frisby, Simmel's linkage to socialist aesthetics is posited as only one arena of his broader impact upon an antibourgeois counterculture. The maturation of his countercultural thought within the avant-garde milieu of fin-de-siècle Berlin is the subject of chapter 1.

NOTES

1. Walter Kaufmann, *Existentialism from Dostoevsky to Sartre* (New York: Meridian, 1975); see also Walter Kaufmann, *Nietzsche: Philosopher, Psychologist, Antichrist* (Princeton: Princeton University Press, 1974).

2. Thomas Anz, *Literatur der Existenz: Literarische Psychopathographie und ihre soziale Bedeutung im Frühexpressionismus* (Stuttgart: Metzlersche, 1977). Simmel's contribution to the literature of existence is not dealt with by Anz. I chronicle this cultural linkage in chapter 4.

3. A. M. Bevers, *Dynamik der Formen bei Georg Simmel: Eine Studie über die methodische und theoretische Einheit eines Gesamtwerkes* (Berlin: Duncker & Humblot, 1985); Rudolph Weingartner, "Form and Content in Simmel's Philosophy of Life," in *Georg Simmel, 1858–1918*, ed. Kurt H. Wolff, 1959; Mari Steinhoff, "Die Form als soziologische Grundkategorie bei Georg Simmel," *Kölner Vierteljahrshefte für Soziologie* 3, no. 1 (1923): 215–59.

4. Andrew Arato and Paul Briennes, *The Young Lukács and the Origins of Western Marxism* (New York: Continuum, 1979); Löwy, *Georg Lukács—From Romanticism to Bolshevism*; David Frisby, "Introduction to the Translation," in Georg Simmel, *Philosophy of Money*, trans. Tom Bottomore and David Frisby (New York: Routledge, 1990); Jürgen Habermas, "Simmel als Zeitdiagnostiker," in Georg Simmel, *Philosophische Kultur* (Berlin: Verlag Klaus Wagenbach, 1986); Michael Holzman, "Georg Simmel," *Lukács's Road to God* (Lanham, Md.: University Press of America, 1985); Gertrud Kantorowicz, "Vorwort," in Georg Simmel, *Fragmente und Aufsätze* (München: Drei Masken, 1923); Michael Landmann, "Konflikt und Tragödie. Zur Philosophie Georg Simmels," *Zeitschrift für Philosophische Forschung* 6 (1951–1952): 115–33; Georg Lukács, "Die Lebensphilosophie in der Vorkriegszeit (Simmel)," in *Die Zerstörung der Vernunft: Der Weg des Irrationalismus von Schelling zu Hitler* (Berlin: Aufbau-Verlag, 1988); Regina Mahlman, "Dualität des Individuums," in *Homo Duplex: Die Zweiheit des Menschen bei Georg Simmel* (Würzburg: Königshausen & Neumann, 1983); Hartmut Scheible, "Georg Simmel und die '*Tragödie der Kultur*,'" *Die Neue Rundschau* 91, no. 2 (1980): 133–64; Ernst Troeltsch, *Der Historismus und seine Probleme* (Tübingen: J. C. B. Mohr, 1922); Rudolph Weingartner, *Culture and Experience: The Philosophy of Georg Simmel* (Middletown, Conn.: Wesleyan University Press, 1962).

5. See Löwy, "Towards a Sociology of the Anti-Capitalist Intelligentsia," in *Georg Lukács*; Werner Jung, "Variationen des 'Romantischen Antikapitalismus,' " in *Wandelungen einer ästhetischen Theorie—Georg Lukács Werke 1907 bis 1923* (Köln: Pahl-Rugenstein Verlag, 1981).

6. Löwy, "Towards a Sociology of the Anti-Capitalist Intelligentsia," p. 26.

1

THE AVANT-GARDE ORIGINS OF SOCIOLOGY

Simmel's Unity of Extremes, 1880–1900

Our era—which raved about both Böcklin and Impressionism, about Naturalism and Symbolism, about Socialism and Nietzsche—manifests its highest life-stimulus in the form of an oscillation between the extreme poles of humanity.

Georg Simmel, "Sociological Aesthetics,"1896[1]

I resist anything better than my own diversity.

Walt Whitman, "Song of Myself"

A WHITMANESQUE COMMENCEMENT IS APPROPRIATE FOR SEVERAL REASONS, AND not simply because Walt Whitman and Georg Simmel shared cultural attributes—such as a pantheistic cosmology that was given voice through the spiritual discourse of the "soul"—and a similar economic environment of rapid industrialization. From the middle of the nineteenth century, Western high culture became suffused with compassion for the common victims of social iniquity and pitiless self-interest. In the works of Walt Whitman, Leo Tolstoy, Emile Zola, and Gerhart Hauptman, the common lives of working men and women found unyielding expression in tragic dramas and passionate lyric. These authors produced a literary atmosphere shrill with social invective, contemptuous of false conventions, and supercharged with the aesthetics of social compassion. This was the cultural atmosphere of Georg Simmel's intellectual maturation. The young Simmel, no less than most of the literary figures whose dramatic chorus filled the cultural air of Berlin in the late 1880s, was neither a socialist nor a revolutionary. But he was a member of an iconoclastic, often bohemian, and reform-minded German intelligentsia. His immersion in Berlin's Naturalist counterculture in the late 1880s reinforced his interest in historical subject-matter, and, more importantly perhaps, provided him with a style of life wherein art and politics made no attempt to evade one another. Art, long associated with the search for beauty, now cohabited with a volatile spirit of social justice. Art became a civic model of life that prescribed social critique.

SIMMEL AND THE COUNTERCULTURAL COSMOS OF THE LATE NINETEENTH CENTURY

The development of Simmel's intellectual leverage in the 1890s was shaped by a Naturalistic ethics that recognized purely aesthetic approaches to social progress as insufficient. Art intensified the significance of ethics as a category of life. Within the Naturalist counterculture, proletarian and feminist themes gave rise to a new spiritual orientation; cultural refinement was enchained with a gripping repugnance for the bestial self-interest of commercial culture and for social hierarchy. In renouncing the ethical validity of commercial self-interest, Simmel embraced the Naturalists' urge to combat economic injustice and sexual inequality. His interest in politics peaked in the period from 1885 to 1900. Before the turn of the century he wrote several articles on feminism and published in numerous socialist journals. After 1900, with the publication of *The Philosophy of Money*, he turned more exclusively to aesthetics. Certainly, he continued publishing sociological essays and published *Soziologie* in 1908. However, his *Soziologie* lacked the thematic coherence of *The Philosophy of Money*, and at least five of its ten chapters were written before 1900.[2] His turn away from overt political and sociological concerns and toward aesthetics after 1900 was a *tendency* and was in no way exclusive of other interests. His aesthetic concerns coexisted with a continued interest in philosophy, literature, history, sociology, and politics. Here I will simply suggest that Simmel's move from a critical sociology of Kaiser capitalism in *The Philosophy of Money* to aesthetics was an attempt to repackage his critical philosophy in a less obvious, and that meant less overtly political, form.

Despite attempts to periodize Simmel's thought, there is something constant in his thought and pedagogy from the 1890s onward, namely, a unity of two critical perspectives: an intense sociological critique of repressive institutions and an equally robust defense of aesthetic individuality. Aesthetics spurred a sociological ethics, and sociological inquiry was always conjoined to an instructive philosophy of aesthetic individualism. This combination of proclivities is present in very diverse movements of European modernism, from the iconoclastic realism of Gustave Courbet of the mid-nineteenth century to the revolutionary antirealism of the Surrealists.[3] We should also note the nineteenth-century provenance of critical aesthetics.

Individuality historically had been suppressed by the tyrannical institutions of the aristocracy, but, by the end of the nineteenth century, the control of repressive institutions was increasingly being usurped by the bourgeoisie. Therefore, those in the aesthetic counterculture expressed and explored their individual freedom often by means of satire and tragic drama whose intent was an overt savaging of bourgeois conventions. The historical preconditions for modernist aesthetics can best be represented figuratively. If one arrow points aesthetics toward the external goal of social transformation, and another marks the aesthetic direction toward intense introspective and creative individuality, then the quest of modern art can be seen as containing a contradiction. But just as a force acting in one direction can animate one acting in an opposite direction, the sociology of modern art might be seen as a complimentary unity of extremes.

Simmel's thought is expressive of the same crushing conflicts between the individual and social institutions that one finds in the novels of Zola and the dramas of Hauptmann. This was no accident. His intellectual maturation took place in the late 1880s within Naturalist circles in Berlin. The tragic subjugation of the free-willing individual by the forces of social convention that dominated Naturalist literature was the central presupposition of Simmel's sociology and philosophy. However, by the 1890s he responded to tragic Naturalism by championing the heroic individualism of Nietzsche. His espousal of Nietzsche did not entail a renunciation of the political concerns of Naturalism; rather, Nietzschean philosophy deepened his defiance. Nietzsche's ethical individualism was a model for how to resist, if not subdue, conventional economic and sexual hierarchies. It was in this sense, rather than via the glorified life of the vagabond à la Baudelaire, that Simmel was countercultural and semibohemian.

Simmel was a countercultural member of the upper bourgeoisie. His sociology of the stranger might best be interpreted as a self-reflection upon his relationship to his class:

> [The stranger] is fixed within a particular social group, or within a group whose boundaries are similar to spatial boundaries. But his position in this group is determined, essentially, by the fact that he has not belonged to it from the beginning, that he imports qualities into it which do not and cannot stem from the group itself.[4]

Simmel was a member of the bourgeoisie who never belonged to its economic way of life. This enabled him, as he says of the stranger, to produce different pictures of the same object. Simmel's objects were the institutional and ideological edifices of society itself. His ability to see them differently was connected to an outsider's model of freedom and objectivity. "The objectivity [of the stranger]," explained Simmel, "may be defined as freedom: the objective individual is bound by no commitments which could prejudice his perception, understanding, and evaluation of the given."[5] The Naturalist avant-garde embodied this model of freedom; here, social elites created a self-image as outsiders whose aesthetic freedom expressed itself in honest pictures of society. Naturalism was a new objectivity that married aesthetic individualism and social critique, and Simmel's thought was stamped by it.

Simmel's thought, as a particular unity of extremes, was un-Hegelian both philosophically and politically. Philosophically, his thought was fully tied to the period's neo-Kantian moorings of epistemological skepticism. He did not believe that it was possible or desirable to resolve all philosophical tensions. Politically, the ethical individualism of Simmel, like that of Tolstoy, did not prescribe the reintegration of the spiritually elevated individual into society à la Hegel. The gilded degradation of social and moral corruption was to be renounced once and for all. Above all, Simmel's thought sought to balance, rather than resolve, the modernist predilection for social responsibility and ethical individualism. He was aware of the perils of both totalized social ethics and unrestrained individualism. The call to social responsibility and social justice could easily destroy the basis of morality itself, individual free will, by maintaining the self-evident and law-like requirement of a particular social ethics. We find this impulse no less in Edmund Burke's defense of aristocratic institutions than we do in dogmatic Marxism. Conversely, the defense of ethical individualism can easily convert itself into an unconscious sibling of the wolfish selfishness of the bourgeoisie. Like an unknown brother who was put up for adoption, ethical individualism can reinforce the antisocial ethics of economic liberalism by partaking in the sinister myth that self-interest is synonymous with social interest. Simmel's thought avoided both pitfalls. He rejected the ethical reification of class ethics. More specifically, Simmel criticized the ethical presuppositions of Kaiser capitalism while taking issue with the reification of egalitarian morality that he identified with socialism. If he was sympathetic to egalitarian goals, he reminded socialists that equality was not a moral absolute but a free choice. He feared the tyranny of an ethical system that expelled from its domain the basis of ethics themselves: individual free will. Conversely, Simmel renounced as illogical the essential presupposition of economic liberalism, namely, that self-interest was always already social virtue. He cautioned that moral individualism, like that of Nietzschean philosophy, must be distinguished from bourgeois morality. Therefore, through his reception of Nietzschean philosophy, he espoused a model of individual free will that presented Nietzschean ethics as incompatible with the commercial rapacity of the bourgeoisie and the ethical slovenliness of the aristocracy.

Simmel was the brightest academic sun in the Wilhelmine galaxy of

German modernism, and this book interprets his work as illustrative of the polarities found in late nineteenth-century high culture. Various phrases will be used to depict this polarity as a unity of antipodes: introspective Naturalism, practical idealism, Nietzschean sociology, objectictive idealism, and sociological aesthetics. Perhaps most important for our narrative of Simmel's legacy is the understanding of him as a Nietzschean anticapitalist. His thought is explicated as a blend of Nietzschean philosophy (aesthetic resistance to social fate) and sociology (an analysis of social determinism). The fulcrum of his critical sociology was an identification of commercial capitalism as the modern variant of Nietzschean slave morality. To exercise moral freedom, it was axiomatic that one must resist convention, and in the context of Wilhemine society that demanded a conscious transgression of the bourgeois culture (*Bürgerlichkeit*). Both in its form and content Simmel's sociology was a countercultural critique of convention. However, his sociology of commercial culture was not simply a result of the logic of Nietzschean existentialism. It represents the birth of sociology as well. The very foundation of modern sociology in Germany (e.g., Ferdinand Tönnies, Werner Sombart, and Max Weber) was tied to a social analysis of capitalist culture, and Simmel's sociology was, in this regard, no different. What distinguished Simmel's sociological thought was (1) its embrace of Nietzsche's philosophy of life and (2) its bohemian cultural origins. Consequently, Simmel stood out as something more than a mandarin academic. Like the modern artists that he admired as a young man in Berlin, he was an iconoclastic spokesman for a new antibourgeois world.

While this book puts forth a rounded interpretation of Simmel as a Nietzschean anticapitalist, a Whitmanesque forbearance is in order. Like the author of "Song of Myself," Simmel resisted anything better than his own diversity. And, therefore, we must be very circumspect about slavish interpretations. For Simmel possessed a hydra of intellectual talents; he was a paragon of interdisciplinary genius. Walter Benjamin, to whom his interdisciplinary gifts are best compared, remarked that Simmel was at home in every branch of the humanities and could "approach a subject from all sides."[6] Simmel, for instance, exhibited the unusual gift of being able to extract the sociological essence of aesthetics and the spiritual essence of politics. His interdisciplinary reach and his unsurpassed insights about modernity have established him as a classic thinker who deserves his place in the pantheon of European intellectual history.

Simmel's precise placement within this pantheon is problematic because he resists all-encompassing interpretations. Should he be hailed as a great Nietzschean or Kantian philosopher; as a philosopher of history, aesthetics or mass culture; as a social critic; as founder of modern sociology; as a feminist or a precursor to existential Marxism? He was all of these identities and more. Simmel was a polymath who never set out to create a system of thought. His philosophy of life consciously pursued the transgression of disciplinary boundaries. Often his analytical brilliance displayed itself in demonstrations of (1) the impossibility of logical laws of history and (2) the impossibility of bracketing one area of life from any other. At his core, he was an existentialist who, like Immanual Levinus today, defined ethics as the first philosophy. If we cannot hope to represent thoroughly the variance and subtlety of his thought, we can at least grasp the historical underprops of his life in the late nineteenth century. In this chapter, his intellectual progression is broached through the presentation of a series of interpretive horizons: family, academic career, Naturalism, cosmopolitan Berlin, socialism, the generation of 1890, Kant, and Nietzsche. The following examination of these cultural forces is the backdrop for a history of his cultural legacy.

FAMILY AS CULTURAL CAPITAL

A nuanced biography of Georg Simmel has yet to appear. The reason for this is twofold. First, most of Simmel's autobiographical memoranda were destroyed or lost in the Second World War. Georg Simmel's only child, Hans, somehow succeeded in gaining release from the concentration camp Dachau, and emigrated hastily from Berlin to the United States in the late 1930s. He escaped Nazi Germany with his wife and four children. However, he was unable to save his possessions and arranged to have two loads of cargo shipped to the United States via Hamburg. This shipment contained the bulk of his father's memoirs and correspondences. It is unclear whether this cargo was misplaced, confiscated by the Gestapo, or later destroyed by the Allied bombings that reduced much of Hamburg to rubble. To date, Simmel's private effects have not resurfaced. However, the recent founding of the Georg-Simmel-Gesellschaft at the University of Bielefeld and the publication of his collected works bodes well for the future of Simmel scholarship. One of the goals of the Simmel-Gesellschaft is the construction of an archive whose purpose is the central assemblage of Simmel's biographical and intellectual estate. This project portends an ongoing refinement of our knowledge of Simmel's biography and its relationship to his philosophical and sociological work.

The second reason for an incomplete biography of Simmel is purely academic. Most scholars are interested in Simmel's ideas and his status as a founder of the discipline of sociology. The vast majority of Simmel's historiography assumes the irrelevance of his biography to an analysis of his sociology. With respect to the issue of the significance of his biography for an analysis of his thought, this text steers a middle course. Most studies of Simmel's sociological thought not only eschew the integration of biographical materials, they also tend to be expository. Conversely, my analysis of Simmel's thought situates his legacy within a larger cultural and intellectual context: Berlin, European Naturalism, German Social Democracy, Literary Expressionism, radical feminism, the homosexual rights movement, Western Marxism, and the culture of war. And when it is obviously relevant to his cultural reception and political legacy, biographical elements are integrated into my analysis. Simmel's influence upon Georg Lukács and Ernst Bloch, for example, cannot be understood in the absence of a thorough grasp of their shared Jewish descent and economic circumstances. It should not be assumed, however, that his biography and intellectual production are in a relationship of cause and effect. The relationship was much more dialectical. In the context of German academia, for example, his work was perceived as being quite radical, and this altered his academic life history. His inability to secure a professorial position until after he had celebrated his fifty-fifth birthday resulted from an official recognition of the critical character of his work. He was widely recognized as the greatest cultural critic of the present, and while this well-deserved reputation endeared him to radical students in Berlin, it was a tremendous liability in securing a professorial chair.

Before we turn to the theme of Simmel's scholastic life and difficulties within academia, his biographical particulars should be recounted. The patrilineal character of European culture accounts, perhaps, for the paucity of matrilineal and a fair amount of patrimonial knowledge of Simmel's descent. Although baptized in the Lutheran Church, Simmel was of Jewish descent. His paternal grandfather, Isaak Simmel, was a prosperous businessman who was born in 1780 in the Jewish community of Dyhernfurth, Silesia. Isaak eventually moved to Breslau where, as a Jew, he faced legal restrictions on his citizenship. Georg Simmel's father, Eduard Simmel, was born in Breslau in 1810. One of Eduard's earliest recollections was the image of himself as a very young boy upon a horse-drawn wagon while accompanying his father on a business trip. Eduard, like many sons throughout history, embraced the vocation of his father and became a businessman. He was often on the road, and during a trip to Paris in 1832, Eduard was baptized in the Catholic Church. He then took the name Eduard Marie.

In 1838, Eduard Simmel married Flora Bodstein who was then twenty years old. She, too, was a native of Breslau. Furthermore, like Eduard's family, her family was of Jewish descent and, like Eduard, she was baptized as a Christian, although not as a Catholic but as a Lutheran. (Consequently, Georg Simmel had lived knowledge of the Jewish, Catholic, and Lutheran traditions.) Shortly after their marriage, Eduard and Flora resettled in Berlin, where Eduard's business ventures thrived. In the early 1840s, he was the first person to import and distribute for sale fine French jams.

Flush with the success of importing culinary goods for the upper class, he and a group investors founded Felix and Sarotti, a firm that produced fine chocolates. Its products were so well received that the Prussian royal family named Felix and Sarotti its chief supplier of chocolates.

For unknown reasons, Eduard Simmel eventually separated from his partners in the chocolate business. For the Simmel family this proved to be an inauspicious economic divorce. The once prosperous family suffered worsened financial conditions. Georg Simmel recalled that the financial stress was accompanied by psychological correlatives, and this contributed to the memory of an unhappy childhood. Nonetheless, the family was never poor. Real difficulties only arose much later, after Eduard's death in 1874. Georg was fifteen years old. Since Georg was the youngest of seven children, it is safe to assume that most of his siblings were no longer living at home. However, we know very little about the life course of his siblings and few of his surviving correspondences were addressed to them. In any case, Georg Simmel's only child, Hans Simmel, reports that his father recalled this period as one of economic and psychological distress. We can imagine that Georg, unlike those siblings who no longer lived at home, bore the omnipresent weight of his mother's despair.

Georg and his mother were rescued from their distress by a close friend of the family, Julius Friedländer, who was known to Georg and his siblings as Uncle Dol. Although much older than Flora, she welcomed his companionship and the financial and emotional security it provided. Friedländer was extremely wealthy. He had founded the music company Peters, which published a great repertoire of classical music for piano and stringed instruments. Peters not only offered a broad range of music, its publications were also quite cheap, and this created new markets for sheet music, particularly among the learned bourgeoisie. Friedländer eventually consented to sell his portion of Peters for which he received over a million marks. Subsequently, his business acumen was directed toward property management and the acquisition of real estate in and around Berlin.

At least one of Friedländer's business transactions came to involve Georg Simmel in a dramatic way. On November 1, 1886, the National Newspaper ran a story about the attempted murder of Dr. Georg Simmel, who intermittently managed properties while his stepfather was out of the city. Under his temporary administration was the bronze wares factory of a Herr Guggenbüchler. The rent for this property was long overdue and, hence, Friedländer exercised his legal right to evict the tenant. A law enforcement agent informed Herr Guggenbüchler of his eviction on the evening of October 31. Shortly thereafter, Herr Guggenbüchler took a first-class horse-drawn taxi to Simmel's apartment on Landgrafen Street. He engaged Simmel in conversation about the eviction and then, suddenly, pulled out a revolver and fired a shot which missed its target. Simmel ran hurriedly down the hallway toward the street. Guggenbüchler gave chase and fired two additional shots. The first went through Simmel's hat and wounded him on the head and the second struck him on the shoulder blade.[7] We know little more about this incident or about the lingering effects of the injuries. But it is symbolic in many ways. Simmel's best works can be read as a spiritual manual for avoiding the imprimatur of avarice that so often accompanies the possession of private property and the acquisition of wealth. Guggenbüchler's bullets were symbolic of a moral accusation that demanded Simmel's reflection upon the ethical meaning of his membership in Berlin's economic elite. We should not eschew the conjectural insight that Simmel's wounds were not simply physical but were a psychological basis for his future sociology of commercial interiority.

For the purposes of our narrative, Julius Friedländer's relationship to Georg Simmel was significant for two reasons. First, his stepfather facilitated cultural continuity within the Simmel family. Musical and culinary culture surrounded Georg before his father's death. The family's financial difficulties were not so dire that they precluded expenditures on culture. The Simmel household not only included a piano (a cultural marker distinguishing the upper and cultured bourgeoisie from the petite bourgeoisie), the familial budget also afforded young Georg both piano and violin lessons. We can glean some semblance of the familial atmosphere in Hans Simmel's biographical description of his father, Georg, often playing four-handed piano with his sister. This atmosphere would have been alive to other aesthetic refinements and delicacies of decorum. Given his father's business concerns, Georg would have been exposed to the realm of culinary sophistication as well. The joys of aesthetic refinement, which we identify with the cultural hegemony of the upper classes, were a cornerstone of the Simmel household. The intergration of Uncle Dol into the family after the death of Eduard Simmel in 1874 meant the continuation and perhaps intensification of aesthetic diversions. Like Eduard Simmel, Uncle Dol made his living via the commercialization of aesthetic pleasure. Uncle Dol thereby reinforced not only the existing cultural sophistication of the Simmel family but also the integration of commercial life and aesthetic culture that had characterized Eduard Simmel's vocation.

Second, Uncle Dol bequeathed to Georg a life-long condition of economic independence. As the youngest child in the Simmel family, Georg was the sibling in whom Uncle Dol took the most interest. Friedländer became Georg's legal guardian and later adopted him. Upon his death, the bulk of Uncle Dol's inheritance descended to Georg. The vast sums of money that Georg inherited are crucial to an understanding of his thought and legacy. First, the inheritance of vast sums of unearned money placed Simmel among the economic elite. His economic status facilitated reflection upon the ethical meaning of wealth. Indeed, the spiritual meaning of money and social hierarchy were redounding themes of his work. Second, for virtually all of his adult life, Simmel was financially beholden to no one. His work, then, was indicative of a creative mind freed from the financial pressures to conform that typically accompany subordinate positions in labor relations. Furthermore, he was released from the financial and cultural restraints of the economic status quo. No doubt, his intellectual acuity and love of learning were key elements for academic success. Simmel had these in spades. But, if acuity and familial cultural capital were the rich soil facilitating intellectual development, then economic means were like the sun. Without the brilliant light of a sizeable inheritance, it is unlikely that Simmel's critical and sociological perspicacity would have blossomed with such repletion. His inheritance facilitated a rich cultural life in Berlin unencumbered by the normal demands of a hierarchical workplace. His apartment in the upscale section of Berlin, Westend, his extensive collection of Asian porcelains, and his frequent travels to Italy, Switzerland, and Paris would have been impossible if he were financially dependent on the meager remuneration received from the University of Berlin.

The synergy of financial and cultural capital is not, however, merely a fulcrum of his biography. It was perhaps his most important sociological site of critical reflection. His greatest work, *The Philosophy of Money*, was an extended and arguably unrivaled rumination on the copula of intellectual and financial capital. His sympathy for socialism, in part, rested on his assertion that economic impoverishment ensured intellectual impoverishment. He maintained, moreover, that economic liberalism placed the human intellect in the service of avarice and egoism. This impoverished the foremost philosophical concern of humanity: ethics. Conversely, Simmel remonstrated, as if drawing upon autobiographical experience, that the possession of money does not always stamp the human soul with avarice. Clearly, his economic independence afforded distance from the ideology and cultural hegemony of the status quo. If he was not interested in acquiring money, he was totally enveloped by the aesthetic cultivation endowed by its possession.

Simmel conceived of his cultural development as deriving from a polemical spurning of the economic, cultural, and political status quo. His son Hans recalled not only his father's disdain for the cultural atmosphere of the bourgeoisie but for aristocratic politics as well. In one of a series of reminiscences, Hans recounts a story of his father joking about the sad absence of royal assassins in Germany: "Is there really no Ravaillac in Germany?!" intoned father to son (Ravaillac was the murderer of King Henry IV of France).[8] Georg Simmel was equally vehement in his disdain for the cultural predominance of the petit-bourgeoisie. On account of his economic independence, his scholarship refined this sociological polemic with little fear of economic retribution. He was a prototype of his own sociological portrait of the stranger: a bourgeois whose freedom, intellectual mobility, and objectivity derived from a lack of commitment to the ethics of the bourgeoisie.

His penchant for social critique endeared him to radical students in Berlin. He embodied their unwillingness to cut their conscience to fit the bourgeois and aristocratic fashions of the day. His countercultural legacy would be carried on by students who were either independently wealthy or culturally independent, having established their own cultural institutions. No doubt their radical ethics of free will, like his own, were facilitated by economic and cultural privilege.

BERLIN AS CULTURAL CAPITAL

In addition to situating Simmel's thought within the context of his familial culture, his intellectual maturation must be understood in relation to the atmosphere of Berlin. By the late nineteenth century Berlin had eclipsed Paris as the political, economic, and military capital of continental Europe. Culturally it was emerging as a cosmopolitan city of world significance. Georg Simmel was born in Berlin in 1858, the youngest of seven siblings and spent all but the last four years of his life in Berlin's environment of commercial and cultural phantasmagoria. His date and place of birth contributed to his absorptional sociology of modern culture, and he was fully aware of this.

> The development of Berlin from a large city to a world city in the years around and after the turn of the century corresponds with the period of my strongest and most expansive intellectual development. . . . Perhaps, if I had lived in a different city, I also may have achieved something valuable; but my particular intellectual achievements, which I successfully brought to fruition in these decades, undoubtedly were connected to the Berlin milieu.[9]

Simmel was also cognizant of the fact that his cultural legacy was tied to the University of Berlin, where he was one of the most well-known and beloved pedagogues. His countercultural influence was impossible, he believed, at any other German institution save Munich University.

Simmel's birthplace is illustrative of the experiential wealth that contributed to his sociology of modernity. His house was located at the northwest corner of Leipzig and Friedrich streets. During Simmel's lifetime, these two streets emerged as two of the most important commercial corridors in Berlin. This location was also adjacent to the heart of old Berlin or *Stadtmitte* (literally, city-center). The subway station *Stadtmitte* was later constructed not far from his family's apartment. In addition to the location of his birth, the year of his birth, 1858, located him in the center of modern

German cultural and political history as well. At the age of thirteen (as he was experiencing the physiological transition to adulthood), he witnessed the numerous victory parades marking Germany's unification and victory over France in 1870. He thereby experienced Berlin's ascension to the political capital of Europe. Furthermore, his home on the corner of Leipziger and Friedrich streets placed him within walking distance of most of Berlin's cultural meccas. The state orchestra hall, with the accompanying twin churches and large market, was practically across the street. The state opera, Germany's parliamentary building (the Reichstag), the massive Berlin cathedral and royal castle, the Brandenburg gate on Pariser Platz, and Berlin University were all less than fifteen minutes away by foot. Perhaps most important given Simmel's intense interest in the visual arts, the museum island (crowned on one end by the Kaiser-Friedrich-Museum and on the other by Friedrich Schinkel's Altes Museum) provided him with an immediate reservoir of cultural experiences.[10] Friedrich Schinkel's Altes Museum opened in 1830. It is presumably the first museum to be built expressly for the public. The three other museums comprising the museum island were built or under construction during Simmel's lifetime. The Neues Museum opened a year after Simmel's birth in 1859. The Nationalgalerie was dedicated in 1876, and the Kaiser-Friederich-Museum was ready to receive visitors in 1904. The Pergamon Museum first opened its doors in 1901. It was precisely in Simmel's lifetime that Berlin became not only the political capital of Europe but also developed into a world-class cultural center.

The growth of Berlin's aesthetic and political institutions were framed by the rapid acceleration of Germany's capitalist economy, the increasingly phantasmagoric nature of cosmopolitan Berlin, and the emergence of Europe's largest socialist party. Thematically, Simmel's thought was an expression of these historical developments: it combined an interest in the sociology and civics of commercial culture with an intense affirmation of aesthetics as a way of life. Moreover, the themes of many of his early social-psychological essays are derived from his urban and modern cultural experiences. For instance, Simmel interpreted city life as the locus of modern economic and cultural alienation. In his essay "Great Cities and the Life of the Spirit [*Geistesleben*]," he describes the significance and meaning of city life:

> The deepest problems of modern life originate from the attempt of the individual to protect the independence and particularity of his existence (*Dasein*) against the superior power of society, historical tradition, external culture and technology of life. . . . The punctuality, calculability, and exactitude—which the complications and expansiveness of life in great cities force upon one's life style—stand not only in the closest connection to the money economy and its intellectual character, but must

> necessarily color the contents of life and favor the exclusion of every irrational, instinctual, and sovereign characteristic and impulse, which want from themselves to determine the contours of life, instead of receiving them as a general, schematic presentation from the outside.[11]

Simmel conceived of the city as the geographical embodiment of commercial life. Negotiating the punctuality of transportation networks and embracing the calculating intellect demanded by financial life alienated individuals from the sovereign impulse of ethical individuation. Simmel's ruminations about urban life recapitulated the central copula of his social criticism: alienation and the money economy.

Berlin was also significant because it was here that Simmel would spend most of his academic life. In the second half of the nineteenth century there was probably no city in Europe that was changing more rapidly than Berlin. Germany was in the midst of a massive economic and social transformation. Berlin was the administrative and cultural center of this transformation, and after 1871, it was the political and commercial capital of Europe. Berlin was the environmental precondition for his eventual reputation as the greatest sociologist of modernity. But the same cultural forces that stimulated his intellectual brilliance, no doubt, doomed his academic career. Simply put, his cosmopolitanism begat critical assessments of Wilhelmine society and undermined his prospects for professional advancement. Simmel had his pulse on modern culture and, therefore, his engaging lectures drew students who yearned for an understanding of the historical relevance of academic life. But the engaging nature of his thought—expressed in his sociological treatment of such controversial themes as feminism, socialism, alienation, Nietzsche, social hierarchy, poverty, and greed—contributed substantially to his institutional marginalization within academia.

The general contours of Simmel's academic career are well known, although a political understanding of his marginality is underdeveloped. In 1881, at age twenty-four, he received the degree of Doctor of Philosophy having written a dissertation on Kant entitled "The Essence of the Material: Concerning Kant's Physical Monadology." Here he criticized Kant's abstract understanding of materiality; Kant failed to comprehend the existing realities of political and institutional power.[12] This Simmelian perspective prefigures much of our analysis of his work. In the forthcoming pages, we will investigate Simmel's thought as a historical and sociological exposition of Kantian philosophy. Simmel eventually became a private lecturer (*Privat Dozent*) at the University of Berlin in 1885. In this capacity, he was an unpaid lecturer who had to rely on student fees for remuneration. Despite copious publications and a heralded reputation as a lecture, he retained this status for fifteen years. After the publication of his magnum opus, *The Philosophy of Money*, in 1900, the University conferred upon him the title of Extraordinary Professor. This was a purely honorary title. It did not change his status vis-à-vis the institution. He remained an outsider in the Department of Philosophy and still had to rely on student lecture fees, rather than a salary, for remuneration. Moreover, he was still unable to oversee dissertations, and this severely limited his ability to mentor future German academics. His intellectual legacy, although considerable, was correspondingly truncated. It was not until 1914 that he was offered a position as full professor. The acceptance of this position was preceded by serious reservations. The position was at Strasbourg University, and that meant Simmel would have to leave his beloved Berlin in order to gain institutional respect. Four years after accepting the position, he died of liver cancer. His professorship in Strasbourg symbolized his status as an academic outsider. Geographically, Strasbourg removed Simmel from the heart of German political, academic, and cultural life. Then, the Great War intervened and further reduced the significance of his academic pursuits. After the war, Strasbourg once again became part of France. This, too, is meaningful. Even in death, Simmel retained the stigmatic mark of an institutional outsider. He had been physically removed from the center of German culture to non-German soil. This symbolized the cultural fate of his intellectual reputation after the Great War.

Several interpretations have been put forth to explain Simmel's substandard treatment by Wilhelmine academic powers: unprofessionalism, the transgression of disciplinary boundaries, and anti-Semitism. Donald Levine's explanation corresponds with the first of these interpretations:

> Simmel's extraordinary originality may well be connected to his position as a relatively isolated figure. He was, indeed, a "stranger" in the academy. The stylistic manifestations of a marginal position are striking in his written work. Neither in Simmel's text nor in annotations does one find acknowledgement of scholarly predecessors or contemporaries. . . . [For example,] Simmel's was the only entry in the 1890–91 volume of Schmoller's *Jahrbuch* without footnotes. . . . Yet there is evidence that he was disposed toward academic nonconformity from an early age. . . . During his trial colloquium at Berlin in 1884 Simmel showed a conspicuous disregard for academic etiquette.[13]

The incident to which Levine referred was Simmel's public rebuke of Professor Zeller who maintained that the soul was located in the central brain lobe. In a public forum, the student Simmel indiscreetly violated the cultural hierarchy of academic privilege. Students do not rebuke professors. As a result of this insubordination, his appointment as a lecturer was delayed for nearly a year.[14] Lewis A. Coser has contributed additional insights into Simmel's academic difficulties: "The breadth of Simmel's culture, his refusal to be restricted by any of the existing disciplines, perturbed many of the more settled spirits in the academic world."[15] These two interpretations are insightful but limited in their explanatory cache. Most biographers, and here Coser and Levine are typical, fail to provide historical explanations of insubordination and unconventional writing style. His nonconformity was, in part, connected to his economic independence. Frankly, he was financially insulated from the intellectual conventions of the professions. With respect to his style, it should be seen as aesthetic. Simmel saw himself as a sociological artist. And like the literary genius, he felt no need to footnote the inspirational sources of creative activity.

The most prevalent explanation of Simmel's thwarted academic career is anti-Semitism, and, without seeking to deny this explanation, the intention here is to expose its limitations. Academic anti-Semitism was cited by Weingartner, Coser, Levine, and Köhnke as the most powerful explanation of his academic marginality. However, a letter written to the German cultural ministry in 1908 presents an even more complex set of possibilities. The letter opposing Simmel's appointment to Heidelberg University was written by the government official, Dietrich Schäfer, and includes the following statements:

> He is an Israelite through and through. . . . His academic audience sits together. The ladies constitute what is, even for Berlin, a strong contingent. The remaining are students from the oriental world who have become residents, and those who stream in from eastern countries are extremely well represented. His entire manner corresponds with their tastes and leads in their direction. . . . Simmel essentially owes his reputation to his "sociological" activities. . . . To want to establish the "society" as the law giving organ of collective life in place of the state and the church is in my opinion a fateful error.[16]

The anti-Semitic element is clear. In fact, Schäfer further maligned Simmel by referring to him as a "philosemitic" instructor. This was blatant ethnocentrism. But none of his biographers have referenced other elements of this letter. In order to undermine Simmel's reputation as a popular instructor, Schäfer appeals to academic misogyny, an allusion to Simmel's acceptance of female students, publication of feminist essays, and sponsorship of feminist politics. Schäfer, who also lived in Berlin, may have known about Simmel's interest in collecting Asian art. His feminist politics and his art collection may account for the above description of Simmel's "taste." Furthermore, it is not only possible, but highly likely, that the expression "sociological activities" would have been interpreted by the Minister of Culture as "socialist activities"; for it was the socialists who were criticizing the monarchical state apparatus and the holy dogmas of the Christian confessions. Hence, Schäfer referenced Simmel's threat to Christianity. This threat was real. Simmel's early essays were clearly proworker if not prosocialist. Moreover, to government officials, *The Philosophy of Money*, with its scathing critique of the spiritual degeneracy of Kaiser capitalism, surely resembled Marx's *Capital*. Another interesting fact about this letter is that it was four times as long as the letter by Wilhelm Windelband favoring Simmel's appointment to Heidelberg. This may indicate that the conservative cultural forces opposing Simmel's promotion were much more zealous than those favoring his institutional ascent within the ranks of German academia.[17] In the end, the barrier of anti-Semitism is an inadequate explanation of Simmel's inability to procure a permanent academic position, for many other Jews had risen in German academia with far less resistance than Simmel. Minimally, we need to recognize the political barriers to Simmel's promotion. His feminist politics, Nietzschean morality, antibourgeois ethics, and sociological investigations of social hierarchy were a threat to the status quo which had no intention of giving institutional affirmation to a cultural enemy.

REALISM: THE REVOLUTIONARY AVANT-GARDE AND BOHEMIAN COUNTERCULTURE

In the 1880s, Berlin's aesthetic counterculture experienced a Naturalist fever. Simmel was at ground zero of what the authorities perceived as a political plague. Although Naturalism was not a domestic movement, it had a huge impact on German culture, reaching its aesthetic zenith in the dramas of Gerhart Hauptmann. The term was probably imported into the literary realm from French realism, and a cursory examination of the origins of Naturalism in the French fine arts can tell us much about the competing political and philosophical meanings of European Naturalism. The great French art critic of the mid-nineteenth century, Jules-Antoine Castaguary, championed Naturalism and wrote: "The naturalist school affirms that art is the expression of life in all of its modes and degrees and that its sole aim is to reproduce nature in giving it the maximum of power and intensity; it is truth balanced with science."[18] The question that arises from this definition of art is: does the positivist accent on the reproduction of nature undermine the subjective freedom and individuality of expression that has fueled artistic creation from the Renaissance to Romantics? As we shall see, this was a driving concern of Simmel, who wrote extensively on Naturalism.

But, before we turn to Simmel's thoughts on Naturalism and his participation in Berlin's Naturalist counterculture, I want to reference the aesthetic philosophy of Gustave Courbet. Courbet is widely recognized as the greatest representative of French realism. Castaguary, a leading art critic during the French Second and Third Republics, linked the realism of Courbet to the literary Naturalism of Zola. Undeniably, paintings such as Courbet's *Stonebreakers* (1849) and *The Peasants of Flagey Returning from the Fair* (1850) emanated from an aesthetic spirit intent on depicting the vitality and suffering of the lowest classes. This spirit was conscious and countercultural. Its countercultural impact, and that of Naturalism as well, depended on the aesthetic affirmation of *vox populi* within a civilized French culture of bourgeois refinement and aristocratic delicacies. In this respect, Realism and Naturalism share a critical affinity with Enlightenment thinkers such as Diderot and Rousseau who articulated the barbarism underlying civilization. And, let us not forget Candide's revelation about the reason for cheap sugar in eighteenth-century Europe: slavery.

Still, the realist atttitudes of the mid-nineteenth century were much more politically volatile than the social criticism of the Enlightenment. By the beginning of the nineteenth century, rapid changes in the economic realm were solidified by the political marriage of the bourgeoisie and aristocracy. (For example, this marriage of bourgeois top hat and aristocratic tiara was manifest in the relationships of Louise-Philippe and Casimir Périer in post–1830 France and Otto von Bismarck and Gerson Bleichröder in Imperial Germany.) These elites depicted their social superiority through court paintings, portraits, and historical painting. Here, and in most realms of elite culture, there was an absence of historical narratives about humble lives. This cultural absence was pivotal to the moral bearing of Courbet's narrative paintings and Zola's literary Naturalism. Max Buchon's advertisement for the 1850 exhibition of Courbert's *Stonebreakers* gives some indication of the social narrative that French contemporaries perceived in Courbet's paintings:

> The painting of the Stonebreakers represents two life-size figures, a child and an old man, the alpha and the omega, the sunrise and sunset of that life of drudgery. A poor young lad, between twelve and fifteen years old, his head shaven, scurvy, and stupid in the way misery often shapes the heads of the children of the poor. . . . A ragged shirt; pants held together by a breech made of rope, patched on the knees, torn at the bottom, and tattered all over; lamentable, down-at-heel shoes, turned red by too much wear, *like the shoes of that poor worker you know*: that sums up the child.[19]

Buchon's narration explicitly mandates the transference of the artist's point of view into the viewers' lives. This mandate was not the projection of tendentious meaning à la Lukács's essays on realism. Possibly the most important consideration with respect to Courbet's artistry was his partisan point of view, which Buchon properly references as an aesthetic immanence. Courbet was a social apostolate of French anarchism, and his work was a deliberate effort to steer society toward a new anarchist (decentralized, communitarian, and agrarian) way of life.

A letter written to Pierre-Joseph Proudhon in the summer of 1863 gives us some impression of the politcal underpinnings of Courbet's art. The letter was written in the form of aphorisms:

- The man who spends his life amassing a fortune has no business in the intellectual world.
- The superiority of one class over the other does not exist. The only superior man is the man who is superior by virtue of his work and his actions.
- A man who works in the arts must concede nothing to public opinion that is at odds with his own ideas. If he does, his originality does not exist. He chooses the beaten path.[20]

Courbet's anticapitalist partisanship and insistence on aesthetic individuality point to the fact that the tension between aesthetic purity and engaged art was not present here. "I am both objective and subjective," Courbet explained: "I have made my synthesis."[21] For Courbet, there was no opposition between the ethical impulses of *l'art réaliste* and the aesthetic impulses of *l'art pour l'art*. This opposition devoloped with the transition of *l'art réaliste* from the fine arts to the literature. The clinical precision of Gustave Flaubert's novels and the historical objectivity of Zola emphasized an intimate connection to science, and thereby an appreciation for artistic individuation and painstaking artistry correspondingly receded in cultural significance. Moreover, Naturalists distinguished themselves from Courbet in their typical unwillingness to express sympathy for the fated souls whose tragic lives they picturesquely narrated.

Both in terms of real individuals and as ideal types, we need to differentiate the spirit of the revolutionary avant-garde, embodied in Courbet, from the bohemian counterculture of Naturalism. Regarding the crucial question of social change, one favored insurrection and the other the forces of order. We must say from the outset that Simmel refrained from support for revolutionary transformation. He was a member of the bourgeois German intelligentsia that embraced bohemian iconoclasm of the Naturalist counterculture without endorsing socialist revolution.

If the distinction between the revolutionary avant-garde and bohemian counterculture is a fundamental presupposition, it must not occlude important continuities, shared perspectives, and overlapping moods. While Naturalism often eschewed the exogenous partisanship of Courbet's *l'art réaliste*, it retained what Simmel called "an ideal of truth in art" and thereby an immanent call for the moral reformation of social evils.[22] Easily apparent in the art of Courbet was the transformation of the traditional relationship between high art and morality which continued with Naturalism. Whereas high art had previously affirmed the arrogation of the moral authority to the ruling classes, now it expressed a searing hatred for the spiritual depravity of gilded selfishness and social injustice. Naturalism was not revolutionary in the strictest sense. However, it contained, to use the police language of the period, a seditious tendency due to its often honest depiction of what Georg Lukács called "an anticapitalist world outlook."[23] More broadly, the Naturalist counterculture posited itself and constituted itself as a cultural force opposed to tastes and principles of the respectable world. The defiance of respectability was integral not only to the act of creation. Within Europe's bohemian intelligentsia, this defiant posture was the central appeal of an aesthetic way of life.

NATURALISM IN BERLIN: UNRESTRAINED AND UNBRIDLED

The naturalistic movement made its seditious debut in Berlin in the 1880s, and Simmel was at the epicenter of this counterculture. Prior to its debut, the German master of the realist novel was Theodor Fontane, who spent much of his life in Berlin. This great realist chose themes that resonated with the historical period. His narratives highlighted social iniquity and outmoded social mores. Class hierarchies and sexual conventions were often the subject matter of Fontane's books. However, there was no attempt to answer the problems raised through his novels. His realism was social literature but not socialist literature. Nonetheless, Fontane's novels were often received as cultural documents of social critique. And while he was not a socialist, in literary historiography he is widely considered the seminal precursor of German Naturalism, a movement whose radical branches directly linked socialist ideology and German drama.

While in military service in the 1840s, Fontane was a member of the Berlin literary club Tunnel Under the Spree. The members met in cafes and restaurants and gave public readings of their works. In these settings, Fontane read his early poems and in 1850 published two books of poetry. Later he would turn to historical literature, including serial war novels.[24] But he became most well-known and respected for his Berlin novels which typically addressed the unjustifiability of contemporary social conditions. A prime target was the falseheartedness, artifice, and sanctimony of obdurate bourgeois mores. For example, *L'Adultera* (1882) was about a woman ostracized from high society for adultery who descends the class ladder, but gains an appreciation for the spiritual insignificance of counterfeit conventions. The Berlin novels concluded with an unfinished work, *Mathilde Möhring*, about a female member of the lumpen proletariat. Like other masterpieces of the era—*Nana*, *Madame Bovary*, and *Hedda Gabler* come to mind immediately—Fontane's masterpiece, *Effi Briest*, dealt honestly with the faults and virtues of women yearning to transcend their spiritually oppressive social circumstances. Such thematic treatments of social probity and contemporary events gave Fontane's work an existential relevance. Through his novels, his followers experienced the nearness of art to life. Furthermore, Fontane's stylistic brilliance and the lyrical subtly of his prose bore nothing in common with the aesthetic reputation of later socially inspired literature, such as the socialist realism of the 1930s. Fontane's realism, in contrast to its communist namesake, was extolled for its poetic spirit and aesthetic refinement. There was no distinction between aesthetic accomplishment and a thematic treatment of society's merciless conventions.

Fontane was the quintessential man of letters in Berlin. By the 1880s, Fontane devotees, leaders in the arts, dilettanti, and academics, coalesced around a Berlin cultural association known as The Society of the Unrestrained (*Die Zwanglosen*). Fontane took part personally in its summer parties and Friday evening social events. Simmel was a member, as were a group of his close friends: Otto Brahm, Julius Hoffory, Richard Meyer, Otto Pinower, Paul Schlenther, and Max von Walberg. Around 1889, members of this group—led by Hoffory and Simmel—mutinied The Society of the Unrestrained. They preferred a more dionysian social club and founded The Society of the Unbridled (*Die Zügellosen*). Roughly thirty years later, Professor Fritz Mauthner recounted this mutiny in his obituary of Simmel:

> I knew the young university lecturer [Georg Simmel], although I was not close to him. One evening with him, actually it was more than half a night, will remain unforgettable to me, admittedly less as a result of Simmel than a third person [Julius Hoffory]. . . . There was then and still is today in Berlin a society without articles of association. It is a social club of men which call themselves the Unrestrained [*die Zwanglosen*]. Some day someone will talk about the Unrestrained, just as today they talk about the literary group Tunnel Over the Spree. The type of spirit—of which the Unrestrained were progeny—is indicated by a few names from its necrology: Schlenther, Brahm, . . . and the Professor of German philology, Julius Hoffory, who had been Ibsen's model for Eilert Lövborg in *Hedda Gabler*; at that time Hoffroy already had been stricken by the so-called psychological torment that soon made him unable to work and that not much later caused him to die miserably. My memory betrays me concerning the question of whether Simmel participated actively in The Society of the Unrestrained or appeared among us as a guest. In any case, Simmel and Hoffroy united themselves in a half jesting revolution against The Society of the Unrestrained's Friday evenings. They wanted to found The Society of the Unbridled [*die Zügellosen*] and invited me—not coincidentally on a Friday—to a well-known beer house, where I would be "won over." Concerning the intentions of the rebels I can say nothing more than that the Unrestrained tended to go home one hour after midnight and the Unbridled intended to drink until two. Normally a

> quiet scholar, Hoffroy's mental illness led to the impression that under the influence of alcohol he became wild and ebullient and diabolically clever; thus he argued about a new slogan for the Society of the Unbridled, at which time Simmel—with barely audible dialectical humor—maintained the appropriateness of the phrase, "one should drink beer until no earlier and no later than two o'clock." Thus, punctually at two o'clock we set out and wandered through the snow of Potsdamer Street in earnest conversation. Suddenly, after a couple swigs from his beloved flask, Hoffroy fell into a state of believing himself to be Eilert Lövborg incarnate. In a compassionate and thoroughly congenial speech he showered his colleague Tesman (who Georg Simmel now appeared to him to be) with criticism. We recognized these attacks, and Simmel did not have the slightest reason to feel attacked by the outbursts of this sick individual. However, he answered, untroubled by Ibsen's authorial intentions, by proving that, as to the characters of the two figures, Lövborg would be the ideal of unbridledness [*Zügellosigkeit*] and Tesman the ideal of unrestaint [*Zwanglosigkeit*]. They belong to one another just as two to one. And, as always, Simmel remained victorious when he spoke.[25]

Among the many issues that invite discussion here, only two are vital for helping us to grasp Simmel's mentality and cultural influences. First, this cultural rebellion was distilled through Naturalism, in this case Ibsen's *Hedda Gabler* and its leading male protagonists, Jürgen Tesman and Eilert Lövborg. There was an even more substantial connection between The Society of the Unbridled and and the leading Naturalist, Ibsen. Ibsen had based the character of Lövborg on Hoffroy. This, no doubt, intensified a particular countercultural attitude: life itself was an aesthetic creation.

Secondly, while the dramatic impact of *Hedda Gabler* requires an exhibition of Tesman and Lövborg's incommensurable intellectual and ethical tempers, Simmel gives ultimate vivification to their dependence. Simmel's diplomatic resolution to Hoffroy's reproaches was symbolic of the Janus of his own life and work. Simmel was a hard-working bourgeois like Tesman whose apollinian refinement produced the desire for the dionysian freedom of Lövborg/Hoffroy. In *Hedda Gabler*, Lövborg's rogue romanticism demands his banishment from respectable society. Hoffroy, despite being the model for Ibsen's character, does not follow the dramatic script. He does not wait for society's ostracism. Rather, he and Simmel initiated a cultural rebellion against the Tesman-like milieu of the Fontane circle. The model of The Society of the Unbridled was not reactive or reactionary. Paramount was the act of self-definition, unbridled by social convention. Some time after the first meeting of The Society of the Unbridled, Simmel sent a letter to Mauthner. It was signed "in unbridled [*zügelloser*] devotion."[26] Simmel, a wealthy bourgeois by birth, made it quite clear that his cultural loyalties were not those of Tesman, Hedda, and the respectable bourgeoisie of the Fontane circle. He and The Society of the Unbridled remained free from the bits of dogma and the reigns of social convention that bridled German high culture.

As a particular subset of the German intelligensia, The Society of the Unbridled was nearly identical to the most progressive wing of the Naturalist avant-garde in Berlin. According to Hans Simmel, The Society of the Unbridled included, among others, Brahm, Hoffroy, and Slenther. Collectively, these three did more to advance Naturalist drama than any other group of individuals in Germany. The primary foreign influence on German Naturalism in the early 1890s was Ibsen. Hoffroy, Professor of Nordic Philology at Berlin University, was a zealous Ibsenite, and translator and personal friend of Ibsen. One can imagine that his rakish neglect of formality and his insanity after 1889 made him a model of antibourgeois disrespectability. His was also the ultimate countercultural insider. Ibsen fever descended upon Berlin like a heat wave in 1887. Performances of *Ghosts*, *An Enemy of the People*, *The Wild Duck*, and *Pillars of Society* were all staged in that year. *Ghosts* was the first to be performed, and Ibsen was present for its opening on January 9, 1887. Two days later he was honored with a large banquet. We have no knowledge of Simmel's attendence. We do know that future members of The Society of the Unbridled played an important role because Ibsen sent them thanks. Ibsen wrote to Hoffroy on February 4:

> My visit in Berlin and all connected with it I regard as a great and true personal happiness. . . . I ask you, my dear Professor, to accept my most cordial thanks for the large and important share which you had in all of this, and extend a similar thanks to Dr. Brahm and Dr. Slenther.[27]

If Hoffroy was the missionary of Ibsenian drama in Germany, Schlenther and Brahm were the Peter and Paul who established the church. Slenther edited Ibsen's collected works in German.[28] According to Brahm, their lives were forever altered by a 1878 performance of Ibsen's *Pillars of Society* in Berlin. Possibly this was the most fateful event of their lives.

> It so happened one day that we [Brahm and Schlenther] ended up at a performance of *The Pillars of Society* in the tiny "City Theater" on Linden street. Immediately we felt the first premonition of a new poetic world. We felt ourselves, for the first time, confronted with people of our day, in whom we could believe; and we saw the ideals of freedom and truth as the pillars of society rising out of an all-encompassing critique of the present. From then on, we belonged to a new reality art [*Wirklichkeitskunst*], and our aesthetic life welcomed its new content.[29]

Again, Ibsen's Naturalism was experienced not only as a shocking and uncompromising embodiment of the moral power of aethetics; it was an alternative to the celebratory and uncritical culture of the *Gründerzeit*. The scope of historical and theatrical literature of the 1870s rarely presented a historical context beyond that of the bourgeoisie and its conventions. Protagonists did not encounter political predicaments.[30] This dramatic tendency toward social affirmation of the status quo was completely undermined by Naturalism.

Brahm and Schlenther's commitment to an art situated in a real historical context and that raised moral issues such as industrialization and class politics led them, along with Maximilian Harden, Theodor Wolff, Julius and Heinrich Hart, to found The Free Theater [Die Freie Bühne] in 1889.[31] In contrast to the Théâtre Libre in Paris upon which it was modelled, The Free Theater was not a business undertaking. Schlenther proclaimed in his manifesto concerning the genesis of The Free Theater that the intention to bring before the public an avant-garde, experimental, and living theater was not going to be tainted by the cancerous "acquisition of wealth."[32]

The Free Theater is now widely recognized as the seminal institution of German Naturalist drama, but its significance for our narrative lies in its contribution to an understanding of Simmel's interpersonal, cultural, and generational environment. Brahm (b. 1856), Schlenther (b. 1854), and Simmel (b. 1858) all came to maturity in the conservative era of the 1870s. They shared this authoritarian political context and a cultural rejection of its conventions. Beneath the celebratory nationalism, industrial mania, bourgeois faith in science, and slavish belief in the inevitability of progress of the 1870s and 1880s, they recognized the artifice of convention and the moral complacency of the upper classes. And, just as the Socialist Law (1878–1890) sought to repress an economic and political critique of Kaiser capitalism, they experienced imperial culture through Naturalist drama as the suppression of individuality and freedom.

They shared more than an authoritarian cultural context and Naturalist countercultural spirit. They also possessed a shared academic background. They met at Berlin University and studied literature and culture with Professor Wilhelm Scherers.[33] Within the matrix of imperial culture, Simmel and his circle of friends represent a particular substratum of the bourgeoisie: Ph.D.s whose academic training did not lead to social integration but social critique. Simmel broadly defined this Naturalist subculture as a "Sociological Aesthetic."[34] Brahm and Schlenther, paragons of a sociological aesthetics, sought their cultural fortunes outside of academia. Before the establishment of The Free Theater, Brahm was already the theater critic for the newspaper, *Die Nation*, and Schlenther was the lead literary critic for the *Vossische Zeitung*. Simmel remained in academia. But, the spirit of his work in 1890s bore the stamp of Naturalist drama whose denouement often turned on the exposure of the ethical hypocrisy of high society.

SIMMEL AND UNBRIDLED WOMEN

The Society of the Unbridled is significant not only because it establishes Simmel's intellectual maturation within the Naturalist counterculture, but also because it was linked to the milieu in which he met his future wife. The circumstances under which Simmel met Untrud [later, Gertrud] Kinel were illustrative of the countercultural, semibohemian, and iconoclastic atmosphere fostered by the learned bourgeoisie. One of Georg Simmel's close friends in the 1880s was Harald Graef, whose father was a well-known painter. His sister, Sabine Graef, was a gifted and highly accomplished artist as well. In the late 1880s, Georg apparently spent a considerable amount of time around the Graef household, an atmosphere which he described as semibohemian. Sabine, who remained a lifelong friend and to whom Simmel penned one of his final letters in September 1918, recalled her first introduction to Georg Simmel around 1875:

> Georg Simmel, school mate of my brother Harald, first came to our house as a seventeen-year-old gymnasiast. . . . With warmth and cleverness, he consciously entered into a special relationship with every individual family member in the course of his visit. . . . The half-finished, emotional imbalance in me, and the thirst for knowledge (with which I absorbed all intellectual sustenance) won me—not only for my youth but for my entire life—a teacher and the truest of friends, Georg Simmel. He oversaw my intellectual and human development. . . . So he became the friend to me who was always there when I needed him. He always mixed a little scholarly tenderness in with his friendship. He suffered along with me when fate was ill disposed toward me. He felt himself to be a kind of protector. However, when things were going well, he very seldom was able to share delight. He was incapable of jubilation over a success, possessed no belief in luck, and could not put forth a consistent Yes to life. He connected the finest analytical understanding with a warm, helpful disposition. He was a dialectically playful spirit and at the same time a serious person, and he had the stuff of an important scholar with character.[35]

Simmel's comportment in his friendship with Sabine Graef was replicated in other relationships with women. But what shines most brightly is the portrait of Simmel as a unity of extremes. Earnestness often ripens into dispassionate intolerance, and often individuals capable of extreme compassion are overcharged with emotionality and hence less adept at analytical distinctions. Simmel, however, embodied that rare combination of compassion and cold analytical rigor which was accompanied by an inability to give himself over to unbridled optimism. Starkly perceptible in this interpersonal portrait was the outline of his larger philosophical disposition which combined a sociological and analytical exactitude with a politics of compassion.

Simmel's close relationship to Naturalism was illustrated by his membership in The Society of the Unbridled and by the roughly simultaneous founding of this cultural group and The Free Theater in 1889. Harald Graef, along with Simmel, Hoffroy, Brahm and Schlenther, was also a member of The Society of the Unbridled whose primary interest was the discussion of cultural history and the newest literature. The informal group also included Botho Graef (Harold's brother), who later became professor of archeology in Jena, and Reinhold Lepsius, portrait painter and son of the great Egyptologist.[36] As the group's name indicates, members conceived of themselves as intellectuals whose cultural development unfolded via the rejection of the tradition's restraints. Sabine Graef described the cultural spirit within this segment of the German intelligentsia as lacking "bourgeois single-mindedness of purpose."[37] This group was typical of the "young rebels" of the European Generation of 1890.[38]

It was in this cultural environment that Simmel met Untrud Kinel, who was a close friend of Sabine Graef. Sabine and Untrud were the only female members of The Unbridled Ones, and they were formidable intellectuals in their own right. The support for women's intellectual aspirations and access to educational institutions was one of the primary goals of the early women's movement in the 1890s. Simmel embraced these aspirations and throughout his life was a strong advocate for women's intellectual equality. It is clear, moreover, that Simmel conceived of his marriage to Untrud as a partnership of equals, and he came, by the end of his life, to conceive of the feminine principle of love as a new model for civic equality. In his personal life and in his publications, Simmel was an overt critic of the hierarchal character of the patriarchal family. Moreover, throughout his professional life he nurtured intellectual relationships with women. We have mentioned his friendship and support for Sabine Graef. He seems to have provided the same level of encouragement for Untrud's intellectual and cultural aspirations.

Leaving Sabine in the city of lights, Untrud returned from a trip to Paris in March 1889, and after her arrival in Berlin, Georg proposed marriage. The pair were engaged, and on July 11, 1890, they were married by one of Georg's university colleagues, Professor von Soden. The marriage of Georg and Untrud was made financially easier by the death of his stepfather around Christmas of 1889. As a result of a sizeable inheritance, Georg was now an economically independent man. It is very likely that Hoffroy's reproachful association of Simmel and Tesman (Ibsen's caricature of the bourgeois academic specialist) at the first meeting of The Society of the Unbridled in the winter of 1889 referred to Simmel's impending marriage. This critique of Simmel as a bougeois family man was misguided. For, while Simmel embraced a conventional form, marriage, he aspired to give it a new feminist content. His life with Untrud was more than a traditional marriage; it was an intellectual and cultural partnership. By the turn of the century,

Georg was holding private seminars at their Westend apartment. As she had in The Society of the Unbridled Ones, Untrud often participated in these seminar discussions as an intellectual equal. Moreover, by all accounts, Untrud Kinel was no Victorian wallflower lacking courage to flout convention, à la Hedda Gabler. She was an intellectual with her own identity as an author. Under the pseudonym Marie-Luise Enckendorff, she published several philosophical texts: *Concerning the Being and Possession of the Soul* (1906), *Reality and Legality in Sexual Life* (1910), and *Concerning Religiosity* (1919). Georg Simmel's support for Untrud's intellectual aspirations and independent identity was merely one example of his feminist disposition.

As early as 1894, Georg Simmel publically identified himself in print as a feminist. He published an essay entitled "Militarism and the Position of Women," wherein he rejected the proposition that patriarchal roles of the male soldier and female housewife derive from natural law. His critique was explicit. He demonstrated the linkage between militarism and "the overall enslavement of women at this time" and decried the "suppression of the intellectual individuality of women."[39] The essay never mentions Prussian militarism, but the content of the essay was, like much of his work, a civic and ethical critique of the Kaiserreich. Simmel expressed his social critique of other inegalitarian institutions as well. Even before the turn of the century, when women still required the professor's consent to attend lectures at Berlin University, he made a conscious effort to integrate female students and scholars into his private and public seminars. His friendship and intellectual affirmation of intellectuals such as Gertrud Kantorowicz and Margarete von Bendemann, to whom he dedicated *Religion* (1906), was the personal correlative of his public support for women's rights to higher education. He also wrote favorably of female artists such as Kornelie Wagner, Dora Hitz, and Käthe Kollwitz.[40] The ultimate significance of Simmel's feminist writings was twofold: (1) they illustrate the existential character of his thought and pedagogy; countercultural life and intellectual refinement were consciously articulated; and (2) they demonstrate Simmel's willingness to support countercultural values publically and thereby to link academic life and social critique.

This linkage constituted a pedagogical revolution. Hegel, the greatest German intellectual of the nineteenth century, declared: "The State is the actuality of the ethical Idea."[41] The civic goal of academic institutions was to grasp intellectual refinement as political integration. Simmel renounced the conservative premises of Hegelian pedagogy. A fundamental feature of his sociology and philosophy was the proposition that the civic actuation of ethics demanded a renunciation of existing political and economic institutions. The role of the pedagogue was to foster this countercultural conception of social ethics. This existential brand of pedagogy replicated the abiding concerns of European Naturalism which was closely tied to the Women's Question and to the politics of the working class.[42]

ETHICS AS A FIRST PHILOSOPHY

Like the Naturalist counterculture, Simmel was preoccupied with ethical questions. Simmel's *Introduction to the Science of Morals: A Critique of the Fundamental Concepts of Ethics* illustrates this enduring interest. Despite the title, it was hardly an introduction. The text was comprised of two volumes, each of which ran over four hundred pages. Originally published in 1892–93, the text was reprinted in 1904 and 1911.[43] In what became a discursive and thematic hallmark of Simmel's work, the solicitation of moral critique was intensified through the discourse of the soul (*die Seele*), and nowhere was the antibourgeois character of this discourse as thoroughly developed as it was here. While the text was not popular—the first edition ran a mere 500 copies—it was widely read by Simmel's students. It was this text that served as the philosophical foundation of Kurt Hiller's critique of heterosexism and defense of homosexuality. Margarete Susman referred to it often, and Karl Mannheim referenced it in his memorial obituary to Simmel as an acute analysis of the traditional moral life; Georg Lukàcs and Ernst Bloch were also influenced by its philosophical style of moral critique.

Since the political implications of the text are discussed in subsequent chapters, here I restrict myself to a brief analysis of its philosophical premises. The first chapter of *Introduction to a Science of Morals*, entitled "The Ought," established the science of morals on five premises. First, ethics was a conceptual category like any other category. It could not lay claim to philosophical exclusivity. Furthermore, ethics had no ontological basis and no fixed content. In essence, he disarmed ethics of its potential for theoretical imperialism. Having done so, he devoted much of his subsequent intellectual life to the elaboration of an existential philosophy devoted to the examination of the sociological foundation for ethics. Secondly, ethics were a realm of practical idealism. Simmel oscillated between the idealist proposition that "reality is only a concept" and the sociological investigation of "the material content of the . . . concept," which he called the "reality-concept." Simmel's practical idealism reproduced the unified tension of aesthetic individualism and social ethics found in the Naturalist avant-garde. Thirdly, the science of morals linked reality-concepts to behavior and the "order of the feelings" while recognizing that practical experience established an emotional "differentiation within the concept."[44] Simmel's primary interest was an understanding of the affective authority of dominant ethical concepts. Fourthly, the self-evident character of morality was rejected. In this sense, Simmel's philosophy was posthumanist and antiliberal.[45] Unlike the liberal thinkers of the Enlightenment, Simmel's science of morals sought to distinguished itself from natural science. The science of morals could never be a search for natural laws, i.e., Natural Rights and Natural Morality. Morality was by definition antinatural. It was the free and autonomous negation of reified historical reality. Like Naturalists, Simmelian sociology defined naturalized historical conventions in order to clarify the distinction between an autonomous ethical choice and a socially determined one.

Introduction to the Science of Morals was also a defense of philosophical skepticism and a critique of materialism.

> The spiritual clarification of the world is better and more noble than the materialistic clarification, because spirit [*Geist*] is the unknown and in its essence more mystical. . . . Since one cannot protect oneself against the unknown (because we only learn to dominate through apprehension of those things which stand across from us apprehended as controlling powers), veneration and deification structure the spiritual intellect [*Geistige*], which is merely a name for the unknown.[46]

Theoretically, Simmel sustained the Kantian proposition that noumena and phenomena were unknowable in themselves. As a practical matter, however, Simmel's future sociology rejected the proposition that subjectivity was unknowable. In order to determine the ethical validity of individual values, one must reject the proposition that subjectivity is either unknowable or lacks a material correlation. Perhaps the best sociological analysis of spiritual subjectivity was found in his *Religion*, wherein he wholly rejects the proposition of a subjective interiority, and thereby the proposition of the soul's unknowability. His thought was a disunity of extreme propositions: theoretical pessimism about the ultimate knowability of human desire and the moral injunction to seek a practical determination of anthropological desire manifest in history.

Simmel had already established in *Introduction to the Science of Morals* what he would later call his ethics of "the individual law."[47] The "ethical ontology" of religious and social morality was the authority of an original cause: God or social good. For Simmel, these ethical claims denied the "causelessness" and freedom of ethical demands. In contrast to doctrines of fixed truths, his moral philosophy prescribed "theoretical shock, . . . the groundlessness of certain impulses, [and] the break from the teleological progression."[48] This prescription of shock recalls nothing so much as the techniques of the aesthetic avant-garde. The proposition that ethics must be distinguished from rational progressions colored all of his sociological explorations of ethics. The causelessness of ethical freedom (its ultimate basis in a nonmaterial subjectivity) was perhaps most clearly developed in a later text: "as bearers of practical values we possess an unending adaptability of response that can be completely sufficient for every moral demand and that is not determined by a preexisting being."[49] In place of the ethical ontologies of religious and bourgeois morality and in favor of self-determined values, Simmel prescribed individual law.

> The individual moral ideal—as soon as it only carries a general character and as soon as it brings a greater sum of individual experiences and drives to a unity and an equalization—will always have a half "yes" and a half "no" relationship to the real relationships of the social group within which it has shaped itself.[50]

The individual moral ideal was a theoretically groundless collective impulse that maintained personal responsibility to and critical distance from the social group while refusing to depersonalize, reify, and hence dehistoricize, moral concepts. This was another version of Simmel's unity of extremes: neither egoism nor selfless morality, neither reified idealism nor soulless materialism. Simmel's practical idealism was, like Naturalism, a science of the social impact of personal morality.

THE GENERATION OF 1890: NATURALISM AND SOCIALISM

It is imperative for the narrative of Simmel's countercultural legacy that we determine the meaning of his anticapitalism, and to do this we must understand his intellectual development within the Naturalist intelligentsia in the imperialist period. By the early 1890s, Simmel and the Naturalist counterculture in Berlin were moving ever closer to socialist politics. Class conflict in Naturalist drama was probed indirectly, for instance, through theatrical renditions of the German Peasants' War (Julius Brand's *Thomas Münzer*) and the French Revolution (Franz Held's *Ein Fest auf der Bastille*). Reflecting on the aesthetic intentions of Naturalists, Julius Hart wrote in 1893:

> As though seized by a violent disgust for the dancing, laughing, wining-and-dining world of the "ancien régime," art fled from the elegant salons and perfumed boudoirs—wherein our elders were at home ten or twenty years ago—in order to enter the homes of the poor and the oppressed.[51]

Simmel was in the cultural eye of the political storm set in motion by Naturalist drama. When German officials censored Hauptmann's *The Weavers* in 1892, Simmel took a public stand in favor of citizens' right to attend The Free Theater's production of this drama. In fact, many of Simmel's writings in the 1890s expressed sympathy for working class demands and socialist goals.

This cultural nearness to working class politics was never consummated by an overt political affiliation with the Social Democratic Party, however. The reasons for this are philosophical and cultural. Simmel's deep roots in German idealism prohibited an endorsement of the orthodox Marxism of the period. Very much in the tradition of his senior colleague at Berlin University, Wilhelm Dilthey, Simmel's *The Problems of Historical Philosophy* (1892) explicitly criticized the Marxist premise concerning general historical laws. As a sociologist Simmel did share with Marxism the moral terre firma that civic ethics were the highest concern of humanity. However, the Marxist emphasis on collective consciousness and priority on transforming social institutions were far afield from Simmel's first premise, that is, the reflective and self-creating individual as the locus of ethics and institutional transformation: "the accent of life and its development rests not in the sameness of people, but on the absolute peculiarity of individuals."[52] And, yet, the idea of an absolutely free and unique individuality was not the last word on individualism. In "The Individual and Freedom," Simmel maintained that there was a higher form of individualism, namely, ethical individuation or what he called "the metaphysical aspects of the social individual."[53] Simmel conceived of himself as a deadly enemy of bourgeois individualism with its rank celebration of self-interest. Individuation was valid only if it advanced social morality. Economic self-interest, regardless of all the ideological machinations of capitalist ideology, must never be mistaken for ethics.

Simmel was very conscious of the degree to which his philosophical disposition was itself the product of the two great principles of the nineteenth-century economy: unique individuality and the division of labor. The latter called forth an ethical critique of capitalism. He maintained that the monotony and brutality of specialized labor destroyed the creative soul and uniqueness of the individual. At the same time, specialization portended a potential social harmony. He speculated that the increasing appearance of diverse and specialized forms of labor may serve to affirm individuality and "establish the value of its existence."[54] Work would no longer entail exploitation and the suppression of individuality. While Simmel remained an adherent to bourgeois cultural forms (marriage, individualism, and art for art's sake), he filled these institutions with a radically new existential content. Those new contents were no longer ethically compatible with the ideals of the official and semiofficial ideologies of the Imperial period.

Simmel's simultaneous nearness to and distance from socialist politics in the 1890s and the idea of his sociology as a product of the opposing cultural forces of the Imperial period (extreme individualism alongside ethical movements for economic justice) are propositions that are best explored by returning to an original premise. Simmel's thought was a symbol of the cultural milieu of Naturalism in Berlin. Julius Bab, one of the great cultural critics of the Imperial period, began his four volume work on German drama with a section on Naturalism and Gerhart Hauptmann entitled "The Generation of 1890." "No writer before Hauptmann so successfully brought the people to the theater."[55] Hauptmann was one of those rare individuals whose work received both critical and popular acclaim. He immediately became the champion of Berlin's aesthetic counterculture. His theatricality, which he referred to as "social drama," was extremely innovative and well executed. At the same time, his highly crafted works were an example of the art world's unwillingness to accept its secondary status as mere entertainment. Hauptmann's dramas represented the metaphysical dream of the artist aspiring to be the philosopher king of the republic. His dramas were like watercolor canvasses wherein primary colors, as though the distinct realms of aesthetics and political economy, refused to stay in their place, brilliantly blended, and produced an emotionally powerful social critique. In Haupmann's Naturalist dramas and the Expressionist dramas which followed them, dramatic art in Germany announced the clarion call for social change among the German aesthetic intelligentsia.

The popular breakthrough of Naturalism in Germany was Hauptmann's *Before Dawn.* It was his first drama and was staged in October 1889 by Brahm and Schlenther's Free Theater in Berlin. At its core was a validation of the socialist critique of bourgeois decadence and avarice. Julius Bab describes the plot in the following manner:

> Hauptmann's first work, *Before Dawn*, generally depicts poverty which is an entirely specific product of capitalistic social conditions. The community is surrounded by horrible physical and moral depravity; not as a result of need, but rather as the result of the senseless surfeit of the rainstorm of gold which suddenly intoxicated the completely unprepared minds of the primitive peasants, because coal had been discovered under their potato fields.[56]

Often Hauptmann's dramas deal with the dislocations and injustices accompanying Germany's ongoing transition from an agrarian and craft-based economy to an industrial behemoth. Such dramas, however, were more than socioeconomic portraits of Imperial Germany. They symbolized the ethical and aesthetic preoccupations of the progressive bourgeoisie. *Before Dawn* exemplified the moral perplexities facing the bourgeois intellectual who had attained some measure of indignation about social injustices. The protagonist, Alfred Loth, was a sociologist and Social Democrat, who comes to a Silesian village being rapidly transformed by industrialization, specifically mining. He was also an educated bourgeois torn between his friendship for Hoffman, a former friend from his student days who has married into a family that monopolizes the local coal trade, and his sympathy for the poor. The aesthetic/political precept of the drama: the ethical soul was more authentic than class loyalty and the demands of friendship. This prescription, it should be emphasized, comported completely with Simmel's philosophy of life.

Before Dawn also resounded with the sexual predicaments of the bourgeoisie. There was, for instance, a tragic feminist dimension to the play. The only bourgeois character to join Loth's crusade was Helene Krause, Hoffman's sister-in-law. She was convent educated, and one can see her as a symbol of the nonideological origin of socialism: the learned wisdom of simple, if profound, religious compassion. She and Loth were drawn together and fell in love. Reflecting the presence of eugenic thought within Naturalism, Loth ultimately abandoned her when he learned that she came from a family of alcoholics. He will not father children whose hereditary fate was the decadence of alcoholism. Loth's abandonment of Helene might best be seen as a socialist's renunciation of both free will and feminine religious compassion. (But it also represented Hauptmann's Naturalist belief in hereditary alcoholism.) Helene's conversion to abstinence by the end of the play was an example of feminine free will triumphing over biological determinism. Loth's subscription to the historical laws of heredity made him incapable of recognizing Helene's ability to resist fate. Furthermore, Loth's abandonment of Helene symbolized the tension between socialist ethics and immediate tenderness. Thus, Helene's suicide, the denouement, left the viewer with the portrait of the socialist hero who failed to embody compassion in his most immediate relationship. The profundity of Hauptmann's characterizations, like those of Dostoevsky, were their psychological and moral complexity. One rarely encountered uncomplicated exemplars of goodness: Loth facilitated socioeconomic revelations but fell short in the realm of interpersonal ethics; Helene took up the socialist cause but abandoned her family and was rumored to have returned to her hereditary first causes and taken to the bottle. Hauptmann, far from a single-minded social revolutionary, achieved critical and popular success because his complex characters facilitated multiple receptions that turned on a pronounced ambiguity. Naturalism combined two conflicting views of human nature: biological deteminism and the engrained premise of immutability, on the one hand, and the view that human relations were unjust and subject to change, on the other.

One might presume that *Before Dawn* would have aroused the attention of government officials intent on enforcing laws against socialist culture. As it turns out, it was a different Hauptmann play, *The Weavers*, which was written after the 1890 revocation of the Socialist Law, that earned the countercultural honor of being banned by the state. This drama about a weavers' revolt against industrial power looms, poverty, and avarice—called Germany's finest revolutionary drama—was banned by the Censure Section of the Police Headquarters in Berlin in March 1892. This ban again was upheld for a revised version that was submitted to the Censure Section in January 1893. There was no hope for police authorization. Under the threat of jail and legal action, a censure-free rendition of the drama was performed by the Free Theater group at the German Theater in Berlin on February 26, 1893. This was a huge cultural event. It was celebrated by the left and denounced by the right. The Naturalists had thrown down the aesthetic gauntlet. Kaiser Wilhelm reacted to this aesthetic act of political defiance by rescinding his reservation for court boxes at the German Theater. The German Theater thereby lost the patronage of the royal family, but it gained an exponentially larger and more diverse audience, including the prominent Social Democrats Paul Singer and Wilhelm Liebkneckt, who attended the premiere. Under Brahm's direction the German Theater performed the drama nearly two hundred times in the following years.[57] It was a resounding success.

The social fervor aroused by *The Weavers* involved Simmel directly rather than just circumstantially. In the midst of the ban, Simmel published an essay in opposition to censorship in the liberal *Sozialpolitisches Zentralblatt*:

> Hauptmann's play *The Weavers* deserves its place within the register of *our social movement* as if it were the articles of association of a cartel or the proceedings of the Union for Social Politics [*Verein für Sozialpolitik*] themselves. To the same extent as the events to which this paper dedicates itself, this work brings to expression the most profound social movements; the work is a vehicle and symbol of the movements through which every modern expression of life, willingly or unwillingly, must take shape. By depicting the most gripping features of the poverty of the Silesian weavers in the 1840s and their revolt against exploitation, Hauptmann certainly did not intend to foment agitation or make a personal statement by relating the subject matter to the movements of the day. Rather, he was solely interested in a literary problem. However, nothing proves the power of these social movements more than the following acknowledgment [of the primacy of aesthetics]; because it demonstrates how the poverty of the masses and their desire for relief are suppressed even in the hidden and unconscious origins of literary phantasy.[58]

This essay demonstrates that Simmel not only affirmed Naturalism but also understood it as the cultural core of a larger political and social movement within the progressive middle class. The key demand of that movement was for social recognition of the negative consequences of laissez-faire capitalism and support for public reforms that would expand democracy and alleviate poverty.

Secondly, Simmel's defense of avant-garde theater was typical of the ideology of the leading Naturalists of the period. They sought to maintain, at least rhetorically, that Naturalist theater was essentially an aesthetic issue.

Typically we find them seeking to distinguish an aesthetics whose *effect* was political and moral critique from an aesthetics whose *intention* was the promotion of an existing social movement. The reason for this distinction was the rise of proletarian theater. With the revocation of the Socialist Laws in 1890 and animated by the themes of Naturalist theater, intellectuals such as Bruno Wille, Conrad Schmidt, and Franz Mehring helped to establish The Free People's Theater and later The New Free People's Theater in the early 1890s.[59] The cultural overlap of Hauptmann's literary arraignment of the bourgeoisie and socialist transcriptions of Kaiser capitalism was indicated by the fact that Wille's New Free People's Theater staged *The Weavers* three times and Mehring's Free People's Theater staged it seven times. Given this overlap, it was necessary for progressive members of the bourgeoisie to delineate between an embrace of Hauptmann's genuine working-class drama and proselytism for a Marxist world view. For most members of the Naturalist counterculture and the progressive bourgeoisie saw themselves as a moral and cultural elite—an aristocracy of culture rather than blood—that had no intention of submerging their cultural institutions within the movement for Social Democracy. In one of his early essays on Nietzsche, Simmel referred to the cultural disposition of "aristocratic distantness," and this self-conception described the spirit of the progressive bourgeoisie whose claims to cultural leadership depended on a nearness to socialist ethics as much as a distance from working-class culture.[60] The self-conception of the Naturalist counterculture as a moral and cultural elite accounts for Simmel's insistence that Hauptman's subject matter was not an endorsement of a social(ist) movement.

More fundamentally, the political tone and ethical motivation of the Naturalist counterculture and the sponsors of proletarian theater were sharply divergent. Socialists generally sought to forge a collective class identity. Conversely, the aim of the mainline Naturalists who coalesced around Hauptmann was to persuade us of the nobility of individuality. The old weaver's cry—"once in a lifetime a man's got to show what he feels"—was a tocsin decrying the tragic eclipse of individual longing among the lowly.[61] Hauptmann's proletarian lineaments, in sum, take on the contours of the progressive bourgeoisie. The aesthetic treatment of the working class was intended to emphasize the effects of oppression on the individual's spiritual or psychological economy. It was not a summons to a militant collective consciousness. Simmel's interpretation of the play's social meaning resonated with this intonation. He admitted that the "completely new" in Hauptmann's writing was his presentation of the fate of a whole class, rather than merely an individual. At the same time, he argued that Hauptmann's diverse characterization of the working class was akin to a nominalist critique of the socialist presumption of a class identity:

> The doubt of one [worker], the brutality of another, the submissiveness of a third—they are all different radial forms, which point to the same material center and collective class condition. One must reconcile the collective content which shapes the individual life with this collective class condition, although each individual must do so in *their own particular way*. Thereby the attitude, whereby we admit the opposition between the individual's social philosophy of life and their milieu, has achieved its first artistic design.[62]

Immediately apparent here was the untenable nature of Simmel's preceding assertion that Hauptmann's dramas are not tendentious. Hauptmann not only makes the workers' revolt understandable, indeed, his sympathetic treatment of the hellish misery of the weavers makes forgivable the revolt against the bestial greed of their masters. And it is no accident that the local pastor is eating at the home of the fustian manufacturer, Herr Dreissiger, when the rebellious mob makes its impromptu social call. Simmel embraced all of this social commentary. What Simmel did not endorse was an orthodox socialist interpretation of the drama. His reading of the drama displaced an emphasis on class consciousness in favor of an ethical countercultural consciousness whose locus was the ethical and autonomous individual. This reading shared a spiritual and political disposition with anarchists like Courbet, Gustav Landauer, and Leo Tolstoy. This ethics of universal particularity was common within the European avant-garde. For instance, the manifesto of the New Society—a turn-of-the-century Berlin cultural association that included Landauer and cultural critics Heinrich and Julius Hart and dedicated to "the founding of a new world view"—stated: "The core of our world view is the development of knowledge of the identity of the world and the individual [Welt und Ich], the imagination of the world-I."[63] This manifesto expresses a conjunction of aesthetics and ethics which was typical of Simmel's thought as well. As early as 1890, he was theorizing about an ethics of "collective responsibility" from the "standpoint of individualistic realism."[64] Simmel's interest in Naturalist aesthetics boils down to an aesthetic understanding of individual-based ethics created through an investigation and critique of real and material social relations.

Very much in the spirit of Simmel, cultural critic Julius Bab rejected attempts to portray Hauptmann as a "social revolutionary" and instead distilled the meaning of his work in the following way: "It is not the social portrait, not the struggling class, not the shattered social form that interested Hauptmann and that he packed into his dramas, rather it was always the human soul in itself and its divine compassion."[65] During the Imperial period, the discourse of the soul (*die Seele*) and an ethics of compassion were a cultural force field shaping the thought of the German avant-garde, and Simmel's thought was no exception. Simmel's civic orientation derived from a philosophy of compassion. This orientation is ground zero for understanding not only his identification with Naturalism but also the ethical origin of his sociological interests. He chose themes such as patriarchy, social hierarchy, ethical indifference, and the money economy, because they were incompatible with what he called "good will." Good will was a controlling concept of his two volume *Introduction to Moral Science: A Critique of the Fundamental Concepts of Ethics* (1892–1893). Even more tersely than in this work, Simmel's philosophy of compassion and its critical relationship to social institutions was brilliantly revealed in his article "Concerning Greed, Extravagance, and Poverty" (1899), which appeared before the turn-of-the-century in *Ethical Culture: Weekly Periodical for Social-Ethical Reform.* Here Simmel discreetly championed the ethical ideal of poverty that propelled the first Christians and the lives of Buddhist and Franciscan monks. Their deep inner need for a life of "incomparable passion" was contrasted to the "demonic formula" of the capitalist money economy: (1) "indifference toward everything external" and (2) the seduction of extravagant consumerism. Money, the symbol of this era,

> is the most indifferent and most innocent thing in the world. Thus, for those of an ascetic way of life, it is a proper symbol of the devil which seduces us in the masks of harmlessness and impartiality.[66]

For Simmel, the capitalist money economy was neither indifferent nor impartial in its effects, and his sociology of modernity was intent on capturing its spiritual and ethical partiality. Like others within the Naturalist counterculture, the goal of his critique of capitalist culture was not the promotion of socialism but the promotion of higher "spiritual goods" which were incompatible with economic liberalism. For instance, in a different essay, Simmel praised the "hyper-aestheticism" of Naturalism for its attempt to overcome the repulsion, distance, and alienation that characterizes modern relationships. Furthermore, he drew an analogy between Naturalism and scientific tendencies like materialism and positivism. Both sought to overcome the pitiless and unfeeling culture of money through a belief in the unmediated presentation of reality. If the goal was laudable, the philosophical means of achieving it were destined to fail. The cause of this failure was their neglect of the "neo-Kantian . . . medium of the soul."[67]

Simmel was a sociologist of the soul, who throughout his life returned to the subject matter of Naturalism to refine his philosophy. His extensive writings on Naturalism culminated in the posthumous publication of "Concerning the Problem of Naturalism." This essay was an example of what he called his philosophical "Third Way"—"beyond actuality as much as subjective free will."[68] The philosophical ideal of a Third Way was achieved when the "subjective-naturalistic impulse of the artist, his freedom, gives rise to what is needed to meet the objective demands of art: the forfeiture of the contradiction between freedom and necessity."[69] Simmel, as we know, was not an uncritical devotee of Naturalism. While he extolled the Naturalist "truth ideal," he argued that Naturalism, as a philosophy, was based on "a subjective error," namely, the assumption that reality and its reproduction in art must be mechanically and formally similar: "The analogy: the apparent psychological equivalence between historical understanding and the object of study . . . [but] understanding is not reproduction."[70] Simmel, just prior to his death, was still refining his philosophy through a critique of Naturalism. His conception of a philosophical Third Way was possibly the most succinct expression of his thought as a unity of extremes, and it is relevant that his Third Way was developed through an analysis of the feminine principle of love (in "Über die Liebe") and the sociological aesthetics of Naturalism (in "Zum Problem des Naturalismus"). Other Simmel scholars have created a highly developed chronology of his intellectual stages, but it is also necessary to recognize powerful streams of continuity. Major themes—feminism, ethical individuation, Naturalism, monetary culture, and the compassionate soul—were present in his work from the 1890s until his death. As was the case with Courbet's avant-garde aesthetics, Simmel's work combined a penchant for compassionate realism with an unyielding defense of creative individualism. The avant-garde admixture of civics and aesthetic individualism received its most sophisticated expression in his philosophical sociology, which is the subject of our next chapter.

NOTES

1. Georg Simmel, "Soziologische Ästhetik" [1896], in *Das Individuum und die Freiheit* (Frankfurt a.M.: Suhrkamp, 1993), p. 176.

2. David Frisby, *Georg Simmel* (London: Tavistock, 1984), p. 113.

3. T. J. Clark, for instance, links Courbet's art to European modernism: "Realism is an episode against the grain of French art; and therefore its forms have to be extreme, explosive. Hence Courbet's realism; hence Cubist realism which looked back to Courbet as its founding father; hence, finally, Dada." *Image of the People: Gustave Courbet and the Second French Republic 1848–1851* (Greenwich, Conn.: New York Graphic Society, 1973), p. 19.

4. Georg Simmel, "The Stranger," in *The Sociology of Georg Simmel*, trans. and ed. Kurt H. Wolff (New York: The Free Press, 1964), p. 402.

5. Ibid., pp. 404–405.

6. Cited in Gershom Scholem, *Walter Benjamin: The Story of a Friendship*, trans. Harry Zohn (Philadelphia: The Jewish Publication Society of America, 1975), p. 15.

7. See "Berliner Nachrichten," *Nationalzeitung*, 1 November 1896 (Evening Edition).

8. Cited in Hans Simmel, "Auszüge aus den Lebenserinnerungen," in *Ästhetik und Soziologie um die Jahrhundertwende: Georg Simmel*, eds. Hannes Böhringer and Karlfried Gründer (Frankfurt a.M.: Vittorio Klostermann, 1976), p. 260. My biographical sketch of Georg Simmel relies on the information found in this memoir.

9. Ibid, p. 265.

10. On the cultural treasures of the museum island, see David C. Preyer, *The Art of the Berlin Galleries* (Boston: L. C. Page, 1912); on the modernization of Berlin during the late Wilhelmine period, see Annemarie Lange, *Das wilhelminische Berlin. Zwischen Jahrhundertwende und Novemberrevolution* (Berlin: Dietz, 1976).

11. Simmel, "Die Grosstädte und das Geistesleben," in *Brücke und Tür: Essays des Philosophen zur Geschichte, Religion, Kunst und Gesellschaft* (Stuttgart: K. F. Koehler, 1957), pp. 227, 231.

12. See Klaus Christian Köhnke, *Der junge Simmel in Theoriebeziehungen und sozialen Bewegungen* (Frankfurt a.M: Suhrkamp, 1996), pp. 45–46.

13. Donald Levine, "Introduction," in Georg Simmel, *On Individuality and Social Forms*, ed. Donald Levine (Chicago: University of Chicago Press, 1971), pp. x–xi.

14. The most detailed discussion of this incident is found in Köhnke, pp. 54–58.

15. Lewis A. Coser, "Introduction," in *Georg Simmel*, ed. Lewis A. Coser (Englewood Cliffs, N.J.: Prentice-Hall, 1965), p. 3; see Coser's "The Stranger in the Academy," which appears in the same volume.

16. Dietrich Schäfer, 26 February 1908, in Michael Landmann, "Bausteine zur Biographie," in *Buch des Dankes an Georg Simmel: Briefe, Erinnerungen, Bibliographe,* ed. Kurt Gassen and Michael Landmann (Berlin: Duncker & Humblot, 1958), p. 27.

17. Rudolf Weingartner, *Experience and Culture: The Philosophy of Georg Simmel* (Middletown Conn.: Wesleyan University Press, 1962), p. 6; *Buch des Dankes*, pp. 26–27.

18. Cited in James Henry Rubin, *Realism and Social Vision in Courbet and Proudhon* (Princeton: Princeton University Press, 1980), p. 93.

19. Max Buchon, "An Introduction to the *Stonebreakers* and the *Funeral at Ornans*," trans. Petra Chu, in *Courbet in Perspective* (Englewood Cliffs, N.J.: Prentice-Hall, 1977), pp. 60–61.

20. Gustave Courbet, *The Letters of Gustave Courbet*, ed. and trans. Petra Chu (Chicago: University of Chicago Press, 1992), pp. 228–31.

21. Cited in Rubin, p. 79.

22. Simmel, "Zum Problem des Naturalismus," in *Fragmente und Aufsätze* (Münich: Drei Masken, 1923), p. 297.

23. Georg Lukács, "Expressionism: Its Significance and Decline," *Essays on Realism*, trans. David Fernbach (Cambridge: MIT Press, 1981), p. 86.

24. By the 1860s and 1870s his prose was often devoted to the scenes of war: *The Schleswig-Holstein War in 1864* (1865) and *The German War of 1866,* 2 vols. (1869–70). During the Franco-Prussian war, he was taken prisoner while

serving as a war correspondent for the *Vossische Zeitung* and subsequently incorporated these experiences into *Kriegsgefaugen* (1871). In 1878, he finished *Before the Storm*, a four volume historical novel on the Napoleonic age.

25. Fritz Mauthner, "Georg Simmel," *Vossische Zeitung*, October 18, 1918.

26. Cited in Klaus Köhnke, *Der junge Simmel*, p. 83.

27. Henrik Ibsen to Julius Hoffroy, 4 February 1887, in Henrik Ibsen, *Speeches and New Letters*, trans. Arne Kildal (Boston: The Gorham Press, 1910), pp. 106–107.

28. Henrik Ibsen, *Sämtliche Werke*, ed. Paul Schlenther (Berlin: Fischer, 1921).

29. Otto Brahm, "Ibsen in Berlin," in *Kritiken und Essays* (Stuttgart: Artemis Verlag, 1964), pp. 504–505.

30. See Richard Hammann and Jost Hermand, *Gründerzeit. Deutsche Kunst und Kultur von der Gründerzeit bis zum Expressionismus* (Munich: Nymphenburger, 1972).

31. See Katharina Günther, *Literarische Gruppenbildung im Berliner Naturalismus* (Bonn: Bouvier, 1972).

32. Paul Schlenther, *Wozu der Lärm? Genesis der Freien Bühne* (Berlin: S. Fischer, 1890), p. 5.

33. Günther, p. 79; Köhnke, p. 80.

34. Simmel, "Soziologische Ästhetik," pp.167–176.

35. Sabine Lepsius, *Ein Berliner Künstlerleben um die Jahrhundertwende* (Munich: Gotthold Müller, 1972), pp. 63–65.

36. Hans Simmel, p. 251.

37. Lepsius, p. 77.

38. H. Stuart Hughes, *Consciousness and Society: The Reconstruction of European Social Thought, 1890–1930* (New York: Vintage Books, 1958), p. 37.

39. Simmel, "Der Militarismus und die Stellung der Frau" [1894], in *Schriften zur Philosophie und Soziologie der Geschlechter* (Frankfurt a.M.: Suhrkamp, 1985), p. 107.

40. Simmel, "Frauenstudium an der Berliner Universität," [1899]; "Weibliche Kultur" [1902], in *Schriften zur Philosophie und Soziologie der Geschlechter*.

41. Georg Wilhelm Friedrich Hegel, *Philosophy of the Right*, trans. T. M. Knox (New York: Oxford University Press, 1967), p. 155.

42. See, for instance, Gail Finney, "Ibsen and Feminism," in *The Cambridge Companion to Ibsen* (New York: Cambridge University Press, 1994), pp. 89–105.

43. For a detailed editorial history of the text, see *Einleitung in der Moralwissenschaft: Eine Kritik der ethischen Grundbegriffe*, 2 vols. (Frankfurt a.M.: 1989–91), II: 403–11.

44. Simmel, *Moralwissenschaft,* I:18–19.

45. See Simmel's reference to "die blosse Vorstellung der Natürlichkeit . . . bei Rousseau, den Physiokraten und schon wieder in manchen modernen Kreisen." *Moralwissenschaft*, I: 101.

46. Ibid., 45.

47. Simmel, *Das individuelle Gesetz* (Frankfurt a.M.: Suhrkamp, 1987), pp. 74–231.

48. Simmel, *Moralwissenschaft,* I: 43, 44.

49. Simmel, *Schopenhauer und Nietzsche* (Hamburg: Junius, 1990), p. 236.

50. Simmel, *Moralwissenschaft*, I: 91.

51. Cited in John Osborne, *The Naturalist Drama in Germany* (Manchester: Manchester University Press, 1971), pp. 8–9, 5. The translation has been altered.

52. Simmel, "Das Individuum und die Freiheit," in *Das Individuum und die Freiheit* (Frankfurt a.M.: Fischer, 1993), p. 217.

53. Ibid., p. 219.

54. Ibid., p. 219.

55. Julius Bab, *Die Chronik des deutschen Dramas, Erster Teil 1900–1906* (Berlin: Oesterheld, 1922), p. 40.

56. Ibid., pp. 41–42.

57. Brahm, p. 578.

58. Simmel, "Gerhart Hauptmann's 'Webers'" (1892–93), in *Vom Wesen der Moderne: Essays zur Philosophie und Aesthetik* (Hamburg: Junius, 1990), pp. 163–64.

59. See Peter von Rüden, *Sozialdemokratisches Arbeiter Theater (1848–1914): Ein Beitrag zur Geschichte des politischen Theaters* (Frankfurt a.M.: Athenäum, 1973), chapter 4.

60. Simmel, "Friedrich Nietzsche: Eine moralphilosophische Silhouette" (1896), in *Vom Wesen der Moderne*, p. 67.

61. Hauptmann, *The Weavers*, in *Social Dramas*, vol. 1 of *The Dramatic Works of Gerhart Hauptmann*, trans. L. Lewisohn (New York: Huebsch, 1912), p. 351.

62. Simmel, "Gerhart Hauptmanns," p. 165.

63. Heinrich and Julius Hart, *Das Reich der Erfüllung: Flugschriften zur Begründung neuen Weltanschauung* (Leipzig: Dietrichs, 1900), p. 93.

64. Simmel, *Über sociale Differenzierung* (1890), in *Georg Simmel, Gesamtausgabe,* ed. Otthein Rammstedt, vol. 2 (Frankfurt a.M.: Suhrkamp, 1989), p. 111.

65. Bab, p. 43.

66. Simmel, "Ueber Geiz, Verschwendung und Armut," in *Aufsätze und Abhandlungen 1894–1900*, p. 539.

67. Simmel, "Soziologische Ästhetik," p. 175.

68. Simmel, "Zum Problem des Naturalismus," in *Fragmente und Aufsätze*, p. 297.

69. Ibid., p. 297.

70. Ibid., p. 299.

2
PHILOSOPHICAL SOCIOLOGY

Nietzsche, Compassion, and the Capitalist Soul

What must be determined—not in particular, but as a matter of principle–is the a priori element of historical knowledge.
Simmel, *The Problems of Historical Philosophy*

Money has become the God of our time. . . . The most profound essence of the concept of God is reached in its ability to unify the multiplicity and contradictions of the world. . . . Undoubtedly, the psychological functions of the concept of God are similar to the sensations evoked by money. Money increasingly has become an absolutely sufficient expression and equivalent of all values; it elevates itself to a completely abstract summit above the total breadth of the multiplicity of objects. . . . The persuasiveness of money–it is the point of intersection of all values–thus contains a pure psychological, that is to say formal, leveling, which gives deeper meaning to the complaint about money as the God of our time.
Simmel, "Money in Modern Culture"[1]

SIMMEL'S THOUGHT COMBINED A COUNTERCULTURAL ETHICS, A PHILOSOPHICAL critique of historicism, and a sociology of modernity. It is difficult, in retrospect, to imagine this hybrid taking root and flourishing in soils other than those in the intellectual fields of Berlin. Nowhere in Europe in the 1890s was cultural and intellectual ferment more intense. At this time, Berlin was the European cultural capital of what H. Stuart Hughes called an "intellectual revolution" in social theory.[2] Simmel was a key figure in this revolution. However, Hughes's canonical text contained merely two references to Simmel. The intention here is the integration of Simmel's social theory into this revolutionary narrative. For Simmel's intellectual legacy conforms precisely to Hughes' principal themes: Berlin as the locus of intellectual ferment, the revolt against positivism, the critique of Marxism, the recovery of the unconscious, neoidealism, and the transcendence of positivism and idealism.

Simmel was one of Berlin's leading exponents of *Geisteswissenschaften* (the humanities, but literally "science of spirit or intellect"), which was part of a European-wide movement against positivism.

> They used the word [positivism] in a looser sense to characterize the whole tendency to discuss human behavior in terms of analogies drawn from natural science. . . . Hence they used the word positivism almost interchangeably with a number of other philosophical doctrines that they regarded with equal disfavor—"materialism," "mechanism," and "naturalism.[3]

The European epicenter of antipositivism was Berlin University. Its German champion, and the standard bearer of the German idealist tradition, was Professor Wilhelm Dilthey (1833–1911) who founded the fields of *Geisteswissenschaften* and *Lebensphilosophie* (philosophy of life).[4] Dilthey's philosophy of life featured the preeminence of an independent subjectivity whose ethical advancement demanded a highly developed historical and sociological sensibility. Life, a central category of his thought, was conceived as an aesthetics of ethical self-creation whose loftiest goal was "the highest development of social existence."[5] If, on the one hand, Dilthey and Simmel's philosophies of life were a protest of the individual soul against Historicism and monolithic materialist conceptions of history, then on the other hand their methodological concentration on the social psychology of individuals demanded an examination of life within a social-historical reality. Their philosophies of life entailed an appraisal of life-with-others within a historical cosmos.

LEBENSPHILOSOPHIE AS A SOCIOLOGY OF THE SOUL: DILTHEY AND SIMMEL

> *Just as Kant sought the liberation from naturalism, the universal intention of the following study is the preservation of the freedom of the spirit and its form-giving productivity over against historicism.*
>
> Simmel, The Problems of Historical Philosophy[6]

Simmel's thought has already been investigated from several horizons of meaning—familial and cultural background, Naturalism and the nineteenth-century European counterculture, the growth of socialism—but his philosophy of life is understood best in relation to Dilthey. Dilthey was not only Simmel's senior colleague throughout the 1890s. He was the most renowned thinker in the Department of Philosophy at Berlin University, and from 1882 to 1905, he occupied the professorial chair that Hegel once held. He was Imperial Germany's most celebrated representative of the unique blend of philosophical reflection and historical analysis that epitomized German Idealism from the Romantics to Hegel. This style of thought, which Dilthey called *Geisteswissenschaften* and which Simmel referred to as *Erfahrungswissenschaft* (science of experience), is delimited best as philosophical sociology.[7] In any case, the most precise placement of Simmel in the narrative of German intellectual history would be as the intellectual heir of Dilthey. When Dilthey retired from Berlin University shortly after the turn of the century, Simmel became Berlin's leading representative of philosophical sociology, *Geisteswissenschaften* and *Lebensphilosophie*.

Broadly speaking, the *Lebensphilosophie* of Dilthey and Simmel might be conceived as a fin-de-siècle prescience of twentieth-century European existentialism. Like post–World War II French existential thought, *Lebensphilosphie* was a unity of extremes: a defense of the individual locus of ethics and a demand for civic virtue. Philosophy commenced with the presupposition of an intensely introspective self whose ultimate worth derived from a self-created, and hence individuated, social ethics. The ethical denouement of existentialism was nearly identical with the ethical prescription of *Lebensphilosophie*. Dilthey preached responsibility for "public welfare" through "personal morality," and Simmel similarly gave voice to his ethical philosophy with the maxim of "the individual [moral] law."[8] An individuated social ethics, then, was precisely the goal of Dilthey and Simmel's philosophies of life.

As with post–World War II existential philosophy, there was a nonconformist character to *Lebensphilosophie*. It was incompatible with traditional religious ethics which were seen as abstract, dogmatic, and impractical. For instance, in a section of his *System of Ethics* entitled "Practical Philosophy," Dilthey referred to his philosophy as a "polemic against the construction of every morality or ethics which claims to offer a pure formula for all conditions of life."[9] Even a self-constructed morality was insufficient if it did not respond to the historical particularity of life's ethical demands, Dilthey maintained. Simmel, too, renounced ahistorical ethical ideals. He philosophized as a member of a "school of thought concerned with praxis,"[10] and, like Dilthey, rejected abstract moral ideals. This existential approach to ethics was implicitly (Dilthey) and explicitly (Simmel) nonconformist. The eternal verities of traditional religion were ballasts of the Wilhelmine status quo. Dilthey and Simmel not only repudiated the self-evident superiority of traditional morality. They inverted the intellectual hierarchy upon which traditional religious truth-claims stand. Traditional Christian ethics presumed the existence of moral absolutes which transcend history. Historical values, those which make no claim to trans-historical validity, were seen as an evil incarnation of human hubris. The philosophical sociology of Dilthey and Simmel inverted this configuration. Naive and rigid absolute values were savaged in favor of conscious historical values which could respond to the existential and civic needs of contemporary society. In this sense, the *Lebensphilosophie* of Dilthey and Simmel produced a cultural atmosphere encouraging, if not requiring, ethical nonconsent toward status quo ideologies.

In addition to possessing very similar existential ethical philosophies, Dilthey and Simmel shared a neo-Kantian approach to the philosophy of history. Both transferred neo-Kantian thought to the realm of social analysis. They both took up Kant's doctrine that the empirical content of experience was structured by a priori mental categories. Kant hypothesized about the transcendental basis of perception that would explain synthetically the connection between mental forms and empirical objects. The transcendental a priori was the prerequisite for an epistemology of the natural world. The multiplicity of natural phenomena can be ascribed properties only through noumena, i.e., categories of thought: "the principles of possible experience are then at the same time general laws of nature, which can be discerned a priori."[11]

Just as Kant analyzed the manner in which the meaning of empirical objects was shaped by mental forms, Dilthey and Simmel maintained that historical understanding must begin with an analysis of individual mental forms. Dilthey built his philosophy on the proposition that the meaning of historical reality was mediated by subjectivity, what he called "metaphysical knowledge." He said: "Every judgement concerning the existence and composition of external objects is ultimately postulated through the context of thought."[12] This foundational proposition was central to Simmel's philosophy of history as well. Ernst Troeltsch insightfully observed that Simmel's critique of historicism rested substantially upon his "most important concept: the a priori of history."[13] The theoretical premise of Simmel's *The Problems of Historical Philosophy* (1892) was the establishment of the "psychological foundation of historical research," and this entailed, first and foremost, the determination of historical individuals' "psychological a priori."[14] Moreover, the analysis of society found in Dilthey and Simmel's thought normally involved an analysis of the mental forms structuring social institutions. In his essay "Sociology," for example, Dilthey criticized the empirical examination of legal rights, morality, and religion found in the sociology of Comte, Spencer, Schäffle, and Lilienfeld: "Their sociology was not a theory of mental forms which addresses the psychological life below the [empirical] conditions of the social relations of individuals."[15] Dilthey was a historian of consciousness who envisaged society, art, religion, and philosophy as "forms of a philosophy of life and world views."[16]

Simmel's philosophy of history was a continuation of Dilthey's conception of the humanities. Specifically, Simmel declared in the manner of Dilthey that the general a priori categories of natural science (*Naturwissenschaft*) were not applicable to the humanities (*Geisteswissenschaft*):

> In comparison to the formal authority of apprehended spirit [*Geist*], the formal authority of apprehended nature is more widely acknowledged; the former is more difficult to get a hold of historically because it is already spirit.[17]

His primary proposition was that nature and human history were very different objects of study. Unlike natural objects, objects of the cultural sciences were realized human spirit. And the diversity of human life, Simmel surmised in *Concerning Social Differentiation* (1890), meant that neither sociologists nor historians could produce the kind of universally valid categories of understanding that one finds in the natural sciences. Since the meaning of historical reality was relative to the mental forms of particular individuals and specific historical institutions, the creation of universally valid sociological laws was impossible.[18]

Simmel's philosophy of history is best described as a type of social psychology intent on criticizing "naive realism."[19] In chapter Two of *The Problems of Historical Philosophy* entitled "Concerning Historical Laws," he argued that historical laws simplify the complex material of history. Historical laws, like those of positivists and historical materialists, make it possible for "very large internal dissimilarities to appear as similar." Further, numerous elements compose an historical event: "the state, class, religion, culture, production conditions, the position of women, bourgeois freedom and individualities, and innumerable concepts of the same logical level."[20] Historical laws neglect a differentiated examination of each element. Simmel, then, conceived of historical determination as a complex of general factors (group, economic) and psychological factors (personal, ethical, physical, and cultural). General factors can be examined using the methods of natural science.[21] However, the compendium of general and psychological factors of history exist only in the individual soul. Therefore, only an analysis of the individual soul can result in a "unified totality" of historical understanding.[22] But this totality was true only for the specific individual and was not generalizable. "Totality," then, meant differentiated positionality or the examination of an individual's matrix of "value-feelings" (*Wertgefühle*).[23] Historical understanding required individuation, and individuation necessitated the ascertainment of mental forms through which objective factors were experienced. Simmel's philosophy of history also shared sympathies with Wilhelm Windelband's description of philosophy as "a critical science of generally valid values."[24] For Simmel, the science of values was a theory of relativism. "What

I understand as the relativism [of values]," Simmel wrote to Heinrich Rickert, "is a thoroughly positive metaphysical world picture."[25] Simmel's relativistic social psychology was ultimately a product of the early neo-Kantian movement and its program, namely, to establish "philosophy as science grounded in experience."[26] Or, as Simmel wrote later in his life, every experience "finds its border in another categorical world."[27]

Simmel's historical relativism and critique of sociological laws recapitulated the central features of Dilthey's philosophy of history and art. Dilthey's two volume magnum opus, *Introduction to the Humanities* [*Geisteswissenschaften*], proposed a "general law of relativity under which our experience of external reality stands."[28] The correlative of this relativity was the impossibility of a monotheistic or metaphysical approach to historical knowledge. Moreover, Dilthey and Simmel shared a spiritual discourse. Simmel's philosophy of history sought to determine the unique a priori of the individual, or as he put it, "to discover the laws of the life of the soul (*Seelenleben*)."[29] Simmel's studies of Rodin, Rembrandt, Goethe, and Stefan George, for instance, were concerned with discerning the creative motives behind art. Very often he was captivated by what one might call the sociological soul of the artist. One can find immediate precursors of the central features of Simmel's sociological aesthetics in Dilthey's philosophy of art. In *The Imagination of the Writer: Building Blocks for a Poetics* (1887), Dilthey philosophized through the key conception of a "context of the life of the soul (*Seelenleben*)."[30] Simmel's aesthetics replicated not only Dilthey's key concepts, but his method of social psychology as well.

We should not be astonished by Dilthey and Simmel's philosophical similarities. Nearly all of their academic lives were spent together in Berlin University's Department of Philosophy. Dilthey came to Berlin in 1882 and remained until his death in 1911. Simmel began teaching in the Department of Philosophy in 1885 and continued to do so until 1914. We should not be surprised, then, that their works feature not only a similar methodology and discourse but also identical cultural references. Dilthey's *Three Epochs of Modern Aesthetics and Its Contemporary Tasks* (1892), for example, concluded with an explication of the philosophical inadequacies of Naturalism. As we know from the previous chapter, this was a key cultural concern for Simmel as well. Dilthey and Simmel's interest in contemporary aesthetics and culture points to the invigorating and existential character of their thought and legacies. They were essentially philosophers of the present who upheld a vision of life that refused to allow the human spirit to be robbed of its creative vitality. Philosophically speaking, Naturalism, Positivism, and historical materialism elided the significance of individual experience by proposing general laws of history. From the point of view of *Lebensphilosophie*, it was pointless to concern oneself exclusively with the objectivity of human life. Crucial was the pulsating life of the mind and its dynamic relationship to social institutions and collective ideologies. The philosophical sociology of Dilthey and Simmel was a radical transmutation of Hegel's historical idealism with its philosophical delineation of a unitary world consciousness as historical truth. But the significance of *Lebensphilosophie* and Simmel's contribution to it are not discernable simply by looking backward. Simmel's position within and full significance to the history of European philosophy necessitates that we direct our gaze forward as well. Perhaps no one has done so as sagaciously as Fritz Heinemann.

> For Simmel . . . philosophy is also the existential expression of life. Additionally, it is a transition to [later philosophies of] existence. . . . It is the greatness of Simmel, that life is philosophizing, and that he thereby reconquers the essence of the life of philosophy.[31]

Simmel, along with Dilthey and Ernst Troelsch, were the key precursors to Karl Jasper and Martin Heidegger's philosophies of existence.

But beyond Simmel's importance to this narrative of academic philosophy, there was his inspirational legacy outside of academia. His legacy within the political and sexual counterculture distinguishes his *Lebensphilosophie* from formally similar variants of his contemporaries. Simmel's philosophy was unique in its ability to inspire students to transgress the inherently bourgeois and narrow academic meaning of philosophy. In *The Destruction of Reason*, Georg Lukács gives us some insight into Simmel's cultural legacy. The text attacked the *Lebensphilosophie* of Dilthey and Simmel as "a general subjectivism of imperialistic-era philosophy."[32] Simmel's philosophy was said to recapitulate the radical relativism of Dilthey. However, Lukács made poignant distinctions: "Simmel philosophized more resolutely than Dilthey from the standpoint that traditional religions and the old types of metaphysics have collapsed."[33] Furthermore, Lukács suggested that Simmel's commanding generational legacy was framed by the fact that he, unlike his philosophical predecessor, provided *Lebensphilosophie* with an anticapitalist outlook.

THE COUNTERCULTURAL DIFFERENCE: *LEBENSPHILOSOPHIE* AS NIETZSCHEAN SOCIALISM

By presenting Simmel's philosophy in the context of Dilthey's theory of *Geisteswissenschaften*, one danger has been avoided. Too often scholars loose a critical distance from their object of study and disproportionately emphasize originality rather than intellectual debts. However, there is an opposite danger. Scholars can so thoroughly interpret individuals as products of their historical contexts that any sense of originality is lost. The previous section comes dangerously close to transforming Simmel and Dilthey's philosophical similarities into a metaphilosophical identity. This, too, must be avoided. So, here we chart a middle course between the roiling waters. First, the formal similarity of Simmel and Dilthey's categories and strategies of analysis require an admission: the philosophical contours of Simmel's thought were not exceptional for the Wilhelmine period. Second, Simmel is nonetheless an extremely original thinker. His originality resides, first of all, in the objects which he chose to study. He brought new objects of study into the academic arena of philosophy, particularly feminism, fashion, urban culture, outsiders, socialism, and the money economy. The content of these studies regularly included an analysis of the inadequacies of contemporary culture and institititions. In this sense, his sociology contributed to a nonconformist attitude toward life. Third, and crucial for an understanding of his originality, Simmel's thought articulated a rare combination of extant philosophies and cultural ideologies.

Specifically, Simmel was the first major intellectual to combine the antibourgeois thought of Nietzsche with a socialist critique of bourgeois economics. This combination was extremely unusual because most devotees of Nietzsche embraced his denigration of socialism and democracy as herd or slave mentalities. Socialism, so the argument goes, incorporated an egalitarian morality and avoided the existential challenge to construct a superior individuated ethics. Socialists, for their part, were equally repulsed by Nietzschean thought. They interpreted Nietzsche's philosophy as a variant of capitalist individualism. And, generally, Nietzsche's excessively individualist philosophy seemed irrelevant to socialists who observed a need to transform social institutions. The self-evident civic character of individual morality simply went unregistered in Nietzsche's thought, or so it seemed to most socialist intellectuals. Nietzsche's relationship to society was exclusively polemical and negative. Yes, the critique of dogmatic social moralities preceded ethical development in general and self-constructed values in particular. However, the ethical poignancy of social critique was not succeeded by the contemplation of a new institutional and social morality. Consequently, for socialists the healthy worldliness of Nietzschean thought had not broken free from the leash of negative individualism. Nietzsche's philosophy appeared to replicate the civic recalcitrance of the commercial bourgeoisie, and for this reason, the leading socialist thinker of the fin-de-siècle period, Franz Mehring, pejoratively labeled Nietzsche as the "moral philosopher of capitalism."[34]

How was it possible, then, that Simmel combined the incompatible philosophies of Nietzsche and socialism? Erich Przywara, a philosopher of religion and student of Simmel, may provide us with an answer. He defined the uniqueness of Simmel's philosophy in the following way: "Polarity is the objective aporia of existing conditions themselves."[35] This definition remains unsurpassed. The conception of Simmel's thought as an objective aporia is pithy and brilliant. Nietzschean socialism was aporetic because we are inclined to object to the proposition that Nietzschean and socialist thought can overcome their overt philosophical incommensurabilities. How was Simmel able to combine then? Although aware of unmistakable incompatibilities, Simmel, on the whole, was less concerned with differences of dogma than with a sociological analysis of capitalist modernity. He keenly comprehended Nietzschean and socialist thought as two forms of resistance to objective realities of laissez-faire society. As antibourgeois philosophies, then, their heated moral energies reveled in the negation of a shared sociological touchstone.

> Nietzsche sees, in the most ruthless fight of the individual, or socialism sees, precisely in the repression of competition, the conditions for the full development of the individual—either way the same fundamental motive is at work: resistance to the subject becoming consumed and leveled in the social-technical mechanism.[36]

> The radical contradiction of socialism and Nietzsche shows itself to be two antagonistic spiritual dispositions responding to one and the same cultural and psychological fact [atomization].[37]

The polarity of Nietzschean individualism and socialist collectivism were objective responses to bourgeois culture, and this polarity was an objective aporia that Simmel fashioned into a critical philosophy.

Simmel's Nietzschean socialism was, nevertheless, more than an aporetic philosophy born from existing social conditions. It was a countercultural response to those conditions. As a philosophy of life, Simmelian thought unified the two most powerful critiques of bourgeois morality. This is not to say that Simmel uncritically promoted the axiomatic programs of Nietzschean elitism and egalitarian socialism. On the contrary, he was a staunch critic of both. Very often we find in his work a socialist critique of Nietzsche and a Nietzschean critique of conceptual naturalizations within socialist philosophy. But Simmel did argue that Nietzsche proffered a "social-ethical standpoint" and "historical synthesis" for "overcoming the pure isolation of the individual" in liberal society.[38] Most importantly, he enlisted Nietzsche in cultural battle against economic liberalism, emphasizing Nietzsche's loathing for monetary values as an alternative civic ideal.

Simmel was a genius of antibourgeois thought. This did not make him a spokesman for Marxism, however. According to H. Stuart Hughes: "Basically Marxism was to figure in the intellectual renovation of the 1890s as an aberrant, and particularly insidious, form of the reigning cult of positivism."[39] It is technically true, as Hughes asserts, that *Lebensphilosophie* rejected Marxism and its materialist philosophy. However, this antagonistic thesis fails to vouchsafe a more complex comprehension of the politics of the fin-de-siècle German counterculture. Specifically, Hughes's thesis conceals the underprops of a cultural filiation. For example, several of Simmel's early essays appeared in socialist journals: *Vorwärts, Die Neue Zeit, Das freie Wort*, *Sozialistische Monatshefte*, and *Die Zukunft,* and this illumines an elective affinity with Social Democracy: an ethical repudiation of capitalism. Moreover, Simmel's theme of alienation, which was a core element of his sociology of capitalism, was a refinement of Marx's thesis concerning estrangement of labor in modern society. In Simmel's case, then, anti-Marxism was more a philosophical repudiation of materialism than it was a rejection of socialist ethics. Simmel's *Philosophie des Geldes* (1900) was a prime example of how *Lebensphilosophie* renounced Marxist philosophy while at the same time producing a scathing critique of trickle-down bourgeois morality, alienation, the division of labor, and the institutional ethics of Kaiser capitalism. In sum, Simmel's philosophy combined both a philosophical critique of Marxist philosophy and an affirmation of socialist ethics.

We need to keep in mind that Simmel never joined the Social Democratic Party. Nonetheless, if we conceive of socialism more expansively as an ethical rejection of economic liberalism, then Simmel can be said to have endorsed socialism in the broadest sense of the word. For him, socialism meant a rejection of the civic and ethical validity of the capitalist a priori: economic self-interest. Perhaps it is best to think of Simmel's anticapitalism in light of Leo Tolstoy and Gustav Landauer, who both conceived of socialism as the expression of spiritual nobility. Socialism of this ilk denied historical determinism and emphasized the spiritual difficulty of freely willed collective ideals. More than a plea for economic justice or demand for egalitarian eudaemonism, socialism was the deepest expression of personal spirituality. Simmel's interest in socialism and sociology is probably best seen in this light, as the articulation of a feeling of religiosity. This religiosity sought to resolve the fracture "between needs and their satisfaction, between responsibility and action, and between one's ideal picture of the world and the reality" of capitalist society.[40] Moreover, Simmel, like Tolstoy, associated religion with "the feeling-province of love."[41] Shortly before his death he was still working on a philosophy of love. If we are to speak of Simmel as a socialist, then we should do so in relation to a particular subspecie: the compassionate motives of utopian and Christian socialists.

> This is precisely the miracle of love. It does not nullify the being-for-itself of either the I or the Thou. On the contrary, it creates being-for-itself into a condition for the successful nullification of distance and of the egotistical reversion of the will to itself. This is something completely irrational, that evades the otherwise valid categories of logic.[42]

Three fountainheads of Simmelian thought are conjoined in this quote: (1) reason and logic are inadequate for an understanding of value-feelings, (2) any valid philosophy of life transcends the dualism of subject and object and of egoism and altruism by seeking to satisfy simultaneously the individual's need for happiness and social responsibility, and (3) practical philosophy and civic sociology depend upon an ethical analysis of psychic forms.

These central elements of Simmelian thought came together in a monumental essay entitled "Socialism and Pessimism," which appeared the same year, 1900, as his magnum opus, *The Philosophy of Money*, and this essay should be interpreted as the ethical denouement of his sociology of monetary modernity. Heretofore, this essay has been largely neglected, as has Simmel's self-conception of philosophical sociology as an ethical refinement of socialism. Socialism, according to Simmel, was inherently optimistic about the ability of a rational division of possessions to promote general human happiness. This optimistic and rationalistic socialism was destined to fail because it neglected a basic psychological fact: "human beings are distinct emotional beings. . . . Also there is actually no common standard and elevation of the contents of life that can establish emotional equality."[43] We can expect, for example, profoundly different responses to the prospect of a socialistic life with fewer possessions. According to Simmel, socialist optimism was a contradiction; socialism aspired to collective happiness but neglected the reality that economic equality will not produce this because "in our soul always rests a dark conception of the average human lot."[44] For socialism to succeed, then, it must (1) recognize the subjective character of human happiness and (2) prepare for a negative psychological reaction to the socialist goal of material equality. Simmel insisted that these revisions of socialism could be achieved through the "pessimistic advancement of socialism."[45] In particular, socialism must advance a pessimist proposition about the material bases of happiness and the value of human life. That proposition was already a formal element of socialist ideology: the value of human life was not indicated by the class-based distribution of goods. In other words, working-class lives were not less valuable due to material deprivation. Socialism valued life independent of material possessions. According to Simmel, this demonstrated that socialism contains within itself an antimaterialist valuation, a valuation which is pessimistic about our ability to quantify and objectify human life. Far too often this pessimistic and spiritual element of socialism was occluded by another element of socialism: quantifiable and optimistic economic equality. Simmel was not opposed to egalitarian materialism. However, he feared that egalitarian optimism was in danger of extinguishing the antimaterialist and pessimistic elements of socialism. If this happens, socialism was destined to fail. In particular, the success of socialism required an antimaterialist valuation of human life which respected the nonmaterial realm of individuated feelings and spiritualities. Pessimistic socialism would maintain the distinction between the individual and general humanity—a distinction that egalitarianism threatened to banish from civic life—by defending the individual's right to spiritual and aesthetic, i.e., nonacquisitive, self-refinement.

Simmel maintained that a defense of subjective differentiation and spiritual advancement would intensify the significance of socialism in several ways. First, optimist socialism promoted the illusion that happiness and freedom depend solely upon the realization of material goals. Pessimistic socialism guarded against the spiritual bankruptcy of socialist materialism by advancing the goal of individual spiritual cultivation. Second, many individuals justifiably resist socialist eudaemonism because they perceive it as a form of materialistic leveling. By advocating the individual's right to spiritual differentiation, pessimistic socialism removed this legitimate reason for resisting socialist transformation. Third, like an Eastern bodhisattva, Simmel wrote in reference to pessimism: "The path of culture is the path of rising consciousness."[46] But he was quick to emphasize that pessimist socialism was not an absolute pessimism like Hinduism. There was a practical and performative value to the pessimistic advancement of socialism. The immutable tension between sociological and subjective ideals—found in religious renunciations of materialism and Marxist denunciations of religion—could be transcended. Simmel designated this transcendence as the oracle of a "hypertrophic self." Here, hypertrophy alludes to the radiant excess of spiritual conviction. Hypertrophic religiosity, stifled by the narrowness of civic materialism or spiritual consciousness, was an overflowing temperament inspired to seek the reformation of both the political and inner realms.

Three prominent themes in Simmel's early research—social differentiation, the women's movement, and money—directly involved him in both a philosophical and a practical discussion of socialism and its demands. His research on social differentiation began in the mid–1880s and culminated in the publication of *Concerning Social Differentiation* in 1890. This text was clearly influenced by Herbert Spencer's sociological ideas of evolutionary differentiation, whereby human progress was conceived as a movement from homogeneity to heterogeneity.[47] In *Concerning Social Differentiation*, Simmel interrogated "the psychological origins of socialist demands" from the perspective of heterogeneous ethical values.[48] According to Simmel, all ethical values possess a relative character. Their meaning derives from their relation to competing value-feelings, and their legitimacy was never self-evident.[49] The universal character of the socialist ideal of equality was contrary to ethical heterogeneity because it had taken on the appearance of a pure and natural human concept:

> [The socialist notion of equality] is a remnant of the realist concept of natural understanding. . . . The whole idea of the self-evident rights of equality is only an example of the tendency of the human spirit to foresee the result of historical processes (if they exist for a sufficient period of time) as logical necessities.[50]

The socialist demand for equality was, according to Simmel, also a demand for the removal of social differentiation and a demand motivated by resentment and economic envy. However, he concluded, "the cultural values of differentiation" ultimately were not threatened by socialism because our "sensibility for differences" adjusts to social conditions.[51] Despite socialism and the increasing rationalization, standardization, and calculability of modern culture, or because of them, history was leading toward increasing differentiation.[52]

In *Concerning Social Differentiation* Simmel set out to understand the "diversity of mental-moral temperaments" and "plurality of activities" found in modern capitalist society. This text not only celebrated the process of increasing social, moral, commercial, and aesthetic differentiation; it also intended to find the origin of an "actual coexistence of differentiation in the individual."[53] He, like the great economists of industrial society before him, Adam Smith and Karl Marx, came to identify money as the most revolutionary element of modern culture and the source of social differentiation.

> One can view capital, especially the general possession of money, as a latent differentiation. Since the nature of capital is latent differentiation, it has the power to produce an unlimited number of effects. It constitutes itself as a perfectly unified character, because as a pure means of exchange which is perfectly without character, it radiates in the diversity of transactions and pleasures. Moreover, in the form of potentiality, it unifies within itself the whole colorful realm of economic life, just as white appears colorless but contains within itself all the colors of the spectrum. Likewise, money concentrates in *one* point not only the outcomes but also the possibilities of innumerable functions.[54]

The analysis of socialism and money culture found here was accompanied by the contemporaneous publication of political essays which displayed Simmel's identification with and defense of some socialist goals. In a short essay entitled "A Word Concerning Social Freedom" (1892), for instance, he criticized bourgeois individualism and defended workers' rights to organize: "The increase in the standard of living is not only an individual right of the worker, rather it is his social responsibility."[55] Simmel saw the state's defense of the individual labor contract and the correlative ideology of "personal freedom" not only as an intolerable separation of personal rights and social responsibilities, but also as manifesting the narrow interests of religion, philosophers, and the bourgeoisie:

> Personal freedom is an ideal that arose for specific historical reasons. Despite all of the godliness that surrounds it, despite all of the enthusiasm which is tied to it, it is only a means to specific social and personal goals. . . . The church's theological interest in human freedom is to exonerate the author of the world for responsibility for the sins and poverty in it; personal freedom facilitates the speculations of philosophers who see the metaphysical soul as lacking a causal connection with things; finally personal freedom was advantageous to the interest of the dominant class for whom freedom was the condition of their exercise of dominance, and to those who already possessed formidable powers. They stamped it as the ethical ideal for the whole society.[56]

In another article, entitled "World Politics" (1894), Simmel put forth an internationalist and cultural defense of socialism: the bourgeoisie was wrong to view the economic demands of socialism as a simple materialism; ending hunger was the prerequisite for "the production of higher cultural goods."

> The adversaries of the proletariat . . . do not comprehend that not only is the "question of the stomach a question of ethics," rather it is above all an intellectual question. It is a precondition for the development of countless intellects, which the poverty of existence now suffocates.[57]

The cultural-ethical defense of socialist demands was additionally interesting because Simmel published this essay under a pseudonym. Later, his essay on socialism and pessimism was published in Austria. He must have recognized that, at a time when there were no avowed socialists in the German university system, his statements about "class conflict" and "the international division of labor" had reached the border of academic acceptability. Furthermore, it is very likely, though rarely addressed, that Simmel's antibourgeois politics played a significant role in his inability to secure timely promotions.

Simmel's interest in socialism also brought him in contact with socialist feminism. (It must be recalled that the Social Democrats did more on behalf of women's equal rights than any other political party in Wilhelmine Germany.) His article "The Women's Congress and Social Democracy" (1896), for instance, mentioned the socialist-feminists Clara Zetkin and Lily Braun.[58] What this article shared with Simmel's aesthetic sociology and his research on the psychology of socialism was an attempt to develop a cultural analysis of modern society that included a consideration of the effects of capitalism on class and gender relations. His article on the Women's Congress asserted:

> It is the *same* economic social order, *only* with different relationships. . . . The industrial type of production of the present, on the one hand, has torn

> the proletarian woman from the household economy and, on the other hand, has stunted the sphere of activity of the bourgeois woman.[59]

The two terms of emphasis, "same" and "only," were illustrative of Simmel's feminist perspective. His historical prism was mass capitalist culture and its different class refractions, although he dwelt far more on mass culture than class culture. Simmel's interest was the cross-class culture of capitalist exchange. His existentialism did not permit him to reduce the source of anticapitalist or procapitalist values to a class determinacy. Ultimately, the absence of class determinacy was a theoretical asset and a political liability. Simmel's feminism theorized the benefits of economic and political equality for women of all classes. However, this theoretical unification of women's interests had no parallel in the fractured Wilhemine feminist politics which were almost entirely class-based.[60] Therefore, his feminist politics, no less than his distinctive variant of socialist wisdom, lacked organizational agency. His writings suggest that he was undisturbed about such practical barriers to the realization of his public philosophy. He welcomed new worldly subjects into the castle of academia but never transgressed its ramparts to create political vehicles for change. His political iconoclasms were unconnected to organizational politics, and this above all else, would distinguish his cultural politics from the activist politics of his intellectual heirs.

Independent of organizational politics, Simmel consistently mounted an attack on economic individualism. In numerous publications, including "Friedrich Nietzsche: A Moral-Philosophic Silhouette" (1896), "Towards an Understanding of Nietzsche" (1903), "Nietzsche and Kant" (1906), *Schopenhauer and Nietzsche* (1907), and "Nietzsche's Morality" (1911), he struggled assiduously to distinguish Nietzschean individualism from capitalist individualism. This was the central intention of his neo-Nietzschean oeuvre, and its realization as an ethical critique was powerfully expressed in "The Dual Forms of Individualism" (1902). Here, he described the "ideal of freedom and equality, from which the French Revolution originated," as possessing an "inner contradiction."[61] In the eighteenth century arose "the ideal of the pure freedom of the individual" wherein "the society would be converted from the epoch of historical unreason to natural rationality." Simmel called this naturalization of laissez-faire individualism a "disastrous deception."

> This presumption confused the existing, senseless social differences [of aristocratic society] with inequality in general and maintained that freedom, which was supposed to destroy inequality, was the bearer of a general and lasting equality.[62]

Challenging this naturalization of trickle-down morality, an alternative vision of morality arose in the eighteenth century: the rationalism of Kant. For

Kant, the particularity of the individual was not identical to egotistical interests. Moral individuality was tied to a critical affirmation of social interests and mutual obligations. Simmel, drawing on Kant, rejected two myths of liberalism: (1) the myth of political liberalism, that individual freedom was synonymous with equality, and (2) the myth of economic liberalism, that self-interest was automatically synonymous with social interest.

While both economic liberalism and Kantian morality rested upon the "legal and valued equality of the isolated individual," Simmel stressed the difference between these two forms of individualism.[63] The ideal of economic liberalism assumed that natural harmony would arise when the individual was released from all obligations. Conversely, Kantian individualism assumed that the individual represented a general humanity within itself, which meant that individuals were equal in all things and equally valuable. In the nineteenth century, Simmel continues, these two doctrines of the eighteenth century—liberalism and Kantianism—went in two different directions. The presumed unity of individuality and equality found in both doctrines was torn apart. Two tendencies emerged: equality without individuality and individuality without equality. The first tendency was embodied in socialism and it, Simmel added, "lies outside our interests."[64] The focus on individuality without equality was developed by Goethe, Schleiermacher, the Romantics, and Nietzsche. These were the great critics of Kant. These critics were unwilling to accept the "leveling" of differences which dominated Kant's ethical vision of the free individual. According to Simmel:

> That the differentiation of human beings is also a moral demand, that every person has to realize a moral ideal himself and that no two are the same—this was a totally new valuation [of the nineteenth century], a qualitative individualism in contrast to that which placed all value in the form of a free individual.[65]

Ultimately, Simmel's championing of qualitative individualism was indifferent to the distinction (common among philosophers of the era) between the lawful individual ethics of Kant and the differentiated individual ethics of Nietzsche. The most essential element of a life philosophy was self-created morals.

Simmel's ethical philosophy was, then, an aesthetic civics. Ideally, human values would be created by the individual as objects of use for the ethical will. The great ethical task of the will was to transform the "pure negative side of individualism," emerging from liberalism, into "a living and social constitution, which created a positive synthesis of the two types of individualism."[66] This would be a synthesis of the eighteenth-century ideal of equal rights—a pure rational law binding the individual to a higher unity (Kant)—and the nineteenth-century belief that through the recognition of social-historical existence the particularity of individual character can realize its "spiritual-historical direction."[67] Simmel's vision of ethics, then, blended two forms of ethical individualism (Kant and Nietzsche), which were both incompatible with the pure freedom of economic liberalism. Economic individualism and individual rights, the corner stones of bourgeois culture, were quite different from the ethical individuation championed by Simmel. Simmel's version of ethical individuation was not the naive, avaricious, and deistic individualism of Adam Smith, who conceived of a self-interested individualism that automatically functioned like hands on the historical clock of social virtue. For Simmel, economic individualism was, on the contrary, totally incompatible with social ethics.

Much of Simmel's work from 1900 to 1914 was characterized by a Nietzschean anticapitalism that mocked, derided, and resisted the hegemony of bourgeois ideology and bourgeois institutions such as the State and Church.

> Through the decided emphasis that the state places upon conformity and through the over-strained exercise of ecclesiastical means of control, there has been brought about a noticeable advance in the outer Church life. . . . On the other hand, inner and individual religious feeling . . . has withdrawn itself from the official Church to a considerable degree. This is so much the more surprising, because the need for religion, in and of itself, does not seem to have lessened at all. . . . At the present time this longing assumes an aesthetic character.[68]

What did he mean that religiosity has assumed an aesthetic character? As we know, Simmel generally identified with the transgressive aspirations of the European avant-garde. This transgression was moral leadership and authentic religiosity. The artist connected the "painful and fragmentary in real life" to the "fundamental needs of the soul."[69] But aesthetics alone were not a viable strategy for filling the spiritual vacuum created by Money-Church-State nexus.[70] Those who sought an outlet for spirituality exclusively in the aesthetic realm "[would] learn that this field is also too limited."[71] Only an aesthetics of civic individualism or "a moral aristocracy"—the seminal prescriptive concept in *Schopenhauer and Nietzsche*—could bring a new theory of spiritual life into existence.

ACADEMIA AND THE POLITICS OF NONCONFORMITY

Simmel's politics affected his academic career. At the age of forty-two and after the publication of *The Philosophy of Money*, the Department of Philosophy at Berlin University did provide a slight promotion from *Privatdozent* to *Extraordinarius*. This honorary title meant very little in practical terms. He was still excluded from participation in departmental affairs and was entitled to no institutional remuneration. Moreover, his pedagogical value was still determined by student fees. By 1900, Simmel had published six books and over seventy articles, and his work had been translated into four foreign languages. He was unquestionably one of the most popular lecturers at Berlin University. Despite his academic accomplishments, for over a decade Simmel unsuccessfully sought to obtain an *Ordinarius* or professorial position whenever and wherever a seat in philosophy became vacant.

What was the reason for his inability to garner a position? The academic reasons were manifold. The sociological nature of his philosophy was out of step with the analytic emphasis of many neo-Kantians. His rejection of religious eschatology and ontology in favor of Nietzschean sociology did not endear him to cultural conservatives. In *The Problem of Historicism*, Simmel's contemporary, Ernst Troeltsch, damned Simmel as "a child and darling of modernity with all its dreadful diseases and weaknesses."[72] Troetsch's condemnation recalls Foucault's understanding of the discursive medicalization of confinement. In this case, the diseased and immature Simmel was not so much confined as banished from collective legitimacy. His antibourgeois interest in noncanonical philosophers like Nietzsche made him culturally suspect and intellectually incompatible with theological and analytical thinkers of the period. For example, in a 1911 letter to Heinrich Rickert he puts forth a scathing critique of Rickert's assertion that actions are a "pure nothing": "Your argument is useful only as a formal-logical argument," wrote Simmel, and "I refuse to enter into" this type of discussion.[73] In another correspondence, he again completely rebuked Rickert's philosophical terre firma stating, "from logic alone nothing can be won. From this point one can expound the most profound differences between us."[74] Simmel preferred to defend the existential proposition that life, history, and social existence, not logic, must be the starting point of philosophy. In *Schopenhauer and Nietzsche*, he expressed admiration for the vitalist and elitist philosophy of Nietzsche.

> [For Nietzsche], life is absolutely an empirical and historical phenomenon. The enigmatic blossoms for which it strives are the soul and its contents. This striving enables its meaning to extend beyond its earthly limits, but life as such remains absolutely captive to the earth; it remains the child of the earth and the ideal of nobility remains the most sublime sublimation whose form of life-process is development, a select elite, and cultivation.[75]

Most importantly, the earthly Simmel made it unambiguously clear that he did not deem analytic neo-Kantianism worthy of engagement. Undoubtedly his dismissal of hegemonic neo-Kantianism was well-known among academic philosophers and must have been seen as both a threat and an affront. Did he mean it otherwise? Simmel's strong personality and ethical convictions resulted in more than a contentious friendship with Rickert. Interpersonal conflicts with colleagues also may have contributed to his institutional stagnation at Berlin University.

In an attempt to provide an explanation for Simmel's academic stagnation, Rudolph Weingartner has pointed to a letter of dis-recommendation written by a university official, Dietrich Schäfer. The letter was addressed to the cultural minister of Baden in response to Simmel's application in 1908 for a position in the philosophy department at Heidelberg. On the basis of this letter, Weingartner has pointed to anti-Semitism as the reason for Simmel's academic ostracism. In addition to this letter, Simmel's correspondences corroborate this explanation. One of Simmel's missives mentions "anti-Semitism as a principle difficulty."[76] Schäfer's letter of dis-recommendation seems to confirm Simmel's suspicions. It condemned him as an "Israelite" and someone drawn to "Oriental" and "Eastern" art. His intellectual perspective was referred to as "philosemitic." While Weingartner concludes that anti-Semitism was not the sole explanation for Simmel's academic vicissitudes, it is the only sociological explanation he and other Simmel scholars put forth.[77]

This explanation is inadequate for a number of reasons. In the vita that he provided Berlin University, Simmel identified his religion as Evangelical (he, like his parents, had been baptized). Furthermore, some German Jews had risen in German academia with a much less distinguished publishing and pedagogical record than Simmel's. Schäfer's letter itself, as well as other sources, indicate that anti-Semitism was simply one accepted code for circumscribing and marginalizing Simmel's antibourgeois values. There were strong indications of this that Weingartner did not reference. The letter, for instance, stated that Simmel stands against "our German, Christian, classical culture," and described Simmel's sociological perspective as follows:

> To want to establish the "society" as a law-giving organ for human collective life in place of the State and the Church is in my opinion a disastrous error. It is not right that this direction of thought should now become officially accepted, especially at a university which has a significance for the State and Empire like Heidelberg does for Baden and Germany.[78]

For an uninitiated university official, Simmel's sociological methodology would have appeared identical to socialist materialism. Simmel would have appeared as a fifth column of the rising power of the Social Democrats. Such a presumption was not unjustified since Simmel's sociological philosophy was indeed inextricable from his antibourgeois ethics. Consequently, Simmel was unable to procure one of the two seats at Heidelberg, despite a strong endorsement from Max Weber and Dekan Hampe, a government official in Karlsruhe. Hampe's letter of endorsement documents Simmel's complex reputation and the powerful forces resisting his academic ascension:

> One cannot ascribe him to any general current of thought; he has always gone his own way, above all with the utmost sagacity but also with an essentially negative and destructive critique. . . . [Still] powerful forces are working against the employment of Simmel . . . because Simmel appears to be too relativistic and not sufficiently dedicated to a belief in the Bible.[79]

It was not, in fact, Simmel's supposed "philosemitic" thought that was dangerous, but his polyvalent and thorough rejection of bourgeois values.

Simmel was well aware of his reputation and tried to lobby for a new understanding of his intellectual disposition. He was, of course, the caricature of a wolf in sheep's skin. In a letter to Max Weber soliciting help in securing the position at Heidelberg, Simmel wrote:

> In certain circles the idea exists that I am an exclusively and indeed destructive spirit and that my lectures are directed only toward negation. Perhaps I need not inform you that this is a hideous untruth. My lectures are directed at the positive and at the demonstration of a profound understanding of the world and of spirit. They are a total renunciation of polemic and critique in favor of diverging positions and theories.[80]

This missive was a study in damage control and was an attempt by Simmel to recast his powerful critique of Wilhelmine culture in a positive pedagogical light. That his philosophy was equally an optimistic rendering of Nietzsche's philosophy of yea-saying and a nonpolemical sociology of modernity did not influence his historical reception. For his optimistic and analytical responses to monetary culture *were* radical negations of mainstream Wilhelmine culture.

It was this radicalism and not his participation in certain Jewish circles that determined his academic destiny. While his parents were Jewish converts to Christianity, his philosophy contains nothing that is characteristically or exclusively Jewish.[81] Rather, anti-Semitism was the coded pariahdom and cultural circumscription of his multifaceted antibourgeois disposition. His reputation as a destructive thinker was, to a great extent, an accurate description of his ethical critique of Wilhelmine society. Writing to his friend Karl Joël, he described life in Wilhelmine Germany in the most uncompromising way: "Daily it becomes clearer that we live among barbarians."[82] This was the Simmel that his friends and colleagues knew. The Simmel that Joël knew is alluded to in his review of Simmel's *The Philosophy of Money:* "Nietzsche is not the philosopher of the present, rather the philosopher against the present. That is his inner appeal, his power, and his ethic."[83] Joël was not really speaking of Nietzsche but Simmel who had taken Nietzsche's mantel. Simmel had now supplanted Nietzsche as Germany's greatest thinker against the present.

In a memoir about Simmel, another friend and a former student Margarete Susman described the academic atmosphere of twentieth-century

Wilhelmine Germany, and this provides further insight into Simmel's intellectual reputation.

> It was a time that no longer and never again knew what reality is because it possessed no real problem vis-à-vis reality. The concrete reality of life for the intellectual members of the upper strata, as long as they were not stirred by socialism, proceeded unproblematically.[84]

Simmel was deeply stirred by socialism. This, above all else, differentiated him from the other members of academia and endeared him to radical students. And, it is not only conceivable but quite likely, that his uncompromising antibourgeois philosophy of life created a collegial and intellectual rift between himself and the preponderance of German academic philosophers. He was the closest thing Germany possessed to an academic activist, and his travails within the bourgeois church of academia symbolize, if tragically, his success in developing a philosophy of social critique. Simmel was the Archie Schepp of his day: a man whose iconoclastic virtuosity posed a discordant threat to the conventional rhythms of the academic status quo.

Simmel was an intellectual intermediary between the bourgeois sphere of academia and working-class politics. The venue for this mediation was Berlin University, but the larger political and cultural context was equally significant. By 1905, the Social Democratic Party was the largest party in Germany, and by 1912 it controlled over 110 seats in the Reichstag. Class culture predominated in Wilhelmine politics. Nowhere was this clearer than in the women's movement. The feminist Organization of German Women (BDF), for example, eventually renounced its support for the women's suffrage in this period because the proletarian women's movement included it in their platform. It was imperative that all forms of bourgeois culture distinguish themselves from socialism. As Simmel put it, "one can hardly express one's unreserved sympathy with Labor as against Capital without being immediately set down as a socialist."[85] He, nonetheless, was able to resist the cultural imperative that ethical philosophy distance itself from a critique of capitalism and other cultural dominants. The idea of entrusting a professorial position at Berlin or Heidelberg University to an iconoclastic dissenter naturally was repugnant to university and state officials. However, the same trait that ensured marginalization—a critical and nonconformist attitude—endeared him to students who sought liberation from the academic prison house of intellectual conformity.

THE THIRD WAY: KANT, NIETZSCHE, AND SIMMEL'S CONTEMPORARIES

I argued before that Simmel's uniqueness was most evident in his rare combination of extant philosophies and cultural ideologies. His amalgams of Nietzsche and socialism and pessimism and socialism were historically unusual and philosophically revolutionary. If Simmel's thought radiated a spiritual agency, its revolutionary lessens escaped the insolent narrowness of excessive zeal. Perhaps this was because he consistently sought to combine the best ethical components of incompatible world views. In light of this combination of ethical doctrines, a controlling idea of this manuscript has been Simmel's remarkable preference for the unity of extremes: absolute individuality and selfless civics; praise for aesthetic originality and a prejudice for historical art; and philosophical idealism and an objective analysis of social institutions. Simmel, particularly after the turn of the century, designated his enthusiasm for unities of extremes as a third way. By the end of his life, he was describing his philosophy of love and his aesthetic philosophy as a third way. Like a chemist of critical thought, Simmel often brought together two seemingly incompatible thinkers to create a new mental compound. Indeed, his composite of Nietzschean and socialist thought must be regarded as a third way that is splendidly inventive rather than merely epigonic.

Another example of Simmel's philosophical chemistry was his conjunction of Kant and Nietzsche. While he admitted that "in their cast of mind and composition of values an irreconcilable contradiction existed between the two thinkers," he alternatively insisted that, seen together, they "possess the spirit of a third way."[86] The fabrication of a moral philosophy featuring Nietzsche and Kant went against the grain of academic philosophy. A philosophical accord between Nietzsche and Kant was impossible, according to most of his contemporaries. Furthermore, Simmel's espousal of Nietzsche as a philosopher equal in rank to Kant was a judgement not shared by his neo-Kantian contemporaries. This low esteem for Nietzsche among academic philosophers would not be shared by the cultural avant-garde. After the turn of the century, a new generation of students came under the thrall of Nietzschean philosophy. As the greatest academic proponent of Nietzschean thought, Simmel became a gigantic figure among radical students. His sponsorship of Nietzsche as a moral philosopher, then, endeared him to a younger generation and alienated him from his academic contemporaries.

Simmel's philosophy was a cultural document of the neo-Kantianism of the period. Kant predominated not only in Simmel's books but also in his correspondences:

> In general we revolve around the assumptions of Kant's theory of knowl-

edge like squirrels in a cylinder. . . . When will the genius come who will liberate us from the power of the subject as Kant has liberated us from the power of the object? And, what will be the third power?[87]

The unity of Kant and Nietzsche was Simmel's "third way."[88] This third way was both a cultural politics and an academic territory particular to Simmel. As a cultural politics, his search for a third way—beyond the spiritual emptiness of bourgeois society and mechanistic Marxism—was thematically similar to two contemporaneous cultural movements: the *Völkisch* ideologies of the Right and the aesthetic politics of the Left Expressionists.[89] However, the linkage of Kant and Nietzsche gave Simmel's philosophy a unique cultural inflection. His sociological and critical inclinations contrasted sharply with the analytical neo-Kantianism of the Marburg School. His unusual conjunction of Kant and Nietzsche also distinguished his philosophy of religion from other thinkers of the period who sought to establish a closed philosophical system.[90]

For example, one of Simmel's neo-Kantian contemporaries, Hermann Cohen, was dismissive of Nietzschean philosophy, viewing it as a withdrawal from scientific and scholastic rigor. Cohen asserted that the discipline of philosophy could never coincide with the emancipatory cultural interests of Nietzschean scholars.[91] Whether Cohen had Simmel in mind is unknown, but it is very likely given their shared political tendencies. Like Simmel, Cohen defended an ethical version of socialism in contrast to the socialist materialism of the SPD.[92] Cohen, however, was strident in his insistence on the incompatibility of Nietzschean individualism and ethical socialism. Clearly, Simmel was a prime candidate for this line of criticism. But Simmel's defense of Nietzsche's relevance was less a defense of individualism (in fact Simmel criticized Nietzsche's inability to appreciate the spiritual significance of altruism[93]) than a critique of disinterested philosophy. Through Nietzsche's philosophy, he celebrated the relevance of scholarship to life.

Even before the turn of the century, Simmel found himself defending the sociological relevance of Nietzsche. In his 1897 review of Ferdinand Tönnies's *The Nietzsche Cult*, he criticized Tönnies's "vulgar misconception whereby Nietzsche is presented as the practical ideal of egoism."[94] Tönnies's sociological analysis of Nietzschean egoism was particularly disturbing to Simmel. Nietzsche, according to Tönnies, was a naive social scientist who possessed no understanding of economic realities or legal institutions.[95] This ignorance of social conditions redounded from Nietzsche's egoism, master morality (*Herrenmoral*), and pathos of distance (*Pathos der Distance*). In sum, Nietzsche's primary philosophical doctrines legitimized the ethical indifference of the bourgeoisie and the German aristocracy. The truth was, intoned Tönnies, cultures must be judged by the amount of compassionate syncopation they bring to the tragic symphony of life. Nietzsche was "the enemy of compassion" and thereby was a philosophical conductor of the "repression and exploitation of . . . wage slaves."[96] Furthermore, Nietzsche's antipathy for democracy fortified the plutocratic politics of Kaiser capitalism.

Throughout much of his academic career, as though responding to Tönnies's radical critique, Simmel sought to distinguish Nietzschean individualism from economic individualism. He accomplished this by positioning Nietzsche as a critic of bourgeois values. It appeared to Simmel "as though a [socialist] party line prohibited Tönnies's recognition . . . of the moral-philosophical meaning of Nietzsche."[97] Simmel's unique proposition—that Nietzschean philosophy and democratic socialism were merely ideologically incompatible—underlay his rebuke of Tönnies's civic interpretation of Nietzsche. Simmel admitted that striving for a higher morality will necessarily place one in a struggle against the leveling of mass moralities. However, in a uniquely Simmelian fashion, he maintained that the contradiction between noble-minded morality of Nietzsche and democracy was not definitive in practice or theory. There was no reason why these two elements could not coexist as a practical politics. And in Simmel's thought, they coexisted as a theory of social critique. But this coexistence stood in defiance of Tönnies and orthodox Marxists, who posited Nietzschean philosophy and social democratic politics as a contradiction.

How do we resolve this disparity in Nietzsche's reception? It should not be appproached as a zero sum game. Tönnies's interpretation of Nietzsche's civic deficiencies was powerful and precise. From Tönnies's penetrating point of view, Simmel misinterpreted Nietzsche who explicitly renounced the moral significance of social democracy and neglected the plight of wage slaves. Conversely, Simmel interpreted Nietzsche from a sociological standpoint outside of Nietzschean thought per se, namely, in relation to hegemonic bourgeois society. From this perspective, Simmel configured Nietzsche and socialism in an elliptical relationship.[98] They were foci that lie far apart ideologically but function as mutually reinforcing coordinates of an antibourgeois style of life. The best example of Simmel's theoretical and practical reconciliation of spiritual striving and socialist egalitarianism was found in his essay "Socialism and Pessimism" (1900).

One way to understand the elliptical reciprocity of Nietzsche and socialism is by analogy to another duo of thinkers, Nietzsche and Kant, who were also perceived by Simmel's contemporaries to be incompatible.

> Kant and Nietzsche are both moralists—thinkers who perceive values in the determinable action and existence of humanity. . . . Morality was Nietzsche's central interest, just as it was for Kant. . . . However, in cast of mind and in their composition of values, there exists an irreconcilable contradiction

> between the two thinkers, which no one can simply talk away. Yet, a comprehensive examination of the present reveals that their relationship was not merely conflictual. They posses the spirit of a third way. Yes, they would fight one another until the last breath. For us, however, Kant's solution to moral problems in no way appears incompatible with Nietzsche's solution.[99]

This moral conjunction of Nietzsche and Kant exemplified Simmel's proclivity to affirm doctrines that appeared irreconcilable to his academic contemporaries. One example of his tendency to construct a philosophical third way appeared in "Socialism and Pessimism," which amalgamated the doctrine of egalitarian materialism and the idealist proposition that human happiness was independent of material possessions. Simmel served up a similar intellectual ambrosia with his articulation of Nietzsche and Kant. The Nietzschean call for a master morality was conjoined to Kant's egalitarian categorical imperative. If these moral philosophies were incommensurable in theory, they were compatible in practice: social democracy was a conceivable component of a self-created ethics. Seen more expansively, a socially transformative civics, Simmel's highest concern, could draw spiritual sustenance from both Nietzsche and Kant simultaneously. After all, he reasoned, this simultaneity was already a fact of Wilhemine culture: both Nietzschean and Kantian ethics were capacitating cultural and moral critiques of the bourgeois status quo. To Simmel's critical mind, there was a sociological and ethical rationality to the Nietzsche-Kant and Nietzschean-socialist alloys that superseded academic understanding. A concern for higher (nonbourgeois) civic ideals was the constituent element of both philosophical compounds.

Simmel's intellectual castings were repudiated not only by Tönnies but by other sociological minds as well.[100] Most of Simmel's neo-Kantian contemporaries similarly construed Nietzsche as an epicurean egoist. For example, in "Philosophy and Present-Day Culture" (1898), Dilthey forded the precipice between academia and contemporary culture in order to survey the ethical landscape of modernity. This critical task necessarily led him to an assessment of Nietzsche:

> Nietzsche remained a complete dilettante in the use of historical facts for an understanding of the practical contexts of culture. At the same time, he isolated the individual by virtue of his methodological starting point, namely, the cult of genius and great men. He detached the aim of the individual from the development of culture. . . . .So, for him, the individual is detached from the practical contexts of culture, and thereby emptied of cultural contents. Consequently, he forfeits a formal understanding of the relationship of progressive and established elements of culture. And, thus, the greatest [negative] feature of the morality of the modern age lies in the shift of interests to this conception of the individual.[101]

Nietzsche symbolized the shift of modernity toward ahistorical thought and individiualism. Simmel agreed with both Tönnies and Dilthey that it was relatively easy to find logical and civic contradictions in Nietzsche's individualistic world view.[102] Nonetheless, for Simmel, the moral philosophy of Nietzsche, particularly his indifference to society, spoke volumes about the problem of moral development in contemporary capitalist society. According to Simmel, Nietzsche's prescription of indifference expressed a sociological truism, namely, moral development demands indifference to the civic status quo: Manchester liberalism. Moreover, Simmel maintained that Nietzsche promoted personal ideals, but did not sponsor the egoistic eudaemonism that suffuses capitalist culture. Nietzsche's critique of traditional morality was, for Simmel, a positive cultural force because it demanded continual civic development through sociological critique. The reevaluation of all values was not a recapitulation of bourgeois individualism but a rejection of its primary ethical institutions: Christianity and economic liberalism. The Nietzschean will to power synthesized social critique and individual self-transcendence thereby fostering a new social ethics for human kind.[103] Simmel, then, de-emphasized the egotistical component of Nietzschean individualism while preserving the demand for a transgressive personal morality which was incompatible with the moral dogmas of the status quo.

In spite of Simmel's immersion in Kantian philosophy and alloying of Kant and Nietzsche, there were key philosophical questions which he answered with a decidedly anti-Kantian inflection, and this inflection was not in harmony with the philosophy of most of his contemporaries. Like Nietzsche, Simmel opposed Kant's tendency to ground the ethical impulse in reason.[104] Ethics arose from a protean confrontation with preexisting social ideologies, Simmel insisted. The source of this confrontation was the vitalistic soul and its aesthetic desire for a self-realized alternative morality: the transcendence of fate through willful practice. Practice, as conceived by Simmel, was not coterminous with the neo-Kantian prescription that reason serve as the basis of social morality. Instead of rational critique, Simmel called for a sociological critique of all individual values. He refused the conflation, common among his contemporaries, of rational and sociological critique. Simmel believed that claims to reason simply fortified the narrow and authoritarian history of naturalized thought. This critique of rationality was not shared by many of his colleagues. His resistance to the academic rationality of the neo-Kantians was most clearly expressed in his letters to Heinrich Rickert: "From logic alone nothing can be won. From this point is to be expounded the most profound difference between us."[105] This statement is illustrative of the distance between Simmel's philosophy of life and that of other neo-Kantians. Unlike Simmel, Rickert adhered to Kant's ethics and to the rational thesis that there was no ontological contrast between natural science and human culture.[106] Rickert would have the last word in this debate. In 1920, two years after Simmel's death from cancer, he published *The Philosophy of Life: Representation and Critique of the Philosophical Fashions of Our Time*. Here Simmel's philosophical legacy was libeled with the market terminology of "fashion" and with the ethnocentric Christian epithet "cult"; and this despite the fact that Simmel was an overt critic of consumer culture and Christian values.[107]

It must be kept in mind that Simmel's defense of Nietzschean vitalism was not a thorough rejection of Kant. Rather, Simmel rehabilitated Kant's significance by reading him with a Nietzschean sensibility. Simmel's philosophy resisted theoretical closure and conceptual reification by focusing on the dionysian character of noumena which he, like Kant, called the soul (*Seele*). While Kant argued that the limits of practical reason denied direct knowledge of noumena and things in themselves, Simmel affirmed these articles of faith while demanding that all values undergo a sociological analysis. The soul must be judged as a being-for-others. His sociological analysis of the soul was not materialist, however. It was a third way equivalent to Kant's synthetic unity of apperception. Simmel's sociology of the soul kept faith with Marxism in demanding a material analysis of the consequences of values while renouncing (1) the humanist conception of a fixed human nature (equality) and (2) the neo-Kantian proposition that subjectivity was rational and unitary.

Opposition to theoretical closure and metaphysical truth-claims was a hallmark of Simmel's philosophical sociology. His sociology of modernity was a construction of synthetic propositions about how social institutions generally impacted the modern soul. This interpretive construction was conscious of itself as a principle of knowledge and not knowledge itself. According to Kant, experience—apperception—was always already a synthesis. Simmel never abandoned the perspective of Kant's refutation of idealism and materialism in the *Critique of Pure Reason* but simply transferred it from philosophy to sociological theory. While Kant argued that self-consciousness was animated by the consciousness of an object, Simmel took this as the starting point for a philosophical sociology of modernity.

In Simmel's hands, however, Kant's arguments about the source of self-consciousness became a defense of Nietzsche's philosophy of life. Kant's contention that self-consciousness originates through a consciousness of the material realm was descriptive and analytical; Simmel's transference of Kant's version of self-consciousness to the sociopolitical realm was thoroughly prescriptive and confrontational. As with Nietzsche, he prescribed a critical struggle with convention as the basis for self-conscious spiritual development. The pursuit of self-development began with a transgressive sociological critique of bourgeois institutions: capitalism, Christianity, bourgeois sexual morality, and so on. Simmel thereby treated Nietzsche's critique of dogmatic ideologies and institutions as a moral imperative. Here, too, Simmel's philosophical sociology was a unique blend of the two dominant philosophical figures of the Wilhelmine period: Nietzsche and Kant. Kant's emphasis on the golden rule and collective ethics seems totally incompatible with Nietzsche's defense of self-constructed ethics by individuals. Nonetheless, the tension between Kantian and Nietzschean ethics coalesced in Simmel's philosophical sociology. The Nietzschean Simmel maintained that the individual must be the starting point of ethical self-development; however, in opposition to Nietzsche, the sociological Simmel maintained that individual values have always been a collective ethics that demand an evaluation based on their social consequences.

If Nietzsche's iconoclastic path to spiritual self-development was fundamental to Simmel's vision of ethics, Kant's philosophy of apperception was the theoretical terra firma of Simmel's sociology. For example, in an early essay Simmel referred to "sensual empiricism" as a synthetic "overcoming of sensualism" and similarly referred to "empiricism as the constructive principle of knowledge."[108] Kant's antinomies and unwillingness to reify their synthesis as knowledge was the source of Simmel's sociological and political unity of extremes. His cultural politics were as much a Nietzschean defense of the individual as it was a sociological demand for a nonindividualistic ethics. There was always an unresolved tension between his refrain that (1) genuine morality arose as an iconoclastic creation of the isolated individual who opposed the herd mentalities of the status quo, and (2) his demand that the erratic and multiform idiosyncracies of individuated values undergo a thorough sociological evaluation to determine their validity as a civic ethics.

THE PHILOSOPHY OF MONEY (1900)

The Philosophy of Money was a masterpiece of philosophical sociology. It lends itself to a vast number of readings because it touched on innumerable topics: commodification, civic indifference, the tempo of life, the world economy, the division of labor, the increasing specialization and intellectualization of life, the gender of modernity, and the methodology of social science. In its contemporary German iteration, the text runs nearly 800 pages and combines analytical and normative ruminations about the capitalist monetary culture. Most of my examination will concentrate on the normative components of the text, and this will be accomplished in the next section of this chapter. In this section, the intention is twofold: (1) to present Simmel's theory of value as the analytical nucleus of the book and one that was a conscious counterpoint to Marxist theory, and (2) to systematically expose and clarify money as the sociological symbol which is best suited to provide a unitary explanation of the contradictory elements of modernity.

Simmel's theory of value was the analytical core of his study, and this theory turned on a revision of Marxism. In one of his most famous statements, Simmel wrote in the introduction:

> Methodologically, one can express my fundamental intention as follows: to build a framework under historical materialism in such a way that the explanatory value of the inclusion of economic life in the causes of spiritual culture [*geistige Kultur*] is maintained, however such that every economic form is recognized as the result of deeper values and tendencies, of psychological and, yes, metaphysical presumptions.[109]

With few exceptions, the American reception of Simmel's sociology has ignored elements of his work—most notably *The Philosophy of Money*—that are refinements of Marx. Clearly, Simmel was not dismissive of historical materialism (Marxism) and was occasionally very complimentary.

> The science of political economy . . . [and] historical materialism . . . has opened the way to the spiritualization of the manner of looking at history, to spiritualization, indeed, that does not need to come to pass at the price of the suppression and neglect of facts, as in earlier ideological constructions.[110]

He also described historical materialism as a "scientific conception of the world," one that

> rests upon a spiritual and metaphysical basis: it not only mirrors the external, objective existence of material things, but is a product of the human power to form ideas of things, and is dependent upon the inner laws of this power.[111]

Despite his admiration for historical materialism, Simmel was astutely aware of the philosophical naivete that became a part of the Marxist tradition. Historical materialists tended to forget that theirs was an a priori perspective of the image-forming mind. The increasing emphasis on classes, economic conditions, and the food-supply found in political economy was supported by Simmel. But he claimed that historical materialists tended to naturalize their perspective and "interpret phenomena immediately," that is without reference to their own theoretical perspective. They fail to recognize that "matter itself is only an idea"; this comment reflects Simmel's neo-Kantian idealism.[112] Simmel was paradoxically a radical idealist whose methodological and ethical perspectives were radically materialist. His philosophy was a type of practical idealism, and as a cultural critic, he fought to maintain the distinction between his practical idealism and a naive historical materialism. The latter, he repeatedly argued, fortified the externalization of life found in consumer culture and did so at the expense of the creative soul. While affirming historical materialism, Simmel avoided the danger of the metaphysical closure of thought and the oppressive leveling of the individual spirit in the modern world.

Simmel especially praised Marx as the most sophisticated theorist of value and alienation heretofore. For Marx, the valuation of products in capitalist society involved three forms of alienation: (1) the alienation of use value and exchange value, (2) the alienation of humanity from its social nature, and (3) the alienation of human creativity from the producers of value, the workers. Simmel generally embraced the Marxist assertion that exchange, mediated by money, requires alienation. However, he radically altered Marx's conceptions of alienation. While Marx treated utility (use value) as a theoretical terre firma, Simmel rejected this formulation as a naturalization of value. Marx's conception of utility presumed an objective meaning of value. Simmel maintained that an objective and universally valid valuation was impossible to establish; he emphasized the subjective valuation of products and demand. It is desire, not utility, that lies behind the purchase of products. Very often our desire for an object is not based on its use value. For example, the desirability (value) of an object, like a painting, may depend on its beauty rather than its utility.

Simmel neither wholly embraced nor rejected Marx's theory of economic value. He agreed with Marx that monetary exchange *may* result in alienation. The exchange price of an object may confer a depersonalized value that stifles subjective valuation. We can think of the way that advertising can construct a meaning which is independent of both use value and personal meaning. But Marx and Simmel conceived of alienation differently, and this difference was exemplified in their analytical discourse. The central term shared by Marx and Simmel is "Vergegenständlichung," which literally means "to-turn-into-an-object." Marx referred to exchange value as objectified work (*vergegenständlichte Arbeit*) and Simmel to objectified spirit (*vergegenständlichter Geist*).[113] For Marx, the material process of workers' creativity embodied in products was alienated in exchange; for Simmel, exchange was the alienation of human desire resulting from the monetary objectification of value. Three things should be noted here. First, as many of Simmel's contemporaries recognized, *The Philosophy of Money* constitutes a thought-provoking correlate to Marx's *Capital*. Second, Marx's critical focus was the production process and alienation redounding from the dictatorial control of the means of production by capitalists. Simmel's primary locus of analysis was the moment and process of exchange between the consumer and the merchant. This may account for their divergent conclusions. Nonetheless, as theorists of value, they differ markedly. Third, in the same sense that Simmel rejected Marx's interpretive foundation, use value, as an objectification of value, he similarly disputed Marx's labor theory of value, because it presumed that the value of labor was quantifiable. Simmel rejected this Marxist proposition. To quantify the value of labor by reference to the number of hours it takes to produce a product, as Marx's labor theory of value does, neglects the historical mental energy that facilitates production. For example, it may take a professor half an hour to grade a paper, but an objective (hourly) value would not account for the years of study which facilitated the completion of this task. According to Simmel, Marx's objective translation of value required a framework under historical materialism that incorporates intellectual knowledge, and the difficulty of its acquisition, into an analysis of economic value.

Again, keeping in mind their primary sociological foci—Marx/production/worker and Simmel/exchange/consumer—they came to dissimilar analytical conclusions about alienation. In stark contrast to Marx, Simmel maintained that, strictly speaking, alienation was not a necessary result of exchange. Exchange, at least theoretically, may produce a form of justice: the mutual advantage and reciprocal benefit of receiver and giver. This rather optimistic appraisal of exchange was far afield from Marx who interpreted exchange objectively as a multiform process of alienation. Exchange was the material alienation of use and exchange value, of human creativity, and species being. The social nature of production and distribution was contradicted by the asocial character of capitalist control. These elements of Marxist theory were not directly challenged by Simmel, who said little about Marx's assertion that capitalist control of the means of production alienated workers from control of their creative energies and their species being. Generally, we should not see Marx and Simmel as antagonists. Simmel obviously did not see Marx that way. But Simmel did believe that he was amending Marxism with a social psychology of consumer culture. While Marx interpreted exchange exclusively as a process of alienation, Simmel explained the seduction of consumer society. This seduction, Marx and Simmel agreed, flowed from the essence of exchange in capitalist society: products are sold without reference to an ethical examination of production and its consequences. Marx and Simmel further agreed that money was a great symbol of the separation of production and exchange; money sheds all reference to its material origins in production.

In spite of these substantial agreements, Simmel interpreted exchange in consumer culture more narrowly. His analytical conclusion was that alienation was not a necessary consequence of exchange. On the contrary, the satisfaction of personal desire was facilitated by exchange. Simmel's analytical understanding of modern valuation turns on a dialectical Janus. Monetary exchange was the complete objectification of value: objects are reduced to a monetary quantity. But monetary standardization, quantification, and objectification was so thorough in capitalist society that money functioned like an empty form enabling the projection of infinite subjective meanings. Simmel drew an analogy between monetary valuation and the increasing historical significance of the clock. Both add a greater objectivity, precision, and exactitude to life. But neither created a corresponding expansion of exactness in the ethical realm.[114] In fact, the exact opposite was true. The growing objectification of value advanced the subjectification of ethical meaning. The subjectification of value, relativity, was the chief character of monetary capitalism.

> The central concepts of truth, values, objectivity, etc., are rendered by me as the effects of exchange and as the substance of relativism. This relativism is no longer the skeptical dissolution of all stability; rather it means ensuring against skepticism by means of a new concept of stability (as in my *Philosophy of Money*).[115]

For Simmel, monetary exchange was the stable sociological prism producing and explaining the experiential relativism and accompanying sentiments of inner independence and personal satisfaction that comprise consumer society. The commodification of life and objectification of value in monetary society produced subjective freedom, and this, Simmel points out, has been experienced collectively as the elevation of freedom in consumer culture.

In addition to viewing *The Philosophy of Money* as a revision of Marx's theory of value, it should be regarded as a methodological precursor to both Max Weber's theory of ideal types and the Frankfurt School's critique of totality.[116] It is no accident that reference to *The Philosophy of Money* appeared in the first footnote of Weber's *The Protestant Ethic and the Spirit of Capitalism*. Simmel was the sociological mind that established the standard for a self-reflective sociology of the capitalist spirit. In Weber's opinion, Simmel's analysis of capitalist society was simply brilliant. The difference between Weber and Simmel's methodological approaches was not dramatic. While Weber conceived of sociological knowledge as ideal types, Simmel conceived of it as symbolic knowledge. Both were neo-Kantian constructions which consciously repudiated naive empiricism. For Simmel, sociological symbols were synthetic interpretations in a specific sense: like Kant's transcendental propositions, Simmel conceived of sociological understanding as an articulation of the subjective and objective realms. Accordingly, the second half of *The Philosophy of Money* was entitled the "Synthetic Part." Here Simmel set out to realize the neo-Kantian intention to make philosophy a science of experience; the methodological goal of the text was a synthesis of Kantianism and positivism.[117] Like positivism, the sociological Simmel contended that knowledge must be derived from observable facts, in this case, the ubiquitous fact of monetary exchange.

Like the sociology of the Frankfurt School, Simmel's symbolic sociology resisted metaphysical closure through a theoretical language of self-resistance. Although he belongs to a younger generation, the Simmel student Ernst Cassirer understood the sociology of symbolic forms in a similar way:

> Philosophical speculation began with the concept of being. . . . Philosophers attempted to determine the beginning, the origin, and the ultimate "foundation" of all being. . . . What these thinkers called the essence, the substance of the world, was not something which in principle went beyond it; it was a fragment taken from this very same world.[118]

In proposing that the synthetic symbol was only a fragment of the world it was interpreting, as he had in *The Philosophy of Money*, Simmel's sociology accomplished goals that are now routinely associated with critical theory. One symbolic interpretation of society does not exclude others nor does it claim "the perfection of a mechanical interpretation of experience."[119] Simmel left open the possibility of a plurality of perspectives while at the same time exhorting intellectuals with the civic demand for a sociological critique of modernity. Furthermore, Simmel often drew the connection, which is now routinely associated with critical theory, between naturalized truth-claims and authoritarian societies. This connection was examined brilliantly and exhaustively in a section of *Sociology* entitled "Superordination and Subordination." Similarly, as a Nietzschean, he reproached those who habitually attach themselves to traditional authority. This self-imposed servitude undermined ethical free will, denied the presence of a multiplicity of values, and naturalized authoritarian society. Simmel's linkage of naturalized knowledge and authoritarian culture would become a canonical proposition of critical theory. Like contemporary practitioners of critical theory, Simmel was also a critic of theoretical closure. From "the standpoint of science," Simmel wrote, one can "never produce the totality of reality."[120] The best one could do perhaps was to reveal the diversity of historical values and their ability to resist or affirm social determinism.

Writing to Heinrich Rickert in 1898, Simmel proclaimed in reference to *The Philosophy of Money*: "More and more I devote myself to the task of overcoming the naive realism of history."[121] He referred to *The Philosophy of Money* as an "historical value-realism" and, to that extent, the text was methodologically consistent with his philosophy of history with its interest in the personal meaning of history.[122] However, unlike *The Problems of Historical Philosophy,* Simmel's philosophy of money put forth an interpretation of a generally valid empirical a priori of modernity: monetary culture. While Simmel's philosophy of history aimed at demonstrating the impossibility of general historical laws, *The Philosophy of Money* sought the complementary apposition: it strove to be a philosophy of the whole of historical and social life. He treated the monetary culture of capitalism as the empirical and structural determinant of the modern "inner world."[123] Again, this approach constituted a methodological reversal. *The Problems of Historical Philosophy* placed interpretive priority on the discovery of the laws of the soul and how they determined the meaning of historical events. *The Philosophy of Money* sought the reverse: an understanding of how the empirical realities of capitalist culture determined the soul. When the presuppositions of *The Problems of Historical Philosophy* and *The Philosophy of Money* are placed side by side, then, Simmel's sociology of modernity appears as a reversible appliqué. His philosophy of history pointed to knowledge of individual values as the precondition for historical understanding. *The Philosophy of Money* reversed the interpretive priority on the individual's subjectivity and instead constructed an historical sociology whose priority was the analysis of a supra-individual institution: the monetary culture of economic liberalism. This reversibility of critical perspectives was Simmel's aporetic stock-in-trade.

Considering the contradictory elements of modernity, Simmel assigned an insuperable relevance to money as a sociological symbol. The role of sociology was to unmask the essential relationship between seemingly diverse and unconnected institutions, conventions, and psychological routinizations. Only money was suited to provide a unitary explanation of the contradictory elements of modernity. Money was a historical object that framed and articulated many levels of meaning. As the most ubiquitous object of modern life, it was a monad of modernity, namely, an indispensable part that could articulate the whole. As a sociological symbol, it epitomized modern man as an exchanging animal engaged in processes of external reciprocity. Money was a new historical form of objectivity.

In addition, money was the sociological key to unlocking the "contradictions of the modern era."[124] Three contradictions or "antithesis-pairs" were explainable by money as a sociological symbol: (1) the simultaneity of increasing economic interdependence and growing civic indifference, (2) the abetment of subjective valuation by the hegemony of objective valuation, and (3) money as a form of social stability advancing the rapid tempo of modern life. First, the growth of the money economy facilitated the growing interdependence of distant peoples in the world economy. Money bridged distances and expedited exchange. And yet, while increasing economic interdependence, money discouraged reflection on the ethical meaning of human interdependence, because it left no traces of its material origins. Money, then, articulated the historical simultaneity of growing material interdependence in the world economy and increasing civic indifference. Second, money explained other conflicting streams of modernity. In the money economy, objects are reduced to their external, quantitative monetary value, thereby forfeiting their qualitative value. Simmel referred to the cultural consequences of monetary valuation as spiritual leveling and as the loss of the human spectrum of feelings. Conversely, the process of escalating objectification was, as we saw before, accompanied by the potential for increasing subjectification. Greed was the negative manifestation of increasing subjectification. However, there were positive subjectivities as well. The growth of the money economy actually advanced the freedom of the human spirit, because money was a possession that may be endowed with an infinite number of qualitative meanings. Third, Simmel pointed to another "antithesis-pair" (calling it a Hegelian paradox) that could be explained by money as a sociological symbol: money was the stable element of modernity which expedited the rapid tempo of economic and cultural change. Here he drew an analogy between money and the New York stock exchange:

> Its [the stock exchange] sanguine, choleric fluctuation between optimism and pessimism, its nervous reaction to the ponderable and imponderable, the rapidness with which every changing moment is grasped and the last moment is forgotten—all of this represents an extreme increase in the tempo of life; its fever-pitch movement and the concentration of its modifications achieves the striking visibility of the specific influence of money on the course of physical existence.[125]

Money was a sociological symbol of stability and rapid change. It was the stable element that facilitated change. In sum, money was merely a fragment of reality, but it was not an arbitrary starting point for a sociology of modernity. It was the most ubiquitous object in modern society, and only it could provide a sociological explanation of the antitheses that comprised modern life. As such, Simmel conceived of money as the phenomenological a priori of modernity. It was the most necessary material structure of contemporary economics and culture and the only one capable of articulating the myriad contradictions of modernity.

Money, however, was not treated solely as a sociological symbol by Simmel. It was also a philosophical symbol that actualized his methodological demand for self-reflection. Simmel referred to money as a conscious or secondary symbolism. In doing so, he sought to distinguish his philosophical approach to sociology from empiricism and historicism. Historicism was an example of a social analysis that was unconscious of its presuppositions. Simmel's work consistently alludes to the theoretical naivete of historicism, and in *The Philosophy of Money* he characterizes its theoretical unself-consciousness as naive symbolism. Since, for Simmel, all knowledge was symbolic in the sense that it was shaped by a mental category, sociology must be conscious of its subjective structures.

Simmel treated sociology as a creative science, and *The Philosophy of Money* was something akin to a sociological experiment. His hypothesis was that money constituted the best conceptual category for understanding and articulating the diversity and complexity of modern life. The gravity of *The Philosophy of Money,* then, turns less on its empirical substantiation than on what William James would call its truth-value, and, indeed, Simmel's intellectual aria had a ring of truth that resonated with many readers. Simmel set out to articulate the counterpoints and atonal rhythms of monetary culture. His analytical overtures were never dogmatic, and the virtuosity of his execution was witnessed in the varied reception of his sociological overtures, which will be discussed later. Ultimately, the brilliance of *The Philosophy of Money* consisted of Simmel's invention of a new intellectual genre: philosophical sociology. The key signature of this genre was that an empirical object of study, money, was understood as the subjective condition for the articulation of its sociological meanings. Simmel, the minstrel of philosophical sociology, transcribed money into a historical form that completely harmonized the dual need for a sociology of modernity and for a critique of philosophical naturalization. Money was both a subjective (symbolic) methodology and an objective phenomena determining modern social relations.

AN APORETIC SOCIOLOGIST AGAINST THE CAPITALIST SOUL

> *The "slave revolt" that threatens to dethrone the self-willing and norm-giving character of strong individuals is not the revolt of the masses but the revolt of objects. Just as, on the one hand, we have become slaves of the production process, on the other hand, we have become the slaves of the products.*
>
> Georg Simmel, *The Philosophy of Money*[126]

> *Only the money transaction possesses the character of a completely momentary relationship, which leaves no traces, as is the case with prostitution. . . . Money is never an adequate means for affirming a human relationship—like the true relationship of love—whose essence depends on duration and the inner truth of binding powers.*
>
> Georg Simmel, *The Philosophy of Money*[127]

We turn now from a predominantly analytical understanding of *The Philosophy of Money* to extended analyses of its historical and normative conclusions. Simmel's most convincing and intelligent insights into capitalist society dealt with two problems, the first epistemological and the second ethical and spiritual. He was never more perspicacious than in his characterizations of the epistemological difficulty of a sociology of modernity. The major feature of the institutional complex known as capitalism was, according to Simmel, its inability to be understood from a total perspective. As a sociologist, then, Simmel faced an seemingly intractable problem. How can the essence of modernity be signified when its essence is the absence of essence? The explosion of commercial products, the proliferation of diverse perspectives born of liberal individualism, the increasing specialization of jobs and economic functions, and the general phantasmagoria of economic and cultural life in capitalist society placed that society beyond representation. Stated succinctly, capitalist society lacked a fixed essence. How does one represent its lack of an essence, its insubstantiality, its incommensurable diversity and contradictions? Simmel stated in *The Philosophy of Money* that the fragmentary character of capitalist society demanded definitive social interpretations. This demand arose from his insight about the ethical inadequacies of capitalist society. The demand for a rounded interpretation of capitalist culture, he related, "belongs to the valuations and broadest relations of spiritual life."[128] He specified the ethical emptiness of capitalist culture as the source of this spiritual-intellectual demand. Throughout his life he expressed other opinions about the source of the demand for social interpretation. In "The Fragmentary Character of Life," he referred to the need to overcome banal pessimism. In another essay, he lamented: "The technical side of life has won the upper hand over the inner side of life and over human values."[129] This self-imposed demand for an ethical sociology of modernity seemed incompatible with the complexity of modern capitalist society. Paradoxically, it was the lack of a fixed essence that Simmel seized upon as the essential characteristic of capitalism. This lack was simultaneously liberating and demoralizing.

In addition to being an unparalleled rumination on the epistemological difficulties of a sociology of capitalism, *The Philosophy of Money* was an artful and penetrating critique of bourgeois culture and one intent on explaining the enervation, alienation, and suppression of the soul in a rapidly industrializing Germany. *The Philosophy of Money* was akin to an interpretive pendulum oscillating between an individual-based critique of social determinism and a sociological critique of individualism, and he interpreted the bourgeois culture of money from both perspectives. Again, his marvelous analytical and sociological cunning may be best described as aporetic. Accordingly, one reviewer of *The Philosophy of Money* deftly summarized its conclusions as a sociological aporia: "Here money is the great oppressor and the great liberator and the best symbol of this double relationship."[130] Liberation/oppression was a fourth antithesis-pair that was only conceivable through money as a sociological symbol. In what sense did Simmel conceive of monetary culture as social liberation and oppression? Simmel interpreted the hegemony of money as an objective determinism that lacked any fixed meaning. It was a social determinism that liberated individuals from social determinism.

> Money belongs to those powers whose character consists of the absence of character, and which, therefore, can color life with extreme differences.[131]

The possession of money lacked a fixed moral character and thereby facilitated ethical differentiation.

Simultaneously—and here we witness a sociological reversal typical of Simmel's antipodal undogmatic thought—money's lack of a fixed ethical meaning imprinted an emptiness upon the soul, and in this sense, money constituted a form of oppression. Money facilitated egoism and greed by providing no material resistance to them. In this sense it was the great oppressor. Monetary exchange reduced human interaction to a functional relationship. It is a relationship of moral indifference which was terminated by the payment of money. Thereby, monetary exchange led to a terrible degradation of personal value. The classic analogy of this relationship was prostitution.

> The same cultural process of differentiation—which confer a special, immeasurable, and irreplaceable cultural significance for individuality—makes money the standard and equivalent of a diversity of opposing objects; however, money's indifference and objectivity make it appear increasingly unsuitable as the equivalent of personal values. . . . The terrible degradation of women inherent in prostitution is most clearly expressed in its money equivalent. . . . Only the monetary transaction carries the same character of a completely fleeting relationship, that leaves behind no traces, as one finds in the particular character of prostitution.[132]

As we shall see, Simmel located in monetary culture a remarkable contradiction. Pecuniary culture facilitated the historical zenith of personal freedom. At the same time, the zenith of personal freedom coexisted with the historical nadir of human ethics.

Simmel went to great lengths to explain the historical origins of capitalist culture. In most precapitalist societies, production was for use. Exchange was not mediated by money. Capitalism introduced the hegemony of production for monetary exchange, and originally one exchanged goods for an equivalent material value, silver or gold. Eventually, capitalist societies moved from a gold or silver standard—exchange based on the intrinsic and material worth of money—to paper money. In the former case, the use of money still expressed a direct equivalence of value. By contrast paper money expresses the value of commodities quite independent of intrinsic worth. Hence, these two quantities were no longer directly held together in exchange. Both quantities were first assigned a symbolic monetary value and then compared to one another. Simmel located a philosophical principle in the symbolic character of money; paper money was an embodiment of the mind's synthetic ability to unify otherwise incomparable objects. For Simmel, as with Kant, the symbolizing operation of the mind was called analogy.[133]

> Gold and silver are obviously the forms through which money can most easily and certainly become a symbol. Money has to pass through this stage in order to achieve its capacities for power.[134]

This focus upon money's symbolic power as the key to understanding contemporary culture was a revision of two Marxian premises: (1) the proposition that being determines consciousness, and (2) the recognition of the transformation of the valuation of products in capitalism, from use value to exchange value.[135] Simmel argued that if we draw the logical conclusion about the hegemony of exchange value, symbolized by and founded in money, then the assumption that being determines consciousness was refuted. Money was the only material structure that completely divested itself of its "substantive base"; it "completely casts off its economic and moral origin."[136]

> Money is the only cultural creation that is pure power, that has completely abolished its material basis by being absolutely only a symbol. Thus, it is the most signifying of all the phenomena of our time, wherein dynamics have secured the leadership of all theory and praxis. That it is pure relationship (and thereby equally signifying) without its meaning being composed as relationship, is not a contradiction. For power is in reality nothing but relationship.[137]

Money was the relational prerequisite of modernity; it alone was the necessary structure of objective relations. Additionally, money's power of diverse signification followed (1) from its formal purity as an empty content and (2) from its universality as a social standard. Money was analogous to the human body after death. It was an object that could by filled with an unlimited number of meanings. Different cultures project multiple meanings into the lifeless human corpse. Like the human body after death, money was an empty form capable of receiving multiple meanings. From Simmel's point of view, the formal emptiness of money thereby explained the diversity of values as a formal aspect of consumer culture. Money's universality as a medium of exchange, Simmel insisted, removed it from any fixed material meaning. It was materiality as immanent multiplicity. It was not a relationship but the a priori form of relationships. Therefore, it alone symbolized the impossibility of a totalized representation of capitalist culture.

Simmel, then, conceived of money as a material nominalism. Money had no fixed moral meaning and, therefore, facilitated all value-feelings. The accumulation of money and use of money, for instance, could serve communist purposes and capitalist purposes. It could facilitate prostitution or be used by feminists to oppose sexual exploitation. Reflecting on the nominalist character of money, Simmel came to conceive of it as "pure negative freedom," or freedom from social responsibility.[138] This leads us to a consideration of another consequence money's nominalist character. Because it is the absolute negation of determinate materialism, money can be said to have no conscience. In monetary culture, life was determined by an object, money, that shed all traces of moral and material contingency, even while its power consisted in its contingent use. The "pure negative freedom" of monetary culture referred to the pure individualism of monetary society; the individual was now free from any binding ethical or social responsibilities.

In a dramatic revision of Marx, Simmel maintained that, for the first time in human history, monetary culture had thereby razed the deterministic chain of being and having. The mere possession of money no longer determined human consciousness the way that the possession of capital had in the past. Historically, the deterministic relationship between being and having depended upon a fixed object of possession, like land. Land was a possession that strongly determined consciousness and human relations. With the end of the feudal householding economy and the emergence of capitalism, however, land was easily converted into the liquidity of money, freeing the land owner from a landlocked social identity. With money, the deterministic relationship of possession and being "finally falls to pieces altogether."[139]

Simmel's chronicle of the decline of social determinism in monetary culture vouchsafed an epic drama of objectification and freedom. A leitmotif of *The Philosophy of Money* was the historical emergence of a revolutionary form of existential autonomy. Simmel's examination of unfolding human freedom began with the following principle of exchange:

> What we feel as freedom is often actually only an exchange of responsibilities. . . . Therefore, every moral philosophy generally identifies ethical freedom with those responsibilities which imposed on us the particular self or an ideal or social imperative.[140]

Simmel outlined three types of historical responsibility: (1) those related directly to the individual (slavery), (2) those directly related to the product of work (payment in kind), and (3) those indirectly related to the product of work (money). Simmel conceived of these three forms of exchange as regulative principles of a society: the personal principle, the commodity principle, and the money principle. There were political and legal correlatives to this historical transition. In feudal society, relationships of obedience were felt to be something personal. The will of the group was unified under the king with whom one feels a personal identity. Because of its personal nature, obedience is more thorough.

With the rise of political liberalism, individuals become increasingly obedient to impersonal or objective forms of social and economic life. For instance, the individual increasingly was habituated to an objective lawfulness and was less subject to the personal whims of monarchal or aristocratic authority. More and more, personal subordination was reduced in favor of the growth of objective legislation to which everyone was subordinate, even legislators. One can see the growth of objectification in the economic realm as well. In the production process, personal skills such as craftsmanship increasingly gave way to the dominance of mechanical and technical elements. Simmel observed that this growing objectivity of social relations also denoted the increasing irrelevance of subjectivity. Therefore, subordination was no longer total; social hierarchies no longer entailed the type of subjective obedience that generally accompanied personal forms of authority. As we said before, Simmel believed that the complete objectification of life made fewer claims on human subjectivity. The diabolical oppression of human obligations was lessened by monetary obligations. The greatest personal freedom, then, arose in the third stage when personal obligations could be met in a purely objective way with capital payments.[141]

In the capitalist stage of economic history, the personality was no longer determined by hierarchical obligations. Why not? In payment, one's personality can be completely withdrawn. Debt was objectified and depersonalized. And, in contrast to direct obligations to work that one finds in medieval society, an individual's obligations may even be met via another person's money. Thus, the substitution of money payments for direct work requirements and payments in kind was interpreted quite favorably by Simmel: "Money can make—at least in principle—every exchange mutually advantageous for both sides."[142] Here was a positive cultural correlative of the objectification of payment.

> The real moral improvement [of the present] is the result of the cultural process, namely, more and more of the contents of life have become objectified in trans-individual structures: books, art, ideal structures like Fatherland, general culture, the form of life in conceptual and aesthetic pictures, and the knowledge of thousands of interesting and meaningful things—all of these can be enjoyed without one person taking something away from another. The more that values change over to such objective forms, the more space there is in them, as in the house of God, for every soul (*Seele*).[143]

Just as the money economy freed the individual from fixed economic activities, the monetary objectification of culture freed the soul from the determination of the object-realm. Simmel contended that the will, the intellect, and value-feelings attached themselves to reality in ways not determinable by reality; and he believed that the monetary objectification of culture in capitalist society was the apotheosis of this existential indeterminacy. The cultural determinism of money was an auto-denaturalization of its authority to determine its meaning for those who possessed, accumulated, or exchanged it.

Simmel likewise interpreted the development of monetary culture favorably as the struggle for the consciousness of consciousness. The highest level of intellectual development entailed the recognition of a more comprehensive concept of objectivity that includes the subject within it.[144] For Simmel this meant a renunciation of a naive materialism in favor of a symbolic philosophy of freedom.

> If secondary symbols—as they may be called in contrast with the naive symbolism of naive cultural conditions—increasingly replace the immediate comprehension of things and values for praxis, thus is the meaning of the intellect for the conduct of life extraordinarily increased.[145]

Money was the historically unprecedented arrival of "secondary symbolism" as the intellectual a priori of society. By destroying the linkage between possession (*Besitz*) and the soul's essence (*Wesen*), money had created a space for the self-creation of the soul. Monetary culture, as secondary symbolism, could for the first time lead to the denaturalization of all cultural totalities. It could thereby herald an awareness of the diversity of values open to practice. Monetary culture, in essence, made cultural reification conscious, and, thereby, the realm of social institutions was emptied of their deterministic power. Money was a pure form or pure means that "lacks a relation to all immediate values."[146] The total absence of an inherent linkage between objects and individual values, namely, the spiritual petrification of the world, and the unrelatedness of objects, was interpreted as a potential *critical distancing that could bring life closer by denaturalizing cultural absolutes*. When culture was petrified and objectified, it was also demystified, and, thereby, it lost its deterministic hold on the individual. The individual was now free to create his or her own vision of social virtue within the previously despiritualized world of objects. Simmel considered this potential of the capitalist money economy as nothing less than "one of the greatest advances that mankind has ever made."[147]

In light of the miserable lives of the downtrodden during the nineteenth century, nothing could be more quixotic and inaccurate, it might be argued, than Simmel's portrait of Manchester capitalism as the greatest advance of human freedom. This objection may be met by understanding that *The Philosophy of Money* was a crosscut of capitalist culture revealing not only veins of freedom but arteries of moral decay. In an interpretive reversal, typical of this sociological Janus, the last chapter of *The Philosophy of Money* ruthlessly criticized monetary culture, the same culture which pages earlier had been eloquently praised as one of the greatest advances in intellect and human freedom. Here Simmel charged that the cold consequence of monetary culture was an insidious reality: the death of human compassion. Just as emphatically as he celebrated new personal freedoms resulting from monetary culture, Simmel denounced the mordant absence of ethical connectedness and being-for-others in capitalist society.

Several historical interpretations of the monetary demon were provided by Simmel. He investigated the historical balance between emotional and intellectual life. In feudal society, the church and precapitalist land relations provided fixed points of spiritual gratification and social meaning. The church provided the goal of salvation, and there was a balance between emotional gratification and intellect: the more emotional end stations contained in practical life, the more the operation of feeling, in contrast to the intellect, will dominate culture. In the medieval period, the church and agricultural life provided fixed, if unstable, points of emotional gratification. In contrast to these institutions, money culture provided no fixed goal. Furthermore, the possession of property in agrarian and underdeveloped money economies entailed a myriad of interpersonal dependencies, legal restrictions, and communitarian conceptions of the self. In stark contrast, monetary culture was distinguished by the endless search for emotional end-stations, because they were no longer inherent to daily life. This search for emotional gratification was unrequited and therefore gave rise to insatiable greed and conspicuous consumption. Moreover, there was a change between being and possessing brought about by the money economy.

> The more fundamentally and affectively the possession is actually owned, that means made fruitful and enjoyed, the more decisive and deterministic will be the effects on the internal and external nature [*Wesen*] of the subject.[148]

In the capitalist money economy, the affective and organic relation between possession of money—*the dominant form of property*—and subjectivity was lost.

Simmel interpreted this uncoupling in two ways. On the one hand, the uncoupling of the deterministic linkage was called "negative freedom" and interpreted as the unprecedented basis for free self-creation. But in an interpretive reversal, typical of Simmel, he asserted that this potential had not been realized and that monetary culture was less the emancipation of the soul than its total objectification. There was a demonic side, then, to the expansion of individual freedom within monetary culture. This expansion promoted and facilitated a nihilistic inner world. Because money imparted no value system, as previous cultural institutions had, and because it provided no resistance to subjective desires, monetary culture placed the intellect in the service of egoism. This meant the plenary expulsion of moral regulation from social relations. There were other deterministic consequences. Monetary culture signaled the quantitative evaluation of reality wherein all things were equally matters of money. The qualitative life of the soul was more and more supplanted by the social status of quantity and accumulation.

One cultural correlative of the monetary demon was something Simmel referred to as pure intellect. The industrial and financial institutions of the money economy demand ever expanding technological, mathematical, and scientific sophistication. Therefore the highly specialized intellect becomes more and more essential to and characteristic of modernity. Like money itself, intellect becomes a pure means of furthering exchange.

> The spiritual energy contained in the appearance of the money economy . . . is the result of the means-character of money. . . . Money is felt everywhere to be a purpose, and, therefore an extraordinary number of things, which actually possess the character of ends-in-themselves, are forced down to the level of pure means.[149]

There was a causal relationship between money and intellect. When life is structured as a means, then the practical world becomes more and more a problem for intelligence. The best example of this character of modernity was the institutions of banking and the stock market. In the banking industry, practical activity is dominated by calculations. It is no mistake that we tend to think of a "calculating person" as someone who combines intelligence and practical egoism. For this is precisely the nature of the banker. As for the stock market and joint-stock companies, Simmel underscored their ability to simultaneously bridge and enlarge distances between people. A European businessman now could own shares in an African business venture. Thus, the monetary economy of capitalism bridged huge distances. However, the businessman could do so while never meeting the workers or other owners, and never visiting the means of production. In this sense, the monetary world economy, more than any other system in human history, symbolized the ability of capitalists to shed from consciousness the ethical questions implicit in mammonism and exploitive forms of production. Capitalism was a pure means of accumulating wealth. It gave rise to a mathematical intellect whose mental sophistication was completely cut off from the continent of human compassion. The stock market was an institutional manifestation of the pure, compassionless intellect engendered by monetary culture. The calculating members of the stock market may, through their purely rational activity, beget a long-term bullish market. But this market advance can occur at the same time that the material standard of living for the majority of the population is actually in decline. The stock market represented a type of pure rational exchange, indifferent and emotionally unconnected to the economic health of the majority of citizens. Rational egoism and the stock market symbolized the compassionless nature of capitalist money culture. Perhaps Simmel's analysis of pure intellect resembles nothing so much as the conclusions of Rousseau's "Discourse on the Origin and Foundations of Inequality." Like Rousseau, he comprehended the modern culture as expanding rationality ruthlessly applied to self-interest.

> The intellect, in its pure conception, is absolutely characterless, but not in the sense of the absence of an actual essential quality, rather because it stands totally beyond the decisive one-sidedness that constitutes character. This is obviously and precisely also the characterlessness of money.[150]

The absence of moral character was the essential quality of pure intellect (academic and financial) and monetary culture.

Simmel reflected upon the spiritual implications of pure intellect and monetary amorality. The calculating intellect was indifferent to the fundamental questions of spiritual life, which Simmel called the "welfare of the soul."[151] The modern soul was now imprinted with the intellectual and indifferent objectivity of money. The fundamental linkage between intellectualism and money, Simmel concluded, was the reason why one finds strains of anti-intellectualism in thinkers who oppose a calculating vision of life. The spiritual nobility—figures like Carlyle, Goethe, and Nietzsche—were laudable precisely because their moral visions were impenetrable to the rationally self-interested intellect. Simmel also provided a sociological explanation of anti-intellectualism in movements for economic equality. These movements, he believed, were responding to the compassionlessness of the intellect in the money economy.

Simmel used a range of terms and phrases to describe the demonic remoteness of things from people in monetary culture: the reification of culture, objectification, depersonalization, impersonality, indifference, the process of the objectification of cultural subjectivity, and the growth of unfamiliarity, remoteness, and distance. This language was quite similar to that of Marx.[152] Marx may have explained "the phantasmagoric form of the relationship of things," "the magic of money," and "the pure atomistic behavior of humanity in their production process."[153] But it was Simmel who undertook a radical critique of capitalist culture from a position of theoretical skepticism. *The Philosophy of Money* supplanted the economic primacy of production and class and the theoretical primacy of dialectical materialism with the cultural primacy of consumer culture and monetary exchange and the speculative metaphysics of symbolic sociology. But the difference between Simmel and Marx's analyses was not pure. Both, for instance, emphasized the centrality of the division of labor for interpreting the cultural consequences of capitalism. Like Marx, Simmel located modern alienation in the capitalist division of labor.

> Even economic production begins with the inseparability of the personal and physical sides of work. The indifference [of these two] develops only gradually into an antithesis, and as a result of production, products and this transformation, the personal element withdraws more and more. This process, however, liberated individual freedom. As we have already seen, this unfolds to such an extent that nature becomes more objective, more thing-like, and self-lawgiving; so it increases along with the objectification and depersonalization of the economic cosmos.[154]

For Simmel, the positive side of the division of labor, objectification, indifference, and the worldwide impersonal interdependence of individuals was the individual's ability to overcome the "unconsciousness of the natural lawlike" character of social relations.[155] The division of labor and social alienation were positive, Marx and Simmel would agree, to the extent that they contributed to a critical denaturalization of social institutions and hegemonic ideologies.

Money, as a sociological symbol, simultaneously explained the civic extirpation of compassion and the consumer's radical feeling of individual freedom. Modernity was itself a unity of extremes: extreme personal freedom and the nihilistic absence of social morality. The monetary economy was akin to a psychic force hurling simultaneously in opposite directions: money, the great dictator, and money, the great liberator; money, the most ubiquitous source of social determinism, egoism, and indifference and money, the agent of the soul's freedom from social determinism. *The Philosophy of Money,* then, turned on a brilliant and paradoxical analysis of modernity. In Simmel's artful hands, the contemporary culture of money was said to produce simultaneously the total reduction of the individual to the cold deterministic logic of monetary objectification and the individual's complete liberation from social determinism.

The Philosophy of Money is the textual key to understanding both Simmel's ambiguous legacy and his relation to socialist politics. Simmel's cultural prestige stemmed from the fact that his philosophy was, in the language of deconstruction, politically undecidable; *The Philosophy of Money*, for example, could be interpreted as both a socialist and an anti-socialist text, as an anti-bourgeois icon and as a defense of extreme individualism, as a document of philosophical idealism and historical materialism, and as an exclusively aesthetic and an essentially political text. In sum, the dyadic nature of Simmel's sociosymbolic conclusions (his elaboration of historical contradictions and antithesis-pairs) left his sociology of capitalist culture open to numerous interpretations.[156] The source of this undecidability was the antinomies that comprised Simmel's philosophy.

After the publication of the *The Philosophy of Money* in 1900, Simmel's primary academic focus shifted from sociosymbolic philosophy to religious philosophy and aesthetics. This shift is clearly reflected in his seminars. Between 1895 and 1899 Simmel often offered a seminar entitled "Social Psychology with Special Consideration of Socialism." This was the first course on socialism ever held at Berlin University. It was offered once in 1895, 1896, and 1897; twice in 1898 and twice in 1899. After 1899, he never held a seminar with "socialism" in its title. It was as if Simmel felt a need to distance himself from socialism and the radical cultural critique of *The Philosophy of Money*. *The Philosophy of Money* could have been, and most likely was, interpreted by university officials as yet another expression of his interest in socialist politics. The text was, after all, a devastating critique of Kaiser capitalism. So, in place of his seminars on socialism, Simmel offered two seminars on the philosophy of religion in 1900. In 1901 he held his first private seminar on aesthetics.

Simmel's ambiguous legacy is manifest in the socialist reception of *The Philosophy of Money*. The most substantial socialist critique referred to the text's insufficient attention to the role of money in the process of capital accumulation and class society.[157] However, at least one leading socialist intellectual was so inspired by Simmel's analysis of monetary culture that he wrote a book on Simmel's significance to socialism. Dr. Max Adler, perhaps *the* leading theorist of Austrian socialism, was the most prominent defender of Simmel's significance for socialism. In *Georg Simmels Bedeutung für die Geistesgeschichte* (1919), he praised *The Philosophy of Money* for its unique ability to articulate the "enormous multiperspectival character of reality." Simmel balanced the recognition of cultural "diversity on one hand" with the "necessary one-sidedness of interpretation on the other hand."[158] According to Adler, Simmel's ability to theorize the complexity of monetary culture, while rejecting capitalist morality, was exceptional among social theorists of the period.

From another point of view, the text could be read as an antisocialist tract. For instance, a leitmotif of the text was the assertion that more individual freedom exists in consumer culture than ever before in human history. The text was, moreover, a celebration of the elitist ethics of Nietzsche and a critique of naive socialist materialism. One thing is clear, however. While much of Simmel scholarship has focused on his *Sociology* and *Lebensanschauung*, the text that most impressed his intellectual progeny was *The Philosophy of Money*. His readers were most influenced by its last chapter, "The Style of Life," which criticized the nihilism, egoism, and greed of Kaiser capitalism. With the publication of *The Philosophy of Money,* Simmel attained a reputation as Germany's greatest cultural critic. One of his contemporaries commented that with the publication of *The Philosophy of Money* Simmel had supplanted Nietzsche as the greatest "philosopher against the present."[159] Here and there a great leader of countercultural thought strikes a note that resonates with a younger generation of nonconformists. Simmel's magnum opus, largely forgotten today, expressed clearly and with conviction a tumultuous spirit of ethical revolt that endeared him to radical students and foreclosed his institutional ascendency within academia.

SOCIOLOGY: EXAMINATIONS OF THE FORMS OF SOCIALIZATION (1908)—COMPASSION AND DOMINATION

Humility requires that philosophy not suppress Georg Simmel's perspective, namely, that it is astonishing how rarely the history of philosophy acknowledges the suffering of humanity.

Theodor Adorno[160]

Simmel has been interpreted disproportionately as a sociologist, rather than a philosopher or social critic. Accordingly, his *Sociology: Examinations of the Forms of Socialization* (1908) has received boundless scholarly attention, and this scholarly attention is faithful to Simmel's enormous contribution to the development of sociology as an academic discipline. One reason for the academic renown of *Sociology* is clear: it was the first major German work to be assigned the title "sociology." The concept of sociology appeared in his work as early as 1894 in an article entitled "The Problem of Sociology." However, while that article was a mere six pages in length, *Sociology* was a weighty tome whose pagination exceeded 800 pages. The originality, sophistication, and sheer scale of *Sociology* transformed Simmel's academic reputation. Within a year of its publication, he was hailed in a standard reference work as Germany's "most important sociologist."[161] The magnitude of the text for the discipline of sociology was monumental. Its title and content articulated the essence of an academic practice which was widespread by 1908—in the works of Max Scheler, Werner Sombart, Ernst Troeltsch, Max Weber, and others—but which lacked a disciplinary rubric. In addition to his conceptual and academic contributions to the emerging discipline of sociology, Simmel's organizational activities were also significant. The German Sociological Society was established with his support. In 1910, at the organization's first meeting, he was afforded the honor of delivering the opening presentation. This honor reflected the judgment of his contemporaries; Simmel had done more than any other German intellectual to establish sociology as a discipline.

Yet Simmel, who did so much to put the discipline of sociology on the academic map, seemed immune to its widespread allure among German academics. Just when sociology had gained academic credibility, it ceased to be an arena of pressing intellectual concern for Simmel. He quickly withdrew from the activities of the German Sociological Society and in the last years of his life sought public recognition primarily as a philosopher. However, this self-conception did not contradict the perception of his contemporaries who overwhelmingly recognized Simmel's philosophical significance to sociology. Among his intellectual peers, he was recognized as the thinker who lifted the practice of sociology above the mere collection of data and established it as a formidable philosophical undertaking. In another futile attempt to recruit Simmel to the University of Heidelberg in 1914, its faculty wrote to the ministry of culture concerning Simmel's originality.

> Simmel's major service is undoubtedly the revolutionary transformation of the social sciences and their reestablishment on completely new foundations. . . . He has newly established the social sciences. He has drawn their borders, established their methods, created their concepts, and, above all, he has brilliantly carried through an examination of their psychological foundations, a task which was absolutely necessary but never achieved heretofore.[162]

Simmel's significance was not only philosophical and methodological. The thematic contents of Simmel's sociological works were equally original. David Levine has eloquently framed the sweeping significance of Simmel's thought.

> Of those who created the intellectual capital used to launch the enterprise of professional sociology, Georg Simmel was perhaps the most original and fecund. In search of a subject matter for sociology that would distinguish it from all other social sciences and humanistic disciplines, he charted a new field for discovery and proceeded to explore a world of novel topics in works that have guided and anticipated the thinking of generations of sociologists.[163]

Levine's vibrant description of Simmel's original and incomparable contributions to the discipline of sociology are valuable. Indeed, his enthusiasm for Simmel's novel topics is the ground upon which to rejoin our grand narrative of Simmel as a countercultural thinker. In addition to our interpretation of Simmel as an exemplar of philosophical sociology, he has been presented here as a critic of the seductive siren of consumer conformity. Although attuned to the growth of personal freedom in liberal culture, he turned a deaf ear to the false freedom and ethical emptiness of monetary culture. This critique of conformity and false freedom was exemplified in his revolutionary sociological topics. Specifically, his sociological analyses of poverty and superordination advanced a sociological spirit, a hearty call to resist—if only by way of an ethical jeremiad—social hierarchy, and the lifestyle of pitiless self-interest.

In *Sociology*, there was a passionate waterway just below the surface of Simmel's dry and highly analytical prose. A critique of the heartless status quo often lurked behind his cold academic erudition. His investigation of social conditions of the poor, for instance, represented a renewed offensive against the ethical inertia of Christianity. In "The Poor," chapter 7 of *Sociology*, Simmel joined the cultural debate over social morality through an incisive critique of the social consequences of Christian charity. His sociological judgment of Christian alms as a form of subjective egoism foreclosed ethical claims to superiority among upper- and middle-class Christians. Simmel's concept of subjective egoism challenged and defined the social-psychology of Christian charity; charitable Christians was less concerned with the poor than with their own salvation. Giving was merely a means for advancing religious self-interest. Like giving to charities in order to deduct the cost from your taxes, Christian altruism was inauthentic and self-deceptive. Compassion for the poor was obviously secondary to religious self-interest. Simmel's sociology of charity yielded an understanding of corollary problems. Since Christian altruism was voluntary, there was no conference of citizenship and dignity upon the poor. Their rights were reduced to nothing. Such powerlessness fostered humiliation and shame.

Simmel's sociology of the poor also directed attention to the tendency of the modern state to deny the poor a right to participate in their own administration. A state may recognize the right to a minimum standard of living, but here, too, the recognition of the poor as citizens was precluded. Simmel suggested that the poor's powerlessness and humiliation was not inevitable or intractable. An ideal of reciprocity and mutual respect was the ethical underframe of his attitude toward the poor. The poor could be granted more expansive rights, such as the right to confer with the government about their needs. He noted that state assistance to the poor forestalled a spirit of reciprocity and failed to prepare the way for the elimination of the conditions that sustain poverty. Rather than blame the poor for the conditions that contribute to poverty, Simmel entertained the possibility of transforming economic and cultural conditions. In open defiance of Manchester mantras about government intervention, he posited the construction of a society that reduced the chances for impoverishment to an absolute minimum. As Simmel would have it, this civic option was impeded, however, by the unwillingness or inability of many citizens to see poverty as a collective outcome of capitalism.[164] Simmel repeatedly returned to the touchstone of his sociology of the poor: poor citizens deserve rights, but class chasms mitigate against the recognition of these rights.

> The higher one's economic class, . . . the less likely one is to come in contact with the poor; yes, in principle, the existence of the poor is actually excluded. . . . The poor person is formally déclassé. Until the poor receive assistance, class prejudice is strong enough to make poverty, so to speak, invisible.[165]

Incidently, Simmel drew a parallel between his sociology of the poor and the social circumstances of the stranger, who is outside of the society to which he belongs. Of course, Simmel's own life within the bourgeoisie and within academia closely approximated the social alienation experienced by the stranger and the poor. Perhaps this partially accounts for his absorbing interest in and compassion for the outsider.

If the unarticulated aim of *The Philosophy of Money* was resistance to the ravages of nihilism and egoism, *Sociology* embodied wonderfully his impassioned and conscious morality of being-for-others. The text contained an eclectic and distinctive set of theoretical problems and social topics: the theoretical preconditions of sociology, conflict as a process of social integration, spacial relations as the determining conditions of social intercourse, the self-preservation of the group, the constitution of individuality, the fragmentary character of human identity, urbanism and marginality as ways of life, the sociological significance of secrets and secret societies, and the quantitative aspects of sociability. Like an art form characterized by montage, Simmel's *Sociology* refused to cordon off one realm of society from another. Alas, he conceived of the enterprise of sociology as the construction of an art work.[166] His sociological portraits of modernity were rarely composed of primary colors. More often they featured a dazzling interaction of mental and institutional hues. Accordingly, the key concept of Simmel's sociology was interaction (*Wechselwirkung*, literally "reciprocal effect" or "exchange effect"). Much scholarly attention has been payed to the brilliance and/or inadequacy of Simmel's concept of interaction.

This study deviates from the traditional estimations of Simmel's sociology of human interactions. We are less concerned with an assessment of the value or limitations of the concept of *Wechselwirkung* for contemporary sociologists than with an assessment of Simmel's sociological attitude as a personal or ethical outlook. Our approach is analogous to the guiding principle of Kandinsky's aesthetics.[167] While Kandinsky sought the inner meaning of art, we seek to deduce the personal presuppositions of Simmel's sociology. Tönnies appropriately offered an aesthetic metaphor for Simmel's profound erudition; his sociological works were said to be "a special art, characterized by suggestion, shading, halftones, and seemingly magical light effects."[168] Many scholars have commented on the aesthetic qualities of Simmel's sociology, but far too often the underlying spiritual dimension endured burial under the weight of something akin to academic objectivity. To date, his distinctive ethical outlook has not been excavated. Above we uncovered a distinctive ethical viewpoint in his sociology of the poor. A discernable ethical viewpoint was also replete in another section of *Sociology* entitled "Superordination and Subordination." This section, chapter 3 of the text, ran more than a hundred and twenty pages in length, and to this sociology of human hierarchies we now turn our attention.

As if trying to avoid the dangerous association of sociology and socialism, Simmel began his sociology of superordination with a disclaimer: "The moral side of this analysis [of domination] does not concern us here."[169] To a great degree, Simmel does fend off potential charges that his sociology was motivated by political or moral concerns. His investigations of domination and hierarchy contained overtly neutral analyses. We will examine three examples: attention to (1) the interactive or reciprocal character of hierarchal relations, (2) the historical nature of superordination, and (3) the fragmentary nature of social identities. The relationships of superordination and subordination play a constant historical role in diverse societies. Simmel defined them as basic societal forms. However, Simmel emphasized that most relationships of authority do not eliminate the possibility for resistance:

> First, within a relationship of subordination, the exclusion of all spontaneity is actually rarer than is suggested by popular expressions such as "coercion," "having no choice," "absolute necessity," etc. . . . For example, what one calls authority presupposes—to a much greater degree than one generally recognizes—a freedom of the person subjected to authority.[170]

This theoretical proposition was reinforced with corresponding historical examples of reciprocity within hierarchies: ancient slavery, medieval social relations, and the modern labor contract. Simmel did not write extended histories which were founded on his interactive conception of domination. Yet, the social histories of subaltern groups, emerging from the ferment of the 1960s, commenced with a similar presupposition and revolutionized various fields of history. Perhaps the best example of this type of historical scholarship is Eugene Genovese's *Roll, Jordan, Roll: The World the Slaves Made*. According to Genovese, even American slavery was not wholly hegemonic.[171] Spaces for social resistance and cultural creation existed within this institution of domination. Simmel's sociology of domination also calls to mind the thought of the greatest modern theorist of power, Michel Foucault. Like Simmel, who saw obedience and resistance as two sides of domination, Foucault rejected a static and absolute conception of authority and marshaled a flotilla of historical documents to support a revolutionary proposition: institutions of authority both produce and unconsciously facilitate resistance.[172] In comparing Simmel's sociology of power with the premises of social historians and Foucault, there is no suggestion that Simmel was the source of their ideas about power. We simply wish to highlight the forward-looking nature of his sociology.

Second, Simmel completely rejected transhistorical explanations of power and theorized the unfolding history of institutions and ideologies of power. Originally, power derived from direct physical coercion (patriarchy) and personal allegiance (warlord). Domination was primarily a victory over external resistance. Eventually, Simmel hypothesized, real subordination was supplanted by habituated subordination. Authoritarian relationships became codified into traditions: state, class, church, school, family, and military organizations. Personal power was transformed and legitimized by superindividual institutions. This institutionalization of superordination was designed to destroy internal resistance. Perhaps most insightful was Simmel's explanation of how traditions make it possible to experience domination as freedom. There was a correlation between codified authority and the feeling of equality. Christian women, for example, experience the objective idea of the patriarchal family as subordination to a divine principle. Men are also required to subordinate themselves to the principle of God and obey their male roles as well. Christian women experience this as a condition of equality: for both men and women are required to fulfill their divine sex roles, and to that extent, both men and women are equally subordinate to God. Nationalism may function similarly, he argued. The focus on an external enemy or conquered people may transform all men and women into a nobility without changing the social hierarchies that underpin the status quo. When the Spanish state conquered the Moors and expelled the Jews, all Spaniards breathed the same air of superordination.

For his part, Simmel was unwilling to brook compromises with traditional claims to authority. Repeatedly, he compared and contrasted natural laws and human laws. Natural laws were an objectivity indifferent to personal values. Individuals were subject to the laws of nature regardless of their understanding or lack of understanding of it. Natural laws preclude the ethical subjectivity of the individual. Human traditions can function similarly. Their claims to social, scientific, or divine objectivity occlude the development and deployment of ethical free will. Naturalized claims to objectivity were the ideological ballasts of tradition. Simmel treated such claims as bad faith. While he recognized the need for superindividual morals, his sociology of superordination appealed to an ideal of social morality that included a conception of free will. His sociological definition of social mortality consciously acknowledged the individual's right to disobey. Ideally, concepts like truth and justice are meaningful only to the extent that they entail individual's conscious consent. Claims to objectivity which derive merely from social tradition categorically destroy the ethical origin of truth and justice: free will.[173] Obedience to tradition soothes the conscience by relieving individuals of responsibility for the consequences of their decisions. Moreover, respect for traditional moralities is one of the best ways to mask the lust for personal gain. One can maintain that they have not pursued self-interest but have assiduously upheld objective values. This reasoning can also justify brutality. Claims to objective truths often serve to suppress compassion. The reality of individual suffering disappears behind the logic that an objective law must be enforced. Hence, we can see that *Sociology* was constructed on countercultural pilings. The linkages between naturalized conceptions of morality, habituated brutality, and ethical irresponsibility were made explicit. In fact, Simmel constructed a philosophical seawall between obedience to tradition and a sociological ethics of freedom and social compassion.

Third, Simmel was one of the first sociologists to theorize the fragmentary character of the self. An individual's sociological identity was never singular. It was a composite of multiple types of interactions, none of which constituted the whole individual.

> Even in the case of an extremely intimate union—like marriage—we must admit that one is never *completely* married; rather, even in the best cases, only a portion of the person is married, just as one is never exclusively a citizen of a city, exclusively an economic comrade, or exclusively a church member.[174]

As a social scientist, Simmel examined a cross section of individuals and groups and concluded that social identity contained "a multiplicity of contiguously exiting relationships of domination."[175]

> However one draws the line that divides everything thinkable into opposing units, the human being will always contain both of them. Whether it is the realm of ideas or the realm of spatiotemporal events, the divine order or the arena of the anti-Christ, the alienating mechanism of things or their meaning and value which we need in order to live, and the natural-corporeal structure of existence or the cosmos of the soul and history, *duality is not reconciled in man, but meets in him.*[176]

Humans are a compendium of unresolved contradictory characteristics. Even what we call egalitarian relationships involve a reciprocity of superordination and subordination rather than absolute equality. Equality means mutual respect for the other's specialized knowledge and thereby an ongoing interlacing of inferior and superior subject positions.

Before we investigate further Simmel's *Sociology*, we need to pause and consider his insistence that his sociology of domination was detached from "moral" considerations. This attempt to bracket morality from sociology was a performative contradiction in several senses. The idea of a neutral and purely analytic sociology contradicted Simmel's own methodology, which was forged as a defense of the subjective features of scholarship and social existence. We also may approach *Sociology* as a revelation of engaged scholarship by looking at Simmel's stock of sociological examples. For instance, bourgeois housewives were presented as an example of the simultaneity of superordination and subordination. While the bourgeois housewife was socially subordinate to her husband, she was superior to her domestic servants. Because domestic servants were personally subordinate to the housewife, there were few delimitations on the wife's power. Thus, the patriarchal family was far from being a mere instrument of a husband's domination of his wife. Patriarchy within the bourgeoisie facilitated an additional form of superordination: the wives' nearly complete control of domestic servants. In another section of the text, Simmel calls attention to the bourgeois family as an example of social egoism. Rather than an institutional negation of monetary individualism, Simmel interpreted the family as a collective embodiment of egoism. Families were habituated to care only for their own members. Flowing from this cultural logic was the inclination to disregard one's responsibilities to those outside the family. *Sociology* was replete was ethical criticisms of the bourgeoisie. Such criticisms were sociologically valid, but they also articulated his antibourgeois attitudes which were inherently moral.

More than anything else, Simmel's language betrayed his insistence that his sociology of domination was disconnected from moral concerns. He made impassioned references to the "terrible hardships" of the Russian peasantry and the complete "powerlessness" of the "modern factory worker" in regards to the entrepreneur.[177] He seemed especially aware of the humiliatingly harsh conditions of nonreciprocal forms of domination. Once a human relationship precludes any form of resistance by the subordinate party, the very notion of society is annulled. Simmel provided a contemporary example of such an annulment.

> The difference between the strategic positions of the lowest workers and employers in modern giant factories is so overwhelming that the work contract ceases to be a contract in the ordinary sense of the word, because the former is unconditionally subservient to the latter.[178]

Elements of modern capitalist society were so oppressive that they were unworthy of the appellation society. Such sociological taxonomies were absolutely convincing as social science, but they also reflect Simmel's abiding moral sensibilities.

We will mention one more way that *Sociology* signifies a moral and political disposition. According to Simmel, our conception of freedom unfolds from the French Revolution. In the Revolution, the bourgeoisie used working-class support to create an economic and social hierarchy which excluded workers from equality. Nonetheless, the ideals of the French Revolution revealed the connection between freedom and equality. Collective freedom may prevail only where general equality prevails. In the wake of the French Revolution, the oppressed masses initially experienced freedom as an elevation into the ranks of the bourgeoisie. Simmel treated this as an immature moment in a new unfolding consciousness of freedom.

The quest for real civic freedom must eventually push society beyond this conception and to the point where the opportunity for some members of the lower class to rise and become part of the superordinate stratum is no longer experienced as collective freedom. He colorfully described the chance of the best workers to rise into the ranks of the propertied classes as a superficial form of collective freedom and as "a regular bleeding of the working class robbing them of their best blood."[179]

Simmel suggested that the remedy to this underdeveloped conception of freedom was located in socialism. The purely technical character of socialism adheres in the fact that it is "the first proposal for eliminating the eudaemonistic imperfections which arise from historical inequality."[180] Simmel went further than a mere acceptance of the historical relevance of socialism. Through a refinement of anarchist ideas, he fashioned his own utopian conception of society. Proudhoun's goal—a society without subordination and whose cohesion resulted from the free coordination of individuals—can be reached "even if superordination and subordination continue to exist, *provided they constitute a reciprocal sociological formation.*"

> In an ideal organization, A would be subordinate to B in one respect, and B would be subordinate to A in another sphere. Thereby the organizational value of hierarchy would be preserved, while removing oppression, injustice, and the one-sidedness of interaction.[181]

A small-scale example of this ideal, Simmel suggested, was the workers' association that elects its leader. They were subordinate to the elected leader but, through mechanism of democracy, they retained a superordinate position as well. In any case, Simmel's civic ruminations about utopian sociological formations transgressed the boundaries of mere sociological description. In *Sociology*, despite Simmel's stated intentions, countercultural dreams broke through the icy surface of scholarly detachment. His sociology called for new states of mind, the transcendence of historical determinism, and the creation of new civic models. What emerged was not a ringing endorsement of orthodox socialism with its primary focus on class hierarchy. While socialists trained their interpretative guns on one relationship of domination, Simmel realized that social identity was comprised of multiple superordinate and subordinate interactions. Thereby his *Sociology* managed to dramatically expand and substantially complicate egalitarian radicalism.

Simmel's sociological imagination consciously expressed a spirit of defiance against the hierarchical order of Kaiser capitalism. But the task of sociology was not merely negative. For Simmel, sociology was an existential strategy for reasserting the "unity of life's elements . . . [given] the fundamental tear inside of men and inside of the world, and between men and the world."[182] It was monetary culture, superordination, and domination that produced the horrible tears that furrowed the modern soul. And, the impassioned task of the sociologist was to sow the hope of healing.

PHILOSOPHICAL SOCIOLOGY AND NIETZSCHEAN SOCIALISM

The conception of Simmel's thought as a philosophical sociology of extremes (idealist philosophy/objective sociology and autonomous subjectivity/socially determined identities) is not only a regulative idea of this text. It was also Simmel's self-conception. In *The Fundamental Questions of Sociology: Individual and Society* (1917), he described his intellectual genre as "philosophical sociology," and in "How is Society Possible?", a philosophical interlude within *Sociology*, he denoted his theoretical perspective of the "social individual" as a position between two extreme poles.[183]

> The social living person . . . is not partially social and partially individual; rather, his existence is shaped by a fundamental, structuring category of unity, which can not be expressed in an other way than as a synthesis or contemporaneity of two logically contradictory determinations: man is a member of society and a being-for-oneself, both a product of society and a life with its own autonomous center.[184]

The individual was socially determined and self-actualizing. Socialization stamped individuals as specifically human. At the same time, habituation stultified individual freedom. So, the individual comes to self-conception by standing against social norms. This was the reason Simmel believed Nietzschean philosophy possessed sociological relevance. A self-conscious conception of socialization can only be gained by an antisocial perspective, namely, by an individual resisting tradition. This distance from society literally creates ethics and responsibility. For, when the law is unconscious, when custom and habit dominate human subjectivity, habituation to authority is automatic, free will is destroyed, and ethics are impossible. But Simmel's dialectic of the individual and society did not stop with the prescription of an ethics of self-actualization. He cautioned that the demand for a self-created and antitraditional ethics potentially lends support to egoism. The right to personal values can bolster self-envelopment and diminish compassion. Social responsibility and altruism are the essence of morality, and they require that all self-created values be subjected to a rigorous sociological evaluation. In *Sociology*, for instance, Simmel expressed his conviction that all personal values must undergo a civic transformation. Personal values must undergo an assessment of what he called their "objective ideality" (*objektive Idealität*) and "superindividual validity" (*über-persönliche Geltung*).[185] In what Simmel saw as the highest stage of morality, this assessment would not be experienced as a social demand but merely as the norm of the free moral conscience. Simmel's moral ideal, the subjective lawfulness of a freely willed being-for-others, was not a terminal point of the dialectic of individual and society. He stripped the conflict between tradition and self-actualized moralities of the quixotic pretense of resolution.

The allure of Simmel's dialectical sociology boils down to something akin to the attraction of a horseshoe magnet. The conductivity of his thought originated from a polarity of forces: the positive pole of an uncompromising civic consciousness and the negative pole of individual freedom. These apparently incompatible magnetic poles produced a unique sociological electricity. Methodologically, they constituted a complete circuit. In Simmel's work, one often finds sociological interpretations of individuals standing side by side with reflections about the inability of sociology to account for the personal meaning of historical events. There was also an ethical branch of Simmel's magnetic thought which was discharged in a keen awareness of dual dangers: the threat that individualism will devolve into acquisitive egoism and indifference and the danger that the demand for social responsibility, if naturalized by dogma, will deny the individual's ethical free will. What we are calling Simmel's Nietzschean socialism should be seen as the concurrent maximization of individual freedom and social responsibility, and what ultimately made Simmel's thought such a powerhouse of critical energy was its simultaneous revelation of the inadequacies of the two major countercultural ideologies. Nietzschean philosophy only achieved its critical potential when it rose above existential individualism and was articulated as a civic philosophy. Socialism, on the other hand, required a fuller appreciation of individual freedom. This appreciation would come from an understanding of the liberatory potential of the money economy. For socialism to achieve the goal of maximizing individual freedom through economic equality, it must realize how "the specific relationships of a monetary economy deliver the outline or type for which socialism is striving."[186] The heterogeneity of subjective freedoms produced by monetary culture opens the possibility for a future society that advances distributive equality and civic responsibility while not sacrificing the individual's right to spiritual aspirations.

Simmel's compassionate critique of Kaiser capitalism, superordination, and monetary culture was not only powerful but brilliant; it ranks him with Nietzsche and Marx as one of Germany's greatest critics of bourgeois society. One might say that he did for capitalist culture what Marx had done for capitalist production: he undertook an immanent critique that called forth countercultural political practice. His anticapitalism, like Eduard Bernstein's socialism, was ethical. His language of *Geist* (spirit) and *Seele* (soul) was uniquely suited to influence those radical students for whom secular language was inadequate to express the existential affinity of knowledge, anti-capitalist culture, and aesthetic self-creation. It was Simmel, more than any other intellectual in Wilhelmine Germany, who articulated the philosophical basis of left modernism: the existential combination of vanguard politics and avant-garde aesthetics.

NOTES

1. Simmel, "Das Geld in der modernen Cultur," in *Aufsätze und Abhandlungen 1894–1900* (Frankfurt a.M.: Suhrkamp, 1992), pp. 191–92; *Die Probleme der Geschichtsphilosophie* (Leipzig: Duncker & Humblot, 1905), p. vi.
2. H. Stuart Hughes, *Consciousness and Society*, p. 33.
3. Ibid., pp. 37–38.
4. See especially, Wilhelm Dilthey, *Einleitung in die Geisteswissenschaften: Versuch einer Grundlegung für das Studium der Gesellschaft und der Geschichte* [1883] (Leipzig: B.G. Teubner, 1923). This is Dilthey's famous statement about the distinction between the natural sciences and the humanities, or, science of spirit. The goal is an understanding of "external reality . . . as life [Leben], not as a naive representation" (xix). See also, Wilhelm Dilthey, *Die Geistige Welt: Einleitung in die Philosophie des Lebens* (Leipzig: B.G. Teubner, 1924), and a selection of his work under the title *Die Philosophie des Lebens* (Stuttgart: B.G. Teubner, 1961). On Dilthey and Simmel, see Hans-Joachim Lieber, *Kulturkritik und Lebensphilosophie: Studien zur deutschen Philosophie der Jahrhundertwende* (Darmstadt: Wissenschaftliche Buchgesellschaft, 1974).
5. Wilhelm Dilthey, *Das Erlebnis und die Dichtung* (Leipzig: Reclam, 1991), p. 19.
6. Simmel, *Die Probleme der Geschichtsphilosophie* (1905), p. vi.
7. Simmel, "Was ist uns Kant?" in *Aufsätze und Abhandlungeng 1894–1900*, p. 145.
8. Dilthey, "Praktische Philosophie," in *System der Ethik* (Stuttgart: B. G. Teubner, 1958), p. 119; Simmel, *Lebensanschauung* (Leipzig: Duncker & Humblot, 1918), p.154.
9. Dilthey, *System der Ethik*, p. 116.
10. Simmel, "Was is uns Kant?" p. 145.
11. Stephan Körner, *Kant* (Göttingen: Vandenhoeck & Ruprecht, 1980), p. 62. See especially chapter 4, "Das System der synthetischen Prinzipien a priori," pp. 55–85.
12. Dilthey, *Einleitung*, pp. 390, 393.
13. Ernst Troeltsch, *Der Historismus und seine Probleme* (Tübingen: J. C. B. Mohr, 1922), p. 579.
14. Georg Simmel, *Die Probleme der Geschichtsphilosophie* (Leipzig: Duncker & Humblot, 1892), pp. 1–5.
15. Dilthey, "Soziologie," in *Einleitung in der Geisteswissenschaften*, p. 420.

16. Dilthey, *Weltanschauungslehre: Abhandlungen zur Philosophie der Philosophie* (Leipzig: B. G. Teubner, 1931), p. 26.

17. Simmel, *Geschichtsphilosophie* (1892), p. v.

18. Simmel, *Über sociale Differenzierung,* pp. 2, 115.

19. Georg Simmel, "Parerga zur Socialphilosophie," in *Einleitung in die Moralwissenschaft*, II: 391–402.

20. Simmel, *Geschichtsphilosophie* (1905), p. 69.

21. Ibid., p. 24.

22. Ibid., p. 24.

23. In other contexts, Simmel referred to a *Vorstellungskomplex*.

24. Christopher Zöckler, *Dilthey und die Hermeneutik* (Stuttgart: J. B. Metzler, 1975), p. 34. Wilhelm Windelband, "Über Begriff und Geschichte der Philosophie," *Präludien* (1884): 29.

25. Simmel, *Buch des Dankes,* p. 119.

26. Klaus Christian Köhnke, *Entstehung und Aufsteig des Neukantianismus: Die deutsche Universitätsphilosophie zwischen Idealismus und Positivismus* (Frankfurt a.M.: Suhrkamp, 1986), p. 406. Two of the most important neo-Kantian journals, *Philosophischen Monatshefte* and *Vierteljahresschrift*, were founded in 1876 ostensibly by Herman Cohen and Johannes Volkelt.

27. Georg Simmel, "Der Fragmentcharacter des Lebens," *Logos* 7 (1916–17): 40.

28. Dilthey, *Einleitung in der Geisteswissenschaften*, p. 386.

29. Simmel, *Geschichtsphilosophie* (1905), p. 71.

30. Dilthey, *Die Einbildungskraft des Dichters: Bausteine für eine Poetik* in *Gesammlte Schriften* (Leipzig: B. G. Teubner, 1924), 6: 144.

31. Fritz Heinemann, *Neue Wege der Philosophie: Geist/Leben/Existenz* (Leipzig: Quelle & Meyer, 1929), pp. 230–31.

32. Georg Lukács, *Die Zerstörung der Vernunft: Der Weg des Irrationalismus von Schelling zu Hitler* (Berlin: Aufbau, 1988), p. 338.

33. Lukács, *Zerstörung*, p. 354.

34. Quoted from Klaus Lichtblau, *Kulturkrise und Soziologie um die Jahrhundertwende: Zur Geneologie der Kultursoziologie in Deutschland* (Frankfurt a.M.: Suhrkamp, 1996), p. 93.

35. Erich Przywara, *Gott* (Köln: Oratoriums Verlag, 1926), p.162.

36. Simmel, "Die Großstädte und das Geistesleben," p. 227.

37. Simmel, *Schopenhauer und Nietzsche*, p. 289.

38. Ibid., p. 277.

39. Hughes, p. 42.

40. Simmel, "Die Gegensätze des Lebens und die Religion," in *Aufsätze und Abhandlungen 1901–1908,* vol. 1 (Frankfurt a.M.: Suhrkamp, 1995), 302.

41. Simmel, "Die Gegensätze des Lebens und die Religion," p. 297.

42. Simmel, "Über die Liebe," in *Fragmente und Aufsätze*, p. 52.

43. Simmel, "Socialismus und Pessimismus," in *Aufsätze und Abhandlungen 1901–1908*, I: 554, 558.

44. Ibid., p. 555.

45. Ibid., p. 557.

46. Ibid., p. 555.

47. A letter recommending Simmel's promotion from *Privatdozent* to *Extraordinarius* included the statement that "his standpoint is Spencer's evolutionary doctrine." The letter, dated June 3, 1898, was addressed to the Minister of Culture and was signed "Dekan und Professoren: Dilthey, Strumpf, Paulsen, Schmoller, Lenz, Delbrück, Wagner." *Buch des Dankes*, pp. 22–23.

48. Simmel, *Über sociale Differenzierung*, p. 114.

49. Simmel's value-pluralism was influenced by two contemporary sources: Darwinian theory and Wilhelm Dilthey. While Darwinian theory proposed that evolution led to an increasing diversification of species, Dilthey asserted that value-pluralism was "the aim of the preservation of the species" (Zöckler, p. 34). See Simmel's relativist interpretation of Kant's notion of a synthetic a priori in "Über den Unterschied der Wahrnehmungs und der Erfahrungsurteile. Ein Deutungsversuch [Kants]," *Kantstudien 1* (1897): 424–25. The concept of value-feeling (*Wertgefühle*) illustrated Simmel's rejection of a purely rational understanding of subjectivity in favor of a dionysian, heterogenous, and unreasonable view of the noumenal relationship to value forms. The fact that value forms can be identified, however, removed the investigation of morality from pessimism and made possible a science of morals. This science does not rest on the belief in a totalized morality. There is no form of moral forms but multiple value-forms evaluated in the light of their experiential or sociological consequences.

50. Simmel, *Über sociale Differenzierung*, pp. 234–35.

51. Ibid., pp. 235–36.

52. The greatest symbol of modern history is money. Money is a symbol of aporetic phenomenology since it simultaneously represents monolithic calculability and differentiation. We will investigate this further in relation to Simmel's *Philosophie des Geldes*.

53. Simmel, *Über sociale Differenzierung*, p. 291.

54. Ibid., p. 291. For another example of Simmel's early interest in money and culture, see "Zur Psychologie des Geldes" in *Aufsätze 1887–1890*, pp. 49–66.

55. Georg Simmel, "Ein Wort über soziale Freiheit," *Sozialpolitisches Zentralblatt I* (1892): 334.

56. Simmel, "Ein Wort," p. 334.

57. H. M., "Weltpolitik," *Die Neue Zeit,* 12 (1893–94): 165–70.

58. Georg Simmel, "Der Frauen Kongreß und die Sozialdemokratie," in *Schriften zur Philosophie und Soziologie der Geschlechter*, pp.133–39. The essays in this volume are an example of his gender theory, which combined feminist and anticapitalist themes. He addressed the central issues of bourgeois feminism: prostitution, militarism, and women's admittance to the university. If the themes were common to the period, his comments were nonetheless very provocative. For instance, he compared the reduction of women in the "good society" to a monetary "ejaculation-mechanism," which he described as "the most impersonal thing that there is in practical life" (62). His cultural assumptions identify him with bourgeois feminism: the assumption of an undifferentiated female psychology—their inclination toward spontaneity, peacefulness, comraderie, and their disposition to deep emotions—and his tendency to see a common structure of female oppression, regardless of class differences. However, Simmel saw gender characteristics as neither psychological fact nor a biological necessity. In this regard, see also his letter to Marianne Weber in *Buch des Dankes*, pp.132–33.

59. Simmel, *Schriften zur Philosophie und Soziologie der Geschlechter*, p.137, my emphasis.

60. On the bourgeois feminist movement in Wilhelmine Germany, see Richard Evans, *The Feminist Movement in Germany, 1894–1933* (London: Sage, 1976); Barbara Greven-Aschoff, *Die bürgerliche Frauenbewegung in Deutschland, 1894–1933* (Göttingen: Vandenhoeck & Ruprecht, 1981); Nancy R. Reagin, *A German Women's Movement: Class and Gender in Hanover, 1880–1933* (Chapel Hill: University of North Carolina Press, 1995). Concerning the proletarian women's movement, see Jean H. Quataert, *Reluctant Feminists in German Social Democracy, 1885–1917* (Princeton: Princeton University Press, 1979); Werner Thönnessen, *The Emancipation of Women: The Rise and Decline of the Women's Movement in German Social Democracy 1863–1933*, trans. Joris de Bres (London: Pluto Press, 1973); Charles Sowerwine, "The Socialist Women's Movement From 1850 to 1940," in *Becoming Visible: Women in European History*, ed. Renate Bridenthal, et. al. (Boston: Houghton Mifflin, 1987): 399–428.

61. Georg Simmel, "Die beiden Formen des Individualismus," *Das freie Wort* (1901–1902): 397. This essay was greatly expanded and appeared as "Individuum und Gesellschaft in Lebensanschauungen des 18. und 19. Jahrhunderts (Beispiel der Philosophischen Soziologie)" in *Grundfragen der Soziologie (Individuum und Gesellschaft)* (Berlin: G. J. Göschen'sche Verlagshandlung, 1917), pp. 71–103.

62. Simmel, "Die beiden Formen," p. 398.

63. Ibid., p. 399.

64. Ibid., p. 400.

65. Ibid., pp. 400–401.

66. Ibid., p. 403.

67. Ibid., p. 403.

68. Simmel, "Tendencies of German Life and Thought Since 1870," *International Monthly* 2 (1902):176.

69. Ibid., p. 176.

70. See for example Simmel's ethical interpretation of art-for-art's sake, "L'art pour l'art," in *Vom Wesen der Moderne*, pp. 329–41.

71. Simmel, "Tendencies," p.177.

72. Ernst Troeltsch, *Der Historismus und seine Probleme*, p. 593.

73. Georg Simmel to Heinrich Rickert, 8 April 1910, *Buch des Dankes*, pp. 105–106. In a subsequent letter, 4 September 1911, Simmel wrote to Rickert stating that he was enclosing his new book, which "appears with every word to contradict the standpoint of your last *Logos* essay" (108). Simmel apparently was not fearful of expressing his intellectual differences with his friends and colleagues. Rickert eventually responded to Simmel's *Lebensphilosophie* by publishing *The Philosophy of Life: A Representation and Critique of the Philosophical Fashions of Our Time* (1920). This was an ongoing critique of Simmel's philosophical influence on the preceding generation of German intellectuals.

74. Georg Simmel to Heinrich Rickert, 15 March 1917, *Buch des Dankes*, p. 119. On Rickert's defense of objective values, see Guy Oakes, *Weber and Rickert* (Cambridge: MIT Press, 1988).

75. Simmel, *Schopenhauer und Nietzsche*, pp. 335–36.

76. Simmel, *Buch des Dankes*, p. 114. In another letter he asserted that the Jewish theater critic, Julius Bab, was unable to procure employment due to anti-Semitism. Most of his epistolary references to anti-Semitism appear after 1910, although I am not aware of the significance of this fact.

77. Rudolph Weingartner, *Experience and Culture*, p. 6.

78. Dietrich Schäfer, 26 February 1908, in Michael Landmann, "Bausteine zur Biographie," in *Buch des Dankes*, p. 27.

79. Dekan Hampe, 17 February 1908, in "Bausteine," in *Buch des Dankes*, pp. 25–26.

80. Georg Simmel to Max Weber, 18 March 1908, in *Buch des Dankes*, pp. 127–28.

81. Undoubtedly Simmel had a tremendous reputation in Jewish circles and was interpreted as a Jewish thinker. This reputation will be addressed in detail in the last chapter. See Elias Hurwicz, "Simmel als jüdische Denker," *Neue jüdische Monatshefte* 3 (1919): 196–98.

82. Simmel to Karl Joël, 24 February 1902, in *Georg Simmel und die Moderne*, ed. Heinz-Jürgen Dahme and Otthein Rammstedt (Frankfurt a.M.: Suhrkamp, 1984), p. 434.

83. Karl Joël, "Eine Zeitphilosophie," *Neue Deutsche Rundschau* 8 (1901): 812.

84. Margarete Susman, *Die geistige Gestalt Georg Simmels* (Tübingen: J.C.B. Mohr, 1959), p. 2.

85. Simmel, "Tendencies of German Life and Thought Since 1870," *International Monthly* 2 (1902): 99.

86. Simmel, "Nietzsche und Kant" [1906], in *Aufsätze und Abhandlungen 1901–1908,* II: 22.

87. Letter to Graf Hermann Keyserling (1908) in Simmel, *Das individuelle Gesetz*, p. 239. On neo-Kantianism, see Thomas Wylie, *Back to Kant* (Detroit: Wayne State University Press, 1978.)

88. Simmel, "Kant und Nietzsche," in *Brücke und Tür*, p. 185. The combination of Kantian and Nietzschean philosophy served as the fulcrum of Simmel's critique of capitalism and noumenal defense of aesthetic *Lebensphilosophie*. His most sustained description of his philosophy as a third way is found in his *Nachlaß*. Georg Simmel, "Aus dem nachgelassenen Tagebuche," in *Fragmente und Aufsätze*, pp. 1–47. In the last chapter, it will be argued that the war was the social source for the predominance of this very Hegelian language. Compare Hegel's section on conscience and the beautiful soul in *The Phenomenology of Spirit:* "The self of conscience, Spirit that is directly aware of itself as absolute truth and being, is the third self" (Oxford: Oxford University Press, 1977), p. 384.

89. See George Mosse, *Germans and Jews: the Right, the Left, and the Search for a Third Force in Pre-Nazi Germany* (New York: Schocken, 1970); Lewis D. Wurgaft, *The Activists: Kurt Hiller and the Politics of Action on the German Left 1914–1933* (Philadelphia: American Philosophical Society, 1977).

90. Horst Müller compares Simmel's recantation of religious metaphysics to a series of neo-Kantian philosophies of religion, which attempt to salvage religious metaphysics: Max Reischle, *Die Frage nach dem Wesen der Religion* (1889); Paul Natorp, *Religion innerhalb der Grenzen der Humanität* (1908); Hermann

Cohen, *Der Begriff der Religion im System der Philosophie* (1915); Georg Mehlis, *Einführung in ein System der Religionsphilosophie* (1917); Albert Görland, *Religionsphilosophie als Wissenschaft aus dem Systemgeiste des kritischen Idealismus* (1922). Müller, *Lebensphilosophie und Religion bei Georg Simmel* (Berlin: Duncker & Humboldt, 1960), pp. 10–13. Simmel was attacked by Ernst Troeltsch for having jettisoned religious eschatology and embracing relativism. On Troeltsch's critique of Simmel, see Liebersohn, *Fate and Utopia in German, 1870–1923*. (Cambridge, Mass.: MIT Press, 1988), pp.156–57.

91. See Hermann Lübbe, *Politische Philosophie in Deutschland* (Basel: Benno Schwabe, 1963), pp. 111–12.

92. Lübbe, pp. 108–109.

93. Simmel, *Schopenhauer und Nietzsche*, pp. 269.

94. Simmel, review of Ferdinand Tönnies, *Der Nietzsche-Kultus: Ein Kritik* in *Deutsche Litteratur-Zeitung*, 47 (1897): 1645–51.

95. Ferdinand Tönnies, *Der Nietzsche-Kultus: Ein Kritik,* ed. Günther Rudolph (Berlin: Akademie-Verlag, 1990), p. 27.

96. Tönnies, pp. 80, 88.

97. Simmel, review of Tönnies, p. 1647.

98. For a different interpretation of Simmel's defense of Nietzsche, see Günther Rudolph's "Friedrich Nietzsche und Ferdinand Tönnies: Der 'Wille zur Macht' widerlegt von der Positionen eines 'Willen zur Gemeinschaft'" in Tönnies, *Der Nietzsche-Kultus*, pp. 136–37. Rudolph's essay places the Simmel-Tönnies debate within a larger textual context of Nietzsche books published in 1890s Wilhelmine Germany.

99. Simmel, "Nietzsche und Kant," in *Brücke und Tür*, pp. 184–85.

100. On Simmel and Tönnies, see several fine essays in *Simmel und die frühen Soziologen: Nähe und Distanz zu Durkheim, Tönnies und Max Weber*, ed. Ottheim Rammstedt (Frankfurt a.M.: Suhrkamp, 1988); Klaus Lichtblau, *Kulturkrise und Soziologie um die Jahrhundertwende*; Heinz-Jürgen Dahme and Ottheim Rammstedt, "Die zeitlose Modernität der soziologischen Klassiker. Überlegungen zur Theoriekonstruktion von Emile Durkheim, Ferdinand Tönnies, Max Weber und besonders Georg Simmel," in *Georg Simmel und die Moderne*, pp. 449–78.

101. Dilthey, "Die Kultur der Gegenwart und die Philosophie," in *Philosophie des Lebens*, pp. 32, 34.

102. For a more favorable, if still critical, account of Simmel, see Ferdinand Tönnies, "Simmel as Sociologist " in *Georg Simmel*, ed. Lewis A. Coser, pp. 50–52.

103. Simmel, review of Tönnies, pp. 1645–51.

104. The "individual law" followed Kant in treating ethics as conditionless, namely, in denying the material or social-historical origin of ethical considerations. Additionally, the "individual law" derived from the soul and not the intellect, as does Kant's categorical imperative. While the categorical imperative proposed a general social ethics, Simmel affirmed only an individuated social ethics. According to Simmel, the concept of a categorical imperative was contentless and demanded an individual content. This was a nominalist critique of Kantian ethics. Individuated content undermined any possibility of a general imperative. See Georg Simmel, *Einleitung in die Moralwissenschaft*, vol. 2, especially chapter 5, "Der kategorische Imperativ."

105. Simmel to Heinrich Rickert, 15 April 1917, in *Buch des Dankes*, p. 119.

106. Klaus Peter Biesenbach, *Subjektivität ohne Substanz: Georg Simmels Individualitätsbegriff als produktive Wendung einer theoretischen Ernüchterung* (Frankfurt a.M.: Lang, 1988), p. 39.

107. Heinrich Rickert, *Die Philosophie des Lebens: Darstellung und Kritik der philosophischen Modeströmungen unserer Zeit* (Tübingen: Mohr, 1920).

108. Simmel, "Über den Unterschied der Wahrnehmungs und der Erfahrungsurteile. Ein Deutungsversuch [Kant]," in *Aufsätze und Abhandlungen 1894–1900*, pp. 416, 425.

109. Simmel, *Philosophie des Geldes*, p. 13.

110. Simmel, "Tendencies," p. 183.

111. Ibid., p. 181.

112. Ibid., pp. 183, 181.

113. Karl Marx, *Das Kapital*, vol. 1 (Berlin: Dietz, 1974), p. 116; *Philosophie des Geldes*, p. 645.

114. Simmel, "Das Geld in der modernen Cultur," p. 193.

115. Simmel, "Anfang einer unvollendeten Selbstdarstellung," in *Buch des Dankes*, p. 9.

116. The best text on the critical theory of the Frankfurt School is Martin Jay's *The Dialectical Imagination: A History of the Frankfurt School and the Institute for Social Research, 1923–1950* (Boston: Little, Brown and Company, 1973). Compare especially the sections on Max Weber and his theoretical impact on the Frankfurt School to my interpretation of Simmel's effect on Bloch and Lukács. At the beginning of chapter 2, "The Genesis of Critic Theory," Jay writes: "At the heart of Critical Theory was an aversion to closed philosophical systems" (41). This study argues that Simmel was the greatest critic of closed philosophical systems in Wilhelmine society.

117. Köhnke, *Entstehung und Aufstieg des Neukantianismus*, p. 406.

118. Ernst Cassirer, *The Philosophy of Symbolic Forms: Language*, trans. Ralph Mannheim (New Haven: Yale University Press, 1955), p. 73.

119. Simmel, *Philosophie des Geldes* (Frankfurt a.M.: Suhrkamp, 1989), p. 9.

120. Ibid., p. 11.

121. Simmel, *Buch des Dankes*, p. 101. For his critique of historicism, see *Geschichtsphilosophie* (1905), pp. 40–51.

122. Simmel, *Philosophie des Geldes*, p. 624; *Buch des Dankes*, p. 97.

123. Simmel, *Philosophie des Geldes*, p. 10.

124. Simmel, "Das Geld in der modern Culture" (1896), p. 178.

125. Simmel, "Die Bedeutung des Geldes für das Tempo des Lebens" (1897), in *Aufsätze und Abhandlungen 1894–1900*, p. 224.

126. Simmel, *Philosophie des Geldes*, pp. 673–74. This section was added to the second edition of the text.

127. Ibid., p. 513.

128. Ibid., p. 9.

129. Simmel, "Tendenzen im Deutschen Leben und Denken seit 1870," in *Schopenhauer und Nietzsche* (Hamburg: Junius, 1990), p. 9.

130. Paul Hensel, "Eine Philosophie des Geldes," *Der Lotse* 48 (1901): 722–29.

131. Simmel, *Philosophie des Geldes*, p. 654.

132. Ibid., pp. 513, 514, 519.

133. Frisby has read Simmel's analogic approach to the phenomenology of money culture as an example of an Impressionistic sociology. This reading neglects the rigorous theoretical basis of his methodology. I prefer to refer to his analogic methodology as a critical symbolism. It is drawn from Kant's "Analogies of Experience," in *Critique of Pure Reason*, trans. Norman Kemp Smith (New York: St. Martin's Press, 1929), pp. 208–33.

134. Simmel, *Philosophie des Geldes*, p. 170.

135. Ibid., pp. 138, 409.

136. Simmel, *Fragmente und Aufsätze*, p. 44; *Philosophie des Geldes*, p. 411.

137. Simmel, *Fragmente und Aufsätze*, p. 44.

138. Simmel, *Philosophie des Geldes*, p. 422.

139. Ibid., p. 410.

140. Ibid., p. 375.

141. Ibid., p. 377.

142. Ibid., p. 388.

143. Ibid., p. 386.

144. See especially chapter 4, Section II, "Das individuelle Freiheit," *Philosophie des Geldes*. The theme of this section is possession as activity.

145. Simmel, *Philosophie des Geldes*, p. 170.

146. Ibid., p. 169.

147. Ibid., p. 162.

148. Ibid., p. 410.

149. Ibid., pp. 591, 593.

150. Ibid., p. 595.

151. Ibid., p. 596.

152. The following words and phrases are taken from chapter 6 of *Philosophie des Geldes:* "die Vergegenständlichung des Geistes," "Objektivierung," "Entpersonalisierung," "Der Objectivierungsprozeß der Kulturinhalte," "Sachgehalt des Lebens [wird] immer sachlicher und unpersönlicher," "Gleichgültigkeit" and "Indifferenz," "Fremdheit" and "Distanzierung."

153. Marx, *Das Kapital*, pp. 86, 107–108.

154. Simmel, *Philosophie des Geldes*, p. 645

155. Ibid., p. 404.

156. In the "Preface," "Introduction," and "Afterward" of the recent translation of *The Philosophy of Money*, Frisby further discusses the reception history of Simmel's text.

157. See, for instance, Conrad Schmidt, "Eine Philosophie des Geldes," *Sozialistische Monatshefte* 5 (1901): 180–85; "Diese Philosophie des Geldes [hält] es gar nicht einmal für nötig, die verschiedenen Functionen des Geldes, vor allem seine Kapitalfunction zu entwickeln resp. die von den Oekonomen, am besten von Marx hierüber gegebene Entwicklung klar zu recapitulieren, um auf diese Weise ein Bild der der modernen Geldwirtschaft zu Grunde liegenden, sich in ihr und durch sie erhaltenden Klassenverhältnisse zu gewinnen" (181).

158. Dr. Max Adler, *Georg Simmels Bedeutung für Geistesgeschichte* (Wien: Anzengruber, 1919), pp. 12–13.

159. Karl Joël, "Eine Zeitphilosophie," p. 812.

160. Theodor W. Adorno, *Negative Dialektik* (Frankfurt a.M.: Suhrkamp, 1975), p.156.

161. Cited in Donald Levine, "Introduction," p. xliv.

162. In *Buch des Dankes*, p. 32.

163. Donald Levine, "Introduction," p. ix.

164. Simmel, "Exkurs über die Negativität kollektiver Verhaltungsweisen," in *Soziologie*, pp. 533–38.

165. Simmel, *Soziologie,* p. 551.

166. This theme is explored in Barbara Aulinger, *Die Gesellschaft als Kunstwerk: Fiktion und Methode bei Georg Simmel* (Vienna: Passagen Verlag, 1999).

167. Wassily Kandinsky, *Concerning the Spiritual in Art*, trans. M. T. H. Sadler (New York: Dover, 1977).

168. Tönnies, "Simmel as Sociologist," p. 50.

169. Simmel, *Soziologie*, p. 161.

170. Ibid., pp. 161–62.

171. Eugene Genovese, *Roll, Jordan, Roll: The World the Slaves Made* (New York: Vintage, 1976).

172. Michel Foucault, *The History of Sexuality*, vol. 1, trans. Robert Hurley (New York: Vintage, 1980).

173. Simmel, *Soziologie*, pp. 233–39.

174. Ibid., p. 180.

175. Ibid., p. 246.

176. Simmel, *Schopenhauer and Nietzsche*, p. 21 (my emphasis). See also Simmel's *Soziologie*, p. 286: "Als die höchste Auffassung indeß, die diesen Gegensatzpaaren gegenüber angezeigt ist, erscheint mir die andere: alle diese polaren Differenziertheiten als ein Leben zu greifen."

177. Simmel, *Soziologie*, pp. 231–32.

178. Ibid., p. 161.

179. Ibid., p. 260.

180. Ibid., p. 262.

181. Ibid., p. 264.

182. Simmel, *Kant und Goethe* (Leipzig: Kurt Wolff 1916), p. 5. See *Schopenhauer und Nietzsche*, chapter 2, on the will as a foundation for reuniting the fragmentary divisions of human beings.

183. Simmel, *Grundfragen der Soziologie*, p. 71; *Soziologie*, p. 52.

184. Simmel, *Soziologie*, p. 56.

185. Ibid., p. 234.

186. Simmel, *Philosophie des Geldes*, p. 692.

3

AN AVANT-GARDE SOCIOLOGY OF WOMEN

Simmel, Marie Luise Enckendorff, and Marianne Weber

> *The culture of humanity, even its pure objective contents, is not so-to-speak genderless; cultural objectivity is not a domain beyond men and women. In fact, with few exceptions,* our objective culture is thoroughly male. . . . *The belief in a pure human culture, beyond male and female, derives from the following presupposition: the naive identification of human and man that in so many languages has led to the use of the same word for human and male.*
>
> Georg Simmel, 1902[1]

When Georg Simmel began formulating his dynamic sociology of modernity in the early 1890s, he placed gender relations and the social position of women at the epicenter. This was unusual but not unique. Herbert Spencer and Ferdinand Tönnies also integrated an analysis of gender relations into their sociologies of modernity.[2] What set Simmel apart from the other intellectual giants of early sociology was partisanship. He not only theorized the gender of modernity but set out to put the values of the sexual avant-garde into practice. The avant-garde worshiped nothing as much as originality. In this spirit, his sociology of women sought to do more than simply provide an analysis of the half-baked crockery of modern gender relations; his critical kiln fired a new ultramodern institutional terra cotta. Simmel and his wife, who wrote under the pseudonym Marie Luise Enckendorff, occupied an important place within the feminist counterculture, and their political embrace of sensual culture distinguished them from liberal intellectuals like Max and Marianne Weber. Our exposition of Simmel's avant-garde partisanship bears in mind the biographical and historical account of his formative ideas. There was an inextricable and reciprocal connection between his academic work, personal politics, and the avant-garde milieu of fin-de-siècle Berlin. Ultimately, these multiform factors are treated here as moments of the same countercultural pattern of life. His practical interest in feminism was one instance of his overall avant-garde project to liberate the individual from traditional forms of life. In order to maximize ethical free will, Simmel felt himself summoned to criticize slavish deference to petrified conventions. We will examine his feminist sociology, then, while recalling the underlying tenant of his social theory: to Simmel, the denaturalization of social conventions is the propaedeutic of humanity's ethical vocation.

Before launching into a detailed analysis of Simmel's equation of modernity and male culture, I want to adumbrate the specific triangulation of his academic work, personal life, and cultural milieu. First, Simmel's feminism was emblematic of the overlap of academic/objective themes and personal/subjective concerns. His wife and life partner was a leading feminist philosopher. Hence, Simmel's feminist research was the objective correlate of his primary relationship of love. Second, Simmel's feminist social theory was an introspective examination of the ethics of male social psychology, an examination grounded in interpersonal realities but also in a neo-Kantian philosophical milieu. His personal compulsion toward introspection and scholarly style of social psychology drew sustenance from the Kantian directive to undertake an examination of the mental forms that structure experience. The essential novelty of Simmel's philosophical sociology (which he referred to as a "social-psychological" method in his earliest essay on women) lies in his demand that we make conscious the male mental and cultural forms through which we evaluate and know women.[3] If, on the one hand, his introspective approach does not transcend the horizon of current neo-Kantian philosophy, on the other hand, Simmel's feminist approach to social psychology was exceptional among his contemporaries. And this originality reflects his unusual existential dictum that academic thought must be lived if it hopes to acquire significance for life. Third, Simmel's feminist partisanship reflected the gender crisis articulated dramatically in European Naturalism. Even before a formal feminist movement emerged in Germany, Naturalist drama was exploring themes such as female personalities smitten by an unjust patriarchal fate. Simmel's close connection to the Naturalist avant-garde and later to the homosexual lyricist Stefan George, then, set the cultural stage for a sociological denunciation of patriarchal culture. But his sociology of modernity did more than pass judgement on patriarchy. The radical rejection of the male-dominated world—a world which included bourgeois marital conventions and the division of labor underlying consumer capitalism—helped him imagine a new and original vision of cultural revolution: feminine culture. Just as modernist artists actively attacked the institutions of art, such as the autonomous status of bourgeois art which implied a separation of artist and social life, Simmel practiced an avant-garde sociology that sought to remove itself from the webs of its own institutionalization. Philosophical sociology comprehended society by illuminating the practical means for its sublation.[4]

Fourth, perhaps nowhere in the world was the connection between feminist and socialist politics closer than fin-de-siècle Germany. August Bebel, who helped to found the Social Democratic Worker's Party in 1869, was Germany's leading Marxist intellectual into the 1890s. He published *Woman and Socialism* in 1879. Through their leader, then, the socialists had established themselves as the only German political party calling for women's political and economic emancipation. Simmel's pedagogical and theoretical interests in socialism reproduced the currency of sexual politics within German socialism. In essence, Naturalism and socialism were modern cultural fields from which Simmel, the intellectual horticulturalist, wrested social themes transplanting them into a freshly tilled academic garden. Fifth, Simmel's interest in feminism was simply one manifestation of his sociological concern with superordination as a formal element of human societies. And, as we mentioned in the last chapter, this sociology of hierarchy was not merely an analytical curiosity. It was a partisan and personal examination of the ethics and rationality of an inegalitarian modernity in general and patriarchy in particular.

At its best, Simmel's sociology investigated women's social roles as a manifestation of habituated traditions and social construction. If Simmel had dedicated himself exclusively to such examinations of the social construction of sexual roles and identities, he could be dressed in the fashion of contemporary gender theory. This sartorial style, no doubt, would appeal to him, but it would have to be altered to fit his actual feminist framework. For Simmel's feminist theory was a product of its era. Like most early feminists, he theorized through essentialist identities. Thus, his notion of female particularity and ontological otherness was not unique. It was symptomatic of the self-definition of the middle-class German women's movement. We now refer to this type of feminism as cultural feminism, and we have come to contrast the political and theoretical assumptions of cultural feminists to those of gender theory. The inner tension between these two theoretical poles boils down to this: cultural feminists embrace essentialist identities while gender theorists reject them. Most gender theorists presume that sexual roles are socially constructed rather than innate. There are corresponding political differences. Cultural feminists empower women through what gender theorists identify as patriarchal identities, while gender theorists deny any fixed or natural expression of womanhood.

Ultimately, Simmel's feminist sociology could fit into either rubric. His theoretical assumptions were a hybrid containing elements of cultural feminism and gender theory. Consequently, his legacy is ambiguous. To his credit, he did more than nearly any academic theorist of the era to legitimize the strident subjectivities that energized early feminist politics. However, from the perspective of gender theory, the idealized and naturalized visions of women that underwrote his feminist sociology are a problematic political cipher through which to pursue social transformation. The presumption of a static female nature, regardless of the positive attributes ascribed to women, is a formal erasure of the ethical diversity and social complexities within female experience. This static conception may explain Simmel's relative silence about proletarian women and the gendered nature of consumerism and the department store, for example. Furthermore, we are now fully cognizant of the political danger of mobilizing essentialist identities for the purpose of empowerment. Images of mothering and nurturing women may serve as a social critique of the dispassionate self-interest and rational instrumentalism of modernity. Naturalized conceptions of women's ethical superiority may also be used as a wedge to open cultural and political space for women in the public sphere. Yet, these images are just as likely to affirm patriarchy and conservative regimes of power. Indeed, a number of historians have shown how motherhood ideology and ideas of female compassion were mobilized in the development of Nazism.[5] In sum, Simmel's strategy of female empowerment intersected with the symbolic politics of the middle-class German women's movement and was replete with its political ambiguities. In subjecting this ambiguity to critical questioning, I will use the concept of conservative empowerment. This refers to cultural resistance that challenges patriarchy immanently without attacking its essentialist identities.[6]

THE FEMALE PRINCIPLE: SIMMEL AS SEXUAL AVANT-GARDIST

Simmel's writings on women, feminist politics, and the philosophy of love span nearly three decades, from 1890 until his death in 1918. Much of his work on women was grounded in a sociological analysis of sexual differentiation which was an analytical focus of his first essay on women, "Towards a Psychology of Women" (1890). This investigation was itself an intellectual remainder or expansion of his first major work, *Concerning Social Differentiation: Sociological and Psychological Examinations* (1890). But there was nothing inevitable about Simmel's application of differential philosophy to the sociology of the sexes. This application was conditioned by personal and cultural forces. The personal event that coincided with the publication of his first essay on women was nothing less than his marriage in 1890 to Gertrud Kinel, who under the psuedonym Marie Luise Enckendorff, later became a leading feminist philosopher of the era. She and

Sabine Graef had been living and painting together in Paris prior to Simmel's proposal of marriage. Gertrud's intelligence and independent spirit no doubt contributed to her attractiveness to Georg, who in his work seems to favor strong, self-reliant, and cosmopolitan women. We can hypothesize that the prospect of marriage to a self-willed woman produced emotional stirrings that crystalized into his first treatise on interpersonal ethics. Naturalist drama also contributed critical energy. In "Toward a Psychology of Women," he admitted that his thoughts were spurred on by dramatic investigations of marriage like those of *Madame Bovary*, *Hedda Gabler*, and *Effi Briest*.

> The meaning of differentiation for the relations of the sexes is sociologically important in the following respect. For many years in dramas of purpose [*Tendenzdrama*], it has been asserted that marriages which do not derive purely from mutual love would be immoral and could never lead to the well-being of the species. Concerning this controversial contention, one could object that in earlier times and in the lower classes marriages of love almost never took place and, nonetheless, the species has not been damaged. But both assertions are qualified by the knowledge that humanity is becoming more individualized. Within a relatively homogeneous mass of humanity, it was a matter of relative indifference which pairs came together. Under these circumstances, the more distinct individuals were, the more limited were choices that would guarantee perfect offspring. And as it stands, we have no criteria upon which to base this decisive choice except the often insufficient and purely instinctual basis of mutual attraction. Other criteria are merely negative, e.g., on the one hand, hereditary sickness, and on the other hand, sufficient material conditions.[7]

Most interesting here is (1) the way in which Simmel's sociology of marriage is unable to transcend his Naturalist horizon, and (2) his presumption that the hegemonic ideal of love arose with growing individuation. Naturalist drama was suffused with a new domain of the mind: Darwinian science and its relevance to human heredity; and in Naturalist drama, Darwinian science cohabitated with feminist treatments of social probity. A hybrid proposition arose: love is a crucial factor in eugenics. This proposition was not only present in Simmel's earliest essay on women, it became a prominent idea within the women's movement as well. It is a common error to assume that because eugenics presumed immutable human traits that it was exclusively conservative. Eugenics and social Darwinism did reinforce the aggressive politics of ethnocentrism and inequality. In the New Imperialist era, 1880–1900, social Darwinian thought added scientific truth-claims to existing justifications for colonialism, namely, god, gold, and national glory. The Berlin Conference of 1885 brought together European nations to discuss the partition of Africa, yet no Africans were present. Social Darwinian assumptions surely were. More often, however, eugenic thought was politically ambiguous. In Naturalism, it coexisted with progressive energies. Helene Stöcker, the leading radical feminist of the era, mobilized eugenic thinking to oppose the Great War. Margaret Sanger fought for sex education and birth control with the eugenic proposition that the progress of species would be advanced thereby. Similarly, Simmel's early feminism, while progressive, was influenced by social Darwinism. For instance, he speculated that the inclination toward childless marriages among the "highest cultures" may negatively impact the propagation of the species.[8]

Also of interest in the quote above is Simmel's contention that the ideal of love is a product of growing individualization within monetary culture. Much of Simmel's early sociology was influenced by the evolutionary sociology of Herbert Spencer who equated social differentiation within industrial society with social progress. Simmel applied this presupposition to an analysis of love.[9] The loving marriage was a refinement of differentiated, and hence liberated, mutual attraction: "When it appears that a pair of individuals is suitable to one another, because they love one another, at the root of this principle relationship will be the reality that they love one another because they are suitable to one another."[10] Modern love was an expression of instincts liberated by increasing differentiation within monetary culture.

Simmelian feminism rested upon two propositions: (1) sexual hierarchy, far from an objective or eternal reality, was an ineluctable consequence of socialization, and (2) female nature was static and unchanging. These propositions are clearly in tension. As we shall see, however, they were not contradictory. Simmel's most widely read essay on women was "Female Culture."[11] The essay is particularly important because it reveals Simmel's methodological ambiguities. In the 1911 version, Simmel added the following consideration: "For now, I offer no opinion on the subject of whether the masculine character of our material culture arises from the inner essence of the sexes or the physical superiority of men, a matter unrelated to the cultural question."[12] What is to be made of Simmel's severance of the question of essentialism from a critical analysis of culture? Analytically speaking, is it possible to separate these two realms? Don't naturalized conceptions of men and women underwrite the degradation of female culture? If we acknowledge the role of ontological conceptions of gender as a buttress of patriarchal society, then it would seem politically prudent to reject essentialist conceptions rather than deny their relevance. One methodological presupposition available to Simmel was the following: simply affirm that sexual identities are socially constructed rather than innate. As a social ideology, this proposition does not fix female identity and, therefore, facilitates the heterogeneous aspirations of women. No stigma would be attached to nontraditional activities and occupations.

Simmel and German feminists felt no need to take this decisive step. As a matter of fact, their strategy for cultural empowerment was the exact opposite. They totally embraced and celebrated traditional female identities. In contrast to socialist feminist visions of equality, Simmel reasoned that sociology should seek a clearer and more radical differentiation of male and female modes of being.

> The more radically the male and female essence are made to appear divergent, the less the denigration of women, which ordinarily derives from this division, follows from it. Thereby, the female world arises more autonomously on its own foundation, a foundation that is not borrowed from men nor shared with the male world.[13]

Gender differentiation is politically ambiguous, because it can fortify patriarchal disparagement. In Simmel's hands however, the amplification and clarification of gender differences presaged a new feminine chapter of history. Parenthetically, Simmel's ascription of metaphysical and liberatory significance to the feminine prefigures the *ecriture féminine* typical of French feminism in the 1980s. In the work of Hélène Cixous and others, femininity is interpreted positively as the utopian basis of spontaneous creativity in a noninstrumental and nonsexist society.[14] And like Simmel before them, here feminine culture is invoked to disrupt, subvert, and politicize patriarchal power structures. According to Simmel, the problems of the sexes do not originate from essentialized identities per se but the occlusion of authentic and autonomous femininity by male cultural categories. Simmel, for instance, located the degradation of women in the common designation of numerous social deficiencies as "feminine," while outstanding achievements of women are celebrated as "male." This symbolic "complex" of valuation, Simmel maintained, "constitutes the cultural capital of the era."[15] Similar to private property itself, this cultural capital was controlled by men. The recognition of sexual identities as a symbolic discourse of cultural hierarchy and as a code of cultural capital is something we now take for granted. It was exceptional at the time.

Politically speaking, Simmel sought the cultural elevation of woman as ontological otherness, but in order to achieve this, the reigning patriarchal hierarchy of valuation had to be exposed as a historical custom. Accordingly, he historicized and relativized the inegalitarian valuation of men and women (with the intention of raising the cultural status of female culture) while paradoxically retaining a belief in the ahistoricity of gendered identities themselves. This approach achieved its highest expression in "The Relative and the Absolute in the Problem of the Sexes" (1911). Here, presuppositions about the "transhistorical basis" of masculinity and femininity coexist with savage criticisms of current cultural calibrations.[16] The scales of respect were weighted prejudicially in favor of male culture.

> The fundamental relativity in the life of our species rests in the relationship between masculinity and femininity. And, this relationship exhibits the typical process whereby one of a pair of relative elements becomes absolute. We measure achievements and commitments . . . by reference to certain norms. But these norms are not neutral and detached from the opposition between the sexes. On the contrary, . . . their actual historical formation is thoroughly male. If we call those ideas which appear as absolute "the objective simplifier," then the following holds in the historical life of our species: the objective = male.

And Simmel was explicit about the sociological meaning of the male objective simplifier:

> The male sex is not merely superior in relation to the female but acquires the status of *generally human;* this objectivity normalizes the *appearances* of individual males and individual females in the same way. In various cultural transmissions, this is conveyed by the *power-position* of men. If we crudely express this relationship of the sexes as one of master and slave, then it is one of the privileges of the master that he never need think about the nature of that relationship. On the other hand, the position of the slave ensures that inferior status is not forgotten. It is not to be doubted that women lose consciousness of their female-being [*Frau-Sein*] much less often than men lose consciousness of their male-being [*Mann-Sein*].[17]

The emphasis on the appearances (*Erscheinungen*) of femininity and masculinity contains a philosophical subtlety. The concept of appearance is intended to ward off the false notion that patriarchal categories account for the actual value of feminine and masculine aspects of culture. They do not. They are nothing more than dominant subjective cultural norms—"transhistorical and transpsychological abstractions"—masquerading as timeless values.[18]

> From time immemorial, every domination that rests on a subjective all-powerfulness has made it its business to provide itself an objective foundation. That means: to transform might into right. The history of politics, the history of the priesthood, the history of economic systems, and the history of family law are full of examples of this. In so far as the will of the *pater familias* is imposed in the house and appears as "authority," then the husband is no longer an arbitrary exploiter of power but the bearer of an objective law that dictates the transpersonal and general interests of the family. In conformity with this analogy and often within this setting, there develops a psychological superiority, which creates the relationship of domination between men and women by naturalizing male expressions. Thereby, psychological superiority is transformed, so to speak, into a logical superiority.[19]

These conclusions, savaging the historical degradation of women and arbitrary power of men, were never merely analytical or coldly academic. They transcended the academic arena and sought to be the basis for a radical transvaluation of patriarchal culture. In this regard, Simmel's work should be seen as a sociological expression of the avant-garde's "culture of negation."[20] His sociological analyses were intertwined with a civic intention to elevate the status of women by negating long-standing traditions and codes of evaluation.

Before evaluating Simmel's unique conception of female culture, I want to pause and reflect upon the strategy of critique embodied in the quotes above. Elsewhere, this style of critical thinking was labeled philosophical sociology. This style seeks synthetic judgements about the relationship of absolutized values to domination, and in "The Relative and the Absolute in the Problem of the Sexes," this synthetic style was applied to the woman question. The result was a brilliant elaboration of the link between absolute truth-claims and oppressive institutions. This type of elaboration was a hallmark of Simmel's sociology of superordination. In this case, his conclusions were quite radical. For, although he conservatively retained the belief in immutable sexual characteristics, the conclusions drawn from this conservative presupposition were far afield from main stream conceptions of women's proper status. It was Simmel's judgement that the existence of absolute sexual differences did not justify corresponding differences in status and power. This reasoning was inherently at odds with the Christian and social Darwinian sexual politics of the era. These forces transposed biological difference into male superiority, and this transposition immediately included a pledge of allegiance to the male "objective simplifier" and corresponding realms of male dominion: politics, religion, economy, and family. With the clinical precision of a German philosopher, Simmel dispatched the traditional logic behind women's domination as nothing more than rank arbitrary authoritarianism buttressed by sophistry and intellectual alchemy. His was able not only to diagnose the philosophical bases of domination but to link them to existing institutional examinations of the patriarchal affliction. The clarity and sophistication of his analytical synthesis were unsurpassed in the feminist thought of the era.

Up to this point, Simmel's analyses may seem familiar to scholars schooled in cultural feminism and gender theory. Similar to cultural feminists, he prepossessed an ontological conception of gender, and similar to gender theorists he sought a synthetic understanding of the relationship of objectified social norms and hierarchical institutions. However, Simmel's philosophy of the feminine principle parts company from both of these contemporary reference points. For both cultural feminists and gender theorists, the male/female binary is the fountain of thought. Women are analyzed or defined in relation to men. Simmel insisted that this would not do. He sought to determine the "autonomous female principle . . . rooted in the undifferentiated ground of nature."[21] Rejecting generalized notions of equality, Simmel maintained that femininity was a unique mode of life whose identity requires no reference to men. "The significance of sexual difference is only a secondary fact for women. In her femininity, she reposes as if in an absolute substance of being—somewhat paradoxically expressed—indifferent to the existence of men. . . . The absoluteness of her immanently determined sexuality . . . requires no relation to the other sex."[22] Femininity is a thoroughly differentiated and individualized form of life (*Lebensform*). Correlatively, the brutalization of women and the denigration of the female principle are consequences of judging them as an antithetical being, namely, as the antithesis of men. This is femininity in the traditional sense, wrote Simmel. It is a type of femininity that arrogates to male culture the category of the absolute. Conversely, Simmel demanded that femininity be judged and conceived as a self-sufficient mode of being.

Simmel's philosophy of autonomous femininity was the most avant-garde expression of cultural feminism in the annuls of European feminism. He was quite self-conscious of the radical implications of his feminist philosophy. Not only was his conception of female culture an overt renunciation of traditional binary conceptions of femininity and absolutized claims of male norms; it was also explicated consciously as a critique of the primary goals of the middle-class German women's movement. As Simmel put it,

> Insofar as the modern women's movement proposed that women merge into the male life-forms and male forms of achievement, for them the issue is acquisition of a personal share of already existing cultural goods to which they traditionally have been denied access. They want this regardless of whether it is a source of new happiness, new responsibilities, or new forms of personal development. Their struggle is always exclusively for individual persons, regardless of how many millions of people it concerns in the present and future. It is not a struggle for a goal that transcends everything individual and personal. The primary focus of the modern women's movement is how often individual women can realize existing values, not the creation of objectively new values.[23]

While the women's movement sought access to existing male institutions, Simmel championed a radical recentering of modernity on a qualitatively new metaphysical basis. He referred to this transcendent basis as female objective culture and was explicit about the incommensurability of female culture and traditional male values and institutions. The realization of female culture would subvert patriarchal society requiring new forms of responsibility and new conceptions of personal development. An authentic women's movement would eschew the entrenched individualism and conservatism of the middle-class women's movement and adopt an avant-garde activity intent on systemic transformations.

Simmel shared with the mainline feminist organization of the period, *Bund Deutsche Frauenvereine* (Confederation of German Women's Associations, or BDF), a similar rhetorical strategy. For both the Confederation and Simmel, motherhood exemplified an ideal of redemptive alterity. Motherhood ideology underwrote German feminism from the late nineteenth century well into the twentieth century.[24] Most often feminists positioned feminine affection and motherly nurturing as outside the decadence of modernity. The intimate and compassionate domestic sphere was contrasted to the public world governed by the impersonality of the cash nexus and bureaucratic state. It is important to keep in mind that neither the domestic sphere nor the institution of motherhood were autonomous enclaves untouched by modernity. In fact, German feminists themselves often drew resources from illiberal municipal governments and pursued overtly class-based political programs.[25] Motherhood ideology was powerfully mobilized by conservative political movements such as Nazism and much later Reaganism in the United States. Just as Simmel's affirmative response to the Great War demonstrated the possible inscription of his avant-garde thought into conservative politics, so, too, must we insist on the political indeterminancy of his feminist politics. Motherhood ideology was the vanguard conception of German feminism; it was and is also the pervading system of belief in reactionary political movements. As was mentioned earlier, I have developed the idea of conservative empowerment to explain this overlap. Cultural feminists conserve naturalized conceptions of gender in pursuit of social change. Their immanent strategy of empowerment (as opposed to political strategies born of conceptions exogenous to patriarchy, i.e., equality or deontology) is both a strength and a weakness. The practical strength of cultural feminism is its refusal to concede traditional cultural territories occupied by conservatives. The radical differences of men and women are reconfigured to raise the social status of traditional female roles like motherhood. Clearly this strategy has limitations. Victories by cultural feminists are pyrrhic to the extent that they are left defending the architecture of patriarchy, even while they presume to furnish it with a new value-content. The residual conservatism of the maternalist ideology is evidenced by the political program and affiliations of some BDF members: one mainstream leader, Anna von Gierke, later sought and won election to the *Reichtag* as a member of the right-wing Deutschnationale Volkpartei (German National People's Party, DVP); another BDF member, Hedwig Heyl, assumed leadership of the imperialistic Women's Division of the German Colonial Society in 1910. Generally the BDF and its member organizations opposed universal suffrage and instead pursued a class-based property franchise that would guarantee themselves the right to vote.[26]

Without denying the conservative potential of separate spheres ideology or Simmel's place in this tradition, we must be careful not to overstate similarities and thereby elide diverging conceptions of cultural feminism. For instance, some cultural feminists in Germany supported the universal franchise, homosexual rights, and women's right to unwed motherhood; most did not. For our purposes, it is the ideology of motherhood which must be differentiated. Our thesis is that Simmel's variant of this ideology was the most radical rendition of the era. Similar to other feminists of the era, Simmel moored femininity in motherhood. But unlike most cultural feminists, Simmel wanted to do more than elevate women's status, provide them with a justification for public activities, and gain them access to existing institutions. Simmel sought nothing less than a complete revolution in culture. In present society, according to Simmel, male principles represented a universal value system, a "transsexual objectivity" transcending men and women and shaping all social institutions; Simmel called for the displacement of male transsexual objectivity in favor of a female universal.[27] Not only the male principle but also the female principle occupies a position independent of the male/female binary. Both are transcendent norms standing above sexual differentiation while remaining the source from which flows social valuations of the male and the female. In the same sense that the male principle is independent of sexual differences, so too the female principle "is more than feminine. Woman represents the general, substantial, genetic, and comprehensive foundation of the sexes, because she is the mother."[28] As though a phenomenologist of spirit, Simmel analytically described all previous history as the embodiment of the male principle. The realization of the female principle, embodied in motherhood, would be the end of history as we know it. It would brook no compromises with the previous mastery of history by the male principle. As in Hegel's dialectic of master and slave, the victory of the feminine principle would be a comprehensive cultural revolution altering all institutions and ideologies.

A NEW FEMININE CONTINENT OF CULTURE

To will oneself free is also to will others free.

Simone de Beauvoir[29]

Simmel, the sexual avant-gardist, advocated nothing less than an objectively female future. Through the "objectification of female culture, . . . a new continent of culture would be discovered," and thereby the "male monopolization of objective culture" would be resisted.[30] His resistance to male objective culture was connected to his critique of middle-class feminism and its epigonal activism. The cultural visions of German feminists, he maintained, often did not exceed existing male forms. Therefore, the creative energies of German feminism could produce nothing more than a culture of "secondary originality."[31] "All feminist aspirations of this type ultimately proceed from the female desire to have and become and what men have and are," remarked Simmel in reference to the (middle-class) women's movement.[32] He confessed that he had no desire to disparage such aspirations. Assessment of their value, however, simply was not his concern. He wanted to furnish an cogent conception of future culture. He anticipated the progressive formation of female historicity and pondered the conditions facilitative and inimical to this development.

Simmel adumbrated aspects of an objective female culture, and this observation runs counter to much of the existing literature.[33] He anticipated the historical future that might arise from the negation of the "male a priori," and his essays on women often proselytized on behalf of a new political state of mind: the female a priori.[34]

> Women generally comprehend existence from the standpoint of an essential a priori and therefore differently from men, even though these two meanings are not subject to a simple alternative: true or false. Through the medium of their psychological interpretations, the historical world could exhibit alternative understandings of the relationship between the parts and the whole. . . . So I believe that there could be distinctly female functions in the field of history, achievements proceeding from the special perceptual, empathetic, and constructive organs of the female soul.[35]

Simmel maintained that the comprehending nature of female subjectivity, then, could radically alter our understanding of everything from popular movements to undisclosed personal motivations. He also hypothesized a distinctly female domain within medical praxis. Since the comprehension of illness often depends upon the world view of the comprehending subject, female physicians would be able to discover knowledge that is undetectable by men. Consequently, women may produce more accurate diagnoses and a more refined sense of the proper therapy.

The historical and medical professions were not the only spheres receptive to the original accomplishments of women. Simmel speculated about the creation of female culture within the domains of pure science and the arts, but often he did nothing more than recapitulate sexual stereotypes. He reasoned that the undifferentiated and unitary nature of women, for whom the distinction of subject and object does not exist, is best suited to the dramatic arts, because here the total personality is unified. And, not surprisingly, the home was for Simmel the supreme cultural achievement of women. He contended that male nature was more compatible with the contemporary division of factory labor because men are detached from their subjective life. Yet Simmel's other sociological analyses are far more original. The separation of the worker from control of the means of production is seen by Simmel as only one instance of the objectification of modern culture. That general trend is characterized by the movement of culture away from humanity and toward human enslavement to the production of objects. Simmel's understanding of the contrast between alienated factory labor and nonalienated household production was not unlike socialist William Morris's understanding of craft production as more diversified and less alienating.[36] But Simmel conceived of the titanic fight between alienated industrial and nonalienated craft production as a struggle between male and female culture. Thus, the fight for feminine culture was inherently a fight against capitalism. Householding conforms to the immanent completeness of women, namely, their unity of subjectivity and objectivity. As a comprehensive model for production, the female principle, if institutionalized, would subvert the alienation resulting from the division of labor in modern society and call forth more fulfilling modes of human creativity.

Perhaps we best can grasp Simmel's reasoning if we compare it to Tönnies's sociology of modernity. Tönnies also theorized the evolutionary transition from community (*Gemeinschaft*) to society (*Gesellschaft*) in gender terms. The village and especially the household were ideal types of community. Tönnies decried the emergence of modern society as a de-evolution from organic institutions to artificial relationships of civilization and the state. Consequently, he abhorred the introduction of women into the capitalist sphere of production. Their integration into the cold-hearted world of avarice and individualism destroyed the empathetic femininity of traditional communal culture. Like Simmel after him, then, Tönnies set out to comprehend and configure modernity in order to resist its dehumanizing tendencies. He suggested that "the possibility of overcoming this individualism and arriving at a reconstruction of community arises with the same process. The analogy of the fate of women and the fate of the proletariat has been recognized long ago. The growing awareness on the part of women and workers can . . . develop and rise to a moral and humane consciousness."[37] Simmel was captivated by the same problem, and he, too, envisioned female culture as not only a resolution to patriarchy but proletarian exploitation as well. Clearly, women can play no progressive role in a capitalist society whose developments reduce the significance of household productivity and require proletarian men and women to work in tragic occupations. Simmel's concept of objective femininity denoted an alternative cultural principle inimical to capitalist alienation and capable of reconciling the fragmented world created by the division of labor.

Simmel was theoretically circumspect about the prospects for change. In considering the conditions for the realization of female culture, he evaluated the egalitarian demands of socialism.

> For the ideal of an autonomous femininity, one could go so far as to propose that its complete opposite is the nearest condition for its realization: mechanical and excessive egalitarianism in the areas of education, rights, occupations, and behavior. One could mean thereby that since the position and achievements of women for so long have persisted in a relationship of excessive inequality with men—and as a result, the realization of a specific female objectivity has been obstructed—then it is first necessary to pass through a period of the opposite extreme, excessive equality. From this point of view, we must pass through a period of egalitarianism before a new cultural synthesis could arise: an objective culture enriched by the nuances of femininity, just as today there are extreme individualists who are socialists, because they believe that through the process of leveling, socialism will produce a new aristocracy and truly deserving elite, a rule of the best.[38]

Simmel's examinations of egalitarian demands are ambiguous. Clearly, he denigrates them as an excessive and mechanical leveling. And, generally, thorough-going conceptions of egalitarianism are in tension with his cultural feminist doctrine of ontological differences. However, similar to much of the avant-garde, Simmel was animated by the political ideal of an artist/philosopher elite. Therefore, he may have favored an egalitarian society ruled by a truly deserving spiritual aristocracy. We do not know. We do know that following the statement above he switched to the first person and admitted that he would not speculate about the conditions under which female culture might have its best chance of realization. Simmel's unrivaled gift of avant-garde vision coexisted with political stoicism. He exempted himself from consideration of political practices requisite to accomplishing his own feminist aspirations.

Ultimately, future realizations of female culture may be impossible given the heterogeneity of female nature, he speculated. The proposition of female heterogeneity obviously clashes with his overt and operative assumption of fixed female characteristics. As though a soothsayer of problems arising from contemporary deontological gender theory, he concluded that heterogeneity may contradict the idea of an objective female culture and, by extension, political sisterhood as well. Neither the practical deficiencies nor the theoretical circumspection of Simmel's theory of autonomous femininity support Klaus Lichtblau's conclusion that "in practical terms it could be realized only at the pride of an antimodern regression."[39] There is a heavy dose of romantic anticapitalism in Simmel's gender politics. Indeed, his ontological conception of feminine nature was akin to a prelapsarian boulder on the ground of modernity. But, his romantic interest in that boulder must not be dismissed as reactionary and regressive. It was the building material of an alternative future.[40] Furthermore, Simmel's critique of the absolutization of male culture and the male's inability to overcome alienation was inherently progressive. In one of his many essays on women, for example, Simmel speculated about the mental preconditions of heterosexual male attraction.[41] He drew a distinction between older men who were attracted to young girls and those men attracted to women roughly their own age. The former, he hypothesized, were attracted to women as stereotypes; the undifferentiated image of young women was an image of patriarchal control. Through it, men knew and—since knowledge is power—possessed, at least conceptually, all women. Conversely, older women had a history and an identity of their own, and consequently they were less easily subordinated. An attraction to independent older women often indicated a man of higher development who acknowledged women's cultural and spiritual diversity. Moreover, such an attraction indicated a male's capacity for love as mutual respect. Simmel made no attempt to verify his conclusions. And, yet, his ruminations on male domination possessed a truth-value which was thoroughly compelling.

From the vantage point of gender theory, it is far too easy to evaluate Simmel's political strategy of empowerment as merely conservative. Placed in his own historical context Simmel appears as nothing less than a feminist avant-gardist concerned with issues of freedom, power, and new ways of acting. He encouraged women to identify themselves as historical agents who were powerful enough to liberate humanity from the instrumental and alienating essence of modernity. However, the urgency of epochal transformation and the possibility of a radiant new dawn was not the exclusive concern of women. Implicit in Simmel's espousal of a radical modernity was the necessity of a mental revolution within men. The tyranny of tragic history would only be left behind if men accepted a new social metaphysics: the feminine principle. Femininity, moreover, was emblematic of his general disaffection from bourgeois modernity. The stridency and thoroughness of this disaffection was unique within the conservative causeways of German academia.

MARIE LUISE ENCKENDORFF, STEFAN GEORGE, AND THE ETHICS OF MARRIAGE

The spiritualization of sensuality is called love; it is a great triumph over Christianity.

Friedrich Nietzsche, *Twilight of the Idols*

Frau Simmel fought for the majority of women, not in the manner of the women's movement, but from a higher watchtower. She was a philosopher. She bestowed deep thoughts to us feminists in her book about the problem of the sexes. . . . I was astounded by the radicalness of this cultured woman.

Marianne Weber, *Lebenserinnerungen*[42]

Perhaps more than any others, Marie Luise Enckendorff and Stefan George symbolize Simmel's personal avant-garde constellation. Enckendorff, born Gertrud Kinel on March 7, 1864, in Potsdam, did not seem destined to be a writer, but rather a painter. In comparison to most young women of the era, her family background was auspicious. Her father, Adalbert Kinel, had a meteoric career rising from masonry apprentice to president of the Royal Prussian Academy of Architecture.[43] Adalbert had lost his parents at a young age and resolved to educate his three daughters so that they, too, could be professionally successful. Access to official academic institutions was unavailable to young women in Prussia until 1883. So the Kinels sought out the best possible private tutors, and eventually Gertrud was the beneficiary of new opportunities for women in the arts. In the mid–1880s, she studied landscape painting in Berlin with Professor Carl Scherres and portraiture with Karl Stauffer-Bern. By the late 1880s, she had placed several paintings in Berlin exhibitions. Among the gifted young women she met in Berlin was Sabine Graef, whose father was a highly regarded portrait painter and whose mother, Franziska, was also an accomplished painter. Gertrud regularly visited the Graef household. The atmosphere was upper-bourgeois, cosmopolitan, and semibohemian. This milieu also involved Gertrud in the complex of personalities comprising The Society of the Unbridled. Sabine and Gertrud were the only women participating in its sophisticated discussions about literature and high culture. This group included among others Harald Graef, Naturalists Otto Brahm and Paul Schlenther, and Georg Simmel.[44] The attraction and eventual marriage of Gertrud and Georg, then, was not purely accidental. They were both highly-educated members of the upper bourgeoisie with an abiding love of the arts.

When they married in 1890, Gertrud was twenty-six, independent, and a highly accomplished artist. Upon marriage, she conceived of herself as the "comrade of my husband."[45] Simmel married a woman who was the sworn enemy of the Victorian marriage. However, her independence and egalitarian conception of marriage quickly were undermined by several factors. First, only months before her marriage she was living in Paris with Sabine Graef; after the wedding, she moved in with Georg and his mother. Georg's mother, Flora, was jealous and tyrannical, and in this context, Gertrud experienced degradation and a loss of self-confidence.[46] We can imagine that Gertrud and Flora's conceptions of marriage were vastly different. Second, in the first few years of their marriage, Gertrud suffered many physical and psychological ailments. She was tormented by chronic back trouble and afflicted with deep bouts of depression. Unable to paint regularly, she lost the self-confidence and social identity that accompanied her successes in the art world. Third, their son Hans Simmel was born in April 1891, and thereafter the Simmel's struck a traditional compromise. Georg would be the bread winner and Gertrud the manager of the home sphere. This arrangement of responsibilities created the classic conflict, one Marianne Weber eloquently examined in her essay "Occupation and Marriage" (1905). However, the hopeful synthesis promised by Marianne contradicted Gertrud's difficult experiences. The tension between family responsibilities and artistic demands required "a resolution that will never come, never," Gertrud wrote to a friend in 1895.[47] She eventually gave up painting altogether.

As Hans grew older and especially after Flora Simmel died in September 1897, Gertrud Simmel transformed herself into a writer under the pseudonym Marie Luise Enckendorff. Once again she possessed an independent creative identity. She, like Simone de Beauvoir following the Second World War, was one of the great German feminist philosophers of the era. And, just as de Beauvoir's work was intercoupled with, although independent of, that of Jean-Paul Sartre, the full measure of Enckendorff's work requires understanding its affiliation with Simmel's philosophy of life. Enckendorff's intellectual universe was filled with the conceptual spheres and problematic gravities of *Lebensphilosophie*. The central axis of this neoexistentialist philosophy was the creative soul (*die Seele*), its need to realize itself as a new civic morality, and thereby create a new world. As with the Romantic thought of Friedrich Schleiermacher, whose philosophy was the touchstone of Dilthey's philosophy of history, Enckendorff invoked conceptions of an authentic soul alongside explorations of its performative status. "It is the mystery of the soul that we express when we say that the soul is not of this world," wrote Enckendorff in *Concerning the Existence and the Possession of the Soul* (1906).[48] The idea of the soul as a nonalienated and nonfragmented point of origin was the fulcrum of German idealism from Romanticism to *Lebensphilosophie*. The soul was an authenticity untouched by social mediation. Moreover, the distinction between the authentic soul and the artificial world led to multiform attempts (which Enckendorff called *Versuche*) to resolve this unbearable bisection of existence. Fichte healed this painful partition by proposing that the world was the creation of the ego. Hegel maintained that this division was not merely metaphysical but manifest in the slave-master hierarchies of history. Marx believed that the master/slave history would come to an end with the consciousness and institutional realization of species being. With Dilthey and Simmel, we no longer have the development of a universal ideal that, once realized, would resolve the alienation of humanity from the given historical reality. But we do have an operative assumption of a social soul, one whose ethical validity is subject to sociological and civic scrutiny. In all cases, the line of synthetic argumentation showed that the self-conscious subject must become a unity. Enckendorff's unique rendition of unified self-consciousness was the "societal form."

> This form establishes itself above our incompleteness and directs us to the positive in ourselves. . . . This form transforms with us since we are always human beings on our way to becoming human. . . . This form is the polar opposite of life premised on the unworthiness of others. It is the polar opposite of the instrumental use of others as a means to self advancement.[49]

The societal form, as a life model, completed human beings by resolving the tension between the life of the individuated soul and the life of the community. In the societal form, the individual found a higher civic life beyond the opposition of self and other.

Similar to Simmel's philosophical sociology, Enckendorff's social philosophy was implicitly avant-garde. In particular, it was consciously opposed to the atomistic prejudices of the commercial bourgeoisie. Hence, her work reflected divisions within the bourgeoisie itself. Those members of the bourgeoisie who made their living from the accumulation of cultural and intellectual capital often came to identify with a civic index relegating the pure pursuit of money to the lowest moral order. Enckendorff renounced, for example, the instrumental self-interest embodied in liberal economics favoring instead mutual respect and collective advancement. Her philosophy proposed that only when the norms and goals of personal life conform to the collective good of society could a happy, nonalienated community come into existence. Furthermore, her philosophy explicitly renounced traditional morality. "The normal path of life," constrained by traditional conceptions of responsibility and reason, fostered "an inauthentic duty."[50]

In analyzing Enckendorff's contestatory perspective, we need to do more than reduce it to a mere specie of Simmel's thought. Yes, their affinities are remarkable, and this is hardly surprising given the fact that Enckendorff began editing Simmel's work shortly after they were married and participated in the private seminars Simmel began holding at their residence in the years following his mother's death in 1897. However, Enckendorff's cultural valences, while reinforced by Simmelian philosophy, were not exclusively of Simmelian origin. Enckendorff was among the most well-educated and cosmopolitan women of her generation. She was a highly accomplished painter, a member of Berlin's cultural association, The Society of the Unbridled, and was living and painting with Sabine Graef in Paris only months before her marriage. Furthermore, at the time of their marriage, her knowledge of aesthetics certainly exceeded that of Simmel. If her association with Simmel reinforced and refined her philosophical gifts, then his posthumous status as the greatest cultural theorist of modernity owes much to Enckendorff's aesthetic amplitude.

Throughout their married life, Enckendorff and Simmel sustained their avant-garde sympathies through friendships and acquaintances with leading artistic and literary figures. For example, Simmel made several trips to Paris to meet Rodin around the turn of the century.[51] Additionally, the greatest lyricist of the Wilhelmine period, Stefan George, was a close friend and frequent visitor to the Enckendorff/Simmel household.[52] Simmel not only wrote on George, but his influence was also reflected in Enckendorff's work. A George quote graced the title page of *Concerning the Existence and the Possession of the Soul*, and George's style, which has been fashioned a second Romanticism, was echoed in Enckendorff's passionate prose.

> With a full, dark, warm stream of feeling, the soul reaches down to the mysteries and life-secrets of all that is inspired with soul: the life of longing, the life of duty, the life of will, and the life of obligation. In its own heartbeat, it feels the pounding pulse of all humanity; it feels what we hold in common kneeling before the secrets of existence.[53]

Enckendorff's spiritualism and neoromantic imagination reverberated with the restless lyricism found in George's *The Year of the Soul* (1897). Here George celebrated Nietzsche and expressed contempt for the crass commercialism of the Wilhelmine bourgeoisie. Enckendorff and Simmel not only shared these countercultural values. They saw in George's lyrical innovations a model of social morality: the avant-garde artist as civic seer. In one of his many essays on George, Simmel praised *The Year of the Soul* as a "deepening of love" and George as a poet whose creativity lives in "the sphere of the ideal."[54]

What was the sphere of the ideal? It was the cultural world of the avant-garde intelligentsia whose world view could be boiled down to two presuppositions: (1) aesthetic and ethical refinement are symbiotic, and (2) beautiful ethics, so to speak, are only possible from the perspective of the outsider. George was the ultimate outsider. His homosexuality excluded and alienated him from hegemonic gender norms and probably contributed to his public aloofness. George's homosexuality undoubtedly also contributed to Enckendorff and Simmel's cultural subversion of bourgeois masculinity and the Victorian marriage. In the world of the avant-garde, however, social deviation entailed more than punishment. Alienation contributed to a heightened aesthetic that was highly self-conscious and punctuated by a pathos of distance from convention. The aesthetic pathos of distance produced something greater than mere art. Simmel and Enckendorff identified with George because his work symbolized their countercultural philosophies of life: the artist-outsider, through the vatic struggle of creation, transcends intimate and passionate subjectivity and fashions an elite civic morality.[55] Consequently, the avant-garde vision unremittingly posited the conventions of bourgeois high society as hell on earth, a lurid emblem of spiritual corruption, hypocrisy, and decadence.

The sensibility of aesthetic politics is clearly evident in Enckendorff's feminist philosophy. *Reality and Lawfulness in Sexual Life* (1910) outlined a hybrid existential philosophy: "the path of life is nature culture."[56] Through the concept of "nature culture," Enckendorff offered an understanding of the progressive potential of human sexuality, particularly the female erotic. The female erotic is "the principle of soulful sexual love (*das Prinzip der beseelten Geschlechtsliebe*). . . . We have this and nothing else; this and nothing else is actual in our life as an ideal. . . . This norm should be our expression of a world view."[57] According to Enckendorff, the erotic ideal of woman is an immanent, natural, and revolutionary idea of life (*Lebensidee*). It is a "metaphysical position" that must be brought to consciousness and realized in cultural struggle.[58] The fact that it is natural in no way ensures its future historical hegemony. In fact, the struggle for female "nature culture" is constrained by powerful forces of the male-world (*Männerwelt*).

Enckendorff described these reactionary forces through the literary rhetoric of Naturalism, and this language is a marker of the interchangeability of aesthetic and ethical signifiers within the avant-garde. The topos of the female erotic is referred to as a "sexual Naturalism" locked in cultural warfare with two competing Naturalisms: asceticism and sensuality.[59] Enkendorff stated repeatedly and unambigiously that the greatest threat to social transformation was the Christian ascetic world view. The Victorian "Madonna cult," which is the "religious pathos . . . of the Christian marriage," creates a "rift between the physical and the spiritual."[60] Women are made to feel guilty about sexual desire because it is associated with filth and spiritual impurity. This Madonna-whore double bind can only be overcome by admitting the dehumanizing social function of marriage.

> Marriage is the institution in the state . . . that gives men dominion over women. This institution, as you know, does not protect the wife from rape by her husband. Customs and institutions that relate to women are always engaged in constructing the defense of the male world against the naturalness of women. These institutions are the wall separating women from the male world, into which they cannot be assimilated.[61]

In addition to Christian asceticism and its cluster of institutions, the antipodal valorization of pure sensuality is also a threat to the future feminization of culture. Pure sensuality, the ideal that all physical desires are naturally good, is the "Naturalism of the naturally pure," and this false naturalism promotes another fissure within humanity and society.[62] In pure sensuality, carnal desire is devoid of spiritual meaning. In contrast to ascetic Naturalism (sex as impure) and sensual Naturalism (all sexual desire as legitimate), erotic spirituality—"nature culture" or the female metaphysic—resolves the disunion of spiritual purity and physical impurity.

There were obvious cultural and conceptual affinities between Enckendorff and Simmel's feminist politics. For both, a metaphysical conception of woman was the foundation for an alternative future. Enckendorff's language was more radical in this regard. At the end of *Reality and Lawfulness in Sexual Life,* she calls for a revolutionary struggle to explode the existing male metaphysic of humanity. In addition, her radical critique of the middle-class women's movement—they do not recognize the need for a new comprehensive social metaphysic—was borrowed by Simmel in "The Relative and the Absolute in the Gender Problem." Ultimately, however, it makes little sense to assign elemental originality to Enkendorff or Simmel. Rather than contribute to a demarcation of originality, we mention that Enckendorff's substantial contribution to Simmel's sociology of women and feminist politics appears almost nowhere in the existing literature.[63] The absence of any mention of Enckendorff is more than an injustice to her brilliance. It severely constrains the possibility of a rounded interpersonal and cultural understanding of Simmel's thought. His wife, who demanded an independent identity, was not only one of the most sophisticated feminist philosophers of the era. She mourned the loss of her career after marriage and, therefore, was positioned to remind Simmel of the gendered and inegalitarian nature of patriarchal culture. His analysis of modern marriage as the lag of objective culture behind women's spiritual development unquestionably was influenced by his brilliant wife who was tormented by this institution.

> Up to this point, the objective organization of production remains behind the development of individual economic energies. This pattern explains many of the causes of the women's movement. The progress of modern industrial technology has shifted an extraordinary large number of household activities—that were previously the responsibility of women—outside the house, where objects are being produced more cheaply and efficiently. Consequently, many women of the bourgeois class have lost the core of their active lives without other activities and purposes being inserted into areas that so quickly have become empty. The multiple "dissatisfactions" of the modern woman, the waste of her abilities, brings about correlative [mental] disorders and ruination. Their partly healthy and partly unhealthy search to prove themselves outside the home is the result of the fact that technology in its objectivity has progressed more quickly than the possible development of individuals. The manifold unsatisfactory character of modern marriage follows from an analogous relationship. The rigidities of forms and habits of marriage that are imposed on individuals run counter to the personal development of the partners, especially that of the wife who may have totally outgrown them. Individuals now may be inclined towards freedom, understanding, and equality of rights and university education, for which traditional and objectively established marriage provides no authentic opportunity. This can be formulated as follows: the objective spirit of marriage lags behind the subjective development of spirit.[64]

Here, Simmel brilliantly articulated correlative forms of alienation in industrial capitalism and modern marriage. Undoubtedly, Enkendorff contributed to his understanding of the sociological predicaments of bourgeois women. She was certainly a modern woman who was inclined toward freedom and equality and for whom objective marital norms were depressing and hampering. Until she found her independent voice as a writer, marriage was a living hell. Its demands were totally incompatible with her familial and feminist ideal of self-reliance and personal fulfillment. In her writing, she criticized Victorian constraints on female sexual satisfaction and proselytized on behalf of a synthetic understanding of love, one that combined spiritual transcendence and erotic fulfillment. This synthesis, by the way, was the theoretical terre firma of Simmel's philosophy of love. "Love belongs to the great structural categories of existence;" it is a "transindividual" resolution to the sociological contradiction of "altuism and egoism; . . . it stands beyond [the philosophical contradiction] of subject and object," wrote Simmel.[65] Enckendorff's practical conception of love as a civic and philosophical revolution reverberated in Simmel's last works.

Enckendorff's originality was also evident in Simmel's critique of the women's movement as well. Rather than portraying women exclusively as victims, she and Simmel emphasized their complicity in patriarchy. Enckendorff went further. Her avant-garde refrain was more confrontational than Simmel's negation of tradition. This radicalism was manifest in her revolutionary phraseology, but it is also confirmed by Marianne Weber, who was astonished by Enckendorff's radicalism. No doubt this astonishment was a reaction to Enckendorff's political proposition of a female pleasure principle. The spiritualization of female eroticism diverged dramatically from the religious rejection of sensual culture that dominated the bourgeois women's movement. Enckendorff, for instance, experienced the traditional family as an obstruction to the spiritualization of society. Marriage was the prison of humanity's most exalted natural virtue: feminine love. In this regard, her critique of traditional marriage was far more pioneering and vanguardist than that of Simmel, who tended to treat the family as women's natural sphere.[66]

Instead of pursuing these comparisons further, we would do well to return to our thesis: any reconstruction of Simmel's sociology of women must account for the cultural interconnections manifest in Enckendorff and Simmel's partnership. Before and after their marriage, Enckendorff was a key figure in Berlin's upperbourgeois avant-garde. She symbolizes Simmel's deep cultural roots in the aesthetic and politically progressive context of Berlin's avant-garde. Moreover, she illustrates Simmel's lifelong identification and friendship with strong, independent-minded female intellectuals like Gertrud Kantorowicz, Margarete (Susman) von Bendemann, and Marianne Weber. This close connection was announced in his books. He dedicated *Religion* (1906) to Kantorowitcz and von Bendemann and *Goethe* (1913) to Weber. Simmel, however, not only surrounded himself with highly educated women in his private life. He defended their right to a university education and wrote eloquently and sympathetically about their unjust exclusion.[67] Hence, his sociology of women must be underscored with references to his predilection for gifted women and his cultural identification with the sexually progressive avant-garde.

Elements of Enckendorff and Simmel's personal life indicate the limits of their transgression of bourgeois probity. Sometime after the turn of the century, Simmel began a longterm liaison with the writer and poet Gertrud Kantorowicz, and this union produced a daughter, Angi.[68] Simmel resolved never to see his daughter. In part, this decision appears to have been a marital compromise. According to Maragarete Susman, Enkendorff "for certain reasons gave him free reign" with Kantorowicz. However, public admission of his paternity was simply out of the question. The primary concern was to shield themselves from public scorn. Furthermore, Simmel's refusal to see his daughter was a way of reassuring Enckendorff of his dedication to their marriage and shielding her from public humiliation. But this decision was also self-serving and not without dire repercussions. Simmel and Enckendorff's personas as a civic and moral avant-garde would have been destroyed by public revelations of his paternity for an out-of-wedlock birth. In hindsight, their conservatism is understandable. The consequences of their decisions, however, were devastating for Simmel's only daughter, Angi, who never met her father and eventually emigrated to Palestine. Moreover, Kantorowicz was deeply wounded by Simmel's unwillingness to see their daughter, although, according to Susman, she bore this heavy emotional burden with dignity and without enmity.

Simmel's observation that men compartmentalize their lives and, therefore, are more disposed to infidelity, has been seen by one scholar as a convenient justification for his extra-marital activities.[69] This assertion is unconvincing since Simmel was an explicit critic of the separation of one's moral core from objective relations seeing this divergence as a sign of (male) modernity's decadence and spiritual alienation. He was unambiguous: this tragic divergence must be overcome via the establishment of female culture. In the end, it is far too easy to read Simmel's infidelity dogmatically, i.e., to see him as a hopeless product of male culture, and forget that the meaning of this behavior was more complex. It reflects the transgressive instincts of the avant-garde who rejected Victorian family values. Did avant-gardism often justify philistinism? We know it did. But we should not conflate these two categories entirely. Simmel explicitly rejected both "the female slave and Don Juan" as prescriptive models of love.[70] In fact, he conceived of types of transgressive behavior—the extramarital desires of Emma Bovary and Nora's exit from the home at the end of Ibsen's *A Doll's*

House come to mind—that are not merely vulgar. For her part, Susman, a close friend to both Simmel and Kantorowicz, interpreted the situation sympathetically from the perspective of Simmel's existential philosophy.

> Simmel obviously felt guilt about his relationship to his child. From this certainly came the words in his diary: "The great tragedy of morality is this: one often does not have the right to perform their duty." What Gertrud Kantorowicz and her fate meant to Simmel shimmered through many of his works, most clearly in the chapter on secrecy in his great *Sociology* and certainly through his concept of an "individual law." In it he saw the law-like inner unity of life that could neither feel nor adopt a law from the outside. Above all, he attributed the individual law to women, just as generally woman and eros—in all relationships and forms—again and again occupied his thought.[71]

Rather than seeing Simmel's behavior as a sordid violation of inviolable marital fidelity, Susman interpreted it as an example of countercultural morality (the individual law), a morality developed to legitimate female liberation from male culture. Perhaps this reading is too exculpatory, but it has the merit of revealing two things: (1) Simmel was not hypocritically postulating double standards; his concept of an individual law disobedient to ethical conventions was developed for, not against, women; and (2) Susman directs us to the gendered underpinnings of Simmel's existential ethics; the idea of an individuated moral code, created by the soul and indifferent to the objective morals of the status quo, was a philosophical strategy for women's liberation.

The circumstances surrounding Simmel's relationship to Kantorowicz are particularly fruitful for speculation about the existential origins of Enckendorff and Simmel's differing views of marriage. Both were avant-garde critics of banal prudery. Enckendorff targeted the cultural chasm between erotic and spiritual love which she associated with the Victorian marriage and Madonna cult. Furthermore, we can speculate that this emotional chasm existed in her own marriage and that she experienced her husband's infidelity as a tragic symbol of marriage devoid of eroticism. Her cultural solution was not an individuated morality that sanctioned extramarital affairs. In print, at least, she championed a version of marital fidelity that synthesized the soulful and the carnal. Simmel's ideas on morality and the erotic were far less faithful to the institution of marriage. His views were summed up in the seventh chapter of *Goethe* entitled "Love": "Goethe was untrue to women because he was true to himself. . . . His unfaithfulness was self-overcoming. That means obedience to his own law of an always loftier developing life, always building over the past. . . . In this conception, life overtakes its last rigidity."[72] Goethe's *Elective Affinities*, for instance, treated the dramatic conflict of romantic passion and marital law.

Both Enckendorff and Simmel committed themselves to an existential transcendence of this powerful antagonism, but they disposed of this tension in very different ways. In response to a long tradition of female subordination, Enckendorff philosophically dispensed with Victorian morality and advocated marital eroticism. The entrenched attitudes about women in marriage must be overthrown, but marriage itself was a redeemable social form. Female desire can find libidinal space within a reformed convention based on mutual respect. For Simmel, love negates the authority of marital fidelity. Male desire finds authentic satisfaction beyond social regulation. Simmel has totally cast off the restraints of bourgeois sexual convention. Or has he? In doing so, he seems to have rounded the misogynistic circle, returning to a male model of dionysian satisfaction that ignores completely patriarchy and female desire. Perhaps this reservation could be articulated best in the form a question: how does the male will to freedom outside of marriage also will the freedom of married women? Simmel and Susman both put forth an answer. In *Schopenhauer and Nietzsche*, Simmel asserted that existential self-overcoming exceeded mere egoism and produced higher social ideals. Susman maintained that Simmel's ethical model of an individuated morality was a model for female liberation from patriarchal repression. It presented women with a new approach to morality that carved out space for individual expression similar to men's and that stood in contrast to the Victorian matrix: ethical dependence, domesticity, sexual purity, passivity, and religious piety. Furthermore, Simmel criticized the traditional marriage with a wealth of anthropological counter examples. Particularly in "Towards a Sociology of the Family" (1895), he denaturalized the contemporary poor treatment of wives by emphasizing the "unending diversity of marriage forms."[73] History contained numerous examples of the unnecessary "inferiority" of women in "the modern family."[74] All of these arguments merit consideration when assessing Simmel's commitment to the feminist cause. Conversely, it may suffice to recall that Enckendorff interpreted her husband's prescriptive separation of marriage and eroticism as the prototypical symbol of male hegemony.

MARIANNE WEBER: LIBERAL VERSUS AVANT-GARDE FEMINISM

The Simmels and Webers (Max and Marianne) were not close friends, but they were acquaintances. Max Weber and Georg Simmel collaborated in the founding of *Logos: International Journal for a Philosophy of Culture*, and clearly they were familiar with one another's work. This familiarity is indicated by Weber's citation of *The Philosophy of Money* in the first footnote of *The Protestant Ethic and the Spirit of Capitalism*. We also know that Max Weber was a fervent supporter of Simmel's candidacy for academic positions in Heidelberg. Furthermore, there were striking affinities between their wives, Marianne Weber and Gertrud Simmel. Both were leading feminist thinkers. Not surprisingly, the style and content of their works reflected that of their spouses. Similar to Georg Simmel, the great titan of philosophical sociology, Enckendorff's books were philosophical. While they certainly contained commentaries critical of dominant institutions and ideologies, they were driven not by practical but metaphysical considerations. This distinction is somewhat misleading, since for Simmel and Enckendorff the reconfiguration of social metaphysics, i.e., dominant subjective systems of valuation, was the generator of cultural revolution. Marianne Weber's work was analogous to that of her husband, who was the paragon of systematic historical sociology. Marianne Weber's feminist essays dealt with immediate historical problems, like the difficulty of balancing the demands of marriage and the desire for an independent occupation.[75] This practical disposition expressed itself in political activities. She was closely connected to the BDF and later assumed a leadership position in that organization after the death of her husband in 1920.

Marianne Weber is particularly important to our narrative because she was, save Enckendorff, the first major feminist to discern the importance of Simmel's essays on women. Furthermore the Webers's rejection of sensual culture stood in stark contrast to Simmel and Enckendorff who theorized the erotic bases of social change.[76] These differences came to fruition in a lively public debate that broke out between Simmel and Marianne Weber after the 1911 publication of *Philosophical Culture*, which contained Simmel's essays "Feminine Culture" and "The Relative and Absolute in the Gender Problem." In 1913, Marianne Weber responded to the issues raised in these essays by publishing "Woman and Objective Culture."[77] Of the compendium of essays written between 1904 and 1919 and published in *Women's Issues and Women's Thoughts: Collected Essays* (1919), Weber's essay on Simmel was the longest, and this evidenced the provocative nature of his thought as well as the earnestness of her engagement. Weber's perspective was representative of the bourgeois German women's movement. Like Simmel, she was a cultural feminist who believed that there were "specific qualities which distinguish one sex from the other."[78] But Weber added an egalitarian principle. In only the second sentence of her polemical essay, she stated: "Men and women both belong to the genus (*Geschlecht*) of humanity, which through physical and spiritual characteristics distinguishes them from all other species."[79] Here she played on the dual meaning of *Geschlecht*, sex and genus, to emphasize a common humanity. Sexuality, then, becomes not a marker of difference but a symbol of shared humanity as well. Weber objected to Simmel's exclusive fixation on the radical polarity of the sexes at the expense of women's equally significant membership in a shared humanity. Weber was right. One rarely finds sustained elaborations of equal rights in Simmel's work. However, this does not contradict his practical opposition to sexual inequality. He was one of the most progressive professors at Berlin University, welcoming women to his seminars and defending their right to education. There were cultural and theoretical reasons for Simmel's distance from egalitarian demands. First and foremost, the bourgeois avant-garde required a self-conception that was distinct from the socialist vanguard. This distance and elitist self-conception was maintained by downplaying egalitarian demands, which were the crown jewels of socialism and the proletarian women's movement. Secondly, the avant-garde also consciously distanced itself from bourgeois culture, in this case the bourgeois women's movement. Just as egalitarian demands of socialism were stigmatized as spiritually leveling, Weber's call for the expansion of women's rights—buttressed by women's conceptual inclusion in a common humanity—was deemed as nothing more than a call for women's access to a patriarchal world. Both sides of this argument have merit. Simmel's avant-garde feminine philosophy undervalued women's needs for formal equal rights. Conversely, Weber did not adequately wrestle with the possibility that female participation in the existing world could fortify, rather than transform, conservative social institutions. Her residual essentialism carried the false assumption that women's mere entry into existing institutions would inaugurate a more passionate community.

An assessment of the differences between Simmel and Marianne Weber is particularly difficult because their feminist ideas combine contradictory conceptions. Earlier it was pointed out that Simmel's existential philosophy of life was in tension with his essentialist propositions. In this regard, Weber appeared to be the superior *Lebensphilosoph* in one crucial sense: she insightfully insisted that the cultural development of women required transcendence of "the natural unity of being"; women must create an ideal that exceeds their "circle of naturalness."[80] A close reading of Weber, however, demonstrates that she was not challenging the ascription of ontological otherness to women. Her intentions were much more modest. She was not calling into question the natural destiny of women, but the necessary circumscription of this destiny within the domestic sphere.

> Simmel's beautiful picture of a closed and harmonious being can be retained. However, how often is this the sweet wrapper of the women behind which is concealed the agitation and insecurity of growth and struggle? And how often are intellectually gifted women coping with themselves and with the antinomies of life and thought, . . . because they lack the opportunity and ability to realize their intellectual powers in an adequate object? . . . We can grant this to Simmel: it is obviously the meaning

> and destiny of women to be women and to develop their femininity to perfection. However, when this is women's exclusive value, that she has to be completed in herself, then unquestionably a metaphysical non-sense is present in the [so-called] natural organization of countless women.[81]

First, buried in Weber's critique of Simmel is a canard that has been replicated wholly by scholars, namely, that his conception of feminine culture precluded women's participation in the public sphere. This is a misreading of his cultural politics. The pivotal political questions for Simmel were, (1) whether the women's movement would accommodate itself to existing (male) institutions, and (2) whether women would perform the same social functions as men or if they would create totally new (feminine) institutional spheres of activity. He classified the former type of women's participation in the public sphere as an example of "the cultural category of secondary originality."[82] Yet, as an avant-garde thinker, he treated society like a freshly stretched canvass deserving strokes of sociological originality. Nonetheless, he praised activities of secondary originality.

> In broad areas—technology, trade, science, warfare, literature, and art—countless achievements of so-called secondary originality are needed, achievements which take place within given forms and requirements but which nonetheless contain initiative, individuality, and creative energy.[83]

Weber admitted that "Simmel's circumscription of the special spheres of women's cultural work certainly are not small," but she feared that they may be too narrow in light of "logical, methodological, aesthetic and ethical norms" shared by men and women.[84] Here we may have reached a paradigmatic impasse. Simmel's sociology of culture never renounced the presence of shared norms. Male culture was an example of shared norms. Rather, his sociology of modernity unfolded from the metaphysical proposition that shared norms are never neutral or objective. Humanity had only two choices: the male or female a priori. The former was traditional and oppressive, the latter avant-garde and liberating. There was no gender-neutral alternative to these competing poles of objectivity. This relative understanding of objectivity contravened Weber's defense of "transsubjective, transnational, eternal, and collective absolutes, that we knowingly denote as nothing other than general-humanity."[85] For Simmel, even the concepts of equality and general humanity were not gender neutral. A radical choice between male and female culture still had to be made.

Secondly, Weber's numerous references to gifted women denotes her class alignment that was shared with Simmel. Although they represented distinct cultural universes within the upper bourgeoisie, the avant-garde and the bourgeois women's movement emanated social visions far removed from the ambitions matured by proletarian hardship. The proletarian women's movement, led in this era by Clara Zetkin and Luise Zietz, was arguably the most revolutionary component of the SPD. The German proletarian women's movement was in the thrall of egalitarianism: equal rights, equal pay for equal work, the franchise, and, ultimately, economic equality that is only possible via the revolutionary destruction of capitalism. Its *Kulturkampf* was taloned to social upheaval. Conversely, the BDF's charitable activities and moderate attitudes and the avant-garde's metaphysical musings and obsession with originality never reached the revolutionary threshold that marked the egalitarian cultural politics of socialist feminists.[86] Socialist feminists' fierce grapple with capitalist realities largely remained outside the cultural purview of Weber and Simmel, but not entirely. Weber briefly introduced the theme of proletarian women into her debate with Simmel. She concurred with Simmel that mechanical production and motherhood were contrary to one another. But, in a reversal befitting her class context, she concluded that women's nature appeared adaptive and elastic enough not to be harmed by this activity; "Women's powers and gender responsibilities are compatible with the rhythms of industrial work."[87] While at first glance, it seems as though Weber was sympathetic to proletarian concerns that were mere eddies in the stream of Simmel's feminist consciousness, it turns out that the adaptability of women in the industrial realm was merely an argument for expanding the occupational possibilities of middle- and upper-class women. She searched for appropriate expressions of women's nature in objective culture and concluded predictably that women were best suited to perform charity. She claimed that leadership positions in industry and commerce were inconsistent with women's natural and ethical contributions to community. Even more than Simmel, Weber narrowly circumscribed the proper public activities of women.

The differing cultural aspirations of Simmel and Weber ultimately come to expression in their incompatible responses to the separation of subjective and objective culture. Although Weber described industrial women's work as cruel and incompatible with motherhood, she concluded with tragic conservatism that it was "an unavoidable necessity for our cultural development; among the masses it tears the work-life from personal life, but for an always increasing percentage of humanity this facilitates the fulfillment of personal life, if only through unfulfilling forms of work."[88] The tragedy of modernity, its increasing requirement that work be alienated from spiritual improvement, was the historical catastrophe that Simmel dedicated his life to repairing *comprehensively*, that is, not exclusively within the bourgeois realm of art and academia but also in the work-sphere of industrial labor. His lofty intellectual longings contrasted sharply with Weber's dialectical understanding of this tragedy as progress. In Simmel and Marianne Weber's conceptions of female culture, the contrasting cultural profiles of the liberal and avant-garde bourgeoisie stand in starkest relief.

FROM THE FIGHT FOR FEMININE CULTURE TO INTERNATIONAL WAR

Thus, the struggle for the establishment of feminine culture among the sexual vanguard was colored by the priority of philosophical subversion for Simmel, sensual revolution by Enckendorff, and egalitarian concerns by Weber. They shared many presuppositions, most notably, a belief in the transformative potential of women's essentialized identities: love, compassion, and nurturing. Their analyses could not help but reflect the historical-political conceptual machinery of their contemporary period. However, Simmel and Enckendorff conceived of their feminist sympathies as counterposed to Weber and the bourgeois women's movement. The latter lacked a revolutionary and comprehensive metaphysical conception of feminine culture, according to Simmel. For her part, Enckendorff polemicized against the mainline feminists for not grasping the significance of female eroticism to the struggle for social transformation. Generally, Enckendorff and Simmel attacked Christian philosophy and Victorian morality with a vehemence that is absent from Marianne Weber's work. Their sexual radicalism was emblematic of the erotic existentialism found in Berlin's neo-Nietzschean avant-garde. However, the fight for feminine culture eventually took a backseat to different and more pressing realities, most notably, the pursuit of war. In the wake of August 1914, Simmel energetically took up intellectual arms against Germany's cultural enemies. His strident, public defense of German militarism initiated a precipitous decline in his avant-garde reputation.

NOTES

1. Georg Simmel, "Weibliche Kultur" [1911] in *Philosophische Kultur* (Berlin: Wagenbach, 1986), p. 221. This revised version of the 1902 essay was reprinted in *Schriften zur Philosophie und Soziologie der Geschlechter*, pp. 159–76.

2. Heinz-Jürgen Dahme, "Frauen-und Geschlechterfrage bei Herbert Spencer und Georg Simmel," *Kölner Zeitschrift für Soziologie und Sozialpsychologie* 38 (1986): 490–509; Klaus Lichtblau, "Eros and Gender: Gender Theory in Simmel, Tönnies und Weber," *Telos* 82 (1989): 89–110.

3. Simmel, "Zur Psychologie der Frauen" [1890], in *Schriften zur Philosophie und Soziologie der Geschlechter*, p. 51.

4. Peter Bürger, *Theory of the Avant-Garde*, trans. Michael Shaw (Minneapolis: University of Minnesota Press, 1984).

5. Claudia Koonz, *Mothers in the Fatherland: Women, the Family, and Nazi Politics* (New York: St. Martin's, 1981); Robert Moeller, *Protecting Motherhood: Women and the Family in the Politics of Postwar West Germany* (Berkeley: University of California Press, 1993); Nancy Reagin, *A German Women's Movement: Class and Gender in Hanover, 1880–1933.*

6. The concept of conservative empowerment and theoretical delineation of cultural feminism and gender theory appear in my forthcoming essay, "Conservative Empowerment and the Gender of Nazism," *Journal of Women's History,* vol. 12, no. 2 (summer 2000).

7. Simmel, "Zur Psychologie der Frauen,"p. 51.

8. Ibid., p. 52.

9. Dahme, "Frauen und Geschlechterfrage," pp. 490–509.

10. Simmel, "Zur Psychologie der Frauen," p. 52.

11. Simmel, "Weibliche Kultur," *Neue Deutsche Rundschau* 13 (Heft 5, May 1902): 504–15. Guy Oakes mistakenly states that the essay first appeared in 1911. Oakes, "Acknowledgements," in *Georg Simmel*, p. vii.

12. Simmel, "Weibliche Kultur" [1911], p. 221.

13. Ibid, p. 252.

14. See, for example, *The New French Feminism: An Anthology*, ed. Elaine Marks and Isabelle de Courtivron (New York: Schocken, 1981); Toril Moi, *Sexual/Textual Politics: Feminist Literary Theory* (New York: Methuen, 1985).

15. Simmel, "Weibliche Kultur" [1911], p. 220.

16. Simmel, "Das Relative und das Absolute im Geschlechter-Problem," in *Philosophische Kultur: Gesammlte Essais*. Berlin: Klaus Wagenbach, 1986, p. 68.

17. Ibid., pp. 64–65.

18. Simmel, "Weibliche Kultur" [1911], p. 230.

19. Simmel, "Das Relative," pp. 65–66.

20. Renato Poggioli, *The Theory of the Avant-Garde*, trans. Gerald Fitzgerald (Cambridge, Mass.: Belknap Press, 1968), p. 107.

21. Simmel, "Das Relative," pp. 66–67.

22. Ibid., p. 68.

23. Simmel, "Weibliche Kultur" [1911], p. 220.

24. Irene Stoehr, " 'Organisierte Mütterlichkeit'. Zur Politik der deutschen Frauenbewegung um 1900," in *Frauen suchen ihre Geschichte: Historische Studien zum 19. und 20. Jahrhundert*, ed. Karin Hausen (Munich: Beck, 1983), pp. 221–249; Elizabeth Meyer-Renschhausen, *Weibliche Kultur und soziale Arbeit: eine Geschichte der Frauenbewegung am Beispiel Bremens 1810–1927* (Cologne: Böhlau, 1989). See especially "Organisierte Mütterlichkeit," pp. 219–24; Ann Taylor Allen, *Feminism and Motherhood in Germany, 1800–1914* (New Brunswick, N.J.: Rutgers University Press, 1991).

25. See Reagin, *A German Women's Movement.*

26. Ibid., pp. 264–65; on German feminists' retreat from political liberalism, see Evans, *The Feminist Movement in Germany*.

27. Simmel, "Das Relative," p. 89.

28. Ibid., p. 89.

29. Simon de Beauvoir, *The Ethics of Ambiguity*, trans. B. Frechtman (New York: Citadel, 1976), p. 73.

30. Simmel, "Weibliche Kultur" [1911], pp. 250, 252.

31. Ibid., pp. 222, 249–50.

32. Ibid., p. 250.

33. For instance, Oakes concludes: "Simmel's reasoning . . . does not open up the possibility of an alternative female culture. . . . The objectification of female existence, or the femininization of culture, is impossible." Guy Oakes, "The Problem of Women in Simmel's Theory of Culture," introduction to *Georg Simmel*, pp. 3–64, quotation on p. 43. Suzanne Vromen similarly insists that Simmel's concept of culture "was the negation of a possible objective culture for women, the categorical rejection of women's capacity to objectify their existence and to express in external forms their distinctive qualities. . . . Simmel's project ended in a failure for women." Suzanne Vromen, "Georg Simmel and the Cultural Dilemma of Women," *History of European Ideas* 8, nos. 4, 5 (1987): 563–79.

34. Simmel, "Weibliche Kultur," [1911], p. 237.

35. Ibid., p. 235.

36. William Morris, *News From Nowhere* (New York: Penguin Books, 1986); E. P. Thompson, *William Morris: Romantic to Revolutionary* (New York: Pantheon, 1976).

37. Ferdinand Tönnies, *Fundamental Concepts of Sociology* (*Gemeinshaft und Gesellschaft*), trans. Charles P. Loomis (New York: American Book Co., 1940), p. 191.

38. Simmel, "Weibliche Kultur" [1911], pp. 250–51.

39. Klaus Lichtblau, "Eros and Culture: Gender Theory in Simmel, Tönnies, and Weber," *Telos* 82 (1989): 89–110; see p. 96.

40. Rita Felski, *The Gender of Modernity* (Cambridge, Mass.: Harvard University Press, 1995), p. 59.

41. Simmel, "Psychologie der Koketterie," in *Schriften zur Philosophie und Soziologie der Geschlechter*, pp. 187–99.

42. Friedrich Nietzsche, *Twilight of the Idols* (London: Penguin Books, 1990), p. 53; Marianne Weber, *Lebenserinnerungen* (Bremen: Johs. Storm, 1948), p. 380.

43. Angela Rammstedt, "Gertrud Kinel/Simmel–Malerin," *Simmel Newsletter* 4, no. 2 (winter 1994): 140–62. Much of the information in this paragraph is drawn from this essay.

44. Hans Simmel, "Auszüge aus den Lebenserinnerungen," p. 251.

45. Angela Rammstedt, "Gertrud Kinel," p. 149.

46. Sabine Lepsius, "Erinnerungen an Georg Simmel," in Gassen und Landmann, p. 199.

47. Quotation in Angela Rammstedt, "Gertrud Kinel," p.152.

48. Marie Luise Enckendorff, *Von Sein und Haben der Seele* (Leipzig: Duncker & Humblot, 1906), p. 20.

49. Ibid., pp. 125–26.

50. Ibid., p. 107.

51. Georg Simmel, "Rodins Plastik und die Geistesrichtung der Gegenwart," *Vom Wesen der Moderne: Essays zur Philosophie und Ästhetik*, ed. by Werner Jung (Hamburg: Junius, 1990), pp. 263–76.

52. Simmel wrote several essays on George. Georg Simmel, "Stefan George.

Eine Kunst Philosophische Betrachtung" [1898]; "Stefan George, Eine kunstphilosophische Studie" [1901]; "Der Siebente Ring" [1909], in *Vom Wesen der Moderne*, pp. 175–234.

53. Enckendorff, *Von Sein*, p. 86.

54. Georg Simmel, "Stefan George, Eine kunstphilosophische Studie" [1901], in *Vom Wesen der Moderne*, pp. 199, 201.

55. For more on Simmel and George, see Michael Landmann, "Georg Simmel und Stefan George," in *Georg Simmel und die Moderne*, pp. 147–73; Angela Rammstedt, "Stefan George und Georg Simmel," *Simmel Newsletter* 9, no. 1 (summer 1999): 101–103.

56. Marie Luise Enckendorff, *Realität und Gesetzlichkeit im Geschlechtsleben* (Leipzig: Duncker und Humblot, 1910), p. 5.

57. Ibid., pp. 72, 71.

58. Ibid., p. 134.

59. Ibid., p. 50.

60. Ibid., pp. 60, 62–63.

61. Ibid., p. 137.

62. Ibid., p. 51.

63. See, for instance, Lewis A. Coser, "Georg Simmel's Contribution to the Sociology of Women," *Signs* 2, no. 4 (1977): 869–76.

64. Simmel, *Philosophie des Geldes*, p. 644. See similar comments in Simmel, "Der Frauenkongress und die Sozialdemokratie" (1896), in *Schriften zur Philosophie und Soziologie der Geschlechter*, pp. 133–38.

65. Simmel, "Über die Liebe," in *Fragmente und Aufsätze*, pp. 49, 57.

66. During the Great War she criticized "the Prussian God" as a renunciation of early Christianity and praised the "unendingly radical" Christian doctrine of love. Here, too, she was more radical than her husband, who was, at least initially, far more nationalistic. See Marie Luise Enckendorff, *Über das Religiöse* (Leipzig: Duncker und Humblot, 1919), pp. 81, 83.

67. Simmel, "Frauenstudium an der Berliner Universität" [1899], in *Schriften zur Philosophie und Soziologie der Geschlechter*, pp.157–58.

68. Margarete Susman, "Erinnerungen an Simmel," in *Buch des Dankes*, pp. 278–91.

69. Vromen, "Georg Simmel and the Cultural Dilemma," p. 570.

70. Simmel, *Goethe* (Leipzig: Klinkhardt & Biermann, 1923), p. 193.

71. Margarete Susman, "Erinnerungen an Simmel," in *Buch des Dankes*, pp. 282–83.

72. Simmel, *Goethe*, pp. 204–205.

73. Simmel, "Zur Soziologie der Familie," in *Schriften zur Philosophie und Soziologie der Geschlechter*, pp. 119–32. Quotation on p. 125.

74. Simmel, "Zur Soziologie der Familie," p. 132.

75. Marianne Weber, "Beruf und Ehe" [1905], in *Frauenfrage und Frauengedanken: Gesammelte Aufsätze* (Tübingen: J. C. B. Mohr, 1919), pp. 20–37.

76. Klaus Lichtblau, "Eros and Culture," pp. 89–110.

77. Marianne Weber, "Die Frau und die objektive Kultur," [1913], in *Frauenfrage und Frauengedanken*, pp. 95–133.

78. Ibid., p. 95.

79. Ibid., p. 95.

80. Ibid., p. 113.

81. Ibid., p. 115.

82. Simmel, "Weibliche Kultur," [1911], p. 249.

83. Ibid., pp. 221–22.

84. Marianne Weber, "Die Frau und die objektive Kultur," pp.107–108.

85. Ibid., p. 109.

86. See Quataert, *Reluctant Feminists* and Evans, *Comrades and Sisters: Feminism, Socialism and Pacifism in Europe 1870–1945* (New York: St. Martin's Press, 1987).

87. Marianne Weber, "Die Frau und die objektive Kultur," p. 125.

88. Ibid., p. 125.

4

A GREAT WAR OF SPIRITUAL DECISIONS

Simmel and the Ideas of 1914

Through the war, the religious inner-powers have experienced an unmistakable revival and intensification, to such a degree that they demand from everyone a decision about which absolute foundation one now will stand upon.

Georg Simmel, 1915[1]

ALTHOUGH MARGINALIZED IN H. STUART HUGHES'S CANONICAL NARRATIVE OF social theory, Georg Simmel now is recognized as a key figure in what Klaus Lichtblau calls the "geneology of cultural sociology in Germany."[2] He has been heralded for his power of observation as "the first sociologist of modernity."[3] But, however much we know about Simmel's legacy as a sociologist, precious little has been written about his response to the monumental event of the era, the Great War. This is unfortunate, because knowledge of Simmel's response to the war is crucial for an understanding of his countercultural legacy, which is the subject of subsequent chapters. Here, we will continue our narrative of Simmel's life and thought up until his death in 1918. To date, a nuanced account of the development of Simmel's cultural criticism (*Kulturkritik*) during the Great War has gone unmentioned or has been minimized by the vast majority of Simmel's historiography.[4] In fact, serious errors have been made in this area by leading Simmel scholars.[5] To redress these errors this chapter plunges into a study of Simmel's forgotten reactions to the Great War. Our ultimate goal is representative biography.[6] But how representative were Simmel's reactions to this epoch-defining event? Perhaps this question is best answered by keeping the relevant historiography in mind. The question of Simmel's representative relevance to an understanding of war culture will emerge by articulating his place within canonical debates about the "Ideas of 1914," the German mandarins, and the culture wars which accompanied the military conflict.[7] One conclusion to be drawn from Simmel's case concerns the chronology and genealogy of academic culture. Fritz Ringer dates the height of the German crisis of higher learning to the period 1920–1933. Simmel's legacy points to a competing chronology. For Simmel and his left-wing intellectual progeny, the legitimacy crisis of German academics began in August 1914.[8] Simmel's radical progeny experienced the war as the last lament for the passing of an era, an era dominated by aristocratic politics, laissez-faire economics, and Simmel's unrivaled reputation as Germany's countercultural mandarin.

No less astute an observer than Hans-Georg Gadamer recognized "the seismographic accuracy" with which Simmel responded to the meandering of the Wilhelmine *Zeitgeist*.[9] As though seeking to fulfill Gadamer's hypothesis, the analyses of the previous two chapters have roved pensively over the cultural landscape of the Wilhelmine era and charted Simmel's thought in relation to cultural landmarks such as Naturalism, neo-Kantianism, monetary culture, and Nietzschean philosophy. Yet, the mere presentation of Simmel's life within historical settings will never produce the subtlety of a freshly conceived intellectual biography. Instead of just two foci (Simmel and historical setting) in an elliptical relationship, we need the triangulation of a third foci: the individuated meaning of tradition. We labor in darkness, unable to glimpse the cherished underprops of Simmel's life, unless we are mindful of the personal meanings of Simmel's reaction to his historical milieu. The context of war is a case in point. Having determined that Simmel was initially a war enthusiast, we still need to distill the personal meaning of that support by comparing it to the pro-war proclamations of others. One tertiary goal of this chapter is to remind readers that the meaning of prowar sentiments were multiform. War enthusiasts projected a diversity of glorious hopes and ethical aspirations into the mobilization for war. This chapter individuates Simmel's wartime hopes and dreams by comparing them to the cultural imagination of other prowar intellectuals such as Thomas Mann.

Further complicating the task of examining Simmel and other intellectuals' response to the Great War is the change of heart that seized many war enthusiasts after the titanic and ghastly military struggles unfolded. An unchanging relationship to the events of war was the exception. Simmel's variable prowar consciousness illustrated this. So, to grasp this changing consciousness and its relationship to the gruesome pageantry of war, this chapter analyzes Simmel's thought as an "empirical phenomenology," that is, as a series of mental stages that accompanied the unfolding narrative of the Great War.[10] As we shall see, Simmel's prowar consciousness followed a tripartite course of social experience. First, he expressed providential enthusiasm that the war would result in mighty world-historical accomplishments. Like many intellectuals, especially those influenced by Nietzsche, Simmel expressed his support for the war in the language of intellectual spirituality (*Geistigkeit*). Indeed, intellectual spirituality was a favored idiom in the culture wars between pro- and antiwar intellectuals, and one that constituted what T. W. Adorno called a cultural "force field."[11] Simmel's prowar *Kulturkritik* was a particular politicization of the German intellectual spirit. Second, the macabre depredations of war quickly weaned Simmel from an unreserved prowar sentimentality. In less than a year after mobilization, he developed a skeptical self-consciousness and voiced profound pessimism about the benefits of this war. And, third, as a means of overcoming this pessimism, he began to search for an international conception of postwar Europe.

HISTORIOGRAPHICAL PRECIS

Roger Chartier, in a brilliant reversal of traditional teleological interpretations, has written that the French Revolution invented the Enlightenment.[12] His perspicacious methodology of reception has made us more painfully aware of the French Revolution as an unconscious hermeneutic event and one that "naturally" has altered our interpretation of the Enlightenment. What the French Revolution is to the Enlightenment, I wish to argue, the history of National Socialism is to Germany's pre-Nazi history. The historiography of what is referred to here as Germany's spiritual culture was invented by National Socialism and by the subsequent historiography of fascism. This is not, however, a reference to the fact that the German "*Sonderweg*" and its correlative institutions (the authoritarian church, aristocratic state, and patriarchal family) had a positive cultural and historiographical connotation before the Third Reich and a negative one after it.[13] My comments on culture, while complementary with the historiographical reassessments of David Blackbourn and Geoff Eley, are animated by the methodological insights of Chartier. Still, as historians of nineteenth-century Germany, Blackbourn and Eley have been the two historians who have forcefully confronted this historiographical legacy. Eley writes: "Our ability to conceptualize the German past is heavily constrained . . . by the two dates of 1848 and 1933." Blackbourn, in reference to nineteenth-century Romanticism, states that its "political ambiguity has been sawn off by Nazi-pedigree hunters."[14] This study argues that, as a result of both the Nazi movement and the historiography of Nazi culture, the political malleability and heterogeneity of the "Ideas of 1914" have been eclipsed by a decidedly unambiguous teleological linkage between support for the Great War and National Socialism.

In addition to Nazism, there is a second perspectival telos that has contributed to a rigid interpretation of German culture prior to 1914, namely, the First World War itself. For instance, in inventing the cultural precursors of the Great War, Walter Falk's *The Collective Dream of War* transmutes a central element of prewar cultural discourse, the Nietzschean concept of a Dionysian struggle [*Kampf*], from prewar culture to war culture. He does this in relation to the Expressionist poet, Georg Heym, who died before the outbreak of war. This not only obscures the political undecidability of Nietzschean philosophy; it also obscures the historical record. Two of Simmel's students, Kurt Hiller and Helene Stöcker, mobilized Nietzschean philosophy in opposition to the war. Heym was one of Hiller's closest friends in the early Expressionist movement in Berlin, and it is likely that he, too, would have opposed the war, despite, or perhaps because of, the language contained in his 1910 poem, "Dionysus."[15] Stöcker, writing in late 1916, explained the relationship between Nietzschean struggle and the war (*Kampf* and *Krieg*) as follows. "One of the most dangerous psychological transpositions is, for example, struggle and war [*Kampf und Krieg*]. . . . In fact, there is an absolute antagonism between war and [the struggle to create] culture."[16] While it might be natural from the perspective of 1914 to assume that the discourse of struggle constitutes a dream of war, this presupposition reverses the historical record and marginalizes the critical manifestations of Nietzschean philosophy that permeated Wilhelmine culture. More precisely, it marginalizes Simmel's cultural legacy. Simmel's greatest cultural impact was upon the Expressionist avant-garde. Its leaders, Kurt Hiller and Franz Pfemfert, led the antiwar movement and opposed the war from a Nietzschean standpoint.[17] They objected to the transformation of Nietzsche into a reactionary war propagandist. For these intellectuals, Nietzsche's ideal of struggle was inconsistent with the militarist propaganda of German nationalists.

With the exception of Lewis D. Wurgaft and Michael Löwy, most studies of Germany's war culture do not recognize the malleability of spiritual politics.[18] There are good reasons for this. Theologians generally supported German imperialism and hailed war as an element of God's cosmology.[19] Consequently, canonical cultural histories that cover this period, George Mosse's *The Crisis of German Ideology: Intellectual Origins of the Third Reich*, Fritz Stern's *The Politics of Cultural Despair*, and Fritz Ringer's *The Decline of the German Mandarins*, tend to investigate Wilhelmine culture and the spiritualization of the Great War from the perspective of 1933. Their general omission of Simmel's legacy is less important than their tendency to link the discourse of spirituality to fascism. The nationalization of spiritual discourse by the radical right during the Great War, and later with the Nazis, is unmistakable. Further, given the importance of fascism to twentieth-century European history, this teleological hermeneutic is both desirable and to a great extent unavoidable. This study also has been unable to avoid references to European fascism; however, it will attempt to place Simmel's legacy more firmly within context of Wilhelmine culture. By doing so, the equation of spiritual politics and right-wing nationalism will appear inadequate to articulate his polyvalent legacy. As we shall see in our discussion of Simmel's prowar propaganda, spiritual discourse was the cultural battleground of German intellectuals. Nowhere was the battle over the meaning of German spiritualism more pitched and politically indeterminate than among devotees of Nietzsche. This struggle of the German spirit, as it was known during the war, has been chronicled by Steven Aschheim and Hinton Thomas.[20] What has not made its way into print is Simmel as an embodiment of this political indeterminacy. First, his prowar philosophy contributed to the annexation of Nietzsche's legacy by the radical right. Second, his prowar invocations of Nietzsche retained a radical content. Third, Simmel inspired the antiwar philosophy of the neo-Nietzschean avant-garde. This contribution, sorely underappreciated in the historiographies of Nietzsche's reception, will be discussed in the next chapter. To explain Simmel's polyvalent legacy, then, one must place him within a cultural force field with more or less defined boundaries without, however, assuming a cultural totality. Simmel wrote: "The entirety of the world and life, as it is recognizable to us, is lived and is presented as a fragment. . . . The entirety is only a piece, only the piece can be an entirety."[21] The context of our examination of war culture is a fragmentary whole: Simmel's spiritual politics.

This chapter is structured by the complimentary assertions that for decades fascism has dominated the horizon of European historiography and that the historiography of the culture of Wilhelmine society has been viewed from within this horizon.[22] Certainly, this historiographical inclination is just as understandable as the Enlightenment being refracted through the experiential lens of the French Revolution. But we must admit that such perspectival refractions have interpretive consequences. The reception of Wilhelmine culture through the telescope of German fascism has until now meant a general inability to see Simmel's contribution to the left-wing avant-garde. Rather than seeing Simmel's towering legacy working itself out from fin-de-siècle to the culture of war, German intellectual history has been read as a stream leading into the river of fascism. This is unfortunate. Simmel's influence, among other things, was a watershed in the development of counterculteral politics, and here I am thinking of the formative role it played in the lives and intellectual development of Kurt Hiller, Helene Stöcker, Georg Lukács, and Ernst Bloch, to name a few avant-gardists.

Within the historiography of twentieth-century German history, one finds an inclination to associate religion, spirituality, and mysticism solely with the German Right. This historiographical tendency has two internal sources in German culture. The first source is obviously German fascism itself, which came to dominate the linguistic-political force field of spirituality (*Geistigkeit*) in the Weimar Republic. The second source is the secular Left. Before and after the Great War, most left-wing critiques of capitalism and bourgeois culture were absent a spiritual appeal of a certain kind. German socialism, in contrast to utopian socialism, followed Marx in vilifying both Christian anarchism and other spiritual renditions of socialism. Working-class politics were described in secular terms. Despite these secular inclinations, socialist culture did, nonetheless, possess a spiritual logic. This took two different forms, the first being the spiritualization of equality. Equality is more or less a secular term, but within socialist culture it carried an emotional charge that, with varying intensities, affected racial, sexual, and class hierarchies. Secondly, one might say that socialism rested upon a spiritualization of the species, the ecstatic consciousness of species-being. Still, it is very important that in Wilhelmine society and Weimar, this socialist spirit was expressed in decidedly secular terms. Social Democrats (SPD) and members of the newly formed German Communist Party (KPD) were a part of the same anticlerical struggle for moral authority and cultural hegemony that is manifest in the split between avant-garde and church culture. German socialists did not simply negate what Freud calls "oceanic experience" and what William James refers to as the "varieties of religious experience," but they did fail to develop an immanent and positive critique of Germany's spiritual cultures. The historiography of the Wilhelmine German left has, therefore, and with few exceptions, naturally emphasized the secular debates and schisms within the socialist movement.[23] What is marginalized by the historiography of mass movements of the left is the history of the spiritually inclined left whose intellectual godfather was Georg Simmel.

An absence of liberal thought and liberal institutions—i.e., the war socialism of military dictatorship—defined the mentalité of Germany's war culture. Revolutionary socialists like Clara Zetkin drew upon the tradition of socialist pacifism in criticizing the war as a manifestation of greed, profiteering, and capitalist economics in general. Zetkin and other pre-Gramscian Marxists did not treat culture as the primary realm of political struggle. As we know, their elemental realm of politics was economic; culture simply veiled and refracted economic realities. In contrast to her revolutionary analysis, this study emphasizes the fact that the war was culturally, if not economically, characterized by the eradication of economic liberalism. The war intensified the preexisting antiliberal tendencies of bourgeois hegemony in Germany.[24] Despite the validity of the socialist critique of German militarism and economic liberalism, this type of Marxist critique did not and cannot adequately explain the popular appeal of war cultures like those of the First World War and Nazi Germany. In Germany during the First World War, the radical left's critique of economic liberalism was simply one example of the antiliberal mentalité. Similar cultural critiques of economic liberalism and the nearly universal acceptance of political illiberalism during the war, be they conscious or unconscious renderings, had no inherent political color. In fact, during the Great War, laissez-faire conceptions of the self and ideas of a liberal open society were rejected from left to right. The successful description of a cultural structure of war, then, will depend on this study's ability to narrate the complex and multiple political positions that share this common mentalité.

A major component of this mentalité was a religious-instinctual sensibility. The outbreak of war induced the experiential realization of Germany's militarist affections. However, the rapturous sensibility that accompanied the outbreak of the war was conditioned by Germany's historical unconscious, namely, its prewar militarist cultural elements. Although it is unusual to talk about the political structure of a feeling, the affective superstructure of Germany's war culture was both religious and instinctual in content.[25] Despite its noticeable absence in William James's *The Varieties of Religious Experience*, war is a sublime religious experience of the first order. The great German historian, Heinrich von Trietschke, opined in the cultural wake of Prussia's victory in 1871:

> War is elevating because the individual disappears before the great conception of the state. The devotion of members of a community to each other is nowhere so splendidly conspicuous as in war. Modern wars are not waged for the sake of goods and resources. *What is a stake is the sublime moral good of national honor*.[26]

Kant described the sublime as a feeling that combines euphoria and angst. The sublime feeling, in this case the exalted spiritual threshold that accompanied the mobilization for the First World War, confounds representation because it combines two feelings that seem logically incongruous: terror and joy. The experiential complexity of sublime pleasure functions subliminally, like an instinct. Thomas Mann, for instance, not only referred to the intellectual turmoil caused by the war as a loss of the "self-evident and unconscious" basis of culture but to his patriotism as deriving from "cloudy instincts."[27] In an antiwar essay entitled "Humanity," Helene Stöcker likewise concluded that "our new knowledges will be realized in opposition to the old instincts and feelings of the majority."[28]

In his public essays against American imperialism, James stressed the need to develop a feeling that could replace what he called "the instinct for war."[29] James's concept of a war instinct is particularly suitable for understanding Germany in 1914 for two historical reasons. First, the United States was formed through a wave of successful wars against England, Spain, Mexico, and native Americans. Similarly, German nationalism was formed around an affirmative war history: Protestant resistance to Rome,

Blücher's defeat of Napoleon, the wars of the 1860's, Sedan, and Prussian hegemony. Second, James began to theorize about the "instinct for war" in the late 1890s when the United States was moving beyond its national borders in imperialist forays. Germany's entry into World War I was tied similarly to a new imperialist politics and to a cultural instinct for war that had been fortified and fed by a series of military successes. It is important to recognize that the concept of an instinct for war derives from the belief that military success imprints itself on a culture. The instinct for war is not, then, an essentialist presupposition about an immutable German character. It is an argument about the historical construction of a hegemonic culture of militarism. In both the American and German cases, economic success and the emergence of a populist racism combined with a series of military successes to buttress an existing instinct for war.

What makes the First World War a much more significant cultural event for Germany than for the United States is obvious. Germany lost the war and was faced with redefining its national instincts. Germany's death toll was comparatively much larger than that of the United States and the war effort itself more total. After August 1914, the sublimity of war gave way to other realities: cultural self-doubt and a social crisis of revolutionary proportions. Put succinctly, the reevaluation of German culture was called forth by the realities of a revolutionary defeat.

This reevaluation entailed the destruction and refashioning of Germany's spiritual-political unconscious. August 1914 was the transubstantiation of German war instincts. Germany's entry into the war meant that the emphasis on individual redemption found in Judeo-Christian culture was augmented and perhaps superseded by the zealous collective redemption of the nation. The sheer magnitude and inclusiveness of this feeling distinguished it from the prewar culture of war. Certainly there are numerous cultural forces that contributed to the Wagnerian jubilation accompanying Germany's entry into the war. The Junker class ethos, the memory of Sedan, the institutional and cultural prominence of the Germany military, the patriarchal vision of men as warriors, social Darwinian ideologies of racial superiority, the pedagogical socialization for war, and groups like the Imperial League Against Social Democracy and the All German League all contributed to a prewar culture of war.[30] In Germany's intellectual culture we also find various manifestations of a war mentality. We can think of Max Weber and the so-called navy professors (*Flottenprofessoren*) with their staunch support for German imperialism: colonial expansion, a large navy, and a new world politics for Germany. Theobald von Bethmann Hollweg, Germany's prime minister during the war, was motivated by Nietzsche's injunction to defeat inferiors.[31] In a word, major elements of prewar German society conceived of war as politically legitimate and culturally productive. Perhaps the most famous defense of the legitimacy and necessity of war was

General Friedrich von Bernhardi's *Germany and the Next War* (1912) which was published in the wake of the Moroccan Crisis. In addition to lauding the "creative and purifying power" of war, General Bernhardi maintained that "war is not merely a necessary element in the life of nations, but an indispensable factor of culture, in which a true civilized nation finds the highest expression of strength and vitality."[32] Bernhardismus, the idea that war is a legitimate means of politics, highlights the fact that the culture of war was not independent of its prewar determinants.[33]

Nonetheless, it is the contention of this study that the cultural realities of the Great War were quite different from their institutional and ideological precursors. First of all, the prewar culture of war obviously was not enveloped by the possibility and reality of death. To that extent, it is not comparable to the emotional intensity of Great War culture, a culture of life and death. The culture of the Great War represents a shift in the meaning of the "prewar culture of war," and this points to the fact that the cultural precursors of war are not timeless entities. Secondly, in attempting to define the culture of war further, it might be helpful to draw upon the thought of a contemporary of the period, Walter Benjamin. Benjamin contended that "experience is indeed a matter of tradition, in collective experience as well as private life. It is . . . a convergence in memory of accumulated and frequently unconscious data."[34] This contention can be revised with respect to the culture of the Great War. The experience of everyday life during this total war was, in comparison to peacetime society, more consciously a ubiquitous social experience. Minute and previously unconscious aspects of daily life, like going to buy bread, became activities existentially integrated into the social fabric of war.

A WAR OF SPIRITUAL DECISIONS: THE CULTURE OF MOBILIZATION

> *I am conscious of the historical moment in the most robust way, because the conditions under which the Timeless is realized have been completely altered. . . . This opening will reveal a totally new relationship between the realm of ideas and reality. For me, this is the most colossal shock.*
>
> Georg Simmel, September 1914[35]

Simmel was shocked and elated by the outbreak of war. He optimistically regarded the war as a cultural bridge linking his uncompromising critique of monetary culture to popular culture. His wartime writings—particularly those about Mammonism—were, then, very much a continuation of his antibourgeois sensibilities. However, his intellectual reputation was immediately transformed. Yes, his support for the war was *implicitly* radical. But subtle distinctions become less significant during periods of war. Alas, in August 1914, the question concerning one's support or opposition to the war superseded individualized meanings ascribed to prowar pronouncements. Simmel sided with the status quo speaking publically in support of the conflict. "German life has been cleansed of cynicism," Simmel wrote optimistically in November 1914.[36] He further described the war as the spiritual reconciliation of all tensions between the individual and the German nation.

His national socialism, so to speak, broke with key elements of his neo-Nietzschean sociology. In essence, a philosophy of *homo duplex*, ethical freedom via critique of the status quo, had become *homo monopole*.[37] In the culture of war, he rejected his own nonconformist doctrine of "aristocratic differentiation and distance."[38] Distance from tradition was now unnecessary because the war had removed all of the tensions between the civic-minded individual and existing social institutions.

> This inner transformation [resulting from the outbreak of hostilities] has attached itself first of all to a new connection between the individual and the whole nation. . . . You have only one existence in which the most individual and most general combine at every point in a life unity. That the mechanical separation between the two has disappeared is one of the greatest benefits of this great moment, and it once again renders us capable of feeling the organic character of our nature (*Wesen*). . . . In every thought and every feeling a transindividual feeling has sprouted . . . like a sublime social doctrine.[39]

Simmel, then, cherished the outbreak of war as a total reconciliation of the productive tensions in his prewar civic philosophy. Prior to 1914, he philosophized under the general proposition that freely willed social responsibility demanded distance from convention. Without countercultural distance from the naturalized claims of tradition, the individual would mindlessly and slavishly follow habituated values. Habituation is the death of ethics; for the a priori of ethics is choice. Prior to the war, this line of thinking had been the bedrock of Simmel's thought.

In the first stage of his wartime empirical phenomenology, Simmel jettisoned this core element of his countercultural philosophy. His nationalistic response to the war farcically reproduced the conservative reconciliation of the individual and the state whose classic statement was found in Hegel's political phenomenology of the spirit.[40] Simmel even parroted Hegelian language in affirming war culture as "the turn of the world spirit to a new thought."[41] His spirited ratification of the euphoric feeling of mass nationalism totally displaced the philosophy of noble nonconformity. Since the early 1890s, his thought had been structured by the sociological conception of an ethical tension between the individual and societal laws. In August 1914, this long-standing element of his thought ceased to exist. Germany's most recalcitrant academic outsider became a nationalist insider.

Simmel's conservative reaction exemplified the response of most German academics. Like nearly all of the German professoriat, Simmel adapted himself to the task of winning the war.[42] Shortly after the mutual declarations of war, he expressed his nationalistic sentiments to a friend:

> I love Germany just as one loves a person and lends his entire physical and material support to him, and just as one would be unable to tolerate this person's ruination. Such love has nothing to do with the rational "idea," rather it exists on a totally different level. It is an absolute fact of being whose particular measure of stability is only comparable to moral law as Kant and Fichte imagined it.[43]

Much of the existing literature has neglected to consider Simmel's nationalistic espousal of war. His enthusiasm might best be seen under the historiographical panoply of "Ideas of 1914": a devotion to the nation that, like the sublime itself, derived from a feeling that, when brought to conception, exceeded rationality and was experienced as moral law. Johann Plenge, who helped to popularize the nomenclature of "the Ideas of 1914," styled mobilization as the key moment of the "history of political spirit" (*die Geschichte des politischen Geistes*).[44] Taking a page from his book, perhaps the only way to understand the prowar intensity and depth of feeling is to conceive of prowar declarations by intellectuals as the formulation of a religious conviction. Roland Stromberg has deftly described mass prowar declarations as a pseudoreligious revolt of the intellect aspiring to collective redemption by war.[45] Emil Lederer asserted that mobilization had transformed Germany from a secular society to a religious community (from a *Gesellschaft* to a *Gemeinschaft*).[46] To many Europeans, it felt as though the modern alienation and cynicism of the individual had been superseded in favor of the collective intimacy of war.

This transformation was a revolutionary experience. Mobilization initiated what Ernst Troeltsch called "a war of spirit and character . . . [which] marks nothing less than a spiritual revolution [*geistige Revolution*]. . . . In this moment, the ideas of 1914 sprout in us and with us." He added that this "revolution of the entire society" was "no theory"; it was a "secure certainty."[47] The outbreak of war essentially obliterated the culture of doubt that accompanied modernity. Mobilization was political rapture. This was true for those opposed to the war as well. Antiwar intellectuals countered the conservative politicization of spirit with a spiritual politics of their own. They conceived of themselves as "spiritual workers" championing an antiwar "spiritual international" (*geistige Internationale*).[48]

The outbreak of war was more than a spiritual quest for a new religious community. Mobilization produced a democratic political feeling that all were equal. The feeling of egalitarianism was the natural consequence of everyone now sharing the same collective goal of winning the war. All citizens were equal in their subordination to this collective goal.

> As never before, thousands and hundreds of thousands felt what they should have felt in peace time, that they belonged together. . . . Each person was called upon to cast his infinitesimal self into the glowing mass, there to be purified of all selfishness. All differences of class, rank, and language were flooded over at that moment by the rushing feeling of fraternity.[49]

This reminiscence of the novelist Stefan Zweig was echoed in the retrospections of the author Robert Musil who recalled the war as a unifying "religious experience" and as a way of life facilitating the "transcendence of selfishness."[50] These recollections indicate the utopian character of August 1914. It was experienced as an egalitarian resolution to the bourgeois ills of atomization, avarice, and class division. The war was an illiberal horizon. The mantra of economic liberalism (that self-interest is synonymous with social virtue) and its political counterpart—the assertion of particular interests at the expense of the social whole—were rejected almost universally. Intellectuals from left to right experienced the culture of war as a critique of bourgeois self-interest. The war was as a crucible within which a new spirituality—that spurned individualism, the chaos of competitive laissez-faire, social fragmentation, and old social categories—would be forged.

In the culture of war, the division between the public and the private that regulated everyday life in bourgeois civil society was, if not completely uprooted, tremendously condensed. The experience of everyday life during this total war was, in comparison to peacetime society, more consciously a ubiquitous social experience. Previously unconscious aspects of daily life became integrated into the social fabric of war. One historian of the period described the effects of this condensation for women:

> Women's embodied experiences of war, revolution, and demobilization—hunger, stealing, striking, demonstrating, and birthing or aborting—opened the way for the transformations of consciousness and subjectivities. The erosion of civil society and the escalated policing by the pronatalist military dictatorship of the spheres of work, consumption, and sexuality meant that women experienced their bodies as sites of intensified intervention and regulation (and perhaps also as political weapons) during war and demobilization.[51]

It seems that periods of cultural emergency convert the feminist truism—that the personal is political—from an activist strategy to a political and social reality. But in its effects, the most important being an omnipresent ethical or civic intensity, this condensation was not limited to women. It expressed itself in the seeming evaporation of class differences and party antagonisms, in the censorship of speech and print, and in such social programs as compulsory savings plans. Thus, Simmel's prowar response to mobilization must be seen as an inscription of this social reality, a reality in which the longings of the individual were subsumed fully within the collective spirit.

WAR AS AN ABSOLUTE SITUATION

Simmel aptly described the horizon of war as a form of imprisonment. The culture of war was "an absolute situation" that demanded "an absolute decision": "we are imprisoned by an idea."[52] War culture imprisoned a whole generation of intellectuals within the idea of social responsibility. This imprisonment was also an expression of perfect freedom. As though the realization of a Hegelian dream, spiritual and political issues now were synthesized in citizens devoted to the mutual recognition of collective desires. The political primacy of obligation demanded a life and death decision about one's social soul. Stated succinctly, Great War culture was a existential atmosphere that intensified social conceptions of the self. Ludwig Rubiner's philosophy of "with-others" (*Mitmensch*) and Martin Heidegger's notion of "with-world" (*Mitwelt*) are examples of how the culture of war initiated a philosophical transfiguration of German intellectual life toward a radical cultural critique of bourgeois philosophy. Rubiner's philosophy was linked to Bolshevik politics and Heidegger's eventually to Nazi politics. An understanding of these political differences should not obfuscate the degree to which both were essentially different realizations of a shared cultural force field. Both grew from the same soil of Great War culture and were unified in their object of critique: liberal individualism. The self-interested individual was dislodged from the center of philosophy, and the trickle-down theory of social morality, central to economic liberalism, was uprooted. While in clock-maker capitalism the activity of individual avarice was said to be *consequently* a social ethics, the culture of the Great War was circumscribed by a rejection of economic self-interest as a socially acceptable ethics. The war-self was *immediately* and consciously, not speculatively and consequently, a social-self. The consequential view of ethics that predominated in the prewar culture of economic individualism was supplanted by the presence of an "absolute situation." From the trenches to the lack of food on the home front, life was experienced as immediately social and integrative, and this omnipresent element of daily life revealed the fallacy of a capitalist world view.

Total war was an absolute situation in the sense that the self was immediately and unconditionally social.[53] Consequently, the outbreak of war and the decision to support or oppose the war concentrated mental energies on the meaning of decisions themselves.[54] The war gave birth to an existential culture of the deed. The ascension of existential philosophy during the war was not so much a break with Wilhelmine culture as it was the legitimization of the previously marginal avant-garde philosophy of life. In his *Philosophy of the Deed* (1914), the philosophic modernist, Theodor Lessing, identified Simmel's philosophy as the highest dictum of a decisionist philosophy of life.[55] In the culture of war, existential philosophies of life became prominent because they were best suited to articulate the omnipresent life and death decisions of individuals in the clutches of total war. This was particularly true in the cases of Simmel, Kurt Hiller, Georg Lukács, and Carl Schmitt.

We need to emphasize that the historiography of German intellectual history often has undervalued the degree to which the growth of both reactionary modernism and left modernism were fertilized in the fields of war.[56] Existential illiberalism was politically undecidable and was the elemental metaphysics of both left and right politics. Since we will deal extensively with its left manifestations in the next chapter, we will pause here to reflect upon its right manifestation in the work of Carl Schmitt. The major war text of Carl Schmitt, who was a legal scholar and professor in Kiel, was *Political Romanticism* (1918). The subject of this text alone shows the significance of the politics of spirituality during the war. In fact, it was Schmitt's only major text that deals with aesthetic politics. The text is significant not only because it was one of the primary documents of the existential culture of the Great War. It is also a clear example of the fact that those whom Schmitt called decisionists participated in the same cultural sphere in at least one thematic sense: they were opposed to bourgeois materialism. This antipathy for the bourgeois was a form of cultural anticapitalism. We see this spiritual anticapitalism expressed in Simmel's critique of mammonism and the culture of money. Hiller's journal, *Das Ziel*, was likewise filled with vituperative attacks on "the bourgeois type" (*bürgerlicher Typus*).[57] Schmitt's *Political Romanticism* was a variation on this theme. His critique, however, was directed at romantic contemplation, which he identified as the central character of bourgeois culture. Romantic aesthetics and romantic spirituality, he argued, rested upon a type of contemplative irony that never realized itself in a political or referential decision. Schmitt wrote in the introduction to the text: "Only in an individualistic, unresolved society could the aesthetic producing subject transfer the intellectual center into itself; only in a bourgeois world, which isolates the individual in the intellectual life, does the individual refer to itself."[58] Schmitt goes on to refer to the romantic sensibility as a private priesthood in the cathedral of personality. Essentially, his text was a critique of the bourgeois type as romantic spirit. Additionally, the text was a critique of both revolutionary and reactionary romanticism. In place of these two expressions of the romantic *Geist,* Schmitt endorsed the spiritualization of realist politics. In *Political Romanticism,* his philosophy of spiritual realism was expressed in the concept of decision (*Entscheidung*). In *Political Theology* (1922) he would develop the complimentary concept, decisionism (*Decisionismus*). This later became the legal basis of his defense of Hitler's dictatorship.

For his part, Simmel, too, was elated that the war had created a cultural atmosphere that would destroy bourgeois conceptions of the self. But, if illiberal convictions were a defining horizon of war experience, war culture was far from monolithic. The war would call forth a multitude of collectivisms. The culture of war on the home front was a force field of competing collectivisms. Christian nationalism was the most fundamental. It could call on a variety of arguments based on compelling ideas like history, theology, tradition, race, and language. But scores of rival collective conceptions competed for political legitimacy: the war socialism of the army, the socialist nationalism of the SPD, the internationalist socialism of Clara Zetkin, the Christian socialism of Max Scheler and Paul Tillich, the Nietzschean socialism of the *Aktivisten*, the decisionist socialism of Carl Schmitt, the biological socialism of Oswald Spengler, the spiritualist socialism of Rudolf Eucken, and so on. The psychological and economic crises of total war, in essence, legitimized the cry for social cooperation and called forth a plethora of intellectual renderings of illiberal culture. The decisive question was: what kind of illiberalism would shape Germany's future?

STAGE ONE: A WAR AGAINST MAMMONISM

> *No one can serve two masters. Either he will hate the one and love the other, or he will be devoted to one and despise the other. You cannot serve God and mammon.*
>
> Mathew 6:24, Luke 16:13

Far too often historians fail to resist the tendency to view societies—even those in the institutional vice grips of total war—as simply totalitarian. Totalitarian interpretations of history have always been accompanied by an extremely static understanding of power. It is the supposition of this study that all political regimes and circumstances of cultural hegemony create possibilities for cultural expression at the same time that they exclude others. Economic egoism, individualism, internationalism, and pacifism were cultural doctrines that were delegitimzed in the collective atmosphere of August 1914. However, in a Foucauldian sense, the war was also a regime of cultural power which enabled "others" to play their part in shaping prowar culture. This was true of Simmel. The culture of war enabled him to present his critique of monetary culture and the Church in a public forum. He was transformed from a well-known academic intellectual to a public philosopher.[59] In Wilhelmine public culture, Simmel often felt it necessary to suppress or stealthily express his political values by publishing anonymously. His exhilaration at the outbreak of war was not simply a mindless nationalism. It was a mindful recognition that his most cherished political critiques now had a public space. War culture was an atmosphere hospitable to his longstanding ethical repudiation of liberal values.

Simmel expressed his support for the war in a new philosophical critique of "mammonism." His critique of mammonism was a fascinating, complex, and affirmative spiritualization of war socialism, and this critique initiated the first stage of his empirical phenomenology. In late 1914 he gave lectures in Strasbourg, Heidelberg, and Berlin in support of the war. Referring to his reception in Berlin, he wrote Rickert in January 1914: "In a Germany wrestling with naked existence, the interest in philosophy at this time (my lectures were jam-packed) is astonishing and considerable."[60] (This astonishment resulted from an underestimation of his public reputation among students as Germany's greatest critical interpreter of culture.) Later the text of those lectures was published under the title "Germany's Inner Transformation." As the title suggests, Simmel transposed the crisis of the war into a crisis of the human soul; social conflict was translated into a spiritual and cultural question. This transposition was, one might say, the psychological equivalent of Hans Wehler and Fritz Fischer's historiographical emphasis on *innere Politik*. Simmel's creative intervention in the shaping of prowar culture focused almost exclusively on the inner or spiritual meaning of the war.

> The undifferentiated idea of a radically different Germany than the Germany that went into this war, will come about from it. What it possesses of weight and vital meaning the youth cannot completely feel at its depth. They have too little of a past. . . . For the older generation, however, whose life has been formed in the epoch since1870, there is an inestimably wide abyss between the past and the future. We stand before this abyss as if before a decision: one more time to create a life on the basis of new presuppositions and in a new atmosphere or, if we do not have the strength to do so, to become like a useless vestige of the past and be ruined in disorientation.[61]

The war was not defined as external aggression so much as a cultural shock to Germany's existential/instinctual soul, and this measureless shock was not caused by an immediate political or military danger, according to Simmel. The shock was the result of the recognition of the huge preexisting gulf between collective human nature (now made self-conscious via the war) and the spiritual depravity of prewar individualism. Few recognized the depth of this cultural crevasse until it became a broad breach during the war.

Although a specie of political conservatism, the culture of war paradoxically contained countercultural sensibilities that were welcoming to Simmel's critique of modern culture. As a consequence of the war, Simmel reasoned, monetary individualism had been supplanted by a social self that was imbued with a new social purpose, a new sense of responsibility, and a new social metaphysics. "We all seek and collectively hope for a new humanity. . . . The meaning of this feeling has to do with the fact that . . . this war has torn open gates that otherwise probably would have remained closed for a long time."[62] War culture was a door in a dual sense. The war was the grand opening of a new classless culture within a capitalist economy: "With the war, our *Volk* has finally become a unity and a whole."[63] It seemed as though the social fragmentation accompanying industrial capitalism and consumer culture had simply disappeared under the cultural omnipresence of national spirituality. Secondly, war culture was also an opening for Simmel personally. The anticapitalist nature of war culture had exposed the nation to the civic fallacy of economic individualism and to the necessity of a social ethics, or so it seemed to Simmel. This meant that public culture finally was hospitable to Simmel's antibourgeois social theory.

Simmel, however, did not express his critique of economic individualism and monetary culture in the secular language of academic sociology, as he had prior to the war, but in the Judeo-Christian language of "mammonism." This religious language bespoke a cultural commandment of war. War culture demanded an inner language and a language of emotional intensity. Religious language is Western culture's primary discourse of life and death, and the life and death realities of the Great War marked the religious language of spirit (*Geist*) as the predominant discursive force field of war. In order to criticize the debasing spiritual influence of monetary culture, Simmel drew upon a theological metaphor, knowing full well that the Christian denominations in Germany had consistently buttressed the spiritual depravity of Wilhelmine culture.

> In the previous years a phenomenon has gained the upper hand. I will call it mammonism. I do not mean that which is apparently unavoidable for every cultural condition and which is no longer barbaric: money, the means for almost every desire-performance of humanity, the absolute means which germinates into a final value and an end in itself. Mammonism is, however, always a form of subjective desire and a psychological abbreviation of practical functionality. Hence, mammonism also denotes an increase in the so-called objective and metaphysical realms: the worship of money and the monetary value of things have become totally unconnected to practicality and personal desire. Because they never present themselves in pure isolation, one must explain such a phe-

> nomenon with paradoxical piquancy in order to make it recognizable inside of the chaos of the soul. Just as the truly pious pray to their god, not only because they want or hope for something from him, . . . so the mammonist venerates money and holds the monetary consequence of all actions, so to speak selflessly, in pure reverence. . . . In our great cities, this transcendent development of the golden calf and the idealism of monetary values has become endemic. This appears to me to be a more refined and profound danger than all those more materialistic and more avaricious accompanying shadows of the money economy. Our great threat was not the immediate materialism, rather that it transplants itself into all kinds of ethical, aesthetic, and political ideologies.[64]

The war was such an intense experience that even this great critic of theological reifications expounded his cultural ethics in religious language.

Two things must be recognized about Simmel's support for the war. First, his support was a case of conservative empowerment. The war was a context of political empowerment wherein Simmel, the public intellectual, sought to institutionalize his critique of monetary culture. The illiberal milieu enabled Simmel to publically denounce the cultural norms of the commercial bourgeoisie without appearing as a proselyte of Marxist internationalism. Consequently, Simmel was no longer a critic on the margins with an exogenous appraisal of Kaiser capitalism. He embraced the prowar status quo and bored from within. While he proved to be an extreme nationalist who threw the full weight of his formidable intellectual powers behind the prowar status quo, his prowar pronouncements of 1914 were a case of political indeterminacy. His philosophy of mammonism was simultaneously a conservative defense of German militarism and an anticapitalist transposition of the implications of nationalistic Christian dogma. Second, the interpretive reduction of his support for the war to a derivative of the "Ideas of 1914" would be a naive reification of intellectual history.[65] Indeed, his complex response to the sublimity of August 1914 calls into question most intellectual histories of this period. His response to the war indicates that support or opposition to war is a facile basis for evaluating the political meaning of the "Ideas of 1914." In each case, historians must ask about the content of these nationalist ideas. Simmel used prowar religious discourse to denounce capitalist culture. Religious language was a discursive strategy of immanent or conservative empowerment.

In other respects, Simmel's advocacy for the war was an obvious reversal of his countercultural philosophy. In the first phase of Simmel's reaction to the war his strategy of conservative empowerment was mobilized at a cost to his Nietzschean sociology. He no longer defined moral individual resistance to social institutions as the preface of ethics. Prior to the war, he opined:

> Ethics are robbed of their deepest and most precise meaning as soon as they are conceived as a type of sociology. The behavior of the soul in itself and toward itself does not commence at all in its external relationships; the religious movements of the soul serve only its own salvation or damnation; its devotion to the objective values of knowledge, beauty, and the significance of all things stands beyond all connections to other people.[66]

A taste for tradition robs the ethical banquet of life of its spiritual flavor. This view of ethics found in *Sociology* was turned on its head in his *Religion*, wherein religious values were evaluated from a sociological view of ethics. In any case, the strict, if reversible, analytic tension between the individuated soul and the sociological realm was jettisoned in the ethical atmosphere of the war. Simmel's civic ethics of war now insipidly postulated that conflicts between the ethical individual and traditional values were resolved. The tension of extremes, which gave his sociology its critical power and ethical poignancy, had given way to a public philosophy that denied the necessity and legitimacy of social critique.

The outbreak of the First World War was not an intersection of the creative soul and objective spirit but the historical right-of-way of social determinism. In this case, the relationship of the ethical soul to itself *did* commence with the external relations of August 1914. This determinism was not total. Simmel's philosophy of mammonism was an example of the creative avenues opened by the confined causeways of power. But it is very important that Simmel found it necessary to express his critique of monetary culture from within a tradition, Christianity, which his Nietzschean philosophy had so consistently and thoroughly rejected. His initial reaction to the war eliminated the Nietzschean legitimacy of an ethical opposition to tradition. Nietzsche's conception of values, the self-creation of the ethical soul independent of and in opposition to society, could not withstand the pressure to define the self through and within existing society. We might say that the Nietzschean conception of the self carried residues of negative freedom, a conception of freedom that Simmel correctly, if too hopefully, interpreted as being banished by the genesis of war culture. In the culture of 1914, few negative conceptions of the self withstood the pressure to formulate an ethics that was integrative and consciously positive. Simmel, Wilhelmine Germany's nonconformist hero, was no exception.

STAGE TWO: AMERICANIZATION AND DOUBT

1914 was, for those who supported the war, a spiritual renewal which reversed the decadences of prewar culture. Gone were the countercultural contradictions between the aesthetic avant-garde and social convention.

> Our life suffers under the contradiction between a materialistic culture and an aesthetic conduct. . . . We knew long ago that we were ill and were ripe for a recovery which we now desire greatly from the crisis of war. . . . If we are certain of a type of general spiritual result of the war, it is this: an innumerable number of us are now living on the basis of that which is essential.[67]

The crisis of war nurtured a collective feeling that life was now authentic. This authenticity meant not that individual and civic morals were harmonized, as they had not been prior to the war. This was not the stoic harmony of idle chatter. The ethical summons of war required political engagement. For Simmel and many academics, this demanded the voluntary transformation of their intellectual pursuits to meet the obligations of total war. Entangled in the intensifying effects of nationalism and militarism, conformity became a generational spirit. A prowar frenzy initiated the unfolding intellectual stages of war culture and is treated here as an empirical determination of culture. In this case, social determinism does not refer solely to cultural hegemony. Rather, it is important to keep in mind the psychological meaning of hegemony. It was not experienced as a restraint on freedom but as a cultural constraint that produced a positive and integrative feeling of liberation. Prowar culture was hegemonic but not monolithic. German citizens faced difficult and limited choices and most enthusiastically embraced a senseless war. The intense heat of historical determinism, however, does not absolve prowar Germans of responsibility for creating a polarized world—"Germans" versus "our enemies"—which removed the enemy from a community of ethical obligation. Still, the collective behavior of human beings is complex. Even where there is shared action, there is also differentiated psychological meaning. Perhaps there is no monolithic explanation for collective behavior. Nonetheless, among intellectuals, and probably the general population as well, we can identify general trends. August 1914 was experienced widely and naively as the commencement of a new chapter in the glorious history of human progress. Faced with a war atmosphere shrill with the intensity of a religious revival, most Germans, like most Europeans, chose not to break ranks with their countrymen and adopt overtly nonconformist behavior.

The second stage of Simmel's empirical phenomenology, vertiginous despair, followed very quickly after this general enthusiasm. His somber mood about the realities of war was an emotional reversal of the euphoric spirit of 1914. But this second stage was also a continuation and intensification of his nationalist critique of economic liberalism. The outbreak of war had purged Germany of mammonist defilement, he reasoned. Mammonism was an exclusively foreign cultural substance. Simmel, in effect, came to justify German militarism by projecting his image of mammonist impurity upon the enemy. His critique of mammonism, for instance, was formulated as a critique of Americanism:[68] "The most horrible thing imaginable is that this suicide of Europe initiates an act of world history in favor of America."[69] For Simmel, America was the historical realization of his greatest social fear: the world-historical hegemony of economic individualism and spiritless materialism. The rise of America symbolized the slave revolt of products and consumer culture as the trajectory of world history. Americanization was not a new concept, however. It had been central to his earliest formulations about money as a symbol of world history and bourgeois cultural domination. In "Money and Modern Culture" (1896), an adumbration of *The Philosophy of Money*, his cultural sensibilities chafed against the "Americanization of our era."[70] In a variation on a theme, his *Sociology* associated the United States with the brutality of a culture purely motivated by money and with misuses of civic power that result from a society in the clutches of corporate domination.[71] These images of mammonization—half ghastly prophecy and half dehumanizing stereotype—were a cultural reserve that Simmel called up and mobilized on the cultural front. His critique of the spiritless monetary dominant was projected not only upon the United States but England as well. In an article published anonymously in the *Frankfurter Zeitung* in March 1915, Simmel wrote that the war had "unleashed England's hunger for gold."[72] In this manner, his critical commentary on capitalism was used to demonize Germany's enemies. He produced cultural ammunition for a war requiring that national adversaries be removed from the human community of compassion.

Conversely, Simmel's reduction of the enemy to a mere manifestation of monetary decadence was accompanied by a renewed critique of German society. His prewar writings often anatomized the German status quo with clinical precision. His ambitious sociology despatched the perpetrators of Kaiser capitalism in the language of moral revulsion. This political stance was redirected toward Germany's enemies in 1914. However, by 1916, his public writings no longer read like an apologia for German militarism. Public reports of mass deaths transformed Simmel's wartime civic consciousness. He found cultural space for a renewed social critique of German society within the network of militarist ideology—in this case through the category of patriotism.

In two 1915 essays—"Money and Food" and "The Reevaluation of Values: A Word about the Wealthy"—he maintained that it was his patriotic duty to pass judgement on the class character of consumption on the home front.[73] The second essay began with a Nietzschean phrase. However, its critical logic did not refer to existential self-creation in opposition to convention as had been the case in his Nietzschean sociology. Simmel argued that the scarcity of food on the home front evidenced the need to reevaluate capitalist forms of distribution. The basis of this reevaluation was not Nietzschean subjectivity but a new material determination of culture:

> We are returning in a certain sense to the natural economy. Perhaps this will have its most profound consequences for us in that *the present scarcity of foodstuffs has broken the spiritual and absolute sovereignty of money*; the meaning of objects themselves will once again determine our value-consciousness.[74]

Simmel's naturalization of the war economy as a return to a precapitalist "natural economy" is an example of romantic anticapitalism that was rare in his oeuvre. Nonetheless, Simmel's mind was still set in a key critical of the sonorous sonics of bourgeois hegemony. He drew the conclusion that the scarcity of food necessitated a war on the home front, a war on the inequality of consumption. The war on the Eastern and Western fronts was not enough. A third front must be opened within Germany with battle lines ready to assault the economic privileges of the wealthy. Simmel put forth two plans of attack: the immediate implementation of price controls and an egalitarian *Volks*-consumption. In essence, Simmel had transformed the war against external enemies into a war against internal enemies. Here we simply note, once again, that Simmel found conservative theaters for staging his dramatic countercultural ideas. Was this ongoing countercultural drama perceptible through the heavy curtains of Simmel's prowar proclamations, or did the crude facts of total war displace such criticisms from the main stage of history?

We can only speculate about the reception of Simmel's war writings. However, we know that his critical commentaries were no longer expressed in the language of hope by 1915, and this, above all else, distinguishes the second stage of his empirical phenomenology from the first. In July 1915, Simmel wrote Rickert: "In my case, great and beautiful hopes were buried in Flanders."[75] Due to Strasbourg's close proximity to the front, government officials converted many of the buildings of the university into hospitals. Simmel, then, was presented with the consequences of war in the most direct way. His hopes were not so much buried in Flanders as they were drowned in the continuous stream of injured soldiers and corpses filling the former lecture halls of the university. The consequences of a prowar decision were literally laid before his German soul. In the euphoric temporality of 1914, Simmel was engulfed by cultural optimism.

> All material values are now merely the pure superstructure over the most profound spiritual and ideal decisions and decisiveness. Germany's economic willingness to sacrifice is nothing other than that these values place themselves in that hierarchy of precedence.[76]

War culture had established civic conscience as a base determining a new superstructure of antimammonist material values. However, when this essay appeared in 1917 as part of *The War and Spiritual Decisions*, a footnote was amended to the declaration above.

> This comment has been understood as an optimistic deception. It does not mean that mammonism should be regarded as overcome, rather that a certain or uncertain number of people, whose being mammonism has not yet poisoned, have been awakened from their mindless obedience. Through war profiteering and excessive demands, the preceding war years exposed the presence of hoarding and methods of evading war taxes. Hence, one cannot speak of a general overcoming of mammonism. In contrast to this, the war has also revealed what one can call its metaphysical achievement: it is the great separation of light and darkness, on the one hand, and the noble-minded and the vulgar, on the other.[77]

It was obviously his own "optimistic deception" and "mindless obedience" that Simmel was indirectly referencing. The brutalities of battle had broken his war fever. Pessimistic about the war's general impact on culture, he was now cast back on an old formulation: Nietzschean anticapitalism. Knowledge of the realities of war plunged him into the well of an old philosophical tension between the ethically elevated noble individual and dominant values of the vulgar herd. Initially the war was celebrated as a revolutionary resolution to the tension between the individual and society. This feeling of ethical unity with the German *Volk* had vanished by 1915. He now conceived of his antimammonist values as those of a countercultural elite. As a member of this elite, he envisioned himself in a struggle with the monetary herd mentality which still gripped most Germans.

The reintroduction of a Nietzschean anthropology was a radical revision of his prowar strategy of cultural empowerment. In "Germany's Inner Transformation," he used Judeo-Christian language to promote an antimammonist culture. This creative foray, however, contained neither a critique of the Christian herd nor a defense of the noble-minded Nietzschean iconoclast. In his essay "Become Who You Are" (1915), these elements returned but in a new form. Simmel de-emphasized his critique of economic liberalism in favor of a critique of Christianity.

> A realization of that which is spiritually decisive . . . appears in preparation in the religious sphere. In this sphere, however, the realized decision in the depth of the German spirit [*Geist*], i.e., in the depth of the collective and the individual, is still completely in the dark about its substance. . . . The determination with which the German people has gone its own way for three quarters of a century, will hopefully radiate further into this sphere of fundamental spiritual decisions. Nowhere, however, is this determination faced with such a "putrid peace" as in the religious sphere.[78]

The decisiveness of war culture was spiritually preferable to a "putrid peace" because it revealed the spiritual emptiness of traditional religion. Traditional religion kept Germans in the dark about the fundamental nature of spiritual decisions. Simmel portrayed this revelation as the spiritual telos of "the will of the *Volk*." Nietzsche's axiomatic assertion that the individual cannot develop ethically without renouncing the self-evident authority of traditional religion was thereby transformed into a national, as opposed to a merely individual, necessity. It should be kept in mind that this reintroduction of Nietzsche's philosophy of life differed from Nietzsche's social disposition in one significant way. In Nietzsche's case, philosophical individualism tended to reproduce the fundamental characteristic of bourgeois civil society: the separation of the private and public. The private sphere of self-willed ethics does not pertain, except polemically, to the public, and the aesthetic individual rarely displays a reintegrative energy. Conversely, Simmel's return to Nietzsche, animated by the war, expressed a reintegrative energy. Nietzschean sociology was prescribed as a new national civics.

Other war writings reflected the civic resuscitation of Nietzsche's critique of metaphysics and conservative social institutions. In "The Conflict of Modern Culture," he wrote that the "existing religious forms of the religious inner-life" should be "broken through" and "rejected."[79] Denunciations of mammonism and traditional religion were construed as the extraordinary flowering of a new ethic of struggle. "The true prescription of life is struggle in the absolute sense, which is comprehended as the relative contrast of struggle and peace . . . [struggle] is absolute freedom. This remains the divine secret."[80] Simmel's concept of moral struggle had multiple contents. Prior to the war it was the foundation of his Nietzschean sociology. During the war, the primacy of struggle between individual and herd was displaced by a focus on a cultural struggle between Germany and its mammoniacal enemies. To a great extent Simmel's support for the war (or opposition to peace) was a specie of cultural ethnocentrism. It was a self-affirmation, a self-confirmation of "German" philosophical genius. The ontology of ethical struggle was an element of the German philosophical tradition which, during the war, was transmuted into a chauvinistic campaign for cultural hegemony. Furthermore, Simmel celebrated the war because he interpreted it as revealing the truth of his sociological critique of monetary mentalities and ethical complacency. The war was experienced as a call to arms against the mammonization of world history. In this manner, Simmel transposed the war from a question of political differences—the war was beyond political parties and national distinctions—to an exclusively spiritual question about Europe's future.[81]

Simmel's prowar politics were extremely ambiguous. His essays of war were simultaneously a critique of dominant culture—mammonism and traditional religion—and a conservative, nationalistic, and affirmative spiritualization of war. The fulcrum of this political indeterminacy was the metaphysics of struggle. Was the war a struggle against France, Russia, England, and the United States? Or was it a struggle against the commercialization of world culture? From the beginning, it was both for Simmel. To evaluate the representative nature of Simmel's wartime politics we must place them within a particular subcontext of prowar culture, namely, the intellectual and professorial propagandizing of Nietzschean philosophy.

THE WAR OF NIETZSCHE: THE PROWAR PHILOSOPHIES OF SIMMEL AND MANN

> *The impression—that I stand alone among German intellectuals in my belief that the question of humanity can never be resolved politically but only soulfully and morally—is nothing more than an appearance; it rests on a deception. The legitimacy of my way of seeing and feeling has been confirmed by many expressions of the noble Geist; it remains German because it is exceedingly German.*
>
> Thomas Mann, 1918[82]

"The war of 1914 is the war of Nietzsche," Werner Sombart intoned definitively.[83] This was true in several senses. In France and England, Nietzsche became a symbol of German nationalism and militarism. One London bookstore advertised Nietzsche's works with a sign reading "The Euro-Nietzschean War. Read the devil in order to fight him the better."[84] H. L. Stewart's *Nietzsche and the Ideals of Germany* (1915) made Nietzsche responsible for Germany's immoral war and lack of Christian circumspection.[85] The equation of Nietzsche and German militarism was not merely groundless propaganda. The German military high command nurtured this connection by distributing over 150,000 copies of *Thus Spoke Zarathustra* to German troops. Furthermore, there was a dramatic increase in the sale of Nietzsche's works during the war. Save Goethe's *Faust* and the bible, *Thus Spoke Zarathustra* probably was the most popular text carried into war by German soldiers.[86] For intellectuals such as Thomas Mann, Max Scheler, Simmel, and Sombart, the Nietzschean heritage was the cultural lens clarifying perceptions of the issues of European life that gave rise to the Great War. Mann and Sombart, for example, cited Nietzsche as the great defender of German thought, and for them Nietzschean philosophy was central to carrying on a cultural war against the Western enemy. Here we witness striking similarities with Simmel's prowar conceptions. However, dissimilarities are equally striking, and we will pursue these differences in greater detail. Our fundamental observation is this: while Mann and Sombart's politicization of Nietzsche remained chauvinistic and conservative throughout the war, Simmel's initial abandonment of anti-institutional Nietzscheanism in 1914 gave way to new critical Nietzscheanism. By

1915, his nationalistic despondency was punctuated by the reintroduction of a critique of German society. He called on an ethical elite to fight residual mammonism, religious conservatism, and economic inequality in Germany.

Nietzsche's conception of an ethical elite, or nobility of spirituality, was a national anthem in the culture wars. Thomas Mann, for example, wrote, "there is a solidarity of all intellectuals [*Solidarität aller Geistigen*]. . . . This solidarity is organic. . . . It is a comradeship of nobility."[87] This intellectual aristocracy—an aristocracy of spirit rather than blood—was conceived as the cultural corps responsible for maintaining Germany's ideological supply lines. Mann not only mustered and served in this cultural war, he also unsheathed his pen and supplied German warmongers with ramparts of justification. Those ramparts were armored with Nietzschean philosophy. In fact, the mobilization of Nietzschean thought as an ideological stronghold of militarism reached its political zenith in Mann's *Reflections of an Unpolitical Man* (1918):

> The war was not necessary to teach me to see Nietzsche's Germanness. . . . The enormous manliness of his soul [*Seele*], his antifeminism, and opposition to democracy,—what could be more German? . . . Antiradicalism, stated without praise or reproach, is the specific, distinctive, and decisive characteristic or quality of the German spirit [*Geist*]; the *Volk* is indeed unliterary because it is antiradical, or to expresses the purely negative in the highest positive sense, again without praise or reproach, the *Volk* is the *Volk* of life [*Volk des Lebens*]. The concept of life—this most German, most Goethean, and in the most religious sense, conservative concept—is the one that Nietzsche imbued with a new feeling, draped with a new beauty, a new power and new holy innocence, elevated to the highest rank, and had borne to intellectual [*geistige*] dominance. Did not Georg Simmel justifiably maintain that since Nietzsche, life had become the key concept of the modern world view?[88]

Simmel's philosophy was an intellectual prism through which Wilhelmine Germany perceived the monumental legacy and significance of Nietzsche. Here Mann invoked Simmel's philosophy in his strategic construction of a distinctively German culture. In one sense, Mann's invocation of Simmel was entirely appropriate. As it was for Mann, the rhetoric of German difference founded Simmel's prowar pronouncements. In another sense, Mann's use of Simmel to justify his conception of German culture constituted a reversal of Simmel's prewar legacy. Specifically, Mann filled his concept of Germanness with meanings that were not shared by Simmel. For example, Mann defined Germanness as an enemy of feminism, socialism, and cultural radicalism. This was not the Germanness of Simmel who, for more than two decades, had publically aligned himself with feminism and socialism and who had inspired the cultural radicalism of the Expressionist, feminist, and Marxist avant-garde. While the neo-Nietzschean wartime writings of Mann and Simmel fortified militarism by ethnocentric references to German cultural distinctness, their conceptions of Germanness were politically incompatible. Stated differently, prowar Nietzscheanism had no singular meaning.

Mann's *Reflections of an Unpolitical Man*, arguably the most brilliant defense of conservatism since Edmund Burke's *Reflections on the Revolution in France*, forcefully documented the sublime intellectual atmosphere of war culture. As with Simmel, Mann repeatedly refers to the war as an experience of sublimity. This experience of sublimity was couched in Hegelian language as well: the shock of war commenced a new chapter in world history. "When the turning point of personal life accompanied the thundering turning point of history, consciousness became terrifying," revealed Mann in the introduction to his *Reflections*.[89] This terror was only one element of cultural sublimity, a feeling that defies representation because it is composed of opposites. War was simultaneously the terror of mortality and the religious pleasure of social redemption. As a consequence of the war, the community experienced spiritual unity. This social unity was not manifest in a political "social religiosity" but in the spirit of the personality, which Mann called a "metaphysical religion" and "the experience of metaphysical freedom in opposition to political freedom."[90] War culture, then, was paradoxically rendered as the unpolitical intensification of personal freedom.

Like Simmel, Mann transposed Nietzsche's countercultural individualism into a collective politics of spirituality. The war was conceived as a struggle between German (Nietzschean) ethics and Western decadence. Mann referred to Western decadence as a "spiritual [*geistige*] invasion which is possibly by far the strongest and most overpowering political invasion of the West."[91] Furthermore, Mann shared with Simmel the language of spirituality, *Geistigkeit*. Their wartime writings were suffused and circumscribed by the politically malleable discourse of spiritual culture, *geistige Kultur.* The adjective *geistig*, the concept of a German soul, and a references to a *Volk* community were prominent thematic features of their prowar pronouncements.

Generally, war culture had a similar deterministic effect on the ethical self-consciousness of Mann and Simmel. Mann's personal ruminations are therefore relevant to our construction of an empirical phenomenology of war. Mann wrote:

> I remember very well that my enthusiasm at the beginning of the war was considerable. I was driven by the belief that I had to express that which is good and weighty to myself and others. Nonetheless: what growing unrest, what homesickness for *freedom of delimitation*, what torment from the enormous obeisance and disorganization of all discourse, what gnawing

> grief about the lost months, and years! But when the possibility of standing-back, letting-be, and making-of-yourself-from-it has passed, then "perseverance" becomes more an economic than a moral imperative—even when in these cases the will to completion is something absolutely heroic, when "becoming complete" is unthinkable.[92]

The significance of this passage is twofold. First, we see unfolding mental stages that were very similar to Simmel's: the sublimity of 1914 followed by an abyssal soul-searching for a new completion. Secondly, we see that this was a completion that Mann felt would never come. Nonetheless, the longing for this completion was the emotive unconscious of *Reflections*, and the magnitude of this task demanded nearly 600 turgid pages of spirit-wrenching prose. Similarly, in "The Idea of Europe" (1915), which was his formulation of a supranational Germanness, and in his letters, Simmel increasingly expressed his pessimism: "My inner agitation has found no abreaction that can endure the external movement of fate."[93] Simmel and Mann did attempt to reconcile their prowar nationalism with the idea of a future Europe. Generally, such conceptions were thoroughly ethnocentric, however. Simmel's search for a supranational abreaction of pessimism, for instance, was framed by his description of the war as "the reawakened voice of the blood."[94] The transfusion of Nietzschean thought was prescribed as a German basis for a supranational postwar Europe.

There were, however, significant differences between the prowar pronouncements of Mann and Simmel, and here we witness the necessary differentiation of the "Ideas of 1914." By 1915, Simmel desisted from mindlessly fusillading the architecture of the enemy. In the windows of the enemy he also recognized the countenance of traditional German institutions.

> The war will not create a new religion. However this shock, which in so many ways allows that which is inessential to fall away and allows naked resistance to reveal itself, has become what religion really is to the individual: something beyond superstructure and pure abrading. It is the decisiveness that we now experience everywhere in the consciousness of German nationalism. Its pure form renounces all narrow and aggressive chauvinism because it still issues forth from the precariousness of the feeling of self. It is also one of the integuments through which the process of maturity of this genuine feeling of self will grow—if not in the wars of today, then in their future consequences.[95]

If Simmel supported a German cultural imperialism, it quickly became the imperialism of religious self-doubt and the prescriptive rejection of narrow chauvinism. The war revealed the need to jettison the institutions, worldviews, and concepts of morality that structured prewar culture. This meant a critique of "cultural egoism" and a reevaluation of Germany's "historical values."[96] It also entailed a rejection of traditional religion and renewed responsibility for the creation of new civic values. According to Simmel, the war had destroyed religion and made impossible the creation of a new transcendent religion.

In contrast to Simmel's critique of German culture, Mann and Sombart's Nietzschean defense of German belligerency conservatively resisted national self-critique. Erich Heller condemns Mann as having been "caught in the paradoxical enterprise of establishing irony as a mode of ethical, even religious existence," but Heller does not analyze the affective politics of this enterprise as a reintegrative national Nietzscheanism.[97] Mann ironically justified his pronationalism by defending the consciously ironic proposition that the German modernists—Schopenhauer, Wagner, and Nietzsche—put forth an extra-German or supranational critique of bourgeois civilization and Occidental nihilism. German culture had universal validity. For Mann, the war was a continuation of the "ancient revolt of Germany" against "bourgeois democracy, in the Roman-Western sense, and *Geist*."[98] Mann went so far as ironically to describe his defense of Germany as disinterested and contrasted this aesthetic disposition to the political interests of a socialist religiosity.[99] The irony of Mann's aesthetic disinterestedness was its explicit interest in supporting conservative political institutions in German society: the military, capitalism, and the Church. These institutions actually increased their social hegemony during the war. Mann's ironic disposition was, then, deconstructionist, so to speak, in one fundamental sense. It was premised on the untenable self-deception that a disinterested aesthetics and an antipolitical politics contradicted the Western tradition; in fact, they conservatively fortified the central elements of liberal, Western culture. In Mann's case, for example, prowar Nietzscheanism was a buttress for the revived spiritual hegemony that traditional religion assumed during the war.

By 1915 Simmel had come to apply his critique of mammonism and Christian nihilism to German society itself. His recognition of the recidivism of German decadence was not obviated by his prowar and supranational defense of Germanness. Simmel's prowar Nietzscheanism thereby refused the simplistic Germany/Enemy dichotomy found in Mann's magnum opus. Simmel alone aspired to a critique of mammonism, religious nihilism, and national chauvinism within and beyond German borders. Poles apart, Mann's cultural politics participated in the conservative perpetuation of a liberal affective politics. With Mann, a rhetorical emphasis on individual free will ironically became a justification for total war. This formulation of social ethics remitted prowar Germans (who were likely prostrating their free will to the demands of tradition) from a critique of Germany's existing social institutions. Here, an ethics of negative freedom—the individual's moral freedom from determinism—can and did coalesce with support for Germany's most authoritarian and undemocratic institutions. Mann's discursive politics were, like fascist politics, a sublime hybrid of ethical individualism and collective German identities. This paradox coexisted with another. Mann used Nietzsche's self-described antibourgeois philosophy to fortify the dominance of German conservatism, including the bourgeoisie. This was most forcefully carried off through Mann's distinction between a disinterested German aesthetics and the interested politics of socialism and Western intellectuals. Of course, every disinterested position, whether apologia or disapproval, is necessarily a political stance. And generally speaking, the language of aesthetic disinterestedness has served to fortify aristocratic cultural elitism and bourgeois economic hegemony in the modern era.[100] Disinterestedness was an aesthetic world view that not only served the interests of the cultural status quo but was also an instrument of power for political conservatives. Mann's distinction between the lofty disinterested politics of war and the vulgar interests of Western civilization (which he associated with bourgeois materialism, socialism, feminism, and nihilism) recapitulated this political tradition. Thereby, the German aesthetics of individuality were contrasted to the non-German politics of cultural radicalism. The logic of this argumentation was sinister but affective: (1) aesthetic individuality, an essential characteristic delineating Germanness, was used to legitimize a wartime political regime which had suppressed individual rights, and (2) the aesthetic rational for military rivalry served to portray German socialism and feminism as an interested, and thus alien, political force. Furthermore, the language of disinterestedness was calibrated to preclude competing political claims. It was implicitly an assertion of an objective and neutral truth, in the face of which one had no free will. The discourse of disinterestedness, then, conflated German culture and the objective validity of war. Disinterestedness, the claim to being beyond politics, was the rhetorical basis for Mann's objective refusal to grant civic legitimacy not only to socialism and feminism but to any German who opposed the war.

Nonetheless, it is important to keep in mind that the conservative political function of Mann's rhetoric was overlaid with antibourgeois plating. In the collective culture of war, social hierarchies had to be hidden. This was accomplished by promoting nationalism; immense differences were encased in a cultural and political blanket that swaddled all Germans with equal warmth. Sown into the fabric of German nationalism was antibourgeois rhetoric that projected the social evils of capitalism onto Germany's enemies. This was evident in the wartime writings of Simmel and Mann. Other minds, like Sombart and Scheler, also combined an antibourgeois cultural critique with an extremely nationalist and militarist spiritual politics.[101] In this regard, one can think as well of the war writings found in Eugene Diederich's journal, *Die Tat*, and the decisionist philosophy of Carl Schmitt. Lewis Wurgaft has deftly commented that, "Beyond the political disagreements of the leftist and *völkisch* intellectuals, there existed a rich vein of shared assumptions and temperamental affinities."[102] The war was fertile ground for the growth of both *völkisch* nationalism and an aesthetic left, and their antibourgeois affinities were never stronger than during the war itself. The most significant shared assumption was not something intellectual and representable. It was the collective feeling that the war advanced personal freedom through an anti-individualist society. The culture of war—be it through impassioned consent or radical dissent—intensified the ethical and spiritual perception that bourgeois individualism was pernicious.

Both Mann and Simmel mobilized Nietzsche in an effort to illustrate the spiritual and antibourgeois nature of German culture. However, an exclusive focus on this shared strategy disguises fundamental differences between their prowar sensibilities. In Simmel's case, antibourgeois critiques were, by 1915, aimed at the heart of Germany's conservative institutions. This, above all else, was the demarcation between left and right Nietzscheanism. Unlike Mann and other right-wing Nietzscheans, Simmel and his intellectual progeny mobilized Nietzsche's critique of metaphysics and his anti-institutional rendering of freedom to demonstrate the ethical deficiencies of German institutions. Capitalist and Christian institutions were their target. Mann (as well as the fascist tradition), on the other hand, discarded Nietzsche's critique of conservative institutions and used his philosophy to bolster the status quo. While both left and right participated in the same antibourgeois discursive field, the implications of their shared language was dramatic. For Simmel, unlike Mann, Nietzsche's philosophy required a critique of existing forms of social integration in Germany. In fact, there was nothing equivalent to Simmel's critique of German economic inequality and traditional religion in other prowar politicizations of Nietzsche. Simmel was alone among prowar intellectuals in calling for a war on the home front.

STAGE THREE: THE SEARCH FOR A POSTWAR WORLD

Simmel's reflections about a postwar European culture were the mental equivalent of digging out of the trenches of forlorn inner agitation. In order to attenuate—if not eliminate—his inner agitation, it was necessary that he deal with the divisiveness of European nationalism. In this third stage of his empirical phenomenology, he sought to resolve the tension between his unrepentant identification with the "German soul" and the conception of a postwar multinational Europe. But how could his intense identification with Germany and German culture be reconciled with a multinational postwar Europe? First of all, the comprehensive pleasure of ethnocentrism had to be subjugated. This was accomplished less by Simmel than by public revelations about the scale of human devastation. The sublimity of communal war had given way to the violent metahistory of the collective tragedy. His hopes of war nationalism, like the dreams of the lumpen proletariat in a Zola novel, were pinned down by the barrage of fate: senseless slaughter, hunger on the home front, labor unrest, and the German Revolution. Very quickly, the ethical fetidness of military melee dealt a deathblow to his optimism and German ethnocentrism. The devastation of war had a particular effect on Simmel; it exposed the ideology of an integrated *Volk* as an unsustainable fiction. The gulf between higher social values and herd mentalities was still present in Germany. Again he saw himself as the member of a moral elect whose mission it was to rehabilitate Europe by denouncing mammonist institutions and slavish adherence to traditional religious values.

His vision of a postwar Europe was not, then, a prophetic vision of social reconciliation. Unlike Hegel's phenomenology of mind, Simmel's political consciousness did not promise a seamless future integration of the individual into social institutions. On the contrary, his ethical disposition legitimized civic strife. By 1918, his philosophy once again was seasoned with the flavor of a philosophy of extremes: a Nietzschean conception of individual freedom via social critique and a protosocialist demand for the creation of more egalitarian social institutions. The prescribed tension between the individual and the state was not, however, a prototypical case of bourgeois liberalism, i.e., the self-interested individual versus the state. In 1918, Simmel referred to himself as the "mortal enemy of all bourgeois sensibilities [*Bürgerlichkeit*]."[103] His strident rejection of the spiritual and ethical validity of economic self-interest, evidenced early in his association with the Naturalist counterculture, was a heartfelt conviction that he carried with him unto death. Simmel wrote shortly before his death from liver cancer in 1918 that he believed that "the horrifying epoch of the machine age and of exclusively capitalist values is drawing to an end. I believed I had beheld a new spirituality, still weak, without proper orientation, but to my eyes totally unambiguous."[104] This was about as close as he came to envisioning a future resolution to mammonism and the politics of bloodshed.

Simmel's resolute anticapitalism and Nietzschean critique of German conservatism distinguished him from most prowar intellectuals. However, it still remained inadequate for his countercultural progeny who sought institutional correlatives to antibourgeois politics. They interpreted Simmel's support for the war as a bulwark of conservatism protecting the same values and institutions that he claimed to abhor. The great limitation of Simmel's political thought was that it did not specify a linkage to future institutions. Simmel's political philosophy was a practical idealism that operated under the assumption that the ethical transformation of individuals would result in the eventual formation of a new society. As with socialist anarchism—in fact Gustav Landauer's works were great examples of a prewar spiritual left—Simmel's Nietzschean anticapitalism was mired in an affective politics of individual resistance. Simmel never developed a theory of collective agency intent on institutional transformation.[105] The emotive power of Nietzschean socialism and socialist anarchism derived from their critical purity: morality and institutions were barriers to the ethical becoming of the collective individual. While this purity was incredibly appealing to left intellectuals and tremendously beneficial for resistance to logocentric expressions of socialism, it was also a practical liability. The practical necessity of legislating a new institutional order remained in inevitable tension with the perpetual revaluation of all values. Simmel's own philosophy of decisions was ironically characterized by an unwillingness to make positive institutional decisions, for instance, to join an oppositional party or create a political movement. The heroic Dionysian artist-philosopher did not seek the institutionalization of his own values. While Simmel's sociological ethics ensured that self-created values would undergo rigorous civic scrutiny, they also ensured that the realization of these values would not transcend an ineffectual heroic individualism.

Insistence on the deontological character of countercultural values was perhaps Simmel's greatest contribution to a critical and heterogeneous socialism, but it was also, for those who wanted to do more than interpret the world, the source of his political inadequacy. Simmel's critical philosophy of culture never led him to join the SPD nor did he seek to create a cultural movement. As he wrote in *Schopenhauer and Nietzsche*, "in sharp contrast to Kant and Schopenhauer, Nietzsche does not restrict the philosopher to the task of codifying generally practiced or generally required morals; rather, he considers the philosopher as the law-giver who must advance a 'new table' of values."[106] A strategy for the institutionalization of these higher laws was absent from Simmel's work.

In Simmel's cultural politics, then, there were three tensions; the first, between the cultural elitism of the law-giver and the critic of bourgeois inegalitarianism; the second, between heroic individualism and the sociological desire for an institutional change that is probably impossible without a mass movement; and, third, between a Nietzschean philosophy that affirms inner values without concern for their social consequences and a consequential ethical sociology of interiority. A more substantial and collective politicization of Simmel's antibourgeois ethics would be undertaken by his intellectual successors. The politicization of Simmel's antibourgeois conception of culture began in the sphere of gender and reached its political zenith in the culture of war with the formation of a group calling itself the "International of Spirit." As we shall see in the next chapter, Simmel's aristocratic radicalism attained a more concrete institutional outline through his Activist heirs. But these heirs, leaders of the antiwar movement in Germany, would no longer reference their countercultural mentor. Through his support for the war, the great critic of tradition had conservatively surrendered to social fate. Simmel's support for the war rendered him persona non grata in the counterculture. While 1918 was the year of his death, his reputation among the avant-garde was laid to rest by his support for the war in 1914. His prowar activities were a self-inflicted and deadly blow to his countercultural legacy. Now his countercultural heritage would be carried on by a new avant-garde generation.

NOTES

1. Georg Simmel, "Werde, wer du bist," in *Zur Philosophie der Kunst* (Potsdam: Gustav Kiepenheuer, 1922), p. 148.

2. Hughes, *Consciousness and Society*. Simmel's omission is all the more remarkable given his significance to core elements of the narrative, namely, the theoretical critique of positivism. Conversely, Fritz Ringer notes that Simmel's "methodological views exerted a profound influence upon the subsequent development of German sociology." *The Decline of the German Mandarins: The German Academic Community, 1880–1933* (Hanover, N.H.: University Press of New England, 1969), p. 175. Klaus Lichtblau, *Kulturkrise und Soziologie um die Jahrhundertwende*. With regard to Simmel, see especially "Die Umwertung der Werte," chapter 2.

3. David Frisby, *Fragments of Modernity: Theories of Modernity in the Work of Simmel, Kracauer and Benjamin* (Cambridge, Mass.: MIT Press, 1988), p. 2.

4. In Simmel's vast historiography, there exists only one essay dedicated to his war writings. See Patrick Watier, "The War Writings of Georg Simmel," *Theory, Culture, and Society* 8 (1991): 219–33.

5. In the canonical texts of Simmel's historiography, an adequate treatment of his philosophy of war was never undertaken. In fact, much of the scholarship was woefully inadequate or down right wrong. Concerning Simmel's war essays, Peter Lawrence has written:

> [Simmel] was not, like Weber, an enthusiast of the German war effort; nor did he, like Durkheim, indulge in patriotic pamphleteering. And if we turn this into a conjectural exercise, it is not likely that, had Simmel lived longer, he would have made an academic career in a fascist state, like Michels, have been decorated by Mussolini, like Perato, or written in praise of national socialism, like Werner Sombart. . . . Simmel's condemnation of the First World War is both ethical and cultural.

Lawrence, *Georg Simmel: Sociologist and European* (New York: Barnes & Noble, 1976), p. 49. Nicholas Spykman presents an equally misleading portrait of Simmel's response to the war:

> He was a European in the best sense of the term, incapable of narrow chauvinism. . . . Simmel himself remained objective and analytical in the midst of the debacle which befell Europe.

Spykmann, *The Social Theory of Georg Simmel* (New York: Russel & Russel, 1964), pp. xxviii–xxix. In reality, Simmel was a war enthusiast. While he did no pamphleteering, he actively sought opportunities to make public speeches in favor of the war. He contributed political articles to numerous newspapers and generally sought a public role in shaping prowar culture. Furthermore, from a cultural perspective, any complex view of Simmel's political legacy must place it within the cultural force field of national socialisms. My contention is that Simmel's war writings must be treated as one contribution among many nationalist socialisms, with all of the political ambiguity that "national socialisms" implies. In this way, war culture can be understood as the common soil of Weimar's antibourgeois cultural politics. Finally, Simmel, as far as I can gather, never condemned the war. As late as 1918, he was hoping that the enemy would begin another offensive. This, he hoped, would once again galvanize the nation, which at that time was being torn apart by social strife.

In his *Sociological Impressionism: A Reassessment of Georg Simmel's Social Theory* (London: Routledge, 1992), and in *Georg Simmel*, David Frisby briefly discusses Simmel's intellectual life during the First World War, but provides no systematic interpretation of the war's effect on Simmel's social theory.

6. For an excellent example of representative biography, see Gerry Muller, *The Other God that Failed: Hans Freyer and the Deradicalization of German Conservatism* (Princeton: Princeton University Press, 1987), p. 4.

7. On the academic culture wars see Ringer, p.182; Martha Hanna, "The *Kultur* War," chapter 3 of *The Mobilization of the Intellect* (Cambridge: Harvard University Press, 1996).

8. There is a firmly established narrative of the Great War as a watershed of modern memory and modern culture. See Paul Fussell, *The Great War and Modern Memory* (New York: Oxford University Press, 1975); Modris Eksteins, *The Rights of Spring: The Great War and the Birth of the Modern Age* (Boston: Houghton Mifflin, 1989). According to Eksteins, the Great War brought modernism to the European general public. On Simmel's place in this narrative, see Harry Liebersohn, *Fate and Utopia in German Sociology*. As a consequence of the Great War, Simmel's elitist and neo-Nietzschean critique of Kaiser capitalism gave way to the mass-based anticapitalist sociology of Georg Lukács. For a revisionist view of the Great War, see Jay Winter, *Sites of Memory, Sites of Mourning: The Great War in European Cultural History* (New York: Cambridge University Press, 1995). Winter perceives the perseverance and dominance of traditional prewar culture in postwar Europe.

9. Hans-Georg Gadamer, *Truth and Method* (New York: Continuum, 1982), p. 57.

10. The notion of a generational empirical phenomenology is taken from Harold Mah, *The End of Philosophy, the Origin of "Ideology": Karl Marx and the Young Hegelians* (Berkeley: University of California Press, 1987), pp.18–19. Here, it is applied to Simmel and Thomas Mann in the culture of war.

11. Martin Jay highlights the significance of Adorno's concept of *Kraftfeld* in *Adorno* (Berkeley: University of California Press, 1984). My attempt to constitute a linguistic force field of war is based on my reading of primary texts. Secondary texts substantiate this conception. See Wolfgang J. Mommsen, "Der Geist von 1914: Das Programm eines politischen *Sonderwegs* der Deutschen," in *Nation und*

Geschichte, Über die Deutschen und die deutsche Frage (Munich: Piper, 1990), pp. 87–105; Klaus Lichtblau, "Die geistige Revolution in der Wissenschaft," in *Kulturkrise und Soziologie um die Jahrhundertwende*, pp. 420–56.

12. Roger Chartier, *The Cultural Origins of the French Revolution* (Durham: Duke University Press, 1991).

13. See Blackbourn and Eley's Introduction to *The Peculiarities of German History* (New York: Oxford University Press, 1987).

14. Blackbourn and Eley, pp. 44, 239. Also relevant to this historiographical reevaluation is Ann Taylor Allen, "German Radical Feminism and Eugenics, 1900–1908," *German Studies Review* 11 (1988): 31–56. "The story of the German radical feminists also adds to the current reassessment of the history of eugenics, which challenges previous views of this movement as merely a stage in a German *Sonderweg* culminating in National Socialism" (p. 51). One of the leading radical feminists was Helene Stöcker whose relationship to Simmel is discussed in detail in chapter 4 of this study.

15. See Walter Falk, *Der kollektive Traum vom Krieg* (Heidelberg: Carl Winter, 1977), pp. 187–95.

16. Stöcker, *Menschlichkeit, Kriegshefte des Bundes der Mutterschutz* (Berlin: Oesterheld, 1916), pp.14, 23.

17. See, for instance, Franz Pfemfert, "Die Deutschsprechung Friedrich Nietzsches," *Die Aktion: Wochenschrift für Politik, Literatur, Kunst* 5, no. 26 (1915). Simmel's influence upon literary Expressionism is discussed in the next chapter.

18. Michael Löwy, *Georg Lukács—From Romanticism to Bolshevism* (London: New Left Books, 1979).

19. Karl Hammer, *Deutsche Kriegstheologie 1870–1918* (Munich: Deutscher Taschenbuch Verlag, 1971).

20. Steven E. Aschheim, *The Nietzsche Legacy in Germany 1890–1990* (Berkeley: University of California Press, 1991); R. Hinton Thomas, *Nietzsche in German Politics and Society 1890–1918* (La Salle, Ill.: Open Court, 1983).

21. Simmel, "Aus dem nachgelassenen Tagebuche," in *Fragmente und Aufsätze*, p.10.

22. Geoff Eley's *Reshaping the German Right. Radical Nationalism and Political Change after Bismarck* (New Haven: Yale University Press, 1980) is a concerted attempt to investigate German political history from outside the historiographical teleology of fascism.

23. See, for example, Carl Schorske, *German Social Democracy, 1905–1917: The Development of the Great Schism* (Cambridge, Mass.: Harvard University Press, 1955).

24. On the antiliberal tendencies of bourgeois hegemony in Germany, see Blackbourn and Eley, *Peculiarities*.

25. The exception that proves the rule is Agnes Heller's *A Theory of Feelings*, trans. M. Fenyö (Assen: Van Gorcum, 1979).

26. Cited in Louis Snyder, ed., *Documents of German History* (New Brunswick, N.J.: Rutgers University Press, 1958), pp. 259–62.

27. Thomas Mann, *Betrachtungen eines Unpolitischen* (Frankfurt a.M.: Fischer, 1991), pp. 4, 51.

28. Stöcker, *Menschlichkeit*, p. 31.

29. James' notion of instincts distinguishes itself from Freudian psychology in its emphasis on the historical nature of the cultural unconscious. In regard to James's affective theory of anti-imperialism, see George Cotkin, *William James Public Philosopher* (Baltimore: Johns Hopkins University Press, 1990).

30. *Der Reichverband gegen die Sozialdemokratie* and *Der alldeutsche Verband* respectively.

31. Hammer, *Deutsche Kriegstheologie*, p. 39.

32. General Friedrich von Bernhardi, *Germany and the Next War* [1912] (New York: Longmans, Green & Co., 1914), pp. 14, 16.

33. See Helene Stöcker, *Lieben oder Hassen, Kriegshefte des Bundes der Mutterschutz* (Berlin: Oesterheld, 1914). She examines Bernhardismus, gender, and the spiritual consequences of war culture.

34. Walter Benjamin, *Charles Baudelaire: A Lyric Poet in the Era of High Capitalism*, trans. Harry Zohn (London: Verso, 1973), p. 110.

35. Georg Simmel to Margarete Susman, 21 September 1914, in *Für Margarete Susman: Auf gespaltenem Pfad* (Darmstadt: Erato-Presse, 1964), p. 309.

36. Cited in Watier, p. 225.

37. Regina Mahlmann, *Homo Duplex: Die Zweiheit des Menschen bei Georg Simmel* (Würzburg: Königshausen & Neumann, 1983). Mahlmann, like most interpreters of Simmel, does not analyze the impact of war culture on his thought and reputation.

38. Simmel, *Schopenhauer und Nietzsche*, p. 291.

39. Simmel, "Deutschlands innere Wandlung," in *Der Krieg und die geistigen Entscheidungen* (Munich: Duncker & Humblot, 1917), pp. 10–11.

40. "The State is the actuality of the ethical idea. . . . This supreme end has supreme right against the individual, whose supreme duty is to be a member of the state." G.W.F. Hegel, *Philosophy of the Right* (London: Oxford University Press, 1952), pp.155–56; "Frederick II may be mentioned as the ruler who inaugurated the new epoch . . . in which practical political interest attains universality, and receives an absolute sanction." G. W. F. Hegel, *The Philosophy of History* (New York: Dover, 1956), p. 441.

41. Simmel, "Deutschlands," p.13.

42. For a general overview see chapter 2 of Klaus Schwabe, *Wissenschaft und Kriegsmoral: Die deutschen Hochschullehrer und die politischen Grundfragen des Ersten Weltkrieges* (Göttingen: Musterschmidt-Verlag, 1969).

43. Georg Simmel to Margarete Susman, 21 September 1914, in *Für Margarete Susman,* p. 309.

44. Johann Plenge, *1789 und 1914: Die symbolischen Jahre in der Geschichte des politischen Geistes* (Berlin: Springer, 1916).

45. Roland Stromberg, *Redemption by War: Intellectuals and 1914* (Lawrence: Kansas University Press, 1982).

46. Emil Lederer, "Zur Soziologie des Weltkrieges," *Archiv für Sozialwissenschaft und Sozialpolitik* 39 (1915): 347–84.

47. Ernst Troeltsch, "Die Ideen von 1914" [1916] in *Deutsche Geist und Westeuropa* (Tübingen: Mohr Verlag, 1925), pp. 32–33. Also see his essay "Der Krieg und die Internationalität der geistigen Kultur" wherein he writes: "daß Kraft,

Gesundheit und Einheit des States für die Zukunftsentwicklungen wichtiger ist als alle Konsequenz logisch-wissenschaftlicher Gedankmassen" (p. 58).

48. See, for example, the manifesto "Politischer Rat geistiger Arbeiter," *Das Ziel* 4 (1920): 218–23; see also Wilhelm Herzog, "An die geistige Internationale," *Das Forum* (Oktoberhefte 1918): 1–5.

49. Stefan Zweig, *The World of Yesterday* (Lincoln: University of Nebraska Press, 1964), p. 223.

50. Cited in Watier, p. 224.

51. Kathleen Canning, "Feminist History after the Linguistic Turn: Historicizing Discourse and Experience," *Signs* 12, no. 2 (1994): 368–404. There are several excellent social histories of Germany during the Great War. See, for example, Juergen Kocka, *Klassengesellschaft im Krieg: Deutsche Sozialgeschichte, 1914–1918* (Göttingen: Vanderhoeck & Ruprecht, 1978); Ute Daniel, *The War From Within: German Working-Class Women in the First World War* (Oxford: Berg, 1997); Richard Bessel, "German Society During the First World War," chapter 1 of *Germany After the First World War* (Oxford: Claredon Press, 1993); Roger Chickering, "Imperial Germany at War, 1914–1918," in *Imperial Germany: A Historical Companion* (London: Greenwood Press, 1996), pp. 489–512.

52. Simmel, "Deutschlands," p. 20. His description of the war as "an absolute situation" appears in his letters as well.

53. This characterization of war culture may facilitate a new understanding of culture in the Weimar Republic as well. In the Weimar Republic, amid the intellectual ruins of war, the soulful *Mitmensch* bayonetted the already-disfigured heart of bourgeois philosophy. Leading intellectuals produced a cultural force field of competing illiberal philosophies. War culture was a "common" cultural constraint on the freedom of thought through which individual intellectuals created a diversity of philosophies of the social-self. This was then a freedom in and not a freedom from historical determinism. Within this determinism there was undecidability. But like the intellectual freedom that still existed within the contingencies of the Great War, undecidability itself was not free-floating. Political undecidability was circumscribed by a common cultural renunciation of bourgeois philosophy and ethics. Great War culture was to the crises of the Weimar Republic what Hegel's "Introduction" was to his *Phenomenology of Spirit*, a concise adumbration of things to come. The war introduced the fallacy of negative freedom to a whole generation, and this introduction received its highest expression in the antibourgeois philosophies of Benjamin's *Origins of German Tragic Drama* and Heidegger's *Being and Time*.

54. The antibourgeois decisionism of war culture, for example, was a preponderant element of Hiller's "Philosophy of Purpose" (1916), and Schmitt's *Political Romanticism* (1918). Hiller's philosophy of war was essentially an antiwar rendition of Simmel's Nietzschean socialism, while Schmitt's antibourgeois theory of "decisionism" became the legal basis of National Socialism.

55. Theodor Lessing, *Philosophie als Tat,* vol. 1 (Göttingen: Otto Hapke Verlag, 1914), pp. 303–43. Lessing's interpretation is illustrative of Simmel's reception by a younger generation of philosophical modernists.

56. This is true, for example, of Jeffrey Herf's *Reactionary Modernism* (Cambridge: Cambridge University Press, 1984) and Eugene Lunn's *Marxism and Modernism* (Berkeley: University of California Press, 1982).

57. See, for instance, Hans Blüher, "Der Bund der Geistigen," *Das Ziel* 1 (1916): 40–48.

58. Carl Schmitt, *Politische Romantik*, (Berlin: Duncker & Humblot, 1991), p. 24.

59. "My books are so narrow in disciplinary focus that they would only constitute dead weight for your library," Simmel wrote to a friend in 1898. While his critique of monetary culture was in print, its textual form rendered it more a dead weight than a public critique. In the lectures he delivered at the beginning of the war, Simmel expressed this critique to large audiences.

60. Georg Simmel to Heinrich Rickert, 16 January 1915, in *Buch des Dankes*, p. 113.

61. Simmel,"Deutschlands," pp. 9–10.

62. Ibid., p. 28.

63. Ibid., p. 29.

64. Ibid., pp. 14–15.

65. For a sophisticated account of the "Ideas of 1914" and German philosophers, see Hermann Lübbe, *Politische Philosophie in Deutschland*. See especially the last chapter, "Die Philosophischen Ideen von 1914," which contains not only a discussion of Simmel but other *Geist-Politiker*, such as Rudolf Eucken and Max Scheler, who fall outside the scope of this study.

66. Simmel, *Soziologie*, p. 295.

67. Simmel, "Deutschlands," p. 25.

68. See Georg Simmel, "Europa und Amerika. Eine weltgeschichtliche Betrachtung," *Berliner Tageblatt*, 4 July 1915.

69. Georg Simmel to Hermann Keyserling, 25 March 1918, in Landmann, *Das individuelle Gesetz*, p. 243. Simmel's theory of *Amerikanismus* was mentioned in one of the earliest reviews of the text. See Paul Hensel, "Eine Philosophie des Geldes," *Der Lotse 1* (1901): 722–29.

70. Georg Simmel, "Das Geld in der modernen Cultur," *Aufsätze und Abhandlungen 1894–1900*, p. 190.

71. Simmel, *Soziologie*, p. 205.

72. Georg Simmel, "Die Umwertung der Werte. Ein Wort an die Wohlhabenden," *Frankfurter Zeitung*, 5 March 1915.

73. Georg Simmel, "Geld und Nahrung," *Der Tag,* Berlin, 25 March 1915.

74. Simmel, "Die Umwertung der Werte."

75. Georg Simmel to Heinrich Rickert, 15 July 1915, in *Buch des Dankes*, p. 113.

76. Simmel, "Deutschlands," p.15.

77. Ibid., pp. 15–16, footnote 1.

78. Simmel, "Werde," pp.147–58.

79. Georg Simmel, *Der Konflikt der modernen Kultur* (Munich: Duncker & Humblot, 1919), p. 26.

80. Ibid., p. 28.

81. Simmel, "Werde," p. 146.

82. Mann, *Betrachtungen*, p. 580.

83. Werner Sombart, *Händler und Helden: Patriotische Besinnungen* (München: Duncker & Humblot, 1915), p. 53.

84. Thomas, *Nietzsche in German Politics*, p. 128.

85. Herbert Leslie Stewart, *Nietzsche and the Ideals of Modern Germany* (London: Edward Arnold, 1915).

86. See comments by Aschheim, *The Nietzsche Legacy*, p. 141.

87. Mann, *Betrachtungen*, p. 314.

88. Ibid., pp. 74–75.

89. Ibid., p. 6.

90. Ibid., pp. 45, 251, 505.

91. Ibid., p. 26.

92. Ibid., p. 6.

93. Letter to Hermann Keyserling, 25 March 1918, in Landmann, *Das individuelle Gesetz*, p. 243.

94. Simmel, "Die Idea Europa," in *Der Krieg*, p. 72.

95. Simmel, "Werde," p. 149.

96. Georg Simmel to Hermann Keyserling, 18 May 1918, in Landmann, *Das individuelle Gesetz*, pp. 245–46.

97. Eric Heller, *Thomas Mann, The Ironic German* (Cleveland: Meridian, 1961), p. 137.

98. Mann, *Betrachtungen*, pp. 46, 56–57.

99. Ibid., p. 251.

100. See "Towards a 'Vulgar' Critique of 'Pure' Critiques," in Pierre Bourdieu, *Distinotion: A Social Critique of the Judgement of Taste*, trans. Richard Nice (Cambridge: Harvard University Press, 1984).

101. On Scheler and Sombart's friendship and shared Nietzschean inspirations, see John Raphael Staube, *Max Scheler 1874–1928: An Intellectual Portrait* (New York: Free Press, 1967).

102. Lewis D. Wurgaft, *The Activists*, p. 106.

103. Simmel to Keyserling, 18 May 1918, in Landmann, *Das individuelle Gesetz*, p. 246.

104. Ibid., p. 246.

105. See Eugene Lunn, *Prophet of Community. The Romantic Socialism of Gustav Landauer* (Berkeley: University of California Press, 1973); see also Charles B. Maurer, *Call to Revolution: The Mystical Anarchism of Gustav Landauer* (Detroit: Wayne State University Press, 1971); Robert Michels, "Anarchism as Prophylactic," in *Political Parties: A Sociological Study of the Oligarchical Tendencies of Modern Democracy*, trans. Eden and Cedar Paul (New York: Free Press, 1962).

106. Simmel, *Schopenhauer und Nietzsche*, p. 301.

5
THE SUPERSESSION OF SIMMELIAN THOUGHT

Expressionism, Radical Feminism, and the International of Spiritual Workers

IN DAVID FRISBY'S WONDERFUL *FRAGMENTS OF MODERNITY*, SIEGFRIED KRAcauer and Walter Benjamin's political aesthetics are shown to be heavily indebted to Simmel's critical stance toward the new in modern society, particularly to *The Philosophy of Money*.[1] Frisby's work revolutionized the orthodox reception of Simmel as a formal sociologist by excavating his unheralded but monumental contribution to German critical and cultural theory. The narrative of German intellectual history now included an understanding of Simmel's intellectual leverage upon two of modern Europe's greatest cultural critics. Without replicating Frisby's work, this chapter stands on his wide intellectual shoulders in order to gain an even broader perspective of Simmel's sphere of influence among the political avant-garde. What Frisby's treatment substantially leaves unexamined is threefold: (1) Simmel's relationship to and influence upon the greatest modernist movement in twentieth-century German cultural history, Expressionism, (2) Simmel's philosophy as a radical theory of gender and its contribution to radical feminism and the homosexual rights movement, and (3) Simmel's transformation of Nietzschean philosophy into an anticapitalist sociology and the continuation of this legacy in Expressionism, radical feminism, Activism, and the International of Spirit. Furthermore, Frisby's distinctive assessment largely highlights Simmel's posthumous legacy. Hence, he does not account for Simmel's prodigious cultural influences during his lifetime, which is our task. Simmel's living legacy will be demonstrated by examining his pedagogical and cultural importance to Expressionist Kurt Hiller and radical feminist Helene Stöcker. Both studied with Simmel and were influenced by his avant-garde philosophy of life.

Of paramount importance was Simmel's repute as an avant-garde thinker who championed the cultural elitism of Nietzsche. Simmel, in essence, was the prism through which Nietzsche's legacy was refracted into a broad spectrum of cultural politics. Stöcker and Hiller are among the brightest rays. Although uninterested in the actual reception of Nietzsche by Simmel, Bruce Detwiler's concept of "aristocratic radicalism" is a precise description of the unapologetic elitism of the Dionysian artist-philosopher.[2] Our task is the reconstruction of Simmel's unique reception of aristocratic radicalism and its transmission to the Wilhelmine avant-garde. Simmel's transcription of Nietzschean individualism into a sociological and civic philosophy of life no doubt initiated a different Nietzschean legacy than Detwiler is able to theorize by simply speculating on Nietzsche's potential political meaning. In particular, while Nietzsche loathed socialism throughout his life, Simmel affirmed many of its ethical goals. But this ethical affirmation existed side by side in his works with an elitist self-conception that was typical of the avant-garde and incompatible with the egalitarian socialism of Social Democracy. Simmel's hybrid of Nietzscheanism and anticapitalism was particularly appealing to radical middle and upper-class students at Berlin University. In Simmel's pedagogy of life, they found a philosophy that savaged the moral and economic world view of the bourgeoisie. Simmel dispensed the intellectual weaponry requisite to free nascent cultural rebels from convention. However, these students generally did not wish to surrender the sense of superiority that redounded from their class position and cultural capital. In taking up intellectual arms against bourgeois life, they did not want to identify with egalitarian socialism. Simmel's Nietzschean anticapitalism was particularly magnetic because it enabled rebellious students from the upper class to liberate themselves from the hegemony of tradition while strengthening their sense of cultural superiority to the working class. Simmel encouraged them to see themselves as a cultural and civic nobility. This self-predication not only cemented their superiority over the proletariat. It was also a cultural inversion of the traditional European aristocracy. Simmel's philosophy was an implicit polemic against both the *ancienne noblesse* of blood and the bourgeois aristocracy of wealth. He was a patrician of culture who conceived of his peerage as a meritorious royalty of spirit. Those who entered the learned orbit of the Simmel circle breathed rarified air. With Proustian clarity Margarete Susman recalled "the exclusive air" of the Simmel household.

> When I visited Simmel's house for the first time, I felt surrounded by an atmosphere that I had never known before and have never found again. . . . The great work room on the first level, with its view of the garden, was covered with expensive old Persian carpets. Paintings by great masters and many sketches by Rodin hung on the walls. Everywhere in glass cases and in the open there were vases, bowls, and exquisite Buddha figures

> from the Far East, one of which rests still today in my home. I felt strange, but wonderfully moved.[3]

This was the environment of Simmel's private lectures. But, more importantly, it was a milieu that imparted Simmel's aristocratic radicalism. According to Susman,

> The impact of his lectures, like that of his personality, was enormous. I was introduced to a totally new way of life: everything that Simmel was and occupied was an expression of the most refined culture. It was the culture of the beginning of the century which Simmel, like few others, embodied in his own way and which already a decade later in the First World War was bound to collapse.[4]

Simmel introduced students to a new philosophy of life—aristocratic radicalism. This philosophy received its grandest incarnation in the cultural politics of Hiller and Stöcker. As we shall see, however, Simmel's towering reputation within Berlin's avant-garde would be overshadowed by his justifications for war. He came to be seen as a conservative supplicant to a society he had done so much to discredit. Hiller and Stöcker's formation of such wartime organizations as the antiwar Activist League and International of Spirit was a conscious supersession of (what Georg Lukács called) Simmel's "purely mental radicalism."[5] Unquestionably, the Activist movement (and the whole swath of movements that it unified) marked the collapse of Simmel's honorific status within the historic avant-garde.

The Simmelian concept of the soul indicates the unique prewar discursive universe wherein he had an unrivaled bearing. In his philosophy, the modern soul was the locus of creative energy and individuality, and it stood in a polarized relationship to social convention. For example, in a fascinating essay on intellectual history, "Platonic and the Modern Eros," Simmel distinguished the modern concept of the soul from the Greek and Christian conceptions:

> In the course of the centuries, the idea of God needed only to lose its original power in order for the soul, so to speak, to be the lone residual . . . because the soul, as we conceive of it, is the practice of a perpetual creativity.[6]

The profound basis of Simmelian anthropology was a philosophical rejection of God and religion as absolute knowledge. These were merely historical conventions that concealed the substructure of historical reality: the ideal, spiritual realm of the soul. The soul comes to self-consciousness by abandoning the ethical authority of tradition (objectified spirituality) and realizes itself through negating action. This conception of creative action, whether aesthetic or ethical, articulated the avant-garde philosophy of life wherein originality was the superlative value. Simmel's philosophical sociology crowned this avant-garde edifice with a civic capstone. Within the Simmelian counterculture, (for Hiller and Stöcker in particular) the cult of originality was directed toward the establishment of new social institutions. The consummation of soulful creativity was, then, a unity of extremes. It satisfied the human hunger for two kinds of freedom: (1) the individual freedom of artistic inventiveness, and (2) the nonconformist freedom of social critique, which was expressed in the construction of higher notions of civic responsibility.

Simmel theorized the alternative civic spirit that could foster social transformation. His intellectual offspring, however, were far more politically active in seeking the institutionalization of unorthodox life forces. Nonetheless, like Simmel, they treated values as the base of the bourgeois superstructure, and they attacked this base. Thereby, Hiller and Stöcker greatly expanded and radicalized Simmel's critique of the bourgeois spirit, particularly in the realm of gender politics. Hiller was a leader in the homosexual rights movement and Stöcker became the most significant radical feminist of the Wilhelmine era. As titans of the cultural politics of spirit, Hiller and Stöcker created a unique brand of German critical theory whose intellectual gravity owed much to Simmel.

RADICAL PEDAGOGUE AND TEACHER OF THE ARTIST

In preceding chapters, it has been shown that there was an ethical affinity between Marxist and Simmelian critical perspectives. This overlap, I contend, goes a long way toward explaining Georg Lukács's and Ernst Bloch's relatively easy transition to Marxism and Kurt Hiller's lifelong commitment to anticapitalist politics. But the compatibility of Simmel and Marx should not blind us to an important fact of German intellectual history: it was from Simmel, not Marx, that a generation of students learned their critique of capitalism. For over a decade, Simmel was widely recognized as Berlin University's most critical social theorist. His critical sociology and antibourgeois aesthetics undoubtedly established his reputation as Germany's greatest prewar pedagogue. According to the eminent Marxist critic and former Simmel student, Georg Lukács, his mentor was the great instigator of generational nonconformity.[7] Another student voiced her admiration for Simmel's unconventional pedagogy as follows:

> The figure at the Berlin University who towered above all of the pedants and haughty people and who was most recommended by all of the revolutionary-tinged students—because of the clearly declared independence of his intellect [*Geist*]—was Georg Simmel. . . . He sought to extricate me from my bourgeois milieu.[8]

Simmel was a hydra of antibourgeois culture: he was a feminist and one of the first professors to permit women to "unofficially" attend his lectures;[9] he was a Nietzschean opposed to the Church and its ethical doctrine of universal laws; he was an academic outsider who founded the discipline of sociology; his doctrine of civic existentialism combined the nineteenth-century thought of Germany's greatest critics of bourgeois culture, Nietzsche and Marx, and this constituted a frontal assault on the moral and institutional orthodoxies of Wilhelmine society; and he was a philosophical iconoclast committed to modernist aesthetics. His was the language of the aesthetic soul, and before 1914 this language became the basis for the development of an antibourgeois cultural criticism among a generation of radically inclined upper-class students.

Fritz Ringer has noted that there was not one avowed socialist in German academia previous to the establishment of the Weimar Republic. Here we begin our analysis of Simmel's politics and intellectual significance.[10] In a strange sense, Simmel's case provides a revision of Ringer's assertion. Previous to the publication of *The Philosophy of Money*, Simmel had published anonymously his avowedly anticapitalist essay, "World Politics." After the publication of *The Philosophy of Money*, he published an extensive essay expressing his identification with socialism, but this essay was published in the American journal, *International Monthly.* It was never published in Wilhelmine Germany.[11] It seems as though Simmel was not eager to appear as a socialist sympathizer. Nonetheless, between 1897 and 1899, three times he offered a course entitled "Social Psychology with Special Consideration of Socialism."[12] This was, as far as we know, the first time that a course dealing with socialism appeared in the curriculum of Berlin University. After the publication of *The Philosophy of Money* (1900), he never taught a course with socialism in the title. The implications are clear. Given the radical conclusions of his magnum opus, he felt it prudent to distance himself from socialism. There was, then, at least one socialist sympathizer in German academia. His was not the socialism of the SPD, however. It was "lectern socialism."[13] Simmel's nonconformist politics, however, are rarely touched on in English language treatments of his sociology and intellectual fate.[14] This is a remarkable omission because his politics are central to understanding his pedagogical appeal, intellectual legacy, and inability to procure timely promotions. Ringer's research and Simmel's own circumspect identification with socialism point not only to Simmel's politically precarious position within German academia; they indicate the uniqueness of Simmel's academic presence and the rarefied nature of his pedagogy. Simmel was to the prewar generation of radical bourgeois students what Marx was to the proletariat: the intellectual fulcrum of an antibourgeois cultural circle.

In the next chapter, Simmel's remarkable influence on Western Marxism is treated in detail. This chapter spotlights the transfiguration of his countercultural pedagogy into a philosophical weapon of the German avant-garde. David Frisby's works has engaged this legacy. However, Frisby's *Sociological Impressionism: A Reassessment of Georg Simmel's Social Theory* neglects (1) Simmel's aesthetic preferences and (2) his most direct and significant contribution to European modernism.[15] In the visual arts, Simmel preferred Expressionist painting, despite its visual ugliness, to Impressionism.[16] Furthermore, Simmel's greatest impact was upon literary Expressionism which, as a movement, perceived Impressionism as politically conservative. "Impressionism is no longer written on a banner. One imagines it today as less a style than an inactive, reactive, nothing-but-aesthetic way of feeling. In opposition to Impressionism, one must affirm an ethical feeling (i.e., conviction, will, intensity, and revolution)," Hiller stated.[17] The early Expressionists saw themselves as the ethical, political, and emotive supersession of Impressionism. Simmel's contribution to the civic spirit of literary Expressionism was immense. Writing in 1920, the Expressionist, F. M. Huebner, provided this account of the origins of Expressionism:

> Georg Simmel's philosophy prepared the ground for the new [Expressionist] way of thinking. He did not create an original system; rather he created a constant skepticism toward every type of moral and epistemological doctrine of the past. He did this through his working-out of the concepts of Form, Self, and Life [*Form, Ich,* and *Leben*] which proved to be infinitely rich in instinct. And be it as a lecturer before the podium or as an author of texts, he always brought to life the material of thought in the most passionate way. He allowed the philosophical material to herald itself, and he disappeared behind the process of creative intuition. Moreover, he always placed humanity, perhaps not morally, but dynamically in the middle of the his mental functions.[18]

Huebner's historical overview remains one of the most significant accounts of Expressionist self-understanding and establishes Simmel as a cultural vein from which early Expressionist theory was mined and minted. The Expressionist writer, Emil Ludwig, recounted Simmel's cultural significance in his autobiography: "[Simmel] grew, above all other German intellectuals, to the status of the teacher of the artist."[19] Simmel was the philosopher of the Wilhelmine avant-garde.

KURT HILLER AND THE ORIGINS OF LITERARY EXPRESSIONISM

In the tradition of Karl Kraus, the publicist and lyricist Kurt Hiller was the most provocative and creative cultural critic of his generation. His biography conclusively establishes the Simmelian provenance of the Wilhelmine cultural and sexual avant-garde. Over and above this, Hiller is to Simmel what Marx was to Hegel: a political supersession. Expressionism and Activism—movements Hiller founded and publicized—symbolize the generational and political supersession of Simmel's lectern politics. Hiller was part of an avant-garde coterie that wanted to do more than critically interpret the world. They wanted to change it.

Like two other Simmel students—Ernst Bloch and Georg Lukács—Hiller was born into a wealthy family of Jewish heritage. His father and uncle owned and operated a middle-size tie factory in Berlin, and many of Hiller's relatives were successful professionals.[20] Even this cursory reference to three of Simmel's students reminds us that his intellectual influence was greatest among those who shared his class and cultural attributes. Like his renowned progeny, Simmel, too, came from a wealthy bourgeois family, and his inheritance insulated him from the financial vicissitudes of his troubled academic career. But in Hiller's case, his bourgeois class background did not shelter him from overt political activism.

While his critical acumen and aesthetic sensibilities were overtly antibourgeois, Hiller maintained cultural and political distance from the mainline socialist movement. This distance was encouraged by the elitist and antisocialist denunciation of herd mentalities found in Nietzschean philosophy, a philosophy that he, like Simmel, wholly embraced. However, Hiller's critique of Marxist socialism was conditioned by a factor unrelated to Simmel: a familial relationship to Berlin's socialist leadership. Hiller's great uncle was Paul Singer, who had belonged to the Social-Democratic Workers Party since its inception in 1869 and was a public intellectual of some renown by the turn of the century. Like August Bebel, Singer was the son of a Jewish salesman and came to Social Democracy through the struggle for political equality. For nearly twenty years, 1890–1909, Singer was chosen to be the sovereign leader of the yearly congresses of the SPD. Through the repressive Socialist Laws and despite explicit anti-Semitism among Berlin's working class, he was elected to the city's representative assembly whose Social-Democratic faction he led until his death. Singer knew Ferdinand Lassalle, worked with Karl Marx in London, was close friends with Bebel, was an acquaintance of Friedrich Engels, represented Germany at the Second International, worked with Rosa Luxemburg, and was active with Lenin in the executive of the Second International Bureau.[21] He was second only to Bebel in reputation, and his great popularity displayed itself for the last time during his funeral procession in 1911, when hundreds of thousands of Berlin's workers carried him to his grave.[22]

Thus, Hiller's repudiation of Marxist socialism was something akin to an oedipal response. Throughout his life he struggled to establish an original political reputation in the shadow of his uncle, who, he admitted, played a significant role in his life.[23] Antagonism toward his uncle's traditional Marxism denotes a generational desire for new forms of resistance. This temperament is precisely what motivated Hiller's agitation on behalf of the Expressionist and Activist movements. His critique of socialist egalitarianism proceeded from the aristocratic character of his avant-garde protest. Again, Nietzsche provided the German avant-garde with the conceptual calvary required to carry out the revolt of the "unique" against the traditional social order. While Hiller felt "like a poor person in the universe," he made a distinction between "plebeians" and literary "aristocrats" like himself, and this sentiment was at the heart of his antipathy for democratic working-class socialism.[24] In fact, one of his earliest publications included not only a critique of democracy but also a reference to Paul Singer's "conservatism."[25] Hiller claimed that Singer's egalitarian socialism conserved the leveling herd mentalities of Christianity.

If Hiller's familial relationship to socialism was more substantial than Simmel's, so was his intellectual connection to Judaism. Although the cultural influence of Judaism is addressed in detail in the next chapter, an introduction of the issue is requisite here. True, Simmel's social life was often spent in the circle of Jewish intellectuals, as Margarete Susman's memoir points out.[26] But like his parents, Simmel was baptized and eventually married in the Lutheran Church. The clearest literary link to Judaism was his text *Die Religion*, which was part of *Gesellschaft*, a series of social-psychological monographs edited by Martin Buber. In his letters, moreover, Simmel occasionally refered to his own "talmudic astuteness."[27] But his philosophy was largely untouched by Jewish concepts. This cannot be said for many of his intellectual progeny who integrated Jewish heritage into their critical thought. Walter Benjamin and Ernst Bloch, for instance, developed critical theories that were obviously indebted to Jewish theology. Nonetheless, in the eyes of his Expressionist beholders, Simmel was associated with a Jewish cultural identity. Hiller described him as one of the "most important Jews of our century."[28] In what must be one of the most revealing explications of the linkage of Jewish culture and Expressionist culture, Hiller posed the following question in *The Wisdom of Ennui*:

> Are there non-Jewish intellectuals [*Geistige*]? Should not—silence, Aryan imbeciles! silence, Semitic imbeciles!—perhaps "Jewish" and "intellectual" [*geistig*] be considered one and the same? Should "Jew" be considered not an ethnological but a characterological concept? A designation for a race which uniquely germinates between races?[29]

Jews in Germany, he continues, are the hybrid existence of an historical-philosophical idea. What is that idea? Unified diversity, otherness, impurity, namely, everything foreign, polymorphous, versatile, disharmonious, and restless. They are those in between, *das Zwischige*; their style: "stylelessness, namely—spirit [*Geist*]."[30] Jews were a characterological concept of spiritual becoming, soulful vitality, and cultural otherness that exceeds the fixity of style or form. They were spirituality beyond the law and a model of Hiller's cultural politics.

What we find in Hiller's sociological connection of Jewish and critical thought is something akin to W. E. B. Du Bois's contention that the critical insights of African Americans derives from their "double-consciousness." German Jews, like black intellectuals in America, were both inside and outside dominant culture. However, the consciousness of Hiller was not simply "double" but multiple. Like Du Bois, Hiller experienced the critical distance born of an anticapitalist disposition as well as racism, and, like James Baldwin, his critical consciousness was exponentially magnified by being a homosexual. Perhaps the most appropriate analogy can be drawn between Langston Hughes and Hiller. Both confronted the world as ethnic minorities, Leftists, and homosexuals. To this should be added the critical consciousness of a bohemian and artistic lifestyle.

Simmel's philosophy can be understood as an analogue to a Jewish double-consciousness as well. He described his philosophy as a critical "between-station" (*Zwischenstation*), a description which mirrors Hiller's depiction of the Jewish nature of Expressionist thought (*das Zwischige*).[31] The debate about the Jewish nature of Simmel's philosophy is, however, less significant than two incorruptible facts. First, Jewish members of the Expressionist movement contributed original elements of its theoretical and organizational works.[32] Secondly, Simmel had an immense impact on this generation of Jewish intellectuals. Hiller was drawn to Simmel because his philosophy facilitated the perpetuation of a class-cultural disposition of intellectual superiority while offering an iconoclastic, bohemian, liberatory, cosmopolitan, and antibourgeois style of life.[33]

Hiller's first contacts with Simmel came in 1904 when he transferred from Freiburg to Berlin University. In his two-volume autobiography, *Life Against the Times*, Hiller was unambiguous about Simmel's impact upon his philosophy: "among my philosophical teachers, Georg Simmel was undoubtedly the most important."[34] His description of Simmel's philosophical character and intellectual capacity is an indication of Simmel's stature among the Wilhelmine avant-garde.

> Simmel's ruminations were value-free, however, they were not valueless; on the contrary, his analysis of phenomena and his concepts were, by a wide margin, the most subtle that existed at the time. His analyses and concepts were incomparably more sophisticated than those of "historical materialism" and closer to life and of a richer cultural content than those of the neo-Kantians. One could imagine him as Kautsky with a Nietzsche

> interpretation or as Cohen with George propaganda; thereby one knows what separated the universal, perspicacious, and undogmatic Simmel from the others.[35]

Hiller's portrayal of Simmel as a Nietzschean socialist and as a neo-Kantian lyricist re-marks my previous characterization of his philosophy as an aporetic unity of extremes: (1) antisocialist elitism and socialist egalitarianism (Nietzsche and Kautsky), and (2) the dispassionate duty of Kant's categorical imperative and the rejection of universal laws in favor of passionate individuated ethics (neo-Kantian Hermann Cohen and neo-Nietzschean Stefan George). Moreover, Hiller's description indicates Simmel's reputation as a socialist aesthetician.[36]

No one confirms Simmel's impression on German modernism more than Kurt Hiller. Between 1904 and 1908 Hiller attended five or perhaps six semesters of Simmel seminars. During these years, Simmel gave seminars on a wide range of topics, and the titles of those seminars reveal his pedagogical matrix of ideas: "Philosophy of the Nineteenth Century from Fichte to Nietzsche"; "Social Psychology; Ethics and Social Problems; Sociology with the Consideration of Social Problems"; "Aesthetic Practices; The Fundamental Characteristics of Psychology as a Human Science"; "Introduction to Philosophy with Consideration of the Philosophy of Society and History"; "Greek Philosophy; Philosophy of Culture—especially Aesthetic and Social Culture."[37] Two things are notable about the chronology of Simmel's tutelage of Hiller. The winter-spring semester of 1906–1907 was the first time that Simmel taught his philosophy of culture course, and this critical style of cultural philosophy became the blueprint for Hiller's "*Kulturpolitik*."[38] Secondly, from 1905 until its publication in 1907, Simmel was writing *Schopenhauer and Nietzsche*. This means that Hiller studied with a Simmel, who was immersed in Nietzschean philosophy. As a result of his studies with Simmel, Hiller concluded that "Nietzsche . . . is the greatest human being of the last two thousand years."[39]

Hiller's rearticulation of Simmel's reverence for Nietzsche manifested itself most notably in the creation of the literary Expressionist movement in Berlin.[40] The unmistakable linkage between Simmel's philosophical legacy and the origins of Expressionism is confirmed by a little known but highly evidential fact of geography: the first known meeting of an Expressionist group was organized at Berlin University itself.[41] At the beginning of Winter semester 1909–1910, an announcement appeared on the blackboards of Berlin University. It proclaimed the foundation a literary group calling itself "The New Club," and it contained six citations including the following:

- Our fundamental belief is that we are efficacious beings of efficacious powers (Nietzsche).

- We live in an epoch when the people become imbeciles through diligence (O. Wilde).
- In our present age, no one should cower or give way. One must speak and be active, not in order to conquer, but to last at one's post (Goethe).
- Which amusement prepares us for life when we do not take it seriously? (Wedekind).[42]

The manifesto of the group was presented by Hiller's close friend, Erwin Loewenson, at the Club's first public meeting on November 8, 1909. In his lecture, "The Decadence of the Times and the Proclamation of the New Club," Loewenson virtually reiterated Nietzsche's devastating critique of contemporary culture. Decadence was to be criticized through a revaluation of all traditional values, and life was to be given meaning through a reconstruction of superior values, a life of self-creation.

> Decadence is everything that is averse to life, to the virtuosity of solitary strength, to adventure, to the heathen-unapologetic laugh of unrestrained corporeality and to the sensations of spirit-drunken nerves. It is also averse to all that is Christian and antiaristocratic and to that which feels Christian: Buddha, Socrates, and the Greek prophets of morality, Jesus of Nazareth and the Jewish lapse, therefore, everything in Europe that has up until now been saturated thereby: the entire system of European morality. We all groan under the mucky bonemeal of this past: that we know this and consciously fight against it, we thank for the most part Nietzsche.[43]

Other members of the Club, such as Friedrich Schulze-Maizier and Georg Heym, have acknowledged Nietzsche's centrality to the early Expressionists as well.[44] Nietzsche provided the group with a recusant philosophy of life prescribing an aesthetic relationship to ethics; it is the responsibility of a spiritual elite to create their own values. This philosophy fueled the remonstrative life and art of the avant-garde.

For our purposes, the most salient feature of this group was its relationship to Simmel. In a letter to Max Brod, dated February 2, 1910, Hiller stated that the program of the group was based on "Simmel's concept of culture."[45] Moreover, at their first spring meeting, Hiller was elected permanent president of the group. Thus, the most Simmelian member of the group, Hiller, played a crucial role in the development of literary Expressionism and German Activism. In his memoir, the Expressionist Kasimir Edschmid recalled Hiller's aggressive generalship:

> Though one is permitted to judge him as they wish from the vantage point of historical distance, Kurt Hiller cannot be removed from our conception of literary life before the Great War. The literature of preceding genera-

> tions stood groaning under the hailstorm of his slaps in the face. He administered them with such freshness, audacity, cleverness, and loathsomeness that they accurately hit their target.[46]

Hiller's pugnacious and irreverent polemics played a seminal role in emboldening the early Expressionists. But this pivotal function was derived from his unmatched sociological critique of Wilhelmine society. Hiller dominated The New Club, one scholar has commented, because

> his store of political and sociological knowledge was extensive. . . . It was especially in those areas, politics and sociology, that his impact was most strongly felt in his circle and in others. Schulze-Maizir, to cite one patent example, later recalled the leading role Hiller played in his political education.[47]

His storehouse of iconoclastic political and sociological knowledge was, as we know, stocked by his mentor Simmel.

In addition to his role in the establishment of The New Club, Hiller played a decisive part in the inception of key institutions of Expressionist culture. Most significant was his organization of the literary culture of Berlin's cafés. In 1910, Hiller and other members of The New Club began to hold readings at the Café des Westens and Café Kutsche on the Kurfürstendamm.[48] Hiller first advertised these evenings in *Die Aktion* as a "Neopantheistic Cabaret."[49] The cabaret was established "for the adventure of spirit [*Geist*]" and, through his conception of a transgressive spirituality that was beyond the law, Hiller embodied the avant-garde posture against tradition.[50] On the occasion of the first cabaret evening, the linkage between *Geist* and Nietzschean philosophy was confirmed. In the opening address, Hiller quoted Nietzsche concerning the revaluation of all values and spoke of a "new pathos."[51] Perhaps the best way to describe this pathos is as a bohemian elitism whereby the avant-garde celebrated itself as a higher form of human spirituality.

In 1911, Hiller renounced his presidency of The New Club but he continued as a proselyte of literary revolt. His cultural dynamism now displayed itself in the formation of the "GNU Literary Cabaret." As the leader of this group, he continued to organize venues for literary Expressionism. Hiller's reputation as a leading Expressionist cultural critic was also tied to his participation in two journals which are widely recognized as the founding journals of literary Expressionism, *Pan* and *Die Aktion*, established in 1910 and 1911 respectively.[52] It was an editor of *Pan*, Alfred Kerr, whom Hiller repeatedly cited as the guiding light of the movement.[53] While he considered Simmel the greatest philosopher of his generation, for Hiller Kerr was, "after Goethe, Heine, Schopenhauer, and Nietzsche, the greatest

German writer of prose."[54] Kerr, in Hiller's literary hands, resembled nothing so much as the paragon of spiritual politics; he synthesized the practices of aesthetic creation and political morality. In 1911, Hiller helped to found *Die Aktion* after he and Franz Pfemfert ended their association with another journal, *Demokraten*.[55] In contrast to the liberal and diffuse spiritual politics of Kerr, *Die Aktion* became, under the editorship of Pfemfert, an anarchistic call for an antiparliamentarian, unified German Left.

> *Die Aktion* champions the cause of a unified German Left without placing itself on the soil of a particular political party. *Die Aktion* demands the imposing organization of an "Organization of Intelligence" and assists in reestablishing the old gloss to the long tabooed word *Kulturkampf*. . . . In the context of art and literature, *Die Aktion* seeks to build a counterweight to the sad custom of the pseudoliberal press to value newer impulses purely outside the viewpoint of commerce, and to ignore this point of view completely. With complete independence from Right and Left, *Die Aktion* . . . has the ambition to be an organ of sincere radicalism.[56]

Articles often chided the leadership of the German Social Democratic Party (SPD) for their unwillingness to realize their own revolutionary goals. In his capacity as a contributing editor of *Die Aktion*, Hiller was Pfemfert's right-hand man, and he worked with the journal until 1913. Most importantly, the journal expressed the anarchistlike doctrines that framed Hiller's antibourgeois cultural career: direct action, a critique of parliamentarianism, a rejection of apolitical aesthetic intellectuality, and a (self)worship of an intellectually and morally superior leadership.[57]

Hiller's stellar éclat within Berlin's Expressionist culture waxed with the publication of two birth certificates of literary Expressionism: *Der Kondor* (1912) and *The Wisdom of Ennui* (1913). *Der Kondor*, a compendium of Expressionist writings edited by Hiller, was the first anthology of Expressionist verse ever published.[58] In its introduction, Hiller declared the text a manifesto of a new generation of artists and polemically placed the spiritual demeanor of the movement within the force field of existing spiritual institutions. The spirituality of Expressionism was contrasted to the dominant aesthetic, religious, and academic institutions of Wilhelmine culture. Expressionism was, Hiller stated pugnaciously, a "poet-secession" from the pure aestheticism of Stefan George, from religious monasticism, and from academic criticism.[59] There was a neo-Romantic sensibility in the early literary Expressionist movement. However, this was a Romantic sensibility attuned to the rhythms and sensibilities of the modern city. Literary Expressionism captured what Hiller termed "the experience of the intellectual urbanite" in contrast to the exhausted "agrarian emotions" of nineteenth-century Romanticism.[60] Early Expressionism championed and constructed an antiestablishment urban lifestyle intent on resisting the alienation of urban life with a new culture of spirituality.

The aggressive style of Expressionist titans like Hiller typically targeted the moral lassitude and cultural decadence of the dominant institutions of Wilhelmine spirituality, but this critical flurry was often extremely vague and lacking concreteness. For example, in the second volume of *Die Aktion*, Hiller expressed a philosophy that would frame his life's work. In an article entitled "Litteraturpolitik," he extolled politics as spiritual activity.

> *Politik*, in the sense of a definite type of function or definite "Form" of *Geist*, is once again acceptable [but only] in contradiction to pure concepts and the pure enjoyment of the world, and in contrast to that passivity by virtue of which men themselves become objects of appearance, victims of regulations, open only to impressions and react to them with a surrendering nature.[61]

In spite of Hiller's combative disposition, the abstruseness of his politics was a consequence of the recondite nature of its two central tenets: activism and the concept of *Geist*. The philosophy of activism and the notion of spirit (*Geist*) often lacked a positive institutional content that could to be realized. Politics was defined negatively as the opposition to existing institutions. "*Politik* as a form [of *Geist*] will be culturally rehabilitated independent from its present content."[62] The cultural appeal and political insufficiency of early Expressionism lay in the absence of a positive social content: "A direction? *Der Kondor* will not demand a direction."[63] Like anarchism, particularly the personages of Erich Mühsam and Gustav Landauer who frequented Berlin Expressionist circles, the cultural sensibility of early Expressionism relied on a negative rendering of freedom: antiauthoritarianism, anti-institutionalism, and a Nietzschean rejection of absolute truth.[64] Later in life, Hiller defined his philosophy of "pure activism . . . [as] a rigorous 'NO' to exclusive contemplation, *Schöngeisterei*, psychologism, causalism, historicism, pure form, [and] specialization."[65] In part, early Expressionism was a community of cultural rebels whose activist politics turned on negative integration, i.e., negative freedom as positive freedom.[66]

THE SIMMELIAN PROVENANCE OF LITERARY EXPRESSIONISM

The contentlessness of Hiller's Expressionism was given volume through a critique of Simmel. Hiller, it seems, felt it necessary to clarify his relation to

Simmel, who was recognized as the supreme philosopher of the German avant-garde. He did this in his seminal two-volume compendium of essays and aphorisms, *The Wisdom of Ennui*, a text that Paul Raabe calls "the first document of literary criticism of early Expressionist literature."[67] In a pivotal section entitled "Concerning Culture," Hiller explained Simmel's intellectual and soulful contribution to the Expressionist notion of *Kultur*. What makes this section of the text so important historically is that it is probably the same talk that Hiller gave at the first meeting of The New Club on November 8, 1909.[68] Along with Loewenson's "The Decadence of the Times and the Proclamation of the New Club," it was the founding document of literary Expressionism. "Concerning Culture" began:

> In the sixth and last chapter of his *Philosophy of Money*, Simmel speaks of a "Style of Life." The second section of this chapter deals with the concept of culture and the divergence of objective and subjective culture resulting from the division of labor. This is a classic piece of newer German philosophy and a jewel of spiritual intelligence [*Geistigkeit*]. One could only desire to give it a physical form in order to grasp it in a cold-aristocratic patina and place it on a bed of velvet.[69]

While *The Philosophy of Money* has occasioned diminutive regard in German intellectual history, it must now be honored as a thoughtful pedigree of Expressionist culture. Hiller was heavily influenced by various aspects of the book. He drew most fundamentally upon Simmel's distinction between subjective and objective intelligence (*Geist*).

> All culture of things is a culture of humanity, and in language, morals, political constitutions, religious doctrines, literature and technology is the work of countless generations as objectively realized spirit [*Geist*].[70]

In contrast to the predominance of objectified culture, Hiller followed Simmelian philosophy in defining Expressionism as a philosophy of subjective *Geist*, i.e., as "*subjektive Kultur*."[71] Expressionist culture thereby conceived of itself as an articulation of Simmel's epistemology. Furthermore, in Hiller's work and in the broader context of literary Expressionism, Simmel's philosophical metaphysics manifested themselves in the wholehearted integration of his philosophical lexicon; the Simmelian concepts of *Geist*, *Geistigkeit*, and *Seele* became the bedrock of the linguistic force field of Expressionist culture.[72] "*Kultur* remains," Hiller explained, "rightly a definite emotional degree of refinement of the movements and functions of a soul [*Seele*]."[73]

Hiller and the literary Expressionists gave voice to the antibourgeois sociology of *The Philosophy of Money* with its prescriptive priority on *homo noumena*. Simmel produced, according to Hiller, "a portrait of the times in which the content of culture has become an increasingly more objective intelligence."[74] Similar to Simmel, Hiller conceived of modernity as a discrepancy between "civilization" and "culture" and as "a divergence of the objectified spirit and the culture of the individual."[75] This divergence, Hiller wrote with a Simmelian reverberation, "was realized through the division of labor (in production and consumption)."[76] Hiller was captivated by Simmel's unique articulation of industrial modernization and cultural modernism. And, like Simmel, Hiller sought to remedy these social ills with a new aesthetic politics—*Kulturpolitik* as a *Form of Spiritual Intelligence*; this avant-garde politics, in Simmelian fashion, entailed a rejection of those who treat "the money belt" as a "matter of life and death."[77] The zenith of spiritual/intellectual becoming was not only a rejection of the hegemony of monetary concerns. It was, moreover, a renunciation of the "nonintellectuality of the peasant and the bourgeois."[78] Presaging Walter Benjamin, the typical bourgeois was here represented as the feuilleton or dandy lacking in intellectual earnestness.[79] Hiller criticized German "Dandyism" for seeking "the abolition of spiritual intelligence" and continued: "[the German Dandy] protests against protest, he opposes those who are opponents, and he enthusiastically despises enthusiasm."[80] Hiller ruthlessly derided and consciously rejected what he regarded as the two major characteristics of the "hypertrophic cerebral culture" of the bourgeois: moral and political passivity and aesthetic indifference. In place of emotional indifference, he announced a "moral restlessness of intensity" whereby the "whole personality is permeated in all of its expressions."[81] The defiant pathos of intensity and creative dynamism, he contended, was the essence of Nietzsche's philosophy. Here it is refashioned in the regalia of an Expressionist animus.

While Hiller theorized under the panoply of Simmel's antibourgeois turn of mind, he also came to see Simmel as a bourgeois cultural enemy.[82] We ought parenthetically to grasp this conflict as a cultural dialectic unfolding from the avant-garde's requirement for originality. Hiller's critique of Simmel is a window into the complex reception and eventual supersession of Simmelian thought within the avant-garde community. Early Expressionism was largely developed by a group of upper middle-class intellectuals who had earned doctoral degrees. Hiller was one example of a large group of university-trained intellectuals who constructed the institutional framework of Expressionism. Dr. Theodore Lessing, Dr. Friedrich Markus Huebner, Dr. S. Friedländer, Dr. Rudolf Kayser, and Dr. Kurt Hiller were just a few of the early Expressionists who either studied philosophy with Simmel in Berlin or were highly influenced by his philosophy. In fact, academically trained Ph.D.s or M.D.s dominated late Wilhelmine counterculture: Dr. Kurt Tucholsky, Dr. Kurt Pinthus, Dr. Helene Stöcker, Dr. Gustav Wyneken, Dr. Magnus Hirschfeld, and Dr. Rosa Luxemburg. With doctorate in hand, but lacking academic positions, these intellectuals began to advocate a practical relationship between radical thought and political activity. Their heterogenous advocacies set them apart from the conservative culture of the university system. This cultural dialectic—from academic training to extra- and often antiacademic politics—is central to understanding the origin of Expressionism and Hiller's place within it. In *The Wisdom of Ennui,* Hiller referred to the "spirit of the German professor-philosophy" as the "unsoulful phalanx of the exclusively conceptual, the *Hottentotten* of pure reason."[83] Similar to Marx's relationship to Hegel, Hiller conceived of himself as the practical sublation of Simmel elevating his critical philosophy to the level of countercultural reform.

The Wisdom of Ennui, arguably the foundational text of Expressionist philosophical and literary criticism, contained in its two volumes only one page of lyric; it was entitled "As a Result of Simmel's Lectures."

> The differences are illusionary;
> Is therefore the flamingo more noble than the stork?
> Sorrow-ladden I absorb in my chair
> The great analyst Georg.
>
> I sit there, in my brown vest;
> The army of objects encircles me;
> Oh, the problems are never without remains;
> The putrid smoke of indifference encircles me;
>
> What is the meaning of life? This question
> Is silly, yet it exists.
> It pricks me already for seven thousand days:
> I sit helplessly there, in torment, fatally.[84]

Hiller experienced Simmel's fatalistic pedagogy as permeated by a rotten aura of indifference and one that debased sociopolitical understanding. The inebriation of activism, characteristic of the Expressionist avant-garde, passed a death sentence on Simmel's academic passivity. In his 1910 poem "Master Dead, Dedicated to Georg Simmel," Michael Josef Eisler captured the avant-garde's love/hate relationship to their intellectual forefather.

> You come out of my life's loins,
> wherein you repose since primitive beginnings,
> you animate with tireless hands
> in my existence, in my sensibility
>
> in my brief country travels
> your picture tempts me to quietude
> I am not outside your wanderings,
> and where you tower, validates my profit

> the beautiful hours, mild glowing,
> what troubles me toward higher purposes,
> in you finds only form and query.[85]

Simmel was a touchstone of the avant-garde. His thought framed their cultural existence. However, Simmel's philosophical forms were not adequate for revolt outside of academia. For Hiller and others, Simmel's thought was a passive interpretation of the world; the point was to change it. This reception possessed a powerful textual basis in *The Philosophy of Money*. As we recall, Simmel had maintained that the indifference (*Gleichgültigkeit*) produced by monetary culture was not only fundamental to its predominance, but simultaneously facilitated the aesthetic soul's resistance to monetary culture. Indifference could free one from the soullessness of objective, consumer culture and release the creative soul.

Ironically, Hiller quoted Nietzsche's *Untimely Meditations* in his critique of Simmel's indifferent pedagogical disposition:

> Our modern education is therefore nothing that is living, . . . that means: it is actually not a real education, rather only a type of knowledge about education; it remains in the sphere of pedagogical thoughts and pedagogical feelings. It does not become an educational decision. The supposed contrast to this, that which is a real motive and a deed that obviously moves toward expression, means often nothing more than an indifferent [*gleichgültige*] convention. . . . The inner process, that is now the thing itself, it the true education.[86]

Education was, according to Nietzsche, neither obedience to a formal pedagogical technique nor self-expression in a conventional form. Nietzsche's noble pedagogy elicited this commentary from Hiller: "Education, in the contemporary sense, is nothing other than a dead, inorganic, piled-together knowledge . . . ; subjective content has no possibility of successful expression. Form alone determines values."[87] Hiller's philosophy of spiritual intelligence resembled nothing so much as Nietzsche's demand for a life of self-created subjective content expressed in an unconventional aesthetic form. This attitude meant that indifference could play no role in life or scholarship. Therefore, we might perceive Hiller's critique of Simmel as an attempt to move beyond Simmel's academic Nietzschean sociology to Nietzschean politics. This transformation required a renunciation of academic conventionality, namely, the pedagogical form through which Simmel disseminated Nietzschean understanding.

Literary Activism, a term coined by Hiller, developed in Berlin as a response to Simmel's merely academic iconoclasm. But Hiller's rejection of Simmel's sociological rendering of the indifference was not a close reading of its aporetic meaning. For Simmel, the negative character of money—its characterlessness, its aura of indifference, and its loosening of social ties—also produced positive social consequences. "Progress and stagnation can thus lie immediately adjacent to one another," commented Simmel.[88] Alongside the dispiriting emptiness of capitalist culture, there existed a possibility of filling this cultural void with "completely heterogeneous contents of life."[89] Indifference and characterlessness paradoxically provided the cultural space for a passionate and active self-creation. Hiller's new aesthetic temperament was not, then, a simple negation of Simmel's legacy. It was, rather, the preference for and mobilization of one element of Simmelian philosophy, a Nietzschean aesthetics of moral passion, against the other, Kant's indifferent and seemingly selfless ethics. Hiller's Expressionist philosophy was not really a radical break from Simmel's cultural disposition. Simmel had unified Nietzschean and Kantian philosophy to dramatize two competing subjective demands upon the individual; the first, Nietzschean demand was for a self-created ethics in opposition to monetary determinism; the second, Kantian demand was for a self-consciously social morality: hence, his anticapitalist ethics. Simmel viewed his philosophy as a synthesis of these two demands.

Hiller's "new" *Kulturpolitik* exuded a thoroughly Simmelian aroma in calling for a synthesis of creative and political culture. Through the creation of a new anthropography, "the *Eth*," Hiller elucidated the Expressionist lifestyle. This lifestyle was an historically new synthesis of aesthetics and political ethics:

> Just as the aesthetician is distinguished, as you know, from the aesthete, so is the ethicist distinguished from the *Eth*. The aesthetician is someone who pursues the science of aesthetics (he is hence used to being tasteless); the aesthete is someone who has placed the always alert intention of a sublime, untroubled pleasure at the center of his existence. The ethicist practices the science of ethics—oh, if only one existed!—and remains who he is . . . ; the *Eth* knows nothing of the possibility of Imperatives, Formal Principles. Nonetheless, he lives and weaves—in every moment of his consciousness—for an idea; struggles, suffers, bleeds; animates himself and makes himself base. The aesthete and the *Eth* constitute a cultural antinomy.[90]

In his portrait of the *Eth*, a neologism for the ethical pathos of the avant-garde, Hiller again marked the central antinomies of the Expressionist counterculture: aestheticism versus politics, passivity versus the will, formal ethics versus the self-created moral idea, indifference versus enthusiasm, and quietism versus protest. For those living under the demand for a self-created moral direction, "Good Society has no opinion."[91] Furthermore, the demand for self-creation, Hiller maintained, exposed the fallacy of the aesthetics/ethics antinomy. Ethics and aesthetics were not dichotomies but a life-synthesis. Ethics are necessarily a creative process and aesthetics an ethical process, and *Kultur* thereby meant "the synthetic refinement of the totality of spiritual existence."[92] Again, it must be remarked that Hiller's definition of culture as a "synthetic refinement" reiterated the *Lebensphilosophie* of Simmel, that is, life as a unity of extremes: nature and transcendence, self and idea, subject and object, person and cosmos, and being and becoming. In his war diary, Simmel succinctly defined this unity as a "third inexpressibility" and a "third self," and defined the relation of its opposites as an "unsolvable task . . . which commences with the outermost intensification of life."[93]

Hiller, then, was recapitulating Simmel's philosophical filigree in denying the possibility of an *intellectual* reconciliation of the antipodal realm of aesthetics and ethics. For both Hiller and Simmel, the synthesis could only be accomplished existentially through the aesthetic "will." In *The Philosophy of Money* and in *Schopenhauer and Nietzsche*, Simmel had argued that only the aesthetic will was capable of resisting the nihilism of monetary culture and synthesizing the competing demands of negative and positive freedom.[94] Likewise for Hiller, the Nietzschean concept of the "will" became the synthetic weld of aesthetics and ethics. Cultural understanding was not enough. The deed was higher still.

> The Deed—what is it? The Deed is: the thing that changes things. . . . The meaningful issue is who directs the spirits [*Geister*]. Who redirects them, who revolutionizes them, and who transforms them.[95]

Hiller's answer was the Expressionist aristocracy of *Geist*. Above all else, the emphasis on political activism distinguished Hiller from Simmel and other Nietzschean Expressionists like Salomo Friedländer.[96] While Simmel was the template through which Nietzschean philosophy was articulated to Hiller and others members of the counterculture, Hiller and the other Activists brought a heightened rhetorical commitment to culture as a political will to power.[97]

THE MASTER IS DEAD: THE HOMOSEXUAL RIGHTS MOVEMENT

Nowhere was the Activists' political will to power more pronounced than in the realm of gender politics. As we have seen, Simmel was a sophisticated theorist of gender in his own right. He had over the course of two decades published articles on such diverse topics as the sociology of chastity, the psychology of women, prostitution, militarism and the position of women, money and gender relations, and the sexual politics of the Social Democrats.[98] However, his philosophical radicalism in the realm of gender theory was superceded by his intellectual heirs. The dialectic of avant-garde culture—from Simmel's intellectual preeminence in Wilhelmine culture to the ascendancy of Activist Expressionism during the war—is nowhere more pronounced than in Hiller's transposition of Nietzschean philosophy into a politics of gender. Specifically, Simmel's feminist proclivities were unquestionably radical, but they never ventured beyond the realm of liberated heterosexuality. Hiller's gender politics, on the other hand, were directed at the hegemony of heterosexism itself.[99]

Most importantly, it was in the realm of gender politics that Hiller's Expressionist philosophy renounced a purely negative rendering of Nietzschean philosophy to propose an apollonian vision of dionysian freedom. Hiller was a prime example of Nietzsche's tremendous impact on the social history and gender politics of Wilhelmine culture. Nietzsche heralded an existential philosophy wherein the individual develops his or her erotic instincts in the process of ethical becoming. Hiller's dissertation, *The Right over Yourself* (1908), is evidence of how Nietzschean philosophy called forth a new form of scholarship. Scholarship was not, for Hiller, the search for an objective knowledge that, at best, possessed an unconscious relationship to the author. Accordingly, his dissertation grew out of a desire to legitimize his homosexuality. At the base of Hiller's critique of heterosexism was a posthumanist critique of the Enlightenment. He renounced the Enlightenment notion of scholarly objectivity and its epistemology of Natural Laws.

> The forerunners, messengers, and successors of the French Revolution founded their political and legal system on a substructure of demands, which they called "*droits de l'homme*," "fundamental rights," or "innate rights." . . . At the very least, their world view necessarily leads to the inadmissibility of a critique of positive and normative rights. And this is not only a necessity of thought, it is a fact: the more radical representatives of historicism deny that critique and norm formation are part of the tasks of the jurist, and want this science of knowledge confined to dogmatism and history. Thus they produce the present German condition, i.e., what Friedrich Nietzsche meant when he spoke of the "dispiriting influence of our present business of knowledge."[100]

Hiller recognized that the language of Natural Rights exorcised all doubt about the reasonableness of laws in the German Law Book of 1870/1. Consequently, he aspired to develop a philosophy of rights that requires the denaturalization of all so-called natural rights.

> [The critique of natural rights and the] hypostatization of fundamental demands is freedom. Here, freedom is not understood in the actual psy-

chological sense (free will), but the political sense: personal freedom and the voluntary arrangement of life. I want to be free.[101]

Hiller's critique of absolutized rights recalls Simmel's philosophical esssay on women's culture. The denaturalization of so-called natural rights is a new mode of consciousness and the origin of a new social freedoms. Simmel and Hiller generated a critical notion of freedom whose core was radical reflexivity and conceptual denaturalization. In one important sense, however, Hiller's scholastic style diverged from Simmel's cold analytics. Hiller's use of the first person "I" in his dissertation—"I want to be free"—signified a more personal and urgent relationship between his scholarship and his personal life. This existential urgency derived from the hyper self-consciousness of sexual marginalization.

Legal ethics were the central problematic of *The Right over Yourself,* which began with the question: What portion of personal freedom must be given over to the collective? The treatise contained chapters on suicide, self-mutilation, bestiality, and abortion. But its most impassioned defense of personal freedom dealt with homosexuality. The criminalization of consensual homosexuality between adults was the most important example of the unjust punishment of sexual offenses "because here the penally targeted individuals are—in contrast to incestuous individuals—quite numerous, and, in contrast to pimps, they frequently possess a high social and intellectual standing and are capable of being culturally valuable."[102] Hiller cited the socialist poet Oscar Wilde as a homosexual of high social and spiritual value. Of additional interest to Hiller were the so-called "perverse" acts that were not covered by the penal code: mutual masturbation between men, bondage, masochistic and sadistic acts between men and women, lesbianism and tribady, and solitary masturbation in all forms including necrophilia and the sexual violation of statuary. The only two forms of "perverse" sexual exchange under Article 175 of the 1870/1 Penal Code were male homosexuality (pederasty) and bestiality. "Our question," asked Hiller, "is as follows: Is the sexual exchange between persons of the male sex worthy of punishment?"[103]

In attempting to answer this question, Hiller confronted the arguments put forth by Germany's major juristic thinkers. The most common and prevalent argument against male homosexuality was the assertion that it was opposed to nature and natural law. Hiller destroyed these arguments.

> Does homosexual satisfaction actually contradict a natural law? This can only be maintained by those who have never felt a desire. Since one cannot know what kind of thing a "natural law" is, then one should avoid this and similar expressions. Following Kant's interpretation, imperatives and laws of reason must be distinguished from natural laws, which only

> deal with that which has taken place. Therefore, a deviation from a natural law is impossible, because in the same moment that something takes place which apparently contradicts an established natural law, this natural law would be revealed as incorrect; and in order to seamlessly incorporate the new appearance, humanity would have to search for a new natural law . . . "The order and regularity of appearance, which we call nature, we bring to ourselves" [Kant].[104]

Heterosexual desire cannot be considered an immanent or ontological imperative of nature, Hiller continued. The problem with those who maintain the unnaturalness of male homosexuality is that their concept of procreation reverses the teleology of thought. Procreation is projected as a universal desire without asking whether this desire is necessary or universal. Hiller contended that procreation need not be the intention nor the necessary outcome of heterosexual desire. Hence, heterosexual-procreative desire cannot be understood as the exclusive telos of affection. Clearly those who experience the primacy of homosexual desire are in the minority. This, Hiller asserted, is a fact of social psychology. However, it is the great merit of this discipline that it accepts the existence of exceptions. In this regard, he compared homosexual desire to people with red hair. The fact that red hair is less prevalent does not prove a natural law of hair color any more than the predominance of heterosexuality proves that it is a natural law of desire. Exceptions do not confirm the existence of incontrovertible laws. They simply clarify the predominance of particular regimes of desire.

Hiller painstakingly recounted numerous arguments against the legalization of homosexuality: (1) the biogenetic argument that homosexuality damaged the race, (2) the political contention that homosexuality harmed the state, (3) the psychological description of homosexuality as a pathological abnormality, and (4) the aesthetic argument that homosexuality was "dirty" and ugly. He addressed each of these arguments in turn. However, his primary focus was the contention that homosexuality was immoral. Not surprisingly, he turned to ancient Greece to contradict the contention that heterosexuality is normal and self-evident. If homosexuality is immoral then the Greeks must have been "a nation 'without morality,' and must be seen as a nation of criminals."[105] Plato's *Symposium* was cited as an example of the coexistence of homosexual love and citizenship. Moreover, Hiller was emphatic about the fact that existing juristic critiques of homosexuality had not proven the impossibility of homosexual love. From the perspective of a philosophy of rights, Hiller concluded that there was no reason to outlaw the personal freedom of male homosexuality.

In the final chapter, entitled "Morals," Hiller elaborated upon the significance of Georg Simmel's philosophy for the grand conception of the manuscript. The purpose of the study was to demonstrate the impossibility of an objective morality, and to this end he quoted Simmel's *Introduction to Moral Science*: "until now, no singular substantive ethical commandment has always and absolutely conformed to the moral consciousness of humanity."[106] This Simmelian conception of moral-cultural historicity was the controlling idea of Hiller's study. The rhetorical enemy of Hiller's historical view of morality was not onto-theological but practical, that is, it was not science or Christianity but utilitarianism. From a utilitarian perspective, morality and ethical norms are a social necessity. The problem with this view is that it tends to be used in the service of defending an existing set of ethical norms without addressing a central critical question: why should the existing ethical norm "remain the content of the Ought [*Sollen*]"? The answer, Hiller believed, was deftly provided by Simmel. Again, he quoted from Simmel's two-volume *Introduction to Moral Science*.

> It seems to me that it is the immortal merit of Georg Simmel to have demonstrated conclusively that the Ought is nothing more than a psychological function such as "wanting, hoping, knowing" which are "intermediate conditions and mediations between Not-Being and Being."—"If someone sought to maintain that they felt the absolute perfection of egoism as a moral responsibility, then we would be obliged to accept this as an incontrovertible fact just as one would the same statement concerning altruism. The Ought is such a pure formal principle that cannot refuse any content." The attempt to find a ruling principle of moral content or the attempt to demand a monism of ethical purpose will always be futile. The only thing that so-called "moral" behaviors have in common is the "good will" functioning in them. Thus, "with every individuation and perversity of purpose, the good will remains certain and fixed, just as thought remains thought, even in the case of the most abnormal and most abstruse thoughts." This is the only possibility of an ethical Monism. Kant pointed this out; Nietzsche, who was the most unsystematic of all ethicists, dimly perceived it; Stammler took this thought (also without crystal clarity) into the realm of the philosophy of rights; Simmel alone perfected this understanding of morals.[107]

Simmel's discovery (that the moral imperative was a form of good will that facilitated an infinite number of contents) framed Hiller's legal scholarship. More importantly, Hiller transposed Simmel's ethical philosophy into political activism on behalf of homosexual rights. While borrowing from Simmel's intellectual trousseau, Hiller had superceded the sexual radicalism of his mentor.

Given the limited research on Simmel's contribution to Wilhelmine culture in general, it is not surprising that his substantial influence upon Expressionist gender politics has not been explored. What is surprising is the relative dearth of interest in Hiller himself, and this despite the fact that his critique of heterosexism was an integral part of his Expressionist agit-prop. Wolfgang Paulsen is one of the only scholars who places Expressionism in a gendered context. He systematically interprets it as a generational rejection of "bourgeois family-hell."[108] However, in his section on Hiller, he says nothing about Hiller's particular contribution to Expressionist gender politics and neglects to mention his important essay "Homosexuality and German Prejudice," which appeared in *The Wisdom of Ennui*.[109] Consequently, Paulsen and many other scholars overlook this fundamental element of the Expressionists' critique of bourgeois culture. Despite the enormous amount of research on German Expressionism, this important source of Hiller's dominant stature within the movement has not been tapped. By Hiller's own admission, his unsurpassed philosophical analysis of the juristic technologies of gender contributed to his reputation as the most critical theorist of early Expressionism.[110]

Simmel was neither disgusted nor threatened by Hiller's homosexuality and engaged research. On the contrary, Simmel kindly read Hiller's doctoral work, and, unable to serve as his doctoral advisor, introduced him to Heidelberg University Professor Gustav Radbruch, under whose mentorship Hiller received his Ph.D. in Jurisprudence.[111] Why was it necessary for Hiller to transfer to Heidelberg? His professor of jurisprudence at Berlin University, Franz Liszt, had rejected his doctoral work because it reproduced the academic style of Simmel's philosophical sociology. Thus, regardless of Hiller's multiform activism, his work is inextricably linked to and indebted to Simmel.

HELENE STÖCKER: BEYOND SIMMELIAN FEMINISM

Even those scholars who integrate a discussion of gender politics into their scholarship on Expressionism fail to examine something far more significant: Simmel and Hiller's contribution to gender politics outside the Expressionist movement.[112] Hiller was close friends with both Helene Stöcker and Magnus Hirschfeld. Like Hiller, Stöcker studied philosophy with Simmel at Berlin University, although from 1896 to 1899, and brought an activist mentality to academia. She was part of the first group of women who matriculated at Berlin University when it was opened to women in 1896. Already in 1894, she was a member of the commission whose purpose was the construction of a Library of the Women's Question. In 1896, she founded the Organization Researching Women at Berlin University and presented the first public speech of the organization entitled "Friedrich Nietzsche and Women." By 1898, she was a featured speaker and officer of the left-wing Union of Progressive Women's Organizations and, by 1902, she was undertaking speaking engagements throughout Germany to solicit support for regional women's organizations. She was present in Hamburg on January 1, 1902, as a founding member of the Organization for Women's Right to Vote, which was the first women's organization in Germany to organize and lead a strike (in Crimmitschau in 1903). Eventually she became critical of the conservative leaders of the women's rights movement. She founded the League for the Protection of Mothers in 1905 and for the rest of her life in Germany served as the editor of its accompanying journals, *Mutterschutz* (1905–1907) and *Die Neue Generation* (1907–1932). Due to Stöcker's efforts between 1906 and 1909, regional organizations of the League were established in Munich, Leipzig, Stuttgart, Bremen, Hamburg, Breslau, Dresden, Freiburg, Görlitz, Liegnitz, and Mannheim, contributing to a combined membership of around 4,000 members.[113] The League's greatest institutional accomplishment was the establishment of maternity homes in Frankfurt and Berlin in 1908. These maternity homes provided unwed and mostly working-class mothers with material and psychological support. In 1911, Stöcker internationalized her work on behalf of unwed mothers and their children founding the International Union for the Protection of Mothers and Sexual Reform.

Very much in the tradition of *Lebensphilosophie*, Stöcker was dedicated to the reform of conventional morality, particularly the double standards of bourgeois morality.[114] She worked on behalf of a "New Ethic," as she called it, of maternal love that embraced all mothers and children as legitimate and affirmed the erotic life of women. She elaborated upon the League's comprehensive purpose in a 1905 letter:

> It establishes for itself the following tasks: to discuss the problem of love, marriage, friendship, parenting, and prostitution as well as all of the connected problems of morality and the entire sexual life—not only from a historical, legal, and medical perspective, but also from a social and ethical perspective. It should, through a life-affirming world view, energetically combat the existing harms and evils in this sphere. And, it should help to procure the victory of a more profound examination into the connection between the economic and spiritual [*geistigen*] factors.[115]

Her primary interest in the nexus of economics and spiritual factors brought her in close proximity to the Social Democrats who considered the Women's Question a part of larger social questions. In fact, socialists August Bebel and Lily Braun were prominent sustainers of the League. What must be resisted, however, is the natural inclination to assume that both the Social Democrats and Stöcker conceived of the larger social sphere, within which the Women's Question was articulated, in an identical fashion. A leading Stöcker scholar contends that the larger social question was the question of class conflict.[116] This contention mistakenly turns a critical affinity—interest in the cash-nexus of culture—into an identity. In the proceeding discussion, it will be argued that Stöcker was representative of the avant-garde critique of bourgeois culture typical of Simmel's philosophical sociology.

No doubt Stöcker's Nietzschean feminism was strengthened and enriched through her contacts with Simmel and Simmel's students.[117] Coincidentally, the years that she attended Berlin University correspond precisely to the period in which Simmel was most interested in feminism. Although she cited Wilhelm Dilthey as her most significant philosophical influence at Berlin University, her political understanding of his *Lebensphilosophie* was underpinned by her attendance of Simmel's lectures as well.[118] In 1899, she left Berlin University because a key member of the Philosophy Department, presumably Dilthey, refused to work with female doctoral students. This was a professorial prerogative until 1908. Simmel's subordinate academic status did not entitle him to direct doctoral projects. But, in a letter to the *Vossische Zeitung*, dated December 21, 1899, a "university teacher" anonymously protested the exclusion of Stöcker: "Rarely has such an important step in intellectual culture, such as the admission of women to the university, been accompanied by so little harm!"[119] The letter was written by Simmel.

Simmel's strident defense of the classic feminist demand for access to a university education is not proof of strong personal ties to Stöcker. Still, the traces of a mutual and cyclical intellectual, if impersonal, relationship are quite strong. Stöcker's article "Feminine Erotic" (1903) appears to be a response to Simmel's "Feminine Culture" (1902). Simmel's essay was a fascinating amalgam of a biological conception of sexual difference and a radical critique of biological determinism.

> Doubtless the physiological-sexual quality, with the immediacy of its radiating physical impulses and concomitants, is the source of the sublimest and most spiritual peculiarities of the female soul. . . . Just as the physical-sexual functions of humans gradually have constituted themselves as special organs (while in lower animals the entire body participates in propagation), thus the progressive evolution of the feeling of love will be increasingly demarcated from the residual functions of the soul. Consequently, this feeling will interfere less and less in a diversionary and tyrannical way. A particular variation of this scheme is realized in those women who have differentiated femininity, in the sense of soulful sexuality, from femininity in the sense of general physical qualities—so that the former could totally disappear without diminishing the latter.[120]

Simmel clearly elided female biology and the culture of love. But he maintained that the female nature and the female soul possessed an objective cultural meaning which could thoroughly transform society. While female culture arose from a biological source, it was not imprisoned by its source. On the contrary, it could positively threaten the dominant male/monetary culture. In female culture, Simmel located an immanent opposition to monetary culture: "specialization, which generally characterizes our professions and our culture, is thoroughly and entirely a male essence: to hone yourself to an entirely one-sided achievement, which is distinguished from the united personality."[121] The feminine principle of the erotic was thereby celebrated as cultural negation of the male principles of monetary heartlessness and the division of labor. Simmel's political prescription for the masculine character of culture was not only the rhythm of the feminine soul and feminine spiritual intelligence, however. His concerns included legal and economic equality. The political demand for economic and sexual equality, while typically subducted under the weight of an elitist vision of culture, was an integral part of Nietzschean anticapitalism.

What must be emphasized is Stöcker and Simmel's shared discursive force field. As a research assistant for Dilthey, Stöcker was schooled in *Lebensphilosophie.* Moreover, Simmel and Stöcker shared the touchstone of Nietzschean philosophy. In fact, her interest in Nietzsche preceded her matriculation at Berlin University in 1896. Her first exposure to Nietzschean philosophy seems to have been a small brochure by Ola Hanssons entitled *Nietzsche, His Personality and His System.*[122] Additional attributes were common to the Berlin avant-garde. First, her familial background was typical of other members of the political and aesthetic avant-garde. Like Simmel and most of his intellectual progeny, she came from a solidly middle-class family. Her father owned a factory that produced goods sold in the family's haberdashery in Elberfeld, Westphalen.[123] Secondly, while her earliest essays indicate a familiarity with John Stuart Mill, there was always a socialist, if anti-Marxist, element to her feminism. She was nineteen when she first encountered August Bebel's *Woman and Socialism*, and her work is peppered with the influence of socialist feminism. We also know that she studied with the anticapitalist sociologist Werner Sombart. Thirdly, like Hiller, she was a Nietzschean intellectual who sought a political meaning for Nietzsche outside of academia. In 1892 she moved to Berlin, attended a Gymnasium, and shortly thereafter began political activities among middle-class feminists. She attended Berlin University from 1896 to 1899 and in 1901 received her Doctorate in Philosophy in Bern. For the next forty years she lived and worked as a professional activist.

As was typical of early German feminism, Stöcker's feminist essays—"The Modern Woman" (1893) and "Women's Thoughts" (1894)—used motherhood ideology to promote feminism. In an immanent fashion, nineteenth-century feminists deployed elements of patriarchal ideology, in this case women's primary identity as mothers, to ameliorate the oppressive effects of inegalitarian institutions. For instance, motherhood ideology was used often to justify charitable and political activities outside the domestic sphere. Patriarchy was a discourse of power, then, that not only restrained women but also facilitated a new agency and freedom of movement. Stöcker critically redeployed conservative conceptions of women, derived from biological identities, for the purpose of creating a new culture of gender which was not sex specific. In "Women's Thoughts" (1894), Stöcker adopted an immanent strategy for reconceptualizing female sensuality.

> The new future must emanate from women. It will be the harmony of the spiritual and the physical nature of humanity, which until now has only been comprehended in art; it will thereby glorify the entire human life. Moreover, the eternal agonizing bifurcation between responsibility and personal preference, between material and spirit, and between sensuality and knowledge will disappear. If humanity has until now been split into enemy camps—man and woman, reason and sensuality—then they now will unite a new true bond of higher harmony.[124]

We have no proof of Stöcker's intellectual affect on Marie Luise Enckendorff or Simmel but the philosophical similarities are striking. The central discourse of Stöcker's strategy of empowerment was the language of love. While love was associated with feminine biology, she sought to raise this feeling to the level of a cultural concept. Love was thereby lifted up from its presumed biological origin and elevated to cultural enterprise mediated by the intellect.

Similar to Simmel, Stöcker fought for a new feminine morality which was incompatible with both the mainline feminist movement and egalitarian socialists. In "Nietzsche's Misogyny" (1901), for instance, she employed Nietzschean philosophy to promote the then novel idea that female love can and should entail sexual pleasure for women. The old ascetic morality of the church fathers saw love of the sexes as something sinful and women as something vile and impure. Conversely, Nietzsche understood that the beautiful countenance of Christian women concealed her "spiritless" disposition. Christian women are denied "the spiritualization of sensuality" which is "the most beautiful victory over the asceticism of Christianity."[125] In describing love as "spiritual sensuality" she demonstrated the synthetic character of the oppositional politics of the period; the spiritual politics of Berlin's avant-garde sought culture conceptions that unified intellect, spiritual development, and the pleasure of the body. Her spiritualization of passion transgressed Victorian morality by demanding the sensual and intellectual equality for men and women. "To be a person of higher, brighter, existence-happy culture," she implored, "this Nietzsche demands of both sexes."[126] In light of the applicability of Nietzschean philosophy to the women's movement, attempts to depict him exclusively as a misogynist were misguided, concluded Stöcker.

Typical of the Wilhelmine avant-garde, Stöcker's spiritual politics were framed by an elitist sensibility and by gendered assumptions. She conceived of love as an aristocratic doctrine that was incompatible with the mores of the status quo. Furthermore, she did not problematize patriarchal carry-overs in Nietzsche's philosophy.

> Nietzsche's ideal was explained in the following words: "Thus I want man and woman: the former fit for war and the latter fit for birth, however, both fit to dance with head and foot."[127]

Stöcker's radical agency intervened to place primacy on the third fitness: the terpsichorean talent to spiritualize sensuality. It was her cultural contribution to claim Nietzschean philosophy as the collective property of men and women. But in doing so, she retained elements of an essentialist world view. She was a cultural feminist. Her cultural production gives weight to the Foucauldian contention that the power of an institutionalized discourse does not have predetermined repressive effects. In her hands, an often misogynist Nietzschean philosophy and the patriarchal engendering of "love" became productive constraints critically reinscribed in the fight for new feminist institutions. This was, however, the productivity of a conservative empowerment which recalls the paradox of conservative radicalism found in Simmel. For example, while she sought a radical elevation of "motherhood" to the status of "intellectual [*geistige*] labor," this cultural strategy reproduced the patriarchal identities of the male warrior and the female caregiver.[128] In this sense, her feminism was both constrained and produced by the master discourse of patriarchy whose gendered suppositions she never entirely renounced.

Nonetheless, the paradoxical effect of the radical refraction of patriarchal roles and ideals through Nietzschean philosophy was a cultural politics that consciously challenged fundamental patriarchal institutions. She maintained that female love included the right to spiritual autonomy. In 1905, Stöcker founded the League for the Protection of Mothers and its corresponding journal, *Mother Shelter* [*Mutterschutz*], *Magazine for the Reform of Sexual Ethics;* she did so to provide mothers and wives with the "spiritual affirmation" that they were not receiving in the patriarchal family.[129] Her advocacy of sex education, birth control, the right to abortion, free love, sexual pleasure, homosexual rights, and defense of so-called illegitimate children was a powerful rebuke to the marital morality of Christian patriarchy and the middle class women's movement alike. At the same time, her demand for expanded freedoms was conjoined to a call for sexual responsibility.[130] On the whole, her politics inhabited the political geography of the avant-garde: in opposition to the bourgeois status quo and was predicated on a sense of cultural superiority to Marxist socialism. As a matrix of values, Stöcker's cultural politics were by far the most radical of the era.[131] They were so radical that the mainline feminist BDF refused to admit her League into their umbrella organization when she applied in 1909. She was rejected by her sisters who had no intention of endorsing such programs as homosexual rights and the legitimacy of births out of wedlock. While the discursive system of patriarchy framed Stöcker's political subjectivity, we can see that the meaning of these concepts was in no way fixed. Her zealous defense of the ideal of motherhood, for instance, was coterminous with a critique of the institution of marriage. Thereby, one patriarchal ideal served to dislodge the dispiriting effects and necessity of another.

The political indeterminacy of patriarchal discourse was, to reiterate a central contention, a result of its refraction through the discursive force field of neo-Nietzschean culture, and the political gravity of this force field was provided substantially by Simmel's philosophy. While Stöcker published Nietzschean-feminist essays previous to her matriculation at Berlin University in 1896, the essays published after her matriculation were increasingly suffused with the language of spiritual politics (*Geist-Politik*). This indicates the influence of Simmel's cultural politics in particular and *Lebensphilosophie*—Nietzsche, Stefan George, and Dilthey—in general. Stöcker worked closely with Dilthey in preparing his biography of Schleiermacher. It was Simmel, however, who provided Stöcker with a more political conception of *Lebensphilosophie*. A leading Stöcker scholar characterized Simmel's influence in the following manner: "The conceptual reflections of *Lebensphilosophie* to which she was introduced by Dilthey, she undergirded as a student of the philosopher and sociologist Georg Simmel."[132] A close reading of Stöcker's early essays registers this influence. The principle adjective of Simmel's cultural politics, *geistig*, was rare in her pre–1896 essays. Other elements of the discursive force field of the Simmel circle—such as *seelisch, die Seele*, and *das Genie* (soulful, soul, and genius)—were infrequently used in her early works but became the common coin of her linguistic politics after 1900. In "Motherhood and *geistige* Labor" (1902), for example, she spoke of "soulful motherhood" and the "genius of love."[133]

As was mentioned above, evidence of their shared cultural concerns is found in Stöcker's essay "Feminine Erotic" (1903), which appears to be a response to Simmel's "Feminine Culture" (1902).[134] However, there was a more substantial intertextual connection as evidenced by Stöcker's "The Love of Personality" (1904).

> Recently in a fine essay about women, Georg Simmel laid down the valuable acknowledgement that questions of gender are for many highly-

> placed men the earthly remains which bind them to an underdeveloped condition; with very few exceptions men are unable to rise above the perception of women as a gendered essence.[135]

Here, she further argued that women must have a poetic and spiritual content to their life which is just as strong and rich as that of men. Therefore, their relationship to men can not and should not be one of selflessness. The ethic of selflessness cripples the female soul and turns women into mere servants of men. Instead, women must demand their "right to the development of the personality."[136] In proselytizing for a woman's right to their own identity, Stöcker prescribed a life of self-overcoming and self-creation through love. Love was, then, prescriptive in a double sense: as a spiritual content and as formal philosophy of life.

Like Simmel, Stöcker called for the hegemony of the feminine principle. For both, a biological notion of culture was the basis for a new cultural ideal that was accessible to both sexes. Thus, their politics of gender were simultaneously circumscribed by assumptions of sexual-affective difference, and they transcended biological essentialism in proposing the viability of "feminine" attributes as principles for political agency and institutional restructuring. Stöcker developed a variety of cultural constructs, such as the "symbol of the mother god," proffering a new ethical direction for life.[137] Both Simmel and Stöcker sought to elevate feminine love from a feeling of good will to a concept of social transformation. Two things distinguish their politics, however. First, the most important task, according to Stöcker, was to affirm the spirit of love in all its forms—whether it be between an unwed mother and her child or between persons of the same sex. Such conclusions about female culture, i.e., that it requires support for homosexuality and unwed motherhood, radically transcended Simmel's adumbration of a future feminine culture. Secondly, Dr. Stöcker transformed *Lebensphilosophie* into a life of political activism. In dedicating her life to institutionalizing the liberties of love, she exceeded the circumscribed academic sphere of Simmel's avant-garde philosophy.

TITANS OF THE SEXUAL AVANT-GARDE: HILLER, STÖCKER, AND HIRSCHFELD

In Stöcker and Hiller the Simmelian model of the engaged intellectual reached its zenith. Their mutual political activities were among the most important examples of avant-garde politics in Wilhelmine and Weimar society.[138] Stöcker and Hiller were the next generation of left-wing avant-gardists who, like Simmel, espoused a countercultural politics which unified Germany's two most powerful critiques of bourgeois society: Nietzschean and socialist. In Hiller's intellectual history of the period, *Talented Intellectuals and Simpletons: Profile of a Quarter Century*, he recounted his association with Stöcker in an essay entitled "Comrade in Struggle: Helene Stöcker."

> Nietzsche taught her the great *Ja zum Diesseits*, the great Yes to natural instincts, the great Yes to every splendor, colorfulness, and strength. He taught her the joy of greatness found in the strong, thoughtful personality [*Persönlichkeit*]. He also provided her a psychological understanding of all the actions of mediocrity that hinder the advance of the spirit [*Geist*]. . . . From Marxism she drew on neither the materialistic interpretation of history nor the dialectical method. Rather she drew upon its content of purpose, namely, its titanic intentions: the liberation of the proletariat, the abolition of classes, and the realization of a classless society composed of people who are free, responsibly minded, strong, well-intentioned, and tolerant and who seek happiness. The affirmation of this complex of thoughts brought her together with a significant number of Socialist and Communist leaders, with whom she acted collectively, without however surrendering her own philosophical foundation. *Consequently, to the normal citizen she appeared to be a revolutionary, and to those of the Marxist school she appeared to be a bourgeois ideologue. She is a socialist of an idealistic observance—an interesting intersection.*[139]

Reference to the proletarian element of avant-garde culture in Hiller's homage to his activist-colleague was more than a description of Stöcker's cultural disposition. It is a lucid placement of Simmel and his successors within the culture of the Left. This proletarian element of spiritual intelligence, however, was not fully developed until after 1920. Before 1917 and at the cost of being labelled bourgeois ideologues, Hiller and Stöcker steadfastly promoted an antibourgeois neo-Nietzscheanism that rejected dialectical materialism and heralded the realm of gender as a decisive arena of social liberation. After 1917, Hiller and Stöcker continued to focus on gender politics but now had much more political contact with socialists and communists. Most instructive is Hiller's description of Stöcker as an interesting intersection of idealism and socialism. This was the primary characteristic of Simmel's cultural critique as well.

With the exception of Magnus Hirschfeld, with whom they worked closely and extensively, Stöcker and Hiller were Germany's unsurpassed titans of an alternative gender politics for over three decades. They even exceeded Hirschfeld in their significance as left-wing political activists. The publication of Hiller's *Das Recht über sich Selbst* in 1908 was the origin of an intersection of these three intellectuals. Shortly after its publication, Hiller and Hirschfeld initiated a friendship which would be solidified through joint political activities that lasted over two decades.[140] Stöcker was so moved by the text that she published an essay by the same title in late 1908 wherein she recapitulated its defense of individual rights against the interference of the state.[141] Hiller was well aware that this text had established his towering reputation among sexual reformers.[142] It was so highly regarded that over fifteen years later Hirschfeld included an edited portion of it in a monograph of his Institute for Sexual Science, *Zur Reform des Sexualstrafrechts* (1926).[143] Perhaps the most significant of their numerous collaborations in the realm of sexual politics was the formation in 1925 of the Cartel for the Reform of Sexual-Criminal Law.[144] What must be noted is that the working relationship of this triumvirate predates the formation of the Weimar Republic. The political contours of their gender politics originated out of the war.

ANTIWAR ACTIVISM AND THE INTERNATIONAL OF SPIRIT

Spirit and praxis were formerly an antithesis; today these words describe a correlative dependence.

Kurt Hiller, 1916[145]

In 1914, Simmel moved to Strassburg, having accepted his first and last professorial position. This geographical move from the heart of German culture, Berlin, to its periphery symbolized his cultural fate. As a result of his public defense of the Great War, his reputation as the philosophical soul of the avant-garde was destroyed. Yes, this process of decline was underway prior to the outbreak of war. Activists like Hiller and Stöcker viewed Simmel's brand of avant-gardism as incomplete due to its lack of political practice. However, they did so while retaining respect for Simmel's ideas. Before the war, Simmel's pugnacious ideas were often the lens through which the avant-garde surveyed the spiritual putridity of industrial modernization and cultural modernity. This was no longer the case after 1914. Simmel died in Strassburg in 1918, and as a result of the Versailles Treaty, his grave in Strassburg was no longer part of Germany. His burial site metaphorized the epitaphic knell of his eclipsed cultural significance.

The culture of war contributed to the reversal of Simmel's avant-garde reputation. In 1914, with Nietzschean rays of hope filtering through the ruins of the Socialist International, Hiller founded and led the antiwar Activist League (*Aktivistenbund*), a radical offshoot of literary Expressionism. This organization morphed into the International of Spirit (*Internationale des Geistes*) in 1917.[146] As its name suggests, members of this organization viewed themsleves as the vanguard of cultural revolution. Hiller and Stöcker were driving forces behind the antiwar movement and the political program of Activism. For instance, in her wartime essay, "Modern Population Politics," Stöcker used eugenic theory to criticize the war.

> It is a sign of present culture that we no longer recognize the state as the highest authority of violence, that it has developed from an apparatus of rape to an apparatus of supervision, . . . that it increasingly must become a community of national security . . . to force a politics of population in the sense of mass production for the purposes of war. . . . Women are summoned to supply the abundance of living munitions with the sole justification that the war needs them.[147]

In addition to rejecting "motherhood as the military contribution of German women," her eugenic politics were linked to other causes that rendered them incompatible with Nazi eugenics. Most notably, her anti-imperialist, antimilitarist conception of motherhood coalesced with a public defense of homosexuality. Indeed, she worked closely with Hiller and Hirschfeld to legalize homosexuality. In Stöcker's thought, then, patriarchal and eugenic discourses were refracted through the avant-garde discourse of spiritual intelligence, and the result was an antiwar rendition of maternity.

Crucial for our understanding of the Simmelian heritage behind the feminist and Activist avant-garde is an evaluation of its relationship to socialism. Amy Hackett has accurately tied Stöcker's socialist inclinations to the anarchist-socialist Gustav Landauer, with whom Stöcker founded the Central Office for Human Rights in 1917.[148] But this interpretive link is itself an oversimplification of prewar socialist undecidability and bypasses the more expansive political culture of spiritual workers. Prior to 1914, anarchist-socialists, democratic socialists, and communist revolutionaries coexisted under the rubric of Social Democracy. After 1914, Stöcker chose to identify with the anti-imperialist and pacifist portion of the pre–1914 socialist tradition. In doing so, she rejected both (1) the materialism of Soviet socialism in favor of an expansion of individual human rights, and (2) the prowar policies of the SPD. What must be emphasized is that Stöcker's reverence for Landauer is inadequate for understanding the larger cultural matrix within which she worked.

That larger cultural matrix can be telescoped into the core document of the International of Spirit, "The Political Council of Spiritual Workers" ("*Politischer Rat der Geistige Arbeiter*"), which was first published in 1920 in Hiller's wartime journal, *Das Ziel*. The political program of the Spiritual Workers was the result of three conferences. The first took place in Berlin-Westend from August 10 to August 12, 1917. The second was held in Berlin's Nollendorf Casino, November 7 and 8, 1918, only days after the outbreak of revolution in Kiel and Berlin. Subsequent to the framing of the document, another Activist Congress was held in Berlin from June 15 to 20, 1919. Written in the sublime atmosphere of impending military defeat and revolutionary joy, this document was a radical crescendo in the atonal cultural movement of spiritual intelligence. Of course, this document and the

Activists' International of Spirit must be understood in the context of the German Revolution. Inspired by the Russian Revolution, German sailors mutinied in Kiel on November 3, 1918. Their model for revolutionary democracy was the soviets or councils, which in Germany were called *Räte*. In late 1918, workers' and soldiers' councils were established throughout Germany, particularly in the North (Hamburg, Bremen, and Lübeck, etc.), in the industrialized Rheinland (Düsseldorf, Cologne, Duisberg, etc.), and in larger cities such as Dresden, Munich, and Frankfurt. The Imperial Congress of Workers' and Soldiers' Councils took place in Berlin from December 16 to 21, 1918; this was the culmination of initial revolutionary activities. The Activists' Political Council (*Rat*) of Spiritual Workers rode the crest of this revolutionary tide. They tried to position themselves as the cultural vanguard of social revolution and were well situated to do so. Stöcker had been organizing for cultural revolution for over a decade, and through years of aesthetic and political activity, Hiller, too, had honed his avant-garde cultural conceptions.

What was the cultural vision of the *Aktivisten*? Two characteristics of their program are significant: (1) its socialist radicalism, and (2) its synthesis of the disparate cultural movements associated with literary Expressionism. First, the avant-garde, while sympathetic to Marxism, typically positioned itself against the working-class herd. However, as a result of socialist leadership within the council movement, this was no longer possible. As the title of their program suggests, the diverse leaders of the antibourgeois avant-garde now, for the first time, felt compelled to portray themselves as "*spiritual workers*." A puissant critique of capitalism and an impetuous defense of revolution also took center stage, as it had in the Expressionist journal, *Die Aktion*. Their manifesto was an anticapitalist vision of human rights. The program began:

> The guiding star of all future politics must be the inviolability of life. To consecrate creativity, to protect the creator, to purge every form of slavery from the earth, that is our duty. The Political Assembly of Spiritual Workers accordingly fights above all against the subjugation of the totality of people through war service and against the oppression of workers through the capitalist system. The Assembly wants personal freedom and social justice. Resolved to the swiftest and most radical realization of the precepts of human reason, it calls out against those who are half-hearted, cautious, and restrained. It welcomes all methods of revolution which do not lead to the annihilation of cultural goods and to the bloody domination of a minority, i.e., to anarchy.[149]

In the culture of war and revolution, the success and hegemonic power of Marxist socialism necessitated that these self-styled cultural revolutionaries be more forthcoming about their critique of the capitalist system. They did this by coding themselves as workers and by defending socialist revolution. However, the Activists' brand of socialist revolution occupied a specific cultural space within the panoply of available revolutionary doctrines. Their revolutionary vision accentuated a reverence for aesthetic originality, cultural excellence, and an ethical critique of capitalism. This unity of extremes—aesthetic individualism and ethical socialism—was the political paragon of spiritual intelligence. Unwittingly, then, in the year of Simmel's death, the International of Spirit espoused a model of cultural revolution which was originally articulated in Simmel's Nietzschean-socialist philosophy.

In addition to its strengthened anticapitalist self-understanding, the Activists' program, for the first time, synthesizing diverse strands of the cultural avant-garde. Intellectuals who attended the conferences, signed, and presumably worked on the document included the leaders of the Activist wing of early Expressionism (Kasimir Edschmid, Dr. Rudolf Kayser, Rudolf Leonard, Ludwig Meidner, Dr. Kurt Pinthus, Heinrich Mann, René Schickele, Wilhelm Herzog, Dr. Kurt Hiller), Germany's leading sexual scientist (Dr. Magnus Hirschfeld), a leading advocate of Nietzschean philosophy (Lou Andreas-Salomé), the president of Vienna's League of Spiritual Activists (*Bund der geistigen Tätigen*) (Dr. Franz Kobler), Germany's leading Nietzschean feminist (Helene Stöcker), and, among others, the theoretical shaman of Germany's youth movement, *Der Wandervogel* (Dr. Gustav Wyneken). Of the approximately sixty-five signatories, twenty-two held doctoral degrees, which reinforces the contention that the political avant-garde was substantially a movement of middle-class intellectuals who sought political returns on their intellectual capital outside of academia.

The central significance of this assemblage of intellectuals was its synthetic character. It brought together leading theorists of four cultural movements: Expressionism, sexology, the youth movement, and the feminist movement. "Comrades," the program concluded, "support us! Help us to establish the cultural-political radicals on the foundation of the social Republic!"[150] Their program was indeed the most radical European critique of bourgeois culture since Charles Fourier and the Utopian Socialists.

What made the program so radical was the breadth of its critique. The program was divided into seven demands:

1. The Prevention of War: . . . the abolition of military service in all countries and the prohibition of all military establishments.
2. The Just Distribution of All Earthly Possessions: . . . the transformation of capitalist enterprises into a productive worker's association.
3. Freedom of the Sexual Life Within the Borders of Responsibility: . . . thorough control of all men and women over their own bodies. Legal and social equality for unmarried mothers and their children.
4. Abolition of the Death Penalty. . . .

5. The Radical Reform of Public Education. . . .
6. The Separation of Church and State. The elimination of confessional education in all the schools. . . .
7. Securing and Completion of the United German Social Republic . . . *Der Reichstag*: Equal, direct, and secret ballot for all over the age of twenty for both sexes. The electability of women.[151]

All of the major institutions of bourgeois hegemony were assailed: the military, capitalism, patriarchy, heterosexism, education, the church, and political illiberalism. In contrast to revolutionary Marxists, the International of Spirit treated capitalism as one among many bourgeois institutions that must be abolished. And instead of a Marxist vanguard, the Republic would be directed by a spiritual avant-garde. Section Seven of the program included the plan for new political institutions in a German Republic.

> *The Assembly of Spiritual Intellectuals.* It results from neither the appointment nor the election of its members, rather—by authority of the responsibility of *Geist* to help—from its inherent right, and renews itself according to its own law.
>
> *The Government*: In the hands of a committee of trusted people of the *Reichstag* and the Assembly.
>
> . . . *The President of the German Republic*: To be chosen from the Reichstag by the unbinding consent of the Assembly. . . .
>
> The Political Council of Spiritual Workers believes that under this constitution, which perfects democratic designs and guarantees leadership by the best, a politics of freedom, justice, and reason . . . is secured.[152]

The birth of the Activist Congress and its moral vision might best be seen as the defense of a Platonic Republic. The new German Republic would be Platonic in a double sense. As in Plato's *Symposium*, society would affirm the civic legitimacy of homosexuality. Similar to Plato's Republic, society was to be led by an intellectual-moral elite, an assembly of spiritual workers. As we shall see, this vision of revolutionary leadership was unrealistic due to the Activists distance from workers' organizations. Why would socialists place these privileged members of the avant-garde in positions of leadership?

THE EXPRESSIONIST ORIGINS AND CULTURAL FATE OF ACTIVISM

While the political vision of the International of Spirit existed in various strands before the war, it was their opposition to the war that eventually bound the Activists together institutionally. (After the war, Hiller and Stöcker became leading pacifists. In 1919, Stöcker became the vice president of the predominantly liberal and middle-class German Peace Society; in 1921 she was a founding member of the International of Opponents to War Service; and she became a member of the Group of Revolutionary Pacifists (GRP) in 1926. The GRP was founded by Hiller and continued to work with the larger German Peace Society while rejecting its bourgeois conception of peace.[153]) The organizational synthesis of Activists had been largely the brainchild and realization of Hiller, who coined the term *Aktivismus* at the end of 1914 and who presided over the Activist congresses as chairman.[154] As evidenced by his *Wisdom of Ennui*, the origins of Hiller's activist philosophy preceded the war. The culture of war, however, generated a new sense of urgency and possibility. Hiller responded by founding a dissident journal. The first volume was entitled *Purpose, Calls to the Active Spirit* (1916) (*Das Ziel, Aufrufe zu tätigem Geist*) and subsequent volumes went by the name of *Active Spirit!* (*Tätiger Geist!*). Like other antiwar journals such as *Die Aktion* and *Das Forum*, the first two issues of *Das Ziel* were censored by the government after a limited distribution. The intervention of the state increased Hiller's feeling that he was now carrying on a direct cultural struggle. The war was such an important catalyst in Hiller's life that he would write in his 1930 autobiography: "Everything up until the war was just a prelude; my work and my life achievements only then commenced."[155]

Many of the themes of the Activists' Congresses can be traced to the publication of the first volume of *Das Ziel*. The first essay of the volume, from which came the movement's mantra "active spirit," was a reprint of Heinrich Mann's 1910 essay, "Spirit and Deed." The decision to republish this essay was not only a homage to the stepfather of the movement but also an intended affront to the conservative neo-Nietzschean Thomas Mann, with whom Hiller carried on a heated exchange during the war. The antibourgeois character of the movement was represented in essays such as Hans Blüher's "The Crimes of the Bourgeois Type."[156] The synthetic political strategy of the movement, a unified left, was nearly identical to the organizational program of *Die Aktion*. It was announced in Max Brod's article, "The Organization of Organizations." In articles by the leading theorist and a leading activist of the *Wandervogel*, Wyneken and Walter Benjamin respectively, the affiliation of *Aktivismus* and the youth movement was affirmed.[157] Other essays addressed the university system, the war and women, and the population problem. In the second volume of the journal, Helene Stöcker brought together the interests of the youth movement, the women's movement, and antimilitarism in her article, "The Militarization of Youth and Motherhood."[158] While the war razed the foundation of German culture, it also had a productive effect; it unified and legitimized diverse branches of cultural critique.

The philosophical foundation and institutional vision of what he would later call the "Politics of Synthesis" were most forcefully developed by Hiller in a series of war essays whose publication immediately preceded the Activist Congress.[159] The most important document in this regard was his essay "The Philosophy of Purpose," which appeared in the first volume of *Das Ziel*.[160] In proselytizing for the "activity of spirit" (*Aktivität des Geistes*), here Hiller continued his assault on other pretenders to the throne of spiritual intelligence: the secular intellectual of *Gesellschaft*, the Moralist, the feuilleton, and the defenders of l'art pour l'art, whose purveyors were held most responsible for the world war. In contrast to these, he portended a "utopian," "more bodily" and "more soulful" community (*Gemeinschaft*) which celebrated sexual and cultural "differentiation" (*Differenziertheit*). The most remarkable element of the essay, however, was its spiritual language.

> Spirit [*Geist*] is the unavoidable detour to the happiness of paradise. . . . Spirit is the striving for responsibility—to stir others and make them jointly responsible. . . . Spirit would be the moment of the birth of paradise. . . . Spirit is the goal. . . . As spiritual intellectuals, we embrace association. . . . What do we want? Paradise. Who will gain it? *Geist*. What does it need to succeed? Power. How will spiritual intelligence win power? Through union.[161]

The trope of spiritual paradise was a trope of war in a dual sense. It was a product of the war and the weapon of cultural struggle. Its presence indicates that the nearly seamless support for the war by Germany's Christian denominations demanded an antiwar response that claimed the same level of spiritual authority. There was no way for Hiller to express the intensity of his ethical opposition to war culture without resorting to spiritual language. Of course, through the discourse of soul and spirit, Simmel, Hiller, and Stöcker had carried on a struggle for moral authority against Christianity in prewar Wilhelmine culture. Hiller's mobilization of the trope of paradise was an intensification of this cultural strategy. Hiller's discourse of paradise and spirit highlight the fact that the German avant-garde referenced their spiritual intelligence (*Geistigkeit*) in an attempt to usurp the cultural hegemony of Christian spirituality (*Geistlichkeit*). This discursive overlap notwithstanding, the cultural distinction between these two forms of spirituality was strictly maintained. For instance, the political program amended to the end of the "Philosophy of Purpose" included the injunction: "Struggle against the churches as long as they continue to oppose the will of spirit [*Willen des Geistes*]."[162]

In "The Philosophy of Purpose," Hiller was very clear about the most desirable realizations of "the will of the spirit." In what is the antecedent document of "The Political Council of Spiritual Workers," he put forth the following plan for social revolution:

1. *Abolition of War.* . . . War can not be a permissible means to power for *Geist*.
2. *Advancement of Merit* through the Equal Distribution of Material Goods.
3. *Guarantee of an Existence-Minimum for Every Citizen.*
4. *Liberation of All Love.*
5. *Rationalization of Births from the Point of View of Eugenics.*
6. *Restriction of Laws Derived from Interest Groups.*
7. *Abolition of the Death Penalty.*
8. *The Protection from Psychiatry* . . . which can not make . . . a distinction between irregularity (abnormality) and sickness (pathology).
9. *Restructuring of Higher Education.* In place of learning schools, thinking schools; instead of founding education on the past, founding education on the future . . . Admission to this Culture School for the select youth of all levels of the *Volk*.
10. *Creation of a True University of Letters.* . . . Uncovering the real spiritual intellectuals [*Geistigen*] that lay buried under piles of positivistic rubbish almost everywhere. Immunization of the Alma Mater against the dispiriting influences of artisinal-utilitarian disciplines.
11. *Acquisition of Newspapers.* Newspapers can no longer remain advertising ventures dependent upon the weak-spirited disposition of the cretin who reads them, and upon the grubby disposition of the entrepreneur who heads them. The newspapers moreover must become extricated from Capital and become tools of education—the education of the *Volk* through spirit and towards spirit [*Geist*].
12. *Struggle Against the Churches,* as long as they continue to oppose the will of spirit [*Geist*].
13. *Struggle Against the Parliament,* as long as it continues to contradict the will of spirit [*Geist*].
14. *Struggle Against All the Stars of Bourgeois Refinement*, as long as they continue to oppose the will of spirit [*Geist*].

15. *Introduction of a Monarchy of the Best*, i.e., as Plato understood the aristocracy.
16. *Creation of a German House of Lords* equipped with law-making authority, that would consist of the spiritual leaders of the nation.
17. *Constitutional Unity of All States*. Preparation for it: a middle-European organization of states. Preparation for Preparation: our diplomacy will inject spirit [*Geist*].
18. *Absolute Protection of the Freedom of Thought, Speech, and Press* and, when necessary, alliances with every oppositional direction, group, and party.[163]

The most striking feature of Hiller's Activist program is its synthesis of seemingly antipodal extremes: an antiliberal restriction of the capitalist press and a liberal defense of absolute press freedom; political-intellectual elitism and material egalitarianism; a fascistlike discourse of *Volk, Kampf, Gemeinschaft*, and *Führer* and antifascist demands for an international partnership of peace; conservative-sounding appeals to eugenics and an affirmation of homosexual love. These tensions reflect the aporetic extremes of Simmel's thought: social justice and individual freedom.

If we are going to chart the political legacy of Simmel through Hiller, then it is important to understand the marginality of Activism. The marginal geography of spiritual politics on the map of the German Left was solidified by two characteristics of Hiller's program. First, the Activists' derision of parliamentary democracy and support for a new German House of Lords rendered them incompatible with the overwhelming majority of German socialists. The vehemence of Hiller's elitism may not be apparent in the preceding quote. Still, after 1918, he vehemently attacked the herd politics of Marxism from the perspective of a "revolutionary aristocracy" in the tradition of Plato and Nietzsche.[164] Conversely, the electoral strength of the SPD derived substantially from its ideological assertion that only socialists could realize democracy. The Activists' aristocratic radicalism was totally out of step with the electorate. From the egalitarian mindset of social democracy, aristocratic radicalism was viewed as a variant of extreme conservatism.[165] Secondly and concomitantly, the Activists' remained marginal because they neglected the discourse and affective politics of working-class solidarity. The culture of war and the German Revolution heightened the significance of class politics: strikes and sawdust bread at home and the Russian Revolution next door. Still, we can safely assume that the material condition of most of the Activists was not that of proletarian want. Save their ethical rejection of capitalism, the avant-garde elite had little in common with proletarian socialism. In fact, this aristocracy of culture had a much closer relationship to the bourgeois caste of the brain (the university) than the political stratum of the stomach (the proletariat).

Nothing symbolizes the cleft between the Activists and the mass of socialists better than Hiller's extensive essay, "A German House of Lords," which was a plan for the political hegemony of the avant-garde. It first appeared in print during the 1918 Revolution. Obviously, the Activists' Platonic vision of the Republic stood in sharp contrast to the socialists' egalitarian Republic. In the political program of the Political Council of Spiritual Workers, the Activists narrowed this gap by coding themselves as "spiritual workers" and by assigning their Council of Spiritual Intelligence a mere advisory role in the impending Republic. It did not work. No one appointed them the moral aristocracy of a new spiritual House of Lords, and they had no power to appoint themselves. Their Platonic republic was upstaged by the arrival of capitalist democracy, and they were without an electoral base. To the socialists and communists, now holding power, the Activists' claims to the rights of political leadership must have appeared fanciful and laughingly impractical.

The Activists were antibourgeois countercultural workers and naive politicians. Their enormous cultural productivity and soaring intellectual reputation was short lived. As quickly as they had ascended in 1914, their Icarian claims of spiritual, intellectual, and political leadership were drowned in the swelter of the 1917 Russian and 1918 German Revolutions. Simmel died in 1918, and along side him lay Hiller's institutional "Morality of Nobility."[166] What remained of their aristocratic radicalism in Weimar was a powerful matrix of antibourgeois cultural critique marked by pacifism, material egalitarianism, and alternative visions of sexual civility. But it was an aristocracy of spirit that was institutionally and discursively, though not programmatically, similar to the aristocratic spiritualism of fascism. Unlike the Activists, however, the Nazis understood the necessity of a mass base.

SIMMEL AND CULTURAL RECIPROCITY

Just as Simmel was no mere epigone of Nietzsche and Dilthey, Hiller and Stöcker were not learned toadies of Simmel. In fact, in the culture of war, it was Simmel who seemed more influenced by the Activists than the other way around. During the war, Simmel spoke like a convert to Activism. In his *Schulpädagogik*, a collection of lectures given during the war, Simmel wrote about the need for a new educational "elite" and their "aristocratic basis."[167] He described the art and science of pedagogy as a "foundation and service of praxis. . . . I never lose sight of praxis."[168] Of course, this may not reflect direct contact with the Activists. The discourse of praxis, activity, and decisions was a fundamental element of cultural resistance during the war, and the theme of an aesthetic-moral elite was a ballast of Simmel's philosophy. Still, the elective affinities of the Activists and Simmel were never more pronounced than during the war, and this despite their differing responses to this tragic conflict. For example, Simmel's new demand for pedagogical practicality was strikingly compatible with Stöcker's sexual pedagogy. Stöcker and the other radical feminists of the League for the Protection of Mothers and for Sexual Reform (*Bund für Mutterschutz und Sexualreform*) had petitioned the Reichtag in 1906 for the institution of sex education in the schools. In "Sexual Enlightenment," the appendix of *Schulpädagogik*, Simmel gave detailed instructions about the narrative of sexual edification: first natural history, then procreation of animals, and finally the study of human sexuality.[169] He firmly denounced the pedagogy of chastity as a "refinement of head-in-the-sand politics."[170] His vision of sexual enlightenment parallels Stöcker's hard-fought political attempts to have sex education included in the curriculum of the Wilhelmine school system.

The reciprocity between the Activists and Simmel was not merely philosophical but multidimensional. It is very likely that Stöcker and Simmel interacted during the war when Simmel came to his beloved Berlin on March 17, 1916. The occasion was a public lecture in the maximum auditorium of Berlin University. The lecture, entitled "Goethe's Love," was a revision of a chapter by the same name in *Goethe* (dedicated to Marianne Weber). Only months after its presentation, the lecture appeared as an article in Stöcker's journal, *The New Generation.* The content of the article tells us much about the transgressive meaning of love within the neo-Nietzschean avant-garde. Simmel wrote in reference to Eduard in Goethe's *Elective Affinities*: "He was untrue to women, because he was true to himself. His infidelity was connected to unspeakable suffering and to the self-overcoming of forced obedience to the law of his life."[171] He adds that it is tragicomic that the philistine should see this complex and painful transgression of marital law as merely an example of philistinism. Simmel was not a philistine but an immoralist, in the Nietzschean sense. Through the lense of Victorian Christianity, infidelity—particularly on the part of wives—appeared an unambiguous immorality. Conversely, Simmel scrutinized the spiritual meaning of infidelity for both men and women. Stöcker's philosophy of love was even more comprehensive and unconventional. Through her political activities, she asked that the scarlet letter of shame be removed form the "immoral" practices of homosexual love and the love of unwed mothers.

For Simmel, Stöcker, and Hiller alike, love was a solution to the existential problem of freedom. It was a form of good will that guided and constrained human action. It was also a spirit that transcended dogmatic laws of convention. Hiller's defense of homosexuality and Stöcker's feminism derived from an interpretation of spirituality as love. During the war, Simmel, for the first time, entered into a philosophical dialogue about love. In "Platonic and Modern Eros," he challenged Hiller's interpretation of Platonic Eros.[172] According to Simmel, who had read Hiller's *Das Recht über sich selbst*, Hellenistic love was a denial of "modern love" which derives from the concept of the soul (*Seele*). The Greeks, he argued, did not possess the concept of the soul. It arose with Christianity. The death of God heralded by Nietzschean philosophy was the origin of a historical transmutation of culture from the Christian soul into the modern soul. Simmel's reinterpretation of the soul, a foundational concept of avant-garde politics, thereby rejected Hiller's contention that the homosexuality found in Plato's *Symposium* was a manifestation of modern love. But Simmel neither confirmed nor denied the possibility that modern love could be expressed in homosexuality. Unlike his brilliant student, Simmel never challenged the hegemony of heterosexism.

What Simmel did do, however, was provide a unique understanding of how the concept of love comported with a philosophy of spirit. In an extensive manuscript left unfinished at his death, "Concerning Love," love is shown to contradict the indifference and egoism of monetary culture. While monetary culture was alienation of subject and object:

> From the view of the subject-object concept, love reveals most strongly the soulful immanence of our conception of the world. Because when we recognize—as when we value—we feel ourselves embraced by a binding something, . . . which exists beyond subject and object. (We disparagingly and very imperfectly refer to this something as a norm, a measure or a value.) If we love an object, which unlike other human-soulful inspirations carries within itself a latent intention of becoming a lover, then we feel a decisive freedom . . . and a comprehensive something, which is beyond the contradictory extremes of the soul and world.[173]

Love was celebrated as a prescriptive a priori of human relations and as a great structural category of existence. Simmel cautioned that "to positively realize the content of love in this pure being-for-itself . . . is perhaps an insoluble task."[174] However, this is the task he prescribed for the life of spirit: "The loving person is the only truly free spirit."[175] Perhaps it is the paradox of war cultures that they seem to evoke unprecedented ruminations about love and religion. Max Weber, for instance, was writing his sociology of religion during the war, and this only reminds us that titanic events cast intellectuals into intense reflections about ultimate values.

For Simmel, that ultimate value was love. In contrast to monetary modernity, which is characterized by a universal form absent a spiritual content, love was pure spiritual content seeking realization. Like religion, love tenders a continuity to life. It is the antithesis of the deconstructed and phantasmagoric character of modern diversification. Love, for Simmel, became a metaphorical and prescriptive critique of the bourgeois civility of negative freedom.

GEORG SIMMEL

> Love is a binding of the soul, exactly like ethics; the soul no longer belongs in itself to the same extent. It is no longer so free as it was when one was not in love. The ideal task is precisely the counterpart of ethics: the limitation of freedom should be felt as the higher freedom.[176]

In another context he stated that "where there is will, there is always already the absence of absolute freedom."[177] Love was self-delimitation as freedom. Ultimately, Simmel's musings about love appear to be compensatory: "the true trans-vital love raises itself out of the life of the species."[178] His reflection about love enabled him to psychologically transcend the necessity to contemplate the tragedy of the Great War.

THE POLITICS OF LOVE

Simmel, Hiller, and Stöcker's writings were refractions of Nietzsche's thought. However, their unique contributions to the history of sexual politics were not lessened in luminosity by being derivative of Nietzsche. In them we can locate three typologies of the gender politics of spirit: Simmel, the philosopher of cultural feminism; Stöcker, the radical embodiment of feminist activism; and Hiller, the great critic of the moral and legal hegemony of heterosexism. In Stöcker, Hiller, and Simmel the feeling of good will was raised to a concept of compassion and social transformation. Life-affirming compassions—be they in Simmel's conception of the erotic, Hiller's notion of Eros, Stöcker's politics of love, Wyneken's pedagogy of Eros, or Friedländer's conception of love—were the affective politics of avant-garde spirituality.[179] In each case, there was a political connection between love as a solution to modern alienation and love as a politics of sexual liberation. Nietzschean socialism and the ideal of self-created principles of compassion became the basis for a political recognition of such sexually and economically marginalized elements of society as homosexuals and unwed proletarian mothers.

If elitism was the great historical folly of Simmel and the Activists, then the spiritual politics of compassion were the bold sagacity of the avant-garde. As a cultural politics, Jochen Schulte-Sasse's interpretation of Nietzsche is a felicitous description of Wilhelmine cultural radicalism:

> Nietzsche's dream turns out to be the dream of avant-garde art, namely, that art might be employed to sublate its representational nature and to open a space of structural independence. In this sense, Nietzsche's statement that "Dionysus speaks the language of Apollo; and Apollo finally, the language of Dionysus" is the poetic veiling of a culture-revolutionary dream.[180]

Simmel expressed his revolutionary dream in a similar language: "Around the Apollonian clarity of cool thought danced the Dionysian happiness of the unheard power gained by the soul."[181] The cultural dreams of Simmel and the Activists were more anticapitalist in content and more radical in terms of gender than those of Nietzsche. In Nietzsche there were mere traces of Activist cultural politics:

> Neighbor love, living for others, and other things can be a protective measure for preserving the hardest self-concern. This is the exception where, against my wont and conviction, I side with the selfless drives: here they work in the service of self-love and self-discipline.[182]

What was an exception for Nietzsche—the genius and conviction of social compassion—was the self-imposed rule of neo-Simmelian politics. Not perhaps since Charles Fourier's *The New Theory of Society*, with its critique of the bourgeois tyranny of the passions, had anyone on the Left undertaken a comparably thorough and compassionate critique of bourgeois culture.

THE NEW AVANT-GARDE

As we have seen, Simmel's philosophical sociology was a source of inspiration for literary Expressionism and the conceptual trousseau of the most political wing of the movement: *Aktivismus*.[183] Activism was a rejection of Simmel's academic bifurcation of mental radicalism and political activism. In his memoir of Simmel, Hiller recounted the cultural dialectic of the avant-garde in the following way.

> The transformation of the social world was not an essential characteristic or purpose of Simmel. . . . My demarcation from him, which necessarily remains, and the ovation, which I—the servant of logos—offer to him, do not contradict one another. The Activist angle of vision that rejects him is one completely different from the one that says yes to him, in remaining and newly strengthened veneration.[184]

In the life-work of Kurt Hiller, Simmel's philosophy was criticized and rearticulated as an existential philosophy of political Activism. Moreover, two of his students, Hiller and Stöcker, formed organizations which were the cultural bulwark against the reactionary moral purity movements of the period.[185] In the Weimar Republic, they would maintain their "preeminent position of intellectual (and moral) leadership within the sex reform movement."[186] Simmel's pedagogy and thought was an avant-garde well spring of countercultural capital endowing Expressionism, the homosexual rights movement, radical feminism, and antiwar Activism. These were not the only areas of German culture in which his influences were felt. As we shall see in the next chapter, his avant-garde philosophy also influenced the birth of Marxist critical theory.

NOTES

1. Frisby, *Fragments of Modernity*.

2. Bruce Detwiler, *Nietzsche and the Politics of Aristocratic Radicalism* (Chicago: University of Chicago Press, 1990). On the reception of Nietzsche in Germany, see Steven E. Aschheim, *The Nietzsche Legacy in Germany, 1890–1990* (Berkeley: University of California Press, 1992). My work augments that of Detwiler and Aschheim by arguing that Simmel transformed aristocratic radicalism into an anticapitalist sociology. This transformation influenced a broad spectrum of radical students and political groups in Wilhelmine Germany.

3. Margarete Susman, "Erinnerungen an Simmel," in *Buch des Dankes*, pp. 279–80.

4. Ibid., pp. 279–80.

5. Georg Lukács, *Die Zerstörung der Vernunft: Der Weg des Irrationalismus von Schelling to Hitler* [1955] (Berlin: Aufbau-Verlag, 1988), p. 364.

6. Georg Simmel, "Der platonische und der moderne Eros," in *Fragmente und Aufsätze*, pp. 129, 132.

7. Georg Lukács, "Erinnerungen an Simmel," in *Buch des Dankes*, pp. 171–76.

8. Edith Landmann participated in Simmel's first seminar on aesthetics, which was held at his apartment in Charlottenburg. She reports that Simmel, through his long time friend, Gertrud Kantorowicz, invited her to travel with him to Munich. She states: "Es war dies aber doch für bürgerliche Begriffe ein zu unerhörtes Ansinnen, ich konnte es nicht annehmen. Simmels Interesse an mir erlähmte allmählich, zumal er auch hörte, daß ich philosophisch eher in Opposition zu ihm war." Can we assume that Simmel's interest in Landmann's transgression of bourgeois conventions was more than academic? Edith Landmann, "Erinnerung an Simmel" in *Buch des Dankes*, p. 208.

9. Nonetheless, in a letter to Heinrich Rickert, dated 19 July 1898, Simmel complained about the presence of female students:

> They disturb the unity of the auditorium. Here I am actually referring not to the listeners but to myself. I love it when the auditorium is practically colorless and indifferent. The duality of the formal appearance and their colorful clothes disturbs me. (*Buch des Dankes*, p. 96)

The reaction to the presence of women is emblematic of Simmel's aporetic relationship to pecuniary-consumer culture. Money creates indifference, which in turn facilitates thought. However, consumer culture also gives rise to an enormous number of colorful and alluring objects. As with the rise of the division of labor, the phantasmagoric nature of objects stems from a desire for individuation. Simmel approves of individuation if it is an ethical individuation. In the case of the division of labor and consumer products, individuation facilitates a sense of negative freedom which is incompatible with ethical individuation. In *Philosophy of Money*, Simmel states that it is not the revolt of the masses that threatens the ethical individuation; "[it is] the revolt of objects. Just as we have become the slaves of the production process, so we have become the slaves of the products" (pp. 673–74). Were his female students, perhaps dressed in the latest consumer fashions, unconsciously apprehended by Simmel as a slave revolt of consumerism against ethical individuation? Did these slaves revolt against the consciousness of their master, monetary culture, or was their revolt conservative?

10. Fritz Ringer, *The Decline of the German Mandarins*.

11. Georg Simmel, "Tendencies in German Life and Thought Since 1870," trans. W. D. Briggs, in *International Monthly* (New York, 5/1902): 93–111, 166–84. The first half of the essay was published for the first time in German in 1990. It is amended to the reissue of *Schopenhauer und Nietzsche* (Hamburg: Junius, 1990), pp. 7–33.

12. Kurt Gassen, "Vorlesungen und Übungen," in *Buch des Dankes*, pp. 346–47.

13. Heinz-Jürgen Dahme, "Georg Simmel und Gustav Schmoller: Berührungen zwischen Kathedersozialismus und Soziologie um 1890," *Simmel Newsletter*, vol. 3, no. 1 (summer 1993): 39–52.

14. For example, Nicholas Spykman's *The Social Theory of Georg Simmel*, Donald Levine's forty-page introduction to Georg Simmel, *Georg Simmel: On Individuality and Social Forms*, P. A. Lawrence's extensive description of Simmel's life and work in *Georg Simmel: Sociologist and European*, and the essays contained in Lewis A. Cosner's *Georg Simmel* say almost nothing about Simmel's existential anticapitalism. David Frisby's work is clearly the exception. In his *Georg Simmel* socialist thought is properly portrayed as central to Simmel's life and work. Frisby, however, does not systematically treat Simmel's aesthetic socialism and its fate in the context of war culture.

15. David Frisby, *Sociological Impressionism*. I have found no reference wherein he refers to himself as an Impressionist. Further, Simmel had little or no impact upon the largely French artistic movement known as Impressionism. If Simmel's philosophy is to be given an aesthetic color then one would have to say it was a pink philosophical Expressionism. According to Kurt Hiller, the distinction between philosophical Impressionism and philosophical Expressionism is significant because the former implies an intuitive social theory lacking critical self-consciousness about sociological concepts.

16. Simmel, *Der Konflikt der modernen Kultur* (München: Duncker & Humblot, 1918).

17. Hiller, *Die Weisheit der Langeweile: Eine Zeit und Streitschrift*, vol. 1 (Leipzig: Kurt Wolff, 1913), p. 103.

18. Friedrich Markus Heubner, "Der Expressionismus in Deutschland," in *Expressionismus: Der Kampf um eine literarische Bewegung*, ed. Paul Raabe (Zürich: Arche Verlag, 1987), p. 139.

19. Emil Ludwig, "Geschenke des Lebens. Ein Rückblick," in *Buch des Dankes*, p. 156.

20. Hiller, "Herkunft und Kindheit," in *Leben gegen die Zeit. Logos* (Hamburg: Rowohlt, 1969), pp. 11–24; hereafter as *Logos*.

21. Hoerst H. W. Müller, "Nachwort. Zielcourage in Person: Kurt Hiller," in *Leben gegen die Zeit. Eros* (Hamburg: Rowohlt, 1973), pp. 177–78; hereafter as *Eros*.

22. Thomas Meyer, ed., *Lexikon des Sozialismus* (Köln: Brand, 1986), p. 545; Hiller, *Logos*, pp.18–19.

23. Hiller, *Logos*, p. 56.

24. Ibid, p. 9.

25. Kurt Hiller, "Öffener Brief an Dr. Georg Zepler," *Die Aktion* 1 (20 February 1911): 10–12.

26. Margarete Susman, *Die geistige Gestalt Georg Simmels* (Tübingen: J.C.B. Mohr, 1959).

27. Georg Simmel to Heinrich Rickert, 26 July 1915, in *Buch des Dankes,* p. 114.

28. Hiller, *Logos,* p. 339.

29. Kurt Hiller, *Die Weisheit der Langeweile: Eine Zeit-und Streitschrift*, vol. 2 (Leipzig: Kurt Wolff, 1913), pp. 52–53.

30. Ibid., p. 52.

31. Simmel, *Fragmente und Aufsätze*, p. 149.

32. See Wolfgang Paulsen, *Deutsche Literatur des Expressionismus* (Bern: Peter Lang, 1983), pp. 37–38.

33. Hiller's sense of intellectual superiority was important to his self-conception and politics, and he goes to exaggerated lengths to establish it. See, for instance, "Schule," in *Logos*, pp. 24–54.

34. Ibid., p. 388.

35. Ibid., p. 61.

36. Nicholas Spykman's *The Social Theory of Georg Simmel*, the essays found in Lewis A. Coser's *Georg Simmel*, and Rudolph Weingartner's *Experience and Society: the Philosophy of Georg Simmel* are remarkably consistent in their omission of Simmel's socialist aesthetics. While they may make for interesting reading, these texts are unsuitable for an understanding of Simmel's cultural reception in Wilhelmine Germany. Spykman alone examines Simmel's *Philosophy of Money* and here only as a manifestation of his metaphysics. More recent essays, like those found in *Georg Simmel und die Moderne* and *Georg Simmels Philosophie des Geldes*, do not reference the socialist inflection of his work, and they completely neglect his relationship to the origins of the Expressionist movement. See also Rudolph Weingartner, *Experience and Culture: The Philosophy of Georg Simmel* (Middletown, Conn.: Wesleyan University Press, 1962); Dahme and Rammstedt, eds., *Georg Simmel und die Moderne*; Jeff Kintzelé and Peter Schneider, *Georg Simmels Philosophie des Geldes* (Frankfurt a.M.: Hain, 1993); David Frisby, *Georg Simmel*.

37. For a complete list of his course offerings see *Buch des Dankes*, pp. 345–49.

38. Kurt Hiller, "Litteraturpolitik," in *Die Weisheit*, vol. 1, p. 91.

39. Hiller, *Logos*, p. 9.

40. The underrepresentation of Simmel and Hiller and the total omission of S. Friedländer's *Friedrich Nietzsche* and Theodore Lessing's *Philosophie als Tat* from Steven E. Aschheim's *The Nietzsche Legacy in Germany 1890–1990* (Berkeley: University of California Press, 1992) constitutes a critical weakness in its

depiction of Nietzsche's legacy in Wilhelmine society. Part of the problem rests with Aschheim's heavy reliance on Walter H. Sokel's *The Writer in Extremis: Expressionism in Twentieth-Century German Literature* (Stanford: Stanford University Press, 1959). He asserts that this text "remains definitive" (p. 64). I would contend that the definitive scholar of Expressionism is Paul Raabe. The interpretive distance between Raabe and Sokel is most evident in the case of Hiller. In *The Writer in Extremis*, Sokel does not even mention Hiller. This should be compared to all of Raabe's work wherein Hiller is portrayed as a foundational thinker of the movement and its most significant propagandist. On Hiller's originality and his centrality to the development of literary Expressionism, see Paul Raabe, "Das literarische Leben im Expressionismus," in Paul Raabe, ed., *Die Zeitschriften und Sammlungen des literarisches Expressionismus 1910–1921* (Stuttgart: J.B. Metzlersche, 1964), pp. 1–22. Aschheim's most glaring English-language historiographical omission is Lewis D.Wurgaft's *The Activists: Kurt Hiller and the Politics of Action on the German Left* (Philadelphia: American Philosophical Society, 1977). The idea for Wurgaft's superb text was formulated in a graduate seminar taught by Fritz Ringer. The dissertation, from which the text is drawn, was directed by H. Stuart Hughes and read, at least in part, by George Mosse and Martin Jay. More important than its pedigreed brush with brilliance, however, is its content. It is very clear about the centrality of Nietzschean philosophy to literary Expressionism and about Hiller's seminal influence in constructing this linkage. My work traces Hiller's philosophy back to Simmel's Nietzschean socialism. In this regard, my research is not only a critical revision of Aschheim's treatment of the Nietzschean legacy in literary Expressionism; it is also a revision of his sixth chapter, "Nietzschean Socialism: Left and Right," which fails to reference Simmel's original and path breaking synthesis of socialism and Nietzschean philosophy.

41. The information contained in this paragraph is drawn from two sources: (1) Juliane Habereder's *Kurt Hiller und der literarische Aktivismus* (Frankfurt a.M.: Lang, 1981), especially chapter 2, "Im Vorfeld des Aktivismus"; and (2) Roy F. Allen, *Literary Life in German Expressionism and the Berlin Circles*, especially chapter 4, "Der Neue Club."

42. Quoted in Habereder, p. 37.

43. Ibid., p. 37. Drawing upon archival material, Habereder does an excellent job of establishing the friendship of Loewenson and Hiller. See, for example, her interpretation of their exchange of letters, which preceded the foundation of the New Club (pp. 35–36).

44. Allen, p. 82, note 67.

45. Quoted in Habereder, p. 42.

46. Kasimir Edschmid, *Lebendiger Expressionismus: Auseinandersetzung, Gestaltung, Erinnerung* (Wien: Kurt Desch, 1961), p. 193. This quote is drawn from Edschmid's chapter on "Literary Visionaries," pp. 192–95.

47. Allen, pp. 76–77.

48. On the place of the Café des Westens in the cultural life of Expressionism, see Ernst Blass, "The Old Café des Westens" in Paul Raabe, ed., *The Era of German Expressionism* (Woodstock N.Y.: Overlook Press, 1974), pp. 27–35.

49. See, for example, *Die Aktion* 2 (27 February 1911): 58.

50. Quoted in Habereder, p. 43. While Wurgaft emphasizes Hiller's cultural

relationship to *Pan* and *Die Aktion*, Habereder focusses on his role in founding the literary clubs.

51. It is probable that Hiller borrowed the concept of "das neue Pathos" from Stefan Zweig. Zweig's article, "Das neue Pathos," *Das literarische Echo* 11 (1909): 1701–1708, is arguably the first Expressionist manifesto. The significance of this Expressionist self-description is indicated by the fact that it eventually became the title of an Expressionist journal; *Das neue Pathos* was founded in 1913 and was edited by Hans Ehrenbaum-Degele, Robert R. Schmidt, Ludwig Meidner, and Paul Zech. The Nietzschean resonance of the concept is substantiated in Salomo Friedländer, *Schöpferische Indifferenz* (München: Georg Müller, 1918). The Introduction to this text begins with the following quote from Nietzsche's *Will to Power*: "The will to power is not Being [*Sein*] and it is not Becoming [*Werden*]. Rather, it is a pathos—the most elementary fact of existence—out of which Becoming and realization [*Wirken*] are yielded" (xiii). For a brief history of *Das Neue Pathos*, see Paul Raabe, ed., *Die Zeitschriften und Sammlungen des literarischen Expressionismus*, pp. 44–45.

52. On Hiller's role in the founding of *Die Aktion* see Alexandra Pfemfert's "The Birth of *Die Aktion*" in Raabe, *The Era of German Expressionism*, pp. 35–37. See also Franz Jung's "Franz Pfemfert and *Die Aktion*" and Hans Brunningen's "*Die Aktion* in Vienna" in the same volume.

53. See Hiller's numerous accolades for Kerr in *Logos, Die Weisheit der Langeweile*, and *Köpfe und Tröpfe*. In the first text, he even struggled to establish a familial relationship to Kerr, asserting that they were distant cousins.

54. Hiller, *Logos*, p. 353; on Kerr and Hiller, see Wurgaft, pp. 20–21.

55. The dispute initiating their departure from *Demokraten* seemed to center around Hiller's critique of democracy.

56. *Die Aktion*, 2 (27 February 1911): 58. No author is given. We can assume that it was written by Pfemfert with the oversight of Hiller.

57. Pfemfert was closely linked to Berlin's anarchist circles. For a short but incomparable analysis of anarchist politics in this period, see "Anarchism as Prophylactic," in Robert Michels, *Political Parties: A Sociological Study of the Oligarchical Tendencies of Modern Democracy* [1905], trans. Eden and Cedar Paul (New York: Free Press, 1962).

58. The canonical anthology of Expressionist lyric is Kurt Pinthus, *Menschenheitsdämmerung, Symphonie jüngster Dichtung* (Berlin: Rowohlt, 1920). Hiller's anthology preceded this publication by eight years.

59. Hiller, ed., *Der Kondor* (Heidelberg: Richard Wiessbach, 1912), pp. 5–9.

60. Ibid., p. 8.

61. Hiller, "Litteraturpolitik," p. 138. It is noteworthy that here Hiller, like Simmel, rejected experiential Impressionism in favor of an Expressionist philosophy of the iconoclastic, existential individual.

62. Hiller, *Die Weisheit*, vol. 1, p. 91.

63. Hiller, *Der Kondor*, pp. 7–8.

64. This cultural association is valid, I believe, notwithstanding Hiller's critique of anarchism in *Die Weisheit*, vol. 2: "Mit dem Satz, der Anarchismus bedeute einen psychologischen Irrtum, ist vordergründig zwar gemeint: Es sei die Hoffnung, nach Aufhebung der Zwangsnormen werde sich der menschliche Verkehr schon

von selber menschlich regeln . . . diese Hoffnung sei irrig, da sie eine zu zahme Struktur der Seele voraussetze; alle animalischen Instinkte brächen vielmehr hervor" (p. 14).

65. Hiller, *Eros*, p. 73.

66. Wolfgang Paulsen, drawing on Walter Falk's concepts of "creativism" and "destructivism," defined Expressionism as follows: "Der Kreativismus der voraufgehenden Generation führte in den Destruktivismus, der in seiner reinsten Form völlig unproductiv ist und nach Mitteln und Möglichkeiten verlangt, das Negativ in ein Positiv zu verwandeln." This aptly captures my interpretation of Hiller, who more than any other Expressionist sought a positive meaning for Nietzsche's critical philosophy, not only in art, but also in the realm of politics. See Paulsen, *Deutsche Literatur des Expressionismus*, p. 34. The theoretical foundational of Paulsen's study is Walter Falk, *Der kollektive Traum vom Kriege. Epochale Strukturen der deutschen Literatur zwischen 'Naturalismus' und 'Expressionismus'* (Heidelberg: Carl Winter, 1977).

67. Paul Raabe, "Verzeichnis der Mitarbeiter," in the reissue of *Die Aktion* [1911], 1 (1961): 61.

68. The talk that Hiller gave on November 9, 1909, was entitled "Das Wesen der Kultur." This text has not been found. However, Hiller dates the essay "Über Kultur" to November 1909, and there is good reason to believe that it is the same text as "Das Wesen der Kultur." "Über Kultur" was first published in *Der Sturm* 1 (1910): 187–88, 196–97, 203–204. It was then reprinted in *Die Weisheit der Langenweile*, vol. 1, pp. 49–71.

69. Ibid., p. 49.

70. Ibid., p. 50.

71. Ibid., pp. 54–55.

72. See the phrases contained in chapter 6, "Der Stil des Lebens," of *Philosophie des Geldes*: "den höchsten Gipfeln der Geistigkeit," and "den Unterschied . . . von Geist und Seele" (pp. 624, 647).

73. Hiller, *Die Weisheit*, vol. 1, p. 55.

74. Ibid., p. 51.

75. Ibid., pp. 53, 55.

76. Ibid., p. 51.

77. Ibid., pp. 90–91.

78. Ibid., p. 66.

79. For his critique of the culture of the feuilleton, see, for example, *Die Weisheit*, vol. 2, p. 48.

80. Hiller, *Die Weisheit*, vol. 1, p. 69.

81. Ibid., p. 62, 70.

82. Ibid., p. 67.

83. Ibid., pp. 66–67.

84. Ibid., p. 37.

85. Michael Josef Eisler, *Der Elfenbeinturm* (Berlin: Otto von Holten, 1910), p. 19.

86. Quoted in Hiller, *Die Weisheit*, vol. 1, pp. 58–59.

87. Ibid., pp. 60–61.

88. Simmel, *Philosophie des Geldes*, p. 645.

89. Ibid., p. 598.

90. Hiller, *Die Weisheit*, vol. 1, p. 25.

91. Ibid., p. 68.

92. Ibid., p. 70. The phrase reads: "die synthetischen Verfeinung der Gesamtheit eines geistigen Dasein."

93. Simmel, "Aus dem Nachgelassenen Tagebuche," in *Fragmente und Aufsätze*, pp. 4–46.

94. The concept of the will is particularly central to *Schopenhauer und Nietzsche*. Although Simmel has often been portrayed as a tragic and pessimistic philosopher, this text clearly demonstrated that Simmel was intent on using Nietzschean philosophy to criticize philosophical pessimism. The central element of this critique was Nietzschean concept, *der Wille*. See particularly chapter 4, "Schopenhauer. Der Pessimismus."

95. Hiller, "Kultur und Tat," in *Die Weisheit*, vol. 1, p. 74.

96. Friedländer attended Simmel's philosophy seminars in Berlin, and, unlike Hiller, he maintained Simmel's emphasis on creative indifference in his text *Schöpferische Indifferenz* (1918). Still, Friedländer was, alongside Hiller, one of the greatest disseminaters of Expressionist Nietzscheanism. See, for instance his *Friedrich Nietzsche: Eine intellektuelle Biographie* (1911) and his essays, "Dionysisches Christentum," *Die Weissen Blätter* 4 (1913); "Individuum," *Tätiger Geist! Zweites der Zieljahrbücher* (1917–18): 264–81. His *Psychologie (Der Lehre von der Seele)* (1907) is an example of the centrality of the discourse of the soul in the antibourgeois aesthetic sphere of Wilhelmine culture.

97. For a detailed discussion of the Expressionist origins of Activism, see Wurgaft, pp. 11–22. Hiller believed that the original document of Activism was Heinrich Mann's "Geist und Tat," *Pan*, November (1911): 137–43.

98. On Simmel's gender politics, see chapter 3 of this study. See also the essays in Georg Simmel, *Schriften zur Philosophie und Soziologie der Geschlechter*. For an interpretation of Simmel's sociology of women, see Lewis A. Coser, "Georg Simmels vernachlässigter Beitrag zur Soziologie der Frau," in Dahme und Rammstedt, *Georg Simmel und die Moderne*, pp. 80–91.

99. On Hiller and the homosexual rights movement, see James D. Steakley, *The Homosexual Emancipation Movement in Germany* (Salem, New Hampshire: Ayer Company, 1975).

100. Kurt Hiller, *Das Recht über sich selbst: Eine strafrechtsphilosophische Studie* (Heidelberg: Carl Winter, 1908), p. 2.

101. Hiller, *Das Recht*, pp. 1, 3.

102. Ibid., p. 67.

103. Ibid., p. 69.

104. Ibid., p. 71.

105. Ibid., p. 78.

106. Ibid., p. 103.

107. Ibid., pp. 106–107. The quotes within the quote are, as I said, to Simmel's *Einleitung in der Moralwissenschaft* (1892).

108. Paulsen, *Deutsche Literatur*, pp. 29–38.

109. Hiller, "Homosexualismus und Deutscher Vorentwurf," in *Die Weisheit*, vol. 2, pp. 24–45. This essay revisited the themes of *Das Recht über sich Selbst.*

110. See Kurt Hiller, "Aus einem Brief," in *Georg Heym: Dokumente zu seinem Leben und Werk*, p. 88. Here, Hiller suggests that Expressionism appealed to those who were looking for an articulation of sexuality and philosophy. No one articulated this linkage better than Hiller himself.

111. Kurt Hiller, "Erinnerungen an Simmel," in *Buch des Dankes*, pp. 257–67; see also Hiller, *Logos*, pp. 67–69.

112. The notable exception is Wurgaft's *The Activists*, pp. 36–38, 61.

113. Christl Wickert, *Helene Stöcker 1869–1943: Frauenrechtlerin, Sexualreformerin, und Pazifistin* (Bonn: Dietz, 1991), p. 69.

114. See for instance, Petra Rantzsch, *Helene Stöcker (1869–1943) Zwischen Pazifismus und Revolution* (Berlin: Der Morgen, 1984), pp. 48–52.

115. Cited in Wickert, p. 67.

116. Ibid., p. 68.

117. Stöcker's interest in women's issues predated her matriculation at Berlin University. See her essays "Die moderne Frau" (1893) and "Frauengedanken" (1894), which were reprinted in *Die Liebe und die Frauen* (Minden: Bruns' Verlag, 1906), pp. 19–30. In the first essay, she argues that society must move beyond the dogmatic ideal type of modern woman as housewife and whore and recognize her "cerebral" capacities. Not unlike the English utopian socialists, she sought a harmonious type of human being who combined love and intellect. This conception of humanity would facilitate women's "right to freedom and love." Compare these to Simmel's earliest essays on gender: "Zur Psychologie der Frauen" (1890), "Einiges über die Prostitution in Gegenwart und Zukunft" (1892), and "Ein Jubiläum der Frauenbewegung" (1892) in *Schriften zur Philosophie und Soziologie der Geschlechter*, pp. 27–91.

118. The sources of *geistige Kultur* were overdetermined and were in no way limited to Simmel. In a seminar from Kurt Breysig, Stöcker heard her first lecture on Nietzsche. Moreover, Dilthey's philosophy contained many of the discursive elements that dominated the culture of *Geist-Politik*. On Stöcker's academic life at Berlin University, see Wickert, *Helene Stöcker*, pp. 27–39.

119. Simmel, "Frauenstudien an der Berliner Universität," in *Schriften zur Philosophie und Soziologie der Geschlechter*, pp. 159–60.

120. Simmel, "Weibliche Kultur," in *Schriften zur Philosophie und Soziologie der Geschlechter*, p. 69.

121. Ibid., p. 162.

122. Wickert, *Helene Stöcker*, p. 23.

123. For a fuller biographical account of Stöcker, see Wickert, *Helene Stöcker*; see also Amy Hackett, "Left-Wing Intellectual and Sex Reformer," in *When Biology Became Destiny: Women in Weimar and Nazi Germany*, ed. Renate Bridenthal, Atina Grossman, and Marion Kaplan (New York: Monthly Review Press, 1984), pp.109–30; for a discussion of Stöcker's politics in the context of Weimar, see Atina Grossmann, *Reforming Sex: The German Movement for Birth Control and Abortion Reform, 1920–1950* (New York: Oxford University Press, 1995).

124. Stöcker, "Frauengedanken," in *Die Liebe und die Frauen*, p. 27.

125. Stöcker, "Nietzsches Frauenfeindschaft," in *Die Liebe und die Frauen*, p. 71.

126. Ibid., p. 71.

127. Ibid., p. 71.

128. See her essay "Mutterschaft und geistige Arbeit," in *Die Liebe und die Frauen*, pp. 84–89.

129. Stöcker, "Foreword," in *Die Liebe und die Frauen*, p. ix. In 1907, as a result of political conflicts within the *Bund für Mutterschutz und Sexualreform*, Stöcker founded a new journal, *Die neue Generation*. The title indicates the close connection between the youth movement and the cultural politics of the period. Gustav Wyneken, leader of the youth movement, was clearly a *Geist-Politiker*, and his central concern was a pedagogy of spirituality. More will be said about this association below.

130. Concerning Stöcker's politics in the context of the Kaiserreich, see Ann Taylor Allen, "Mothers of the New Generation: Adele Schreiber, Helene Stöcker, and the Evolution of the German Idea of Motherhood, 1900–1915," *Signs* 10, no. 3 (1985): 418–38. Allen's work does not reference the philosophical and discursive cache of Stöcker's politics. Stöcker's support for "free relationships," the cohabitation of unwed couples, was a classic example of an ethical anti-institutionalism. Her endorsement of free relationships was not an endorsement of sexual anarchy, interpersonal egoism, or moral nihilism. Rather, as a Nietzschean, she was far more concerned with the task of ethical self-creation, and this philosophy of life brought her into conflict with dogmatic institutional ethics, i.e., marriage.

131. For a comparison of Stöcker's ideas to other Wilhelmine feminists, see H. Hinton Thomas, *Nietzsche in German Politics and Society 1890–1918* (La Salle, Ill: Open Court, 1983), especially chapter 7, "The Feminist Movement and Nietzsche."

132. Wickert, *Helene Stöcker*, p. 29.

133. Stöcker, "Mutterschaft und geistige Arbeit," in *Die Liebe und die Frauen*, p. 88.

134. Simmel, "Weibliche Kultur," in *Schriften zur Philosophie und Soziologie der Geschlechter*; Stöcker, "Weibliche Erotik" in *Die Liebe und die Frauen*.

135. Stöcker, "Die Liebe der Persönlichkeit," in *Die Liebe und die Frauen*, p. 155.

136. Ibid., p. 155.

137. Stöcker, "Die Neue Mutter" [1902], in *Die Liebe und die Frauen*, p. 83.

138. Yet strangely, their political associations and shared discursive politics have not made their way into their historiographies: neither Simmel nor Hiller are mentioned in Amy Hackett's "Helene Stöcker: Left-Wing Intellectual and Sex Reformer"; there is no discussion of Hiller in Wickert's *Helene Stöcker*; Habereder's *Kurt Hiller und der literarische Aktivismus* and Wurgaft's *The Activists: Kurt Hiller and the Politics of Action on the German Left 1914–1933* do not note the cultural and institutional linkages of these two intellectuals.

139. Hiller, "Kameradin im Kampf: Helene Stöcker," in *Köpfe und Tröpfe: Profile aus einem Vierteljahrhundert* (Hamburg: Rowohlt, 1950), p. 262, my emphasis.

140. Hiller, *Eros*, p. 75. See especially Hiller's "Der Sinn eines Lebens (Magnus Hirschfeld)" in *Köpfe und Tröpfe*, pp. 253–59. Here he describes Hirschfeld as a "mentor-comrade."

141. Stöcker. "Das Recht über sich Selbst," *Die Neue Generation* 4 (1908): 270–73.

142. Hiller, *Logos,* p. 208.

143. Magnus Hirschfeld, ed., *Zur Reform des Sexualstrafrechts* (Leipzig: Ernst Birscher, 1926).

144. Hiller, *Logos*, p. 208. This organization brought together seven organizations: the Department for Sexual Reform in Hirschfeld's Institute for Sexual Science, the Scientific-Humanitarian Committee, Stöcker's League for the Protection of Mothers and Sexual Reform, the German League for Human Rights, the Society for the Knowledge of Gender, the Society for Sexual Reform, and the Union for the Reform of Marriage Rights. A nine-member steering committee was elected, and it included Hiller, Hirschfeld, Stöcker, and the communist Richard Linsert.

145. Hiller, "Philosophie des Ziels," *Das Ziel* 1 (1916): 209.

146. See the introduction to "Politischer Rat Geistiger Arbeiter," *Das Ziel* 3 (1919): 218–19.

147. Stöcker, "Moderne Bevölkerungspolitik," *Die Neue Generation* 12 (1916): 79.

148. Hackett, p. 120.

149. "Politischer Rat geistiger Arbeiter," pp. 218–19.

150. Ibid., p. 222.

151. Ibid., pp. 221–23.

152. Ibid., p. 222.

153. On the pacifism of Hiller and the *Aktivisten*, see Rudolf Leonhard, "Das Problem der Gewalt und der bürgerliche Pazifismus," *Das Ziel* 3 (1920):175–78; "Programm der Deutschen Friedengesellschaft," in *Geistige Politik! Fünftes der Ziel-Jahrbücher* (1924): 167–69; Hiller, "Haager Friedenkongress" *Die Neue Rundschau* 1 (1923): 157–68.

154. An excellent reader of this "radikale geistige Bewegung" is available: *Der Aktivismus 1915–1920*, ed. Wolfgang Rothe (München: Deutscher Taschenbuch, 1969). The date of publication suggests a belief that self-styled German activists of the 1960s had much in common with antiwar *Aktivisten* like Heinrich Mann and Kurt Hiller.

155. Hiller, *Logos*, p. 97.

156. The German title, "Die Untaten des bürgerlichen Typus," carries a double meaning that does not translate smoothly. "Untaten" combines the colloquial meaning, crimes, and its literal meaning, inaction. One of the central crimes of bourgeois intellectuals is their inactivity.

157. Gustav Wyneken, "Schöpferische Erziehung," *Das Ziel* 1 (1916): 121–35; Walter Benjamin, "Das Leben der Studenten," *Das Ziel* 1 (1916): 141–56.

158. Stöcker, "Militarisierung der Jugend und Mütterlichkeit," *Tätiger Geist! Zweites der Ziel-Jahrbücher* 2/3 (1917–1918): 150–66.

159. Hiller, "Die Neue Partei (Politik der Synthese)," *Geistige Politik! Fünftes der Ziel-Jahrbücher* (1924): 115–66.

160. Hiller, "Philosophie des Ziels," *Das Ziel* 1 (1916): 187–218.

161. Ibid., pp. 198–99, 202–203. Similar language can be found in "Logokratie oder Ein Weltbund des Geistes," *Das Ziel* 4 (1920): 217–47.

162. Hiller, "Philosophie des Ziels," p. 216.

163. Ibid., pp. 214–17. Many sections are radically abbreviated. The italicized words in this translation appeared in capitals in the original.

164. Hiller, "Logokratie," p. 235.

165. For the discussion of *Aktivisten* themes which fails to reference the *Aktivisten,* see Bruce Detwiler, *Nietzsche and the Politics of Aristocratic Radicalism*. The Activists represent Wilhelmine Germany's most rigorous realization of Nietzschean *Moral der Vornehmheit*. Their absence from Detwiler's text is a missed opportunity to investigate a collective and anti-Marxist version of Nietzschean aristocratic radicalism.

166. "Nietzsche. Die Moral der Vornehmheit" is the title of the final chapter of Simmel's *Schopenhauer und Nietzsche*.

167. Georg Simmel, *Schulpädagogik*, (Osterwieck: Zickfeldt, 1922), p. 125.

168. Ibid., pp. 2, 4.

169. Simmel, "Anhang über sexuelle Aufklärung," in *Schulpädagogik,* pp. 127–34.

170. Ibid., p. 129.

171. Simmel, "Goethes Liebe," *Die Neue Generation* 12, nos. 3, 4 (1916): 333–35.

172. Georg Simmel, "Der Platonische und der moderne Eros," in *Fragmente und Aufsätze*, pp. 125–47.

173. Simmel, "Über die Liebe," in *Fragmente und Aufsätze,* p. 57.

174. Ibid., p. 69.

175. Ibid., p. 116.

176. Ibid., p. 115.

177. Ibid., p. 122.

178. Ibid., p. 81.

179. See, for instance, Friedländer's *Schöpferische Indifferenz,* chapter 9, "Liebe" and Wyneken, "Jugendliche Erotik," *Die Neue Generation* 12 (1916): 191–98.

180. Jochen Schulte-Sasse, "Foreword" to Peter Sloterdijk, *Thinker on Stage: Nietzsche's Materialism* (Minneapolis: University of Minnesota Press, 1989), p. xx.

181. Simmel, "Der platonische und der moderne Eros," p. 145.

182. Nietzsche, *Ecce Homo*, in *The Basic Writings of Nietzsche*, trans. and ed. Walter Kaufman (New York: Modern Library, 1968), p. 710.

183. *Aktivismus* was the most political ideology of the Expressionist Movement. The first attempt to distinguish *Aktivismus* from *Expressionismus* is found in Wolfgang Paulsen, *Expressionismus und Aktivismus: Eine typologische Untersuchung* (Strassburg: Heinz & Co., 1935). More than the typology itself, this document testifies to the homology of Nazi culture and Thomas Mann's interpretation of Nietzsche. Paulsen's typological distinction was derived from Mann's *Betrachtungen eines Unpolitischen*. In chapter 3, Paulsen draws upon Mann in defining *Expressionismus* as gothic, anti-Western, and antipolitical; *Aktivismus* is French, pro-Western, democratic, and political. Paulsen relies on the poetry of Fritz von Unruh to construct his own ideal type: "die Synthese von Geist und Seele, von Ratio und Religion—von Aktivismus und Expressionismus" (p. 126). His synthetic ideal was apolitical *Aktivismus*. This ideal, with its dubious defiling of Hiller and the Activists as "French," participates in the ascension of German fascism. It is also patently false in its portrayal of Hiller as a supporter of democracy. But this falsehood points to a cultural truth. Paulsen's typological text, like Mann's, was an interested political interpretation of Expressionism that conceived of itself as disinterested and apolitical.

Paulsen's interests are homologous, if nonidentical, with Nazi culture. The Nazis drew heavily upon the Activist language of spirit and soul in their critique of the dispiriting character of secular socialism and bourgeois materialism. Mann and Paulsen, then, were examples of a conservative cultural imperative to refashion Activist language with a thoroughly apolitical and "German" aura. This imperative, and here Paulsen and Mann are unambiguous, was almost exclusively a struggle over the cultural meaning of Nietzsche's reception among the German avant-garde.

Roy F. Allen has argued, with justification, that "Wolfgang Paulsen's *Expressionismus und Aktivismus* was the most penetrating analysis of Expressionist literature to appear before the Second World War. [Its] thesis . . . was to have a considerable impact on subsequent scholarship." While Allen asserts that the Left-wing elision of Expressionism and Nazi culture was "during the late 1930s to the mid–1940s . . . colored in a very conspicuous way by the political conditions of the era," the cultural politics of Paulsen's 1935 text are never referenced. This may tell us something about the political unconscious of Paulsen's considerable impact. See Allen's excellent study, *Literary Life in German Expressionism and the Berlin Circles* (Ann Arbor: UMI Research Press, 1983), pp. 3, 4, 253.

184. Hiller, "Erinnerungen," pp. 258–59.

185. John C. Fout, "Sexual Politics in Wilhelmine Germany: The Male Gender Crisis, Moral Purity, and Homophobia," *Journal of the History of Sexuality* 2, no. 3 (1992): 388–421. Although Fout does not reference Hiller's contribution to the homosexual rights movement, he presents a nuanced picture of political and cultural forces—most notably the moral purity movements—resisting radical cultural movements. "The moral purity movement was in reality a male-dominated, cleric-led response to the growing presence of women of all classes in the workplace and in the public domain" (p. 408). Simmel not only influenced the homosexual rights movement but also the "social-radical," as opposed to the "mainline," wing of the feminist movement. Stöcker's social-radical *Bund für Mutterschutz und Sexualreform.* For a detailed analysis of "social-radical" and "mainline" feminism, see Ann Taylor Allen, "German Radical Feminism and Eugenics, 1900–1908," *German Studies Review* 11 (1988): 31–56. Her distinction between "mainline" and "social-radical" feminists derives from Daniel J. Kevles, *In the Name of Eugenics* (New York: Knopf, 1985), pp. 57–90. Unlike Fout and Allen, who focus on the political programs of the homosexual and radical feminist movements, this chapter contributes to a history of the philosophical underpinnings of theses movements.

186. Grossmann, *Reforming Sex*, p. 16; the reference is to Stöcker and the *Bund für Mutterschutz und Sexualreform*, but it is also applicable to Hiller whose important role as a leader in the sexual reform movement is not addressed by Grossmann.

6

TROPES OF THE COMMUNIST SOUL

Bloch, Lukács, and the Simmel Circle

Simmel has been described repeatedly as a cultural philosopher. With equal justification, one could call him the philosopher of the soul.

Siegfried Kracauer, 1920[1]

STUDENTS REPAY TEACHERS INADEQUATELY, SPOKE ZARATHUSTRA, IF THEY REMAIN mere pupils. Simmel was the Zarathustra of his generation, and this may explain the historical occlusion of his generational significance. Because they paid their debt to their mentor by refusing to remain epigones, Ernst Bloch and Georg Lukács can be and have been studied as if their primary intellectual debt was not to Simmel. This approach, however, severely limits a cultural history of the late Wilhelmine period and transgresses the historical record. In a 1918 obituary of Simmel, Lukács recounted his mentor's historical significance as follows:

> Georg Simmel was unquestionably the most important and the most interesting transitional figure in all of modern philosophy. Therefore, he was—for all the truly philosophical talents of the young generation of thinkers (who were more than purely intelligent or fluid scholars in individual philosophical disciplines)—so exceedingly alluring that there are hardly any among them who for a short or long period of time were not slain by the magic of his thought.[2]

Among radical students of philosophy and culture at Berlin University, Simmel was a core figure in two cultural transitions: from the predominance of spiritual science (*Geisteswissenschaft*) and literary Expressionism in prewar culture to a postwar cultural politics of historical materialism and the New Objectivity (*Neue Sachlichkeit*). This chapter is an account of this generational and cultural transition, from Simmel's practical idealism to the unique brand of Marxism Lukács and Bloch developed in the culture of war. While Simmel's students were not epigones, their intellectual trajectory is best conceived in relation to his thought, which this chapter treats as the historical a priori of twentieth-century German Marxism. My intention is to explain the communist politics and aesthetics of Bloch and Lukács by placing them within a pre–Great War context and by comparing their communist politics to Simmel's socialism. Of primary significance is their intellectual development under Simmel's influence at Berlin University and within Simmel's social circle of assimilated or assimilating Jews. In addition to the letters and publications of Lukács and Bloch, there is another source for reconstructing Simmel's cultural influence, namely, the essays and correspondences of another brilliant Simmel student, Margarete von Bendemann. Her analysis of Simmel, Bloch, and Lukács provides a cogent and intimate understanding of the generational transition to a post-Simmelian communist aesthetics and ethics. For Simmel's acolytes, the culture of war was a caesura and the formative context of a new public philosophy that remained indebted to his protean antibourgeois philosophy of life.

TROPES AND THE CULTURE OF WAR

Tropes are a methodological starting point for assessing the continuity and discontinuity of Simmel's legacy. In the preface to *The Birth of Tragedy*, Nietzsche wrote the following:

> The time in which it was written, in spite of which it was written, bears witness to the exciting time of the Franco-Prussian War 1870–71. As the thunder of the battle of Wörth was rolling over Europe, the muser and riddle-friend who was to be the father of this book . . . wrote down his thoughts.[3]

Why did Nietzsche feel compelled to discuss the context of this text's conception? He contends that it was written "in spite" of the war, and this contention was borne out by the absence of further mention of the war in its content. Nietzsche seems both conscious and unconscious of the war's affect on his book. I suggest that Nietzsche may be the "father" of *The Birth of Tragedy*, but war itself is the "mother" of the tragic trope. That is not to say that the Franco-Prussian war created the tragic trope. It is rather to suggest that wars have an associative relationship or elective affinity to tragic tropes. Due to Prussia's stunning victory, pessimistic tropes played a relatively insignificant role in the postwar German culture of 1871, especially in comparison to the role they would play in the postwar revolutionary culture of 1918. The Prussian victory of 1871 fortified a positive cultural image of war and affirmed political conservatism. Germany's defeat in 1918, in stark contrast, undermined the affirmative cultural image of war and challenged the political and cultural status quo, which now was held accountable for the experiential gulf between the initial sublimity of battle and the subsequent horror of senseless mass deaths and defeat.

What is the significance of these tropes in assessing Simmel's intellectual metempsychosis after his death in 1918? In the culture of the Great War, Simmel's intellectual heirs—in this case, Lukács, Bloch, and Benjamin—drew upon the cultural reservoir of tragic tropes on their way to constructing a communist politics of the soul, *die Seele*. The circumstances of war culture in essence called forth tropes of decline, which in turn framed the political arena of cultural disputes. Perhaps the most popular trope appeared in Spengler's *Decline of the West* (*Untergang des Abendlandes*), and its politics, too, were tied to the concept of the soul.[4] Spengler's text was an epigram of the spiritual turn of mind found in the culture of war. While Spengler's trope of "decline" sounds secular, his prescriptive solution to social decadence was a life-content of political spirituality. The book made a distinction between civilization and *Kultur*. A return to the spiritual-racial origins of German *Kultur*, Spengler argued, would reverse the process of decline. This distinction between civilization and culture corresponded to correlative distinctions among the German avant-garde: the distinction between community [*Gemeinschaft*] and society [Gesellschaft] and between spirit [*Geist*] and law [*Gesetz*].[5] While *Decline of the West* was not published until 1918, Spengler actually conceived and wrote it before the war. It is, then, a prewar critique of cultural decadence that subsequently came to express both the culture of defeat and the pessimism of many intellectuals.[6] Its trope of decline was exemplary of a larger historical a priori of war culture; particularly after 1918, German cultural politics were shaped through or against pessimistic tropes that differentially assaulted the status quo tropes of social optimism, most notably, progress.

Tropes of decline were, so to speak, *tropisms* of a revolutionary and ruinous cultural context, that is, involuntary cultural reflexes of a society in distress. The German events of 1918 (revolutionary upheaval, cultural uncertainty, economic hardship and the pain of defeat) did not create these tropes. They—apocalypse, the Fall, tragedy, and decline—are ancient, if variegated, archetypes of Western culture. But, undoubtedly their significance as an interpretive unconscious of the German historical imagination was renewed and intensified by ashen postwar realities. It is easy to disregard the creative significance of these metahistorical tropes precisely because of their seeming naturalness to Western culture. Moreover, the bias, often unconscious among historians, toward a mimetic understanding of language—i.e., the discourses of decline merely mirrored Germany's immediate postwar historical context—limits our ability to assess the formative, productive, and long-lasting impact of these tropes upon German culture. The naturalization of these tropes and the mimetic bias suppress the fact that no apodictic form for expressing historical reality exists. One should not go so far as Nietzsche and suggest that there are no facts, only interpretations. This overlooks the novelty of the concentration of particular tropes after 1918 and the degree to which they established the bounded cachet or historical force field of cultural debate. Without the broad facts of war and revolution, German culture would not have been constituted by a particular constellation of tropes. This "tropological prefiguration of the historical field," to borrow a phrase from Hayden White, is the backdrop for an intellectual history of the cultural transmutation of Simmel's reputation.[7] Our preliminary conclusions about the political meaning of these tropes stand in stark contrast to the conclusions of the German cultural historian Klaus Vondung.

> Apocalyptic dreams had established themselves in so many of the representatives of the bourgeois educational establishment that even the defeat of 1918 did not destroy them. On the contrary, defeat frequently strengthened the resistance to reality, especially since the subsequent social situation of academics became even more precarious. The revolution of spirit [*Die Revolution des Geistes*] continued to express itself in the elite demands of the "Conservative Revolution" and among academics whose intellectual fortunes were in decline, just as it did in vulgarly articulated declassé revolts. Both revolts flowed into National Socialism or were drawn into it.[8]

Simmel's legacy offers a different wartime narrative and one that is predominantly anti-Nazi. Within and against tragic tropes of war culture, Bloch, Lukács, Benjamin, and Hiller transformed Simmel's legacy of Nietzschean anticapitalism into heterogeneous strategies for resisting Nazi culture.

The affective intensity of the culture of war was nothing less than "the ethical decision for the future," as the Activist Ludwig Rubiner called it.[9] Simmel, as we recall, described the war as the "absolute situation" because it was a collective event that exposed the ethical and sociological character of personal decisions.[10] For Max Scheler, the moral "genius of war" was a "metaphysical awakening out of the stifling condition of a leaden sleep."[11] Outside of the secular Left, the ethical and metaphysical decisions called forth by this absolute situation were substantially shaped by the discourse and tropes of spirituality. The Christian denominations employed a theodicean logic to legitimize the profanity of Christians killing Christians. For others, however, this theodicy of God's goodness and omnipotence was no longer convincing in view of the war. Paraphrasing Fichte, Lukács described the war as the "epoch of perfect sinfulness" and the military draft as "the vilest slavery."[12] The immediate social nature of personal decisions now meant that a personal sin was absolutely and perfectly social. There was no personal evil per se, only epochal evil. Correlatively, Lukács, Benjamin, and Bloch came to reject the ethics of personal redemption in favor of an ethics of collective redemption. This response should not be understood as a self-evident realization of Jewish messianism, nor as a clean break from Simmel's sociological critique of bourgeois interiority. Here, causal priority must be granted to the culture of war, which intensified a multitude of social ethics: nationalism, internationalism, Germanness, socialism, Christianity, and messianism. In any case, the ethical condensation of the personal and the political and of civil society and the state during the war combined with Germany's revolutionary cultural insecurity to solicit a new social metaphysics. Benjamin developed a linguistic metaphysics of the Fall, Lukács researched the "age of the apocalypse," and Bloch began to write through the Christian trope of apocalypse.[13]

The tropes of perfect sinfulness developed in the culture of war—the Apocalypse, decline, the Fall, and tragedy—were the cultural framework of a post-Simmelean anticapitalism. In her memoir, Margarete von Bendemann reflected upon the war and its impact on the postwar generation:

> While for Simmel the soul [*Seele*] was above all independent from and foreign to the external world and was basically an internal world, the word *Existenz* encompasses *from the inside out* all external conditions which structure human life. In the new generation, in place of the soul there appeared not only a different terminology but a totally different reality. After the First World War, thinkers were only left with expressing a chaotic reality as a clear reality and, thereby, consciously or unconsciously, they reached back to the concept of *Existenz*. Culture in Simmel's sense, and even society as he grasped it, no longer existed after the war. And even the individual person had lost his meaning; the salvation of the soul [*das Heil der Seele*], the individual law, and all concepts of a purely personal life were destroyed for this generation.[14]

The concept of the soul, for instance, was the controlling idea of his massive *Critique of the Fundamental Concepts of Ethics*. It became a key conceptual inheritance shaping the communist politics of Lukács and Bloch.[15] The postwar shift from the philosophy of the soul (*Seele*) to the philosophy of *Existenz* may generally describe the intellectual trajectory of Martin Heidegger (*Dasein*) and Lukács (*Ontologie*). However, in the case of Bloch, this description was philosophically inaccurate. He did not reach back to a purely materialist conception of social reality but sought to articulate social chaos through a metaphysics of chaos. Even in Lukács's case, his communist politics were one among many possible realizations of

Simmel's, qua his own, philosophy of the soul. What is incontrovertible, however, is that the revolutionary culture of war was an *Existenz* that transformed Simmel's cultural significance. This transformation was a metempsychosis of Simmel's antibourgeois philosophy of the soul rather than a destruction of it.

JUDAISM AND THE SIMMEL CIRCLE

To treat Simmel as an historical a priori of postwar anticapitalist thought begs the question of dissemination. In previous chapters, it has been argued that Simmel had the greatest impact on well-to-do Jewish intellectuals. Benjamin, Bloch, Hiller, and Lukács were examples of this class and cultural identity. They were all born with a familial surplus (value) of cultural and/or financial capital. Hiller and Lukács were proud of the talmudic scholars in their familial lineages. Benjamin's father was a wealthy art dealer, and Lukács came from one of the wealthiest Jewish families in Eastern Europe. The problem with this bourgeois Jewish identity as an explanatory affinity is its eclectic content. Both Simmel and Lukács came from culturally assimilated families and identified their religion as Protestant on their German vitae.[16] Moreover, both they and their parents had been baptized in the Protestant faith. Simmel, furthermore, married a Prussian Protestant, Gertrud Kinel, and they were married in the Protestant Church.

At a minimum, Simmel and Lukács confirm the complexity of cultural identity. Concerning his cultural assimilation, Lukács wrote in his autobiography:

> I am from a pure Jewish family. And precisely for that reason, the ideologies of Judaism had hardly any influence on my intellectual [*geistige*] development. . . . In a word, our relation to the Jewish religion was dominated by complete indifference.[17]

Simmel expressed related ideas in a letter to Heinrich Rickert in 1906: "Obviously there are today a slew of Jews, who no longer possess a specifically Jewish style of culture."[18]

This paradox of ethnic identity—pure and indifferent; present and absent—had an analogue in Bloch's description of Simmel:

> Simmel's work contained no Jewish themes. (I interpose that Werner Sombart had always understood Simmel's "Excursus Concerning the Stranger" in *Sociology* as a portrait of the Jews.) Perhaps for that reason Cohen despised Simmel and said to a student who wanted to transfer from Marburg to Berlin: "What could you learn from him?" Although born in an

> assimilated milieu of already baptized parents, Simmel had specifically Jewish, yes Eastern Jewish, gestures and idioms. In this regard, he was an exception among those of his social stratum. Because of his specifically Jewish mannerisms, not simply because his Jewish origins as such, he received his *Ordinariat* very late in life.[19]

What must be concluded is that Simmel's identity was hardly fixed. Marianne Weber disparagingly described him as "typically Jewish, [and] ugly," and Sombart received his work as a sociology of German Jews.[20] Hermann Cohen apparently despised the absence of Jewish concepts in his work.[21] Bloch paradoxically related that Simmel lacked Jewish concepts but spoke in Jewish idioms. Most importantly, perhaps, Bloch understood Simmel as suffering an anti-Semitic predicament. No doubt, Simmel's overtly Jewish mannerisms were exceptional in academia and would have provided a sphere of comfort for other Jewish intellectuals who felt alienated by academic and general anti-Semitism.

But what was Simmel's self-understanding? Did he see and understand himself as a Jew? There is very little evidence that he did. Simmel's son stated in his memoirs that not only did his father have no interest in his Jewish genealogical tree but also had an aversion to discussing his ancestry.[22] Furthermore, the epistolary record clearly shows that Zionism held no allure for him. He viewed it as an unrealizable and unworthy utopia. Instead of separation, Simmel favored the integration of German and Jewish culture. Simmel wrote to a young Russian student in 1897: "The question of Jewish culture does not concern rising above but fusing with another culture, and by fusing, a third culture is created out of two peoples."[23] Simmel was unambiguous. Jews should participate in and integrate into German cultural life. It seems that Simmel was so well integrated into German culture that his past Jewish identity had little meaning to him. In *From Georg Simmel to Franz Rosenzweig: Studies of Jewish Thinkers in German Culture*, Hans Liebeschütz admits that Simmel "had no conscious relationship to Jewish traditions."[24]

JEWISH *EMBOURGEOISMENT*

If, because of the protean content of his identity, we are unable to contentedly label Simmel a Jewish thinker, it remains indisputable that the upper-class culture of Jews and assimilated Jews was the context for the dissemination of his thought. In other words, while Simmel did not see himself as a Jew, prototypical Jewish thinkers like Bloch and Rosenzweig certainly did. Simmel's Wilhelmine context was overdetermined: Berlin as the political capital of twentieth-century Europe, rapid industrialization, Naturalism and

Expressionism, the SPD as the world's largest socialist party, and Berlin University. Still, the most intimate context of dissemination of his thought was Jewish cultural circles, and at the center of Simmel's circle was Margarete (Susman) von Bendemann. Like Marie Luise Enckendorff, Helene Stöcker, and Marianne Weber, von Bendemann provides an example of Simmel's support for feminist intellectuals. She began attending Simmel's lectures at Berlin University in 1900 and was invited to attend his private seminar on aesthetics in 1901. Simmel became von Bendemann's primary intellectual mentor. At the private seminars she befriended Gertrud Simmel, who regularly participated in her husband's Westend seminars.

The Simmel and von Bendemann residences in Berlin's Westend were a salonlike context for the coalescence of intellectuals in Berlin. In their house, related Michael Landmann, the Simmels "brought together the intellectual elite of Berlin."[25] From 1905 to 1912, the Simmel and von Bendemann residences were the social sun around which Bloch, Lukács, Buber, Landauer, George, Rilke, and many others circled. Bloch, Lukács, and Simmel, for example, carried on a well-documented correspondence with von Bendemann; as a result of their academic and social contacts, the Simmels and von Bendemann became close friends.[26] Von Bendemann and Simmel were so intimate that Simmel dedicated *Die Religion* (1906), a text solicited by Buber for the series *Gesellschaft*, to her. The resilience of her ties to the Simmel's also is indicated by her second book, *Von Sinn der Liebe* (1912), which was dedicated to Gertrud Simmel. In 1912, a year after her close friends Bloch and Lukács left Berlin and entered the Weber circle in Heidelberg, von Bendemann also left Berlin, returning to Switzerland. She, like Stöcker, thereby made a decision to remove herself from the confines of marriage. Perhaps Lukács and Bloch's intellectual single-mindedness, symbolized by their move to Heidelberg, inspired her to continue her own development as an independent writer. No doubt the culture of the Simmel circle inclined her to go her own way. Simmel's Nietzscheanism, with its emphasis on the responsible freedom of individual decisions, and correlative feminism immeasurably influenced von Bendemann. One intellectual biography of von Bendemann explained her desire for intellectual independence as follows: "Simmel saved the other-being of women from the hegemony of a culture stamped by men."[27] Von Bendemann's resolute political turn toward feminism and religious socialism during the First World War was conditioned by Simmel's philosophy. Like Stöcker, she was a respected intellectual in the pre-Nazi era and developed a unique blend of socialism and feminism contiguous to, but outside of, the Marxist tradition.

Von Bendemann's social circumstances in Berlin symbolize the ethnic and class matrix which characterized the Simmel circle. She was born Margarete Susman in Hamburg in 1872 and moved to Zurich at the age of ten. She was the second daughter in a wealthy Jewish family. Her father was a liberal who had supported the democratic demands of the Revolution of 1848. By the age of twenty she had published her first book of poetry and was, like young Gertrud Kinel (Simmel) and Bloch's future wife, Else von Strizky, an aspiring artist. Her second text of poetry, *Mein Land*, was published in 1901, the same year that she entered Simmel's personal circle and private seminars. From all accounts she was a respected intellectual. In 1906, she married the painter and art historian, Eduard von Bendemann, who was a protestant aristocrat. Their marriage was indicative of the predominant social matrix found in the Simmel circle. Like Bloch and Lukács, she was an example of the *embourgeoisement* of the German aristocracy by well-to-do Jewish intellectuals.[28] *Embourgeoisement* is best understood as the wedding of substantially fixed wealth (land) and aristocratic title to liquid and academic capital. In this matrimonial process, the historiographical question of class agency, *embourgeoisment* versus gentrification, is irrelevant. The marriage of the bourgeoisie and the aristocracy was marked by the liberal compromises of free love. Debt-ridden monarchies and financially troubled aristocrats exchanged titles for cash and/or the prestige of academic capital. The *haute bourgeoisie* willingly interchanged their financial top hats for the assimilating power and cultural cachet of the aristocratic tiara.

Lukács's name contains a rich narrative of this class dynamic. György Löwinger was born in Budapest in April 1885. His father was Director of the Hungarian General Credit Bank, one of the central banking institutions of the Austro-Hungarian Dual Monarchy. When György was five years old, his father, József, Magyarized the family name, Löwinger, to Lukács. József then paid a substantial sum for a noble title in 1901.[29] When György began studying in Berlin in 1909, he made full use of his father's title. He Germanized his name to Georg, and under the noble designation, "Georg von Lukács," he published early texts such as *The Soul and the Forms* (1911) and "Concerning the Poverty of Spirit [*Geist*]" (1912); substantially written in Berlin, these were Simmelean texts through and through. Lukács, who has been called the greatest Marxist intellectual of the twentieth century, was a *parvenu* aristocrat with unparalleled wealth. But, it was not only wealth and an aristocratic title that Lukács carried with him to Berlin in 1909. He received his Doctor of Philosophy from Budapest University in November of that year for his work on the history of modern drama and bourgeois culture. Subsequently he went by the name of Dr. Georg von Lukács. Lukács was an *Idealtyp*—and here I invoke a concept of his mentor, Max Weber—exemplifying the *embourgeoisement* of the aristocracy within the Simmel circle.

Bloch's biography and class phenomenology similarly comport with this historical *Idealtyp*. Like Lukács, Bloch was born in 1885 into a well-to-do Jewish family. His father was an administrative official in the railroad industry.[30] His uncle, a wealthy merchant and manufacturer, evinced wealth in particular branches of the Bloch family tree. The city of Ernst's birth was Ludwigshafen. It was adjacent to Mannheim and a monument to Manchester capitalism. Its cultural architecture bore little resemblance to the beauty of Budapest. In terms of cultural environment and class standing, then, Bloch started a few branches lower than Lukács on the European social stalk. The most obvious social difference was Bloch's absence of aristocratic bearing, and Bloch's family, while firmly middle class, possessed nothing close to the wealth of the Lukács family. Nonetheless, they shared many cultural attributes. Both were of Jewish heritage and from wealthy families. Both completed their doctoral degrees and, unbeknownst to one another, in 1908 decided to move to Berlin to continue their studies with Simmel. They were immediately welcomed into the Simmel circle.

BLOCH AND LUKÁCS

In 1908, Bloch received his doctorate in philosophy from Marburg University. In that same year, he moved to Berlin to continue his studies with Simmel. It was there that he became acquainted with Lukács. They both attended Simmel's private colloquiums in Berlin Westend. Unlike Lukács, however, Bloch's access to familial finances was either terminated or substantially reduced after he received his doctorate. In comparison to Lukács, then, Bloch's class tailoring cut a diminutive figure. Bloch sought to overcome this cultural and financial deficiency by marrying a wealthy Jewish aristocrat, Else von Stritzky. "You know my desire for the social stability of marriage," Bloch wrote to Lukács in 1911; "there certainly must be special reasons for such a premarital decision—outside of (insufficiently intense) love, which has little to do with the contract of marriage."[31] The marriage contract with Herr von Stritzky, completed by May 1913, produced something rare in Bloch's epistles to Lukács: a mood of unbridled, if interested, happiness.

> I recognize Else . . . as a good, aristocratic, noble person . . . of aristocratic blood: today I came to know that she has a hereditary family vault in the Danzig Marien Church dating back to the fifteenth century. It has been abandoned for four generations. I have also learned that the Stritzky's will be next to receive the Russian patent for their old baronial title. Concerning the other, more modest, family line, it can be traced to [jurist, statesman, and historian] Hugo Grotius. I was totally unaware of this lineage of the baroness. Else speaks very rarely about these things, because she is already a noble type. I, however, am something of a *Hans im Glück*—a successful social climber and an aesthete, and, thus, I am pleased about all this. Obviously, I did not need to write all of this right away. But I am so boundlessly happy, you, my dear, great, highly gifted Djoury. Of course, at first we presumedly will receive scarcely more than

> 30,000 Marks. However, Else knows with certainty that she will possess more than a million after the death of her father.[32]

Else offered Bloch more than love, money, aristocratic bearing, and a prized intellectual heritage. As an unemployed scholar in possession of his doctorate, his marriage to Else was the means to carry on the life of a critical intellectual. Just as Simmel discussed the synergy of financial and cultural capital in *The Philosophy of Money*, Bloch was aware that Lukács's gifted intellect was conditioned by cultural and monetary privileges.

The financial gulf between Bloch and Lukács was in part responsible for their increasingly strained relationship after 1913. Already in January 1912, Bloch solicited 10,000 Marks from Lukács's father via Georg, and this because he was unable to borrow 20,000 marks from Else.[33] Even after his marriage in 1913, Bloch continued to solicit money from Lukács. In the context of solicitation, he wrote to Lukács in the spring of 1914 that "it is disgraceful that Wagner had to beg for money."[34] Lukács was not an easy mark. He criticized Bloch's request in light of the massive spending spree that followed his marriage to Else. Lukács eventually ceased to correspond with him by the end of the war.[35] Their correspondence did not resume until after 1945 when Bloch assumed a chair in philosophy in Leipzig and Lukács accepted a similar position at Budapest University. Simmel's students had by then become the most important theorists of political aesthetics in the Communist bloc representing the extremes of communist modernism (Bloch) and communist antimodernism (Lukács).

THE MEANING OF CULTURAL ARISTOCRACY

From the perspective of discursive agency, it might be assumed that the class dynamics that framed the dissemination of Simmel's philosophy were irrelevant to an understanding of his intellectual/discursive legacy. This is not the case. One must account for the social circumstances of discursive dissemination. However, a "theory of social circumstances," as François Furet calls it, is not sufficient for understanding the Simmelian culture of spiritual intelligence (*Geist-Politik*). For, as Furet says of French Revolutionary ideology, the discourse of the Simmel circle "had no objective existence at the social level; it was but a *mental representation of the social sphere*."[36] One could make the case that an emphasis on discursive agency *independent of* social history is partially valid in this case, because Simmel and those he most influenced were members of the *haute bourgeoisie*, and therefore the anticapitalist content of Simmel's legacy patently contradicted the materialist doctrine of the class determinacy of thought. Here, we can recall the examples of Friedrich Engels and Robert Owen, as well.

However, I maintain that Furet was methodologically correct in rejecting both (1) the absolute disjunction, and (2) a mirroring of social history and political discourse. Significant elements of Simmel's conceptual complex were not only compatible with but affirmative of the aristocratic culture that permeated and dominated the field of politics and the institutions of academia. But this does not mean that Simmel and his legacy simply mirrored the cultural predominance of the aristocracy. His affirmation of aristocratic culture was a social demarcation within which he developed his social critique. Aristocratic culture was the cultural delimitation, as opposed to determination, of his cultural critique.

One of the central reasons that Simmel's anticapitalist philosophy took root was because it was formulated as a Nietzschean "Morality of the Nobility."[37] The appeal of Simmel's cultural legacy, then, was modulated through its aristocratic social and discursive matrix. This does not mean that Simmel's philosophy appealed exclusively to intellectuals with aristocratic associations. It means simply that the *Wertgefühl,* or emotive politics, of his philosophy must be seen within the context of a monarchical society. In a word, his discursive identification with the aristocracy was a struggle for cultural hegemony. Simmel's aristocratic radicalism positioned itself as more noble than the nobility of birth, more spiritual than the spirituality of Christianity, and more philosophically rigorous in its antibourgeois ethics than the naturalized ethics of the SPD.

Simmel's self-inscription within an aristocracy of the intellect possessed the emotive appeal of standing-above the competing aristocracies of birth and money. Nowhere was the affective politics of cultural superiority more explicit than in Kurt Hiller's outline of an *Aktivist* Republic, which was derived from Simmel's conception of culture: a German House of Lords, empeopled by an intellectual aristocracy. In the case of Bloch, von Lukács, and von Bendemann, Simmel's language of aristocracy articulated their ambivalent class status. The antibourgeois positionality of these aristocrats of spirit maintained the genteel disdain for the crass materialism of the bourgeoisie. Moreover, Simmel's call for a moral nobility provided his students with the aristocratic and meritorious feeling of transcending the mere superiority of ancestry. Simmel's philosophy was, then, politically ambivalent. Its discourse conserved the affective technology of aristocratic superiority while putting forth a radical social critique of the Church, the aristocracy, and the ethics of the bourgeoisie. To what extent was Bloch and Lukács's conversion to Leninism in the culture of war a conservation of Simmel's civic aristocracy? Both Simmel's anticapitalism and the Marxism-Leninism of Bloch and Lukács presuppose a political elite. Like Hiller, Bloch and Lukács never fully renounced Simmel's doctrine of a civic nobility.

A SOCIOLOGICAL SCIENCE OF THE SOUL

> *The power of institutions appears to be constantly increasing as if it were real being. However, and this is for me the meaning of the war, we must not concede. We must accentuate over and over again that our souls alone are essential, and that even their eternal a priori objectifications are (to use Ernst Bloch's wonderful image) only paper money whose value depends on their conversion into gold.*
>
> Lukács to Paul Ernst, April 1915[38]

Beyond an aristocratic radicalism of spirit, is there any way of reconstructing the specific content of Simmel's thought that predominated in the Simmel circle prior to the Great War? Since Simmel's *Introduction to Moral Science*, *The Philosophy of Money*, and *Sociology* each run over 800 pages and contain a syncretic range of concepts, it might be presumed that Bloch, Lukács, and von Bendemann's reception of his philosophy contained no hegemonic content. In the search for such a content, the works of Bloch and Lukács are of little help. The reason for this is twofold. First, neither Bloch nor Lukács wrote an extensive monograph on Simmel. Secondly, they, like Simmel, often wrote in a fluid literary style that shunned the contemporary academic salience of footnotes. Unlike Hiller's monographs written during this period, Bloch and Lukács's works make few references to Simmel. One might conclude, therefore, that Simmel was not a substantial and principle intellectual influence. But this conclusion is not borne out by epistolary and autobiographical evidence.

In his autobiography, Lukács explained the influence of Simmel on his early work as follows: "Simmel brought the societal character of art into the discussion, and, thereby, he procured a point of view for me. On this basis I examined literature, but in a way that went far beyond Simmel. The actual philosophy of *The Developmental History of Modern Drama* is the philosophy of Simmel."[39] This ambivalent recollection—Simmel as a foundation, but one that he exceeds—was present in Bloch's letters as well. Bloch was unequivocal about Simmel's intellectual primacy. Over fifty years after he left the Simmel circle, he recalled his "friendship with Simmel. . . . He was almost the only living philosopher who subsequently interested me."[40] In 1911, Bloch and Simmel vacationed together for three weeks in Italy. "And there," Bloch recalled with a commercial metaphor, "I had to undertake a general clearance sale of my youthful philosophizing."[41] Notwithstanding Simmel's intellectual primacy, Bloch's personal feelings for his mentor were more ambivalent. "It appears to me that it would be best," Bloch suggested to Lukács in August 1911, "if we physically and mentally remove ourselves as far away as we can from the Simmel circle." Months later he added: "*Habeat* my imprecation and hatred of Simmel."[42] It is very likely that Bloch and Lukács's distancing from Simmel was complicated by their identification with his politics.[43] In any case, the intensity of Bloch's disdain and his desire to distantiate from the Simmel circle is especially remarkable given that Lukács and Bloch had already physically relocated to Heidelberg. Even after they had removed themselves from the Simmel circle geographically, they struggled to free themselves from his intellectual and cultural preeminence in prewar Germany.

The problem with the epistolary and autobiographical record is that it establishes Simmel's seminal cultural role without overtly accounting for the intellectual content of that preeminence. Fortunately, there is one insider's account of Simmel's cultural influence. The unrivaled source for a reconstruction of Simmel's cultural impact is Margarete (Susman) von Bendemann's brilliant *The Spiritual Structure of Georg Simmel* (1959). This was the only full-length manuscript by a member of the Simmel circle. Above all, this text contends that Simmel's conceptual complex was underpinned by a discourse of the soul, *die Seele*.

> At the root of Simmel's relativism was a concern for the suffering of the human being, who seeks himself *in the world*, and who in an arcanumless epoch does not for a moment forget the secret of his existence and the source of his existence. This latter secret, also a third way, was conveyed by Simmel in the name, *Seele*. . . . Clearly the exploration of the *Seelische* served everything that Simmel had written. Through his historically grounded thinking, everywhere the reality of the soul breaks through. What is the soul? Today its name has faded away. The word itself is no longer at home in poetry. It appears to contemporary people—after all the experiences of our time—as incongruous and no longer real. The soul as the innermost nature of the human being, and as a solid substance concentrating everything in itself, no longer appears in contemporary language. Simmel's soul was a last means of fighting back against the disintegration of the powers of life and death. . . . Simmel's whole sociology, wherein "the soul is the image of society and society the image of the soul," rests, thereby, finally on a third way. Because for him, the soul is also a third way, like everything that consciously or unconsciously conveys the experienced duality of life.[44]

Susman's manuscript is an impassioned and lyrical treatment of Simmel as a philosopher of the "soul in the world," who is simultaneously aware of the determining (Nietzsche) and determined (sociological) character of the human being. She saw his discourse of the soul as neoromantic. The soul had been a central concept of German romanticism and Hegelianism in the nineteenth century. It was still a controlling idea of Stefan George's lyric and Expressionist prose in Wilhelmine culture. Simmel's philosophy was part of this larger historical narrative. His philosophy maintained the romantic interpretation of the soul as the dual locus of aesthetics and ethics. In spite of these strong similarities, Simmel's thought should not be classified as romantic.[45] What was new about Simmel's philosophy of the soul was its unique blend of Nietzschean inflections, overt sociological articulations, and antibourgeois values. He was not a neoromantic anti-modernist. He embraced modernity: feminism, Naturalism, Expressionism, urban culture, the diversity of values, and the liberatory potential of the monetary economy. Furthermore, his thought contained no atavistic desire to resurrect a Greek or medieval Christian golden age.

Susman's focus on the discursive primacy of the soul (*Seele, Seelischen, beseelen, seelenhaft*) is unusual in Simmel historiography. It is not unique, however, in the works of his intellectual progeny. In his 1920 essay, "Georg Simmel," published in the international Weber-Simmel journal, *Logos*, Siegfried Kracauer described Simmel as "the philosopher of the soul."[46] Karl Mannheim's elegiac obituary, published shortly after Simmel's death in 1918, honored him as the most important philosopher in Wilhelmine Germany—above Cohen, Windelband, Rickert, and Lask.

> Simmel philosophized beginning with the avowed consciousness that the philosophical conceptual image of reality can only be inadequate: epistemological categories conform to development and then change; truth allows itself to confront truth; and our epistemological ground (with the change of categories) permanently vanishes from under our feet. . . . Chiefly by means of acute analyses Simmel enabled the regularities of a soulful life [*seelischen Leben*] to be investigated. Thus he wrote in the second part of the *Philosophy of Money* the most beautiful pages of social psychology and also brought to the surface with the same psychological acuity the spiritual [*seelischen*] appearances of the moral life (*Introduction to the Science of Morals*). . . . With his writings, he awoke in us the unending desire for the conceptually perceivable world, called forth our revolt against every previous rigid formulation.[47]

In explaining Simmel's rebellious cultural impact, both Susman and Mannheim, moreover, use the terminology of spiritual intellectuality and character (*Geistigkeit* and *Persönlichkeit*). In the previous chapter, it was shown that this discursive legacy was taken up by early Expressionists and the Activists. Susman's definition of character (*Persönlichkeit*) provides further insight into the Simmel's generational legacy. Simmel used the concept of "character" ("*Persönlichkeit*"), she tells us, "as the counter image of bourgeois-capitalist society."[48] By combining Mannheim and Susman's insights, we can reconstruct the incendiary quality of Simmel's thought; it incited the unified strength of epistemological and social revolt. The narrative teleology of what follows is an investigation of

Simmel's philosophy of the soul and its contribution to the communist theory of Lukács and Bloch.

Simmel's solicitation of cultural revolt was given ethical intensity through the discourse of the soul, and nowhere was the anticapitalist character of this discourse as thoroughly developed as it was in Simmel's *Introduction to the Science of Morals*. Originally published in 1894, the text was reprinted in 1904 and 1911.[49] While the text was not popular—the first edition ran a mere 500 copies—it was widely read by Simmel's students. It was this text that served as the foundation of Hiller's critique of the 1870–71 German Law Book. Susman referred to it often, and Mannheim referenced it above as an acute analysis of the traditional moral life.

The significance of *Introduction to the Science of Morals* for establishing a Simmel legacy rests in its use of the discourse of the soul to investigate the ethical viability of capitalism and bourgeois culture. In particular, Simmel turned to Adam Smith's fundamental proposition that "egoism" produces an altruistic society, i.e., by pursuing self-interest one promotes social virtue. Simmel's critique began by debunking the liberal assertion that egoism was "a natural impulse" which deserved the "title of naturalness."[50] The problem with conceptual naturalization when applied to ethics was that it has no fixed content: "Therefore, we cannot immediately accept the Natural as an ideal norm, because nature, on the basis of which our ideas are measured, is in no way unitary and absent contradictions."[51] A related form of conceptual hypostatization was rationality. Most schools of thought, for instance, describe their fundamental propositions as natural and, thereby, as a "fate of rationality."[52] In contrast to Kant and Hegel, who are differently concerned with reason (*Vernunft*), Simmel believed that ethics were fundamentally a question of what values guide existence. It was axiomatic for Simmel that there existed no set of values that were self-evidently rational and in light of which all others could be dismissed as irrational. One could, however, investigate the "material content" of values as a basis for ethical judgment.[53] Simmel called the investigation of the sociological manifestation of values an ethical philosophy of the "social-soul."[54]

Simmel saw the dual hypostatizations—nature and rationality—at work in liberalism and linked these to its psychological authority.

> One observes that what is characteristic in Adam Smith's thought is more a certain giving-oneself-over to the pull of already conceived ideas rather than an intervention in the thought process itself intent on the removal of emerging contradictions. Since he allows the nature of his concept simply to rule itself, he falls victim to his objective principle, the *laïsser aller,* even in his scientific work.[55]

He might have added the discursively relevant fact that Smith rendered the market price of commodities as the "natural price," just as social Darwinists justified *laisser aller* and imperialism as "natural selection." Simmel's focus, however, was a more general analysis of the emotive politics of cultural naturalizations. The objective principles of nature and rationality carry the positive psychological charge of ethical certainty; they serve as a psychological vehicle for granting subjective ideals objective authority. From Simmel's philosophical point of view, no moral concept—be it the socialist concept of equality, the capitalist notion of egoism, or the liberal presumption of natural rights—was natural. Nonetheless, the cultural and ethical authority of *laisser aller* resides in the psychological authority of these hypostatizations.

In place of the traditional categories of reason, nature, and objectivity, Simmel puts forth the noumenal category of *Seelenvermögen*, or spiritual-capital. (The word *Vermögen* is difficult to translate; it carries the dual meaning of capacity and wealth.) Reason, naturalness, and objectivity, he argued, are not "formal spiritual capital [*Seelenvermögen*]."[56] They are simply reifications that lay claim to objective authority by denying the subjective character of values and their "correlate in objective reality."[57] Simmel's ethics rejected reification and instead focused on the correlation of philosophical monisms and institutional monisms. This correlation was the starting point of his sociological science of ethical judgment.

Simmel's philosophy of *Seelenvermögen* was, in essence, a philosophy of practical idealism, and it was used to criticize the ethical institutions of bourgeois culture. Egoism, the bourgeois ethical imperative, was denounced as a sociological tautology, a monism and a solipsism. As such, it destroyed moral differentiation, differences in kind, by reducing everything to itself. Moral differences thus become mere differences in degree which suffocate institutional regimes that could be realized outside of the hegemony of egoism. If greed is natural and fundamental, then the difference between greed and altruism is lost conceptually and institutionally. In capitalist society, the freedom and possibility of moral diversity is sacrificed to the presumed naturalness of egoism and to devastating effect; "There is overall no greater error than that the strength of the individual and the mechanical conquest of the enemy are solely decisive for existence."[58] The competitive principle that might makes right—which is central to capitalism, "natural selection," and imperialism—was tied, in Simmel's view, to egoism and was at the core of capitalism's moral vacuity. He saw an analogy to this competitive ethic in the capitalist-Christian view of the natural world. Instead of seeing our destruction and instrumental use of nature as a necessary evil, Christians see this as an ethical right.

An additional ethical error of bourgeois culture was the positive social role ascribed to the family in capitalist society. Typically, the Wilhelmine family was portrayed by the bourgeoisie as a mediation of egoism and altruism. Capitalist egoism was legitimized through its transmutation into altruistic family values. Conversely, Simmel charged that the patriarchal bourgeois family was "social egoism" or "group egoism."[59] Capitalist family values were effectively asocial in their fortification of egoism. Simmel also identified social egoism in labor unions. (Early unions in fact neglected the plight of women workers and the unemployed outside their ranks.)[60] Just as peace can be preparation for war, group altruism can and did cloak individual egoism. This was certainly the case with the bourgeois family, wherein (1) there was often little concern with families outside itself, and (2) women were treated as prostitutes. In contrast to egoism, patriarchy, instrumentalism, and reification, Simmel championed an altruistic, noninstrumental and antireifying philosophy of "good will." The doctrine of good will explained how divergent deeds could stem from the same ethical value-feeling.[61] It thereby dignified ethical and cultural differences, while maintaining the ethical demand for a social conscience.

Simmel's *Introduction to Moral Science* was not the only text where the concept of the soul served as the axis of a larger and more complex critique of bourgeois culture and philosophy. Many other texts evince the centrality of that concept: "Vom Heil der Seele" (1902), *Die Probleme der Geschichtsphilosophie* (1905), *Die Religion* (1907), and "Der platonische und der moderne Eros" (ca. 1917). In every case, the soul was treated as the modern secularization of religious intensity. The soul was also the foundation for Simmel's philosophical critique of bourgeois and socialist materialism and a basis for a philosophy of affective politics or *Wertgefühle*, value-feelings. Despite the centrality of the concept of the soul to his work, it is noticeably absent in much of his historiography. Seminal English language texts—such as Rudolph Weingartner's *Experience and Culture: The Philosophy of Georg Simmel*, Nicholas Spykman's *The Social Theory of Georg Simmel*, and David Frisby's *Fragments of Modernity*—reference it incidentally or not at all. This absence stands in sharp contrast to the texts about Simmel written by Hiller, Stöcker, Susman, Mannheim, and Kracauer, namely, by those with whom he was intellectually most intimate. The point must be made that it would be un-Simmelian to suggest that an analysis of his thought must precede from one perspective, i.e., the soul. However, even though Simmel's philosophy can be interpreted with little reference to his philosophy of the soul, it is here emphatically maintained that an assessment of his intellectual legacy demands reference to and an understanding of the soul as a conceptual and political complex. Specifically, the soul is a discursive starting point for an intellectual history of Simmel's influence on Bloch and Lukács.

LUKÁCS, BLOCH, AND THE SIMMELIAN SOUL

The concept of the soul is the key to understanding Simmel's influence on Lukács and Bloch before the war. As Lukács related in his autobiography, the foundation of his *The Developmental History of Modern Drama* was Simmel's aesthetic philosophy of sociological interiority. In its methodological preface, Lukács explained his intention to undertake a type of analysis, literary sociology, that was historically rare. The reason given for its absence reads like Simmel's critique of historical materialism. Heretofore, the absence of literary sociology was, Lukács contends, due to the ambition to reduce the social character of literature to the economic relations of an epoch. By contrast, Lukács argued that the sociology of art could not be found by assuming a deterministic economic relationship. The sociological character of art is found in its form. The concept of *Form,* while present in Simmel's work, was Lukács's unique contribution to a European sociology of aesthetics, and it should be seen as the unreferenced precursor of Hayden White's tropics of metahistory.[62] The discursive content of Lukács's first major monograph suggests that his concept of form was inspired by Simmel's *Sociology* whose subtitled was the "Forms of Socialization."

> Sociology, what Simmel called the science of "the forms of socialization," determined the forms through which materializes the economic and social relationships—the extant variety and manner of tempos, accents, and rhythms in the human world of feeling and thought, and the relationship of these worlds to one another.[63]

Lukács applied this methodology to an analysis of art and literature.

> The truly social in literature is: *die Form.* The form generally makes the experience of the author a communicative exchange with the other, with the public. . . . The form-vision of an artist is not in itself an isolated spiritual [*seelische*] appearance, that only becomes active, in its formulative stage. Rather, it is always, with lesser or greater force, an operative factor of his soul-life [*Seelenleben*]. . . . The true form of the true artist is a priori, a permanent form opposite things, something, without which it would not be possible to perceive objects. . . . The form is spiritual [*seelische*] reality.[64]

As it had been in Simmel's sociology, form (whether economic, social, or aesthetic) was viewed as a realization of the soul's vital energy; it was the self-imposed social fate of the aesthetic soul. Similar to Simmel, Lukács interpreted aesthetic forms as a theory of sociological interiority or *Lebensinhalt.*[65] In Simmel's *Rembrandt: An Aesthetic-Philosophical Analysis* (1916), for example, the first chapter, "The Expression of the Soul," contained a subsection entitled *Life and Form.*[66] While forms, be they social or aesthetic, could simply reproduce the values of the status quo, both Simmel and Lukács combed the history of art and literature for aesthetic forms that expressed moral visions useful for social critique. As Simmel had written in

Schopenhauer and Nietzsche, "The most appropriate analogy to Nietzschean principles can be found in the spheres of art."[67] Art contained the countercultural images that distanced us from the existing state of social affairs and thereby facilitated conceptions of alternative worlds. Consequently, Simmel provided Lukács and other students with an activist or existential approach to academic life. The goal of aesthetic studies and sociological analyses was not merely descriptive or objective. Intellectual activity was guided by the desire for social transformation and self-overcoming.

Simmel and Lukács shared, then, more than a common analytic discourse of soul and form. Their sociological aesthetics were concerned with *the construction of an antibourgeois individuation of form.* In this vein, Simmel referred to the "tendency toward individuation" in Rembrandt's aesthetic form.[68]

> This individuation, however, (as I have sought to explain it here as the *from-the-inside-outward,* cultivated and comprehended life) provided the *Form* an other meaning or a different type of necessity than in classical art. Rembrandt's preference for lumpen phenomena—for the proletarian, whose clothes appear ragged in formal, complete, senseless pieces as a result of the accident of their impoverished lots—acted almost like a conscious opposition to the classical principle.[69]

Form was the decisive necessity of human inner life to provide itself with a perspective. There were, for Simmel, two types of form that guide life. The first type might be called fateful form.[70] It was determined by fate and history. Classical art was fateful form: the noncritical identity of art and social fate. By contrast, Simmel prescribed the production of self-created and timeless aesthetic forms to resist historical determinism:

> Form is timeless, because it exists only in the standing-against-each-other and the relating-to-one-another of the contents of perception; and it is powerless, because as form it can produce no effect.[71]

For Simmel, critical aesthetics were mental forms posed against some apprehended social phenomena. However, like an activist seeking the last word, Simmel asserted that the mere *conceptual opposition* of self-constructed ethical forms to social fate was "powerless." Only through life decisions could ahistorical and iconoclastic aesthetics become powerful historical "forms of the society";[72] "the soulful essence" of an aesthetic/ethical form must realize itself in a "life-process in historical development."[73] Once created, timeless ethical forms must enter the social realm against which they are constituted. Negative self-constitution, if it seeks to be politically powerful and ethically effective, must seek its meaning in the social realm of positive freedom. As was the case in his proletarian interpretation of

Rembrandt, Simmel's own soulful form was typically antibourgeois. In its discourse and political proclivities, his philosophy prefigured Lukács's early antibourgeois aesthetics of soul and forms.

Lukács aquired more than Simmel's life philosophy of soul and forms; his aporetic style of interpretation was also a rearticulation. Lukács followed Simmel in asserting that aesthetic production was groundless. Its source was the soul, which was not only a concept but also an undictated energy, a nonconceptual and sociologically undetermined vital cause. Additionally, Lukács, like Simmel, maintained that modern aesthetics were determined by and grounded in bourgeois society. This seeming contradiction—groundless and determined—is emblematic of the aporetic unity of interpretive extremes found in *The Philosophy of Money*. Lukács wrote that in *The Philosophy of Money*:

> [Simmel's] analysis of causality was pushed so far and attained such a degree of refinement as no one before him had managed to do, and at the same time, the envelopment of causality—its self-delimitation and its halting before that which does not allow itself to be caused—is made visual in inimitable sharpness.[74]

Simmel had provided Lukács with a Manichaean model of the uncaused soul and the socially determined soul. This Manichaean character was already manifest in Lukács's *The Developmental History of Modern Drama*. While the theoretical preface to the text asserted the unconditioned nature of aesthetic production, its second chapter maintained the exact opposite: "Modern drama is the drama of the bourgeoisie. . . . The bourgeois drama is the first drama which grows out of a conscious class conflict; the first whose purpose it is to express the affectiveness and way of thinking of a fighting class seeking freedom, power and its relationship to other classes." And, he continued, the "artistic problem is of course only a symptom of the social problem."[75] Lukács's methodological assertions that (1) literary tropes are groundless and not reducible to economic relations, and (2) that modern drama is grounded in bourgeois class society, would appear contradictory if they were not part of a conscious and systematic style of critique. He himself referred to his analysis as paradoxical and as "the eternal conflict of two abstractions."[76] His method is an aporetic unity of incommensurable claims: indeterminacy and determinacy, subjective causality and objective causality, becoming and being. It is no accident, then, that in the second chapter of the drama book where the methodology of paradox and contradiction was developed, Lukács cited *The Philosophy of Money*: Simmel's critical Manichaeanism par excellence. Later Lukács's philosophy of paradox remained a central element of his "Metaphysics of Tragedy."

GEORG SIMMEL

Since Lukács's *The Developmental History of Modern Drama* was founded on Simmelian methodology, it should not be surprising that he wrote Simmel from Budapest about the manuscript. Seeking publication in Germany, Lukács first sent freshly translated versions of the first two chapters of the drama book to Simmel in 1909. While Simmel said that he would be unable to read the entire manuscript, he did suggest several publishers and offered to send the manuscript to the publisher of Lukács's choice, presumably with a cover letter; "Where should I send your manuscript?"[77] From this exchange of letters we can ascertain a mutual self-consciousness of their cultural affinities and one that existed before Lukács moved to Berlin. Specifically, Simmel's response indicates a high degree of self-consciousness about their methodological consonance.

> Incidentally, I will not conceal the fact that the first few pages that I read were *methodologically* very sympathetic. The attempt to derive the inner and sublime conditions of limitation from the external and coarsest conditions appears to me as a fruitful and interesting endeavor. In terms of the content, the duplicity obviously holds true of all that is psychological and which allows with the same plausibility often contradictory conclusions to be derived from the same premise.[78]

Simmel immediately recognized the correlatives of his own methodology in the theoretical premises of Lukács's doctoral work. After the completion of his doctoral work, Lukács became something like a Simmelian apostle. Outside of Berlin, there was no cultural milieu more influenced by Simmel's sociological aesthetics than the Budapest Sunday Circle which first met in 1911.[79] The core of this young group of Hungarian intellectuals were Simmel students: Lukács, Béla Balázs, and Karl Mannheim. They subsequently formed a journal called *A Szellem* (The Spirit or *Geist*) which was modelled upon *Logos*, a journal dedicated to cultural philosophy and founded in 1910 by Weber and Simmel among others.

Despite Lukács's discursive and formal faithfulness to much of Simmel's philosophy, Simmel's intellectual primacy is substantially undervalued in Lukács's immense historiography. Part of the reason for this is that fifty years after Simmel's death, Lukács was himself dismissive of Simmel's influence.

> Max Weber's influence was stronger and came later. Simmel had frivolities. Weber, conversely, wanted to create a comprehensive literary theory without Simmel's frivolities.[80]

One of Simmel's academic frivolities was his interest in the sociology of art. In this regard, Lukács had more in common with Simmel; only the war freed Lukács himself from this frivolity. Having moved to Heidelberg in

1911 to study with Max Weber, Lukács had to justify his interest in aesthetics to Weber. He did so in a typically Simmelian fashion, that is, with a neo-Kantian sociology of aesthetics.

> I should perhaps mention, because it played a role in my good relationship with Weber, that I once said to Weber concerning Kant . . . that the aesthetic judgement possesses no priority, rather the priority resides with being [*Sein*]. "Art works exist. How are they possible?" This is the question I asked Weber, and it made a strong impression on him. It is the fundamental question of my Heidelberg aesthetic fragments.[81]

Simmel may have been frivolous, but apparently his philosophy was not. For Lukács's defense of aesthetics, to which Weber was so receptive, had simply and brilliantly transposed the central question of Simmel's *Sociology*, "How is Society Possible?", into the realm of aesthetics.[82] In its methodology, its political inflection, and its disciplinary frame, Lukács's early work was primarily influenced by Simmel.[83] What made Lukács's intellectual transition from Berlin to Heidelberg relatively easy was a neo-Kantian empiricism that Simmel, Weber, and Lukács shared. They were all equally skeptical of conceptual reificaton. Their works expressed a similar methodological imperative; the content and validity of noumenal laws (be they Simmelian symbols, Weberian ideal types, or Lukácsian forms) must be determined against and through a sociological apprehension of society.

A more refined assessment of the relative influence of Simmel and Weber must begin with a chronology. From around 1906 to 1911, Simmel was a primary influence on Lukács.[84] Simmel's influence was predominant in both *The Developmental History of Modern Drama* and *The Soul and the Forms*. In 1912, Dr. von Lukács—accompanied by Dr. Bloch—left the Simmel circle and joined the Weber circle in Heidelberg. But Lukàcs never jettisoned his focal interest in aesthetics, an academic area that was not a specialization of Weber. Thematically, and in terms of an academic area, Lukács's next three texts—*Heidelberg Philosophy of Art* (1912–1914), *Theory of the Novel* (1916), and *Heidelberg Aesthetic* (1916–1918)—attest to the continuing influence of Simmel. In contrast to his memoirs from the late 1960s, the younger Lukács clearly believed that Simmel was the more original cultural figure. In 1918, the year of his conversion to Marxism, he claimed that the sociology of capitalist culture undertaken by Weber and Werner Sombart rested entirely on the methodological brilliance of Simmel's *The Philosophy of Money*.[85] Twenty-five years later, in "My Path to Marx," Lukács cited Simmel as the person who, more than any other, facilitated his reception of Marx: "The influence of Simmel, whose personal student I had been, gave me the possibility to incorporate that which I appropriated from Marx in this period."[86]

Given their strong political and theoretical affinities, why, then, did Lukács leave Berlin University and Simmel's mentorship? Weber's brilliance and Heidelberg University's intellectual reputation played an important role. But why were these more attractive to Lukács than Berlin and the Simmel circle? One reason for Heidelberg's superior appeal was purely practical. The ambitious Dr. von Lukács sought a German doctorate, and Simmel's academic vicissitudes prevented him from supervising doctoral candidates. While Simmel had been promoted from *Privatdozent* to *ausserördentlicher Professor* after the publication of *The Philosophy of Money* in 1900, he did not become an *Ordinarius*, or full-fledged and well-paid member of academia, until 1914 when he received a position in Strassburg.

Consequently, like Stöcker and Hiller before him, Lukács had to seek a doctorate outside of Berlin and the Simmel circle. Simmel's anonymous letter defending Stöcker's right to seek a doctorate at Berlin University—presumably in opposition to Dilthey, with whom she had been working—was unsuccessful. In order to receive her doctorate, Stöcker left Berlin in 1899 and eventually received a doctorate in philosophy—having written on aesthetics—in Bern. Similarly, Hiller expressed frustration over his inability to have Simmel as *Doktorvater*. In his memoirs, there are two separate descriptions of a meeting at Simmel's flat in Charlottenberg. The meeting concerned the manuscript which would become *Das Recht über sich Selbst*. Simmel recommended Hiller to a young professor in Heidelberg who eventually accepted this work as a doctoral manuscript. By having earned a doctorate prior to studying with Simmel in Berlin, Bloch avoided this problem all together. Simmel's inability to direct doctoral work was, however, a problem for his friend, Dr. von Lukács. It is very possible that Lukács would not have left Berlin in 1911 if Simmel were capable of supervising doctoral students.

But leave Berlin Lukács and Bloch did, carrying their knowledge of Simmelean philosophy with them. (Bloch was now much closer to his home in Ludwigshafen, and he and Lukács often travelled to see opera and theater in Mannheim.) Their cultural impact in Heidelberg was immediate. Paul Honigsheim, an insider of the Weber circle, recalled their arrival:

> [The Baden-Baden "Hegel Club"] became less important, at least for a time, because of the stir caused by the appearance of two "figures from opposite poles," as Marianne [Weber] called them. . . . These were Georg von Lukács and his friend Ernst Bloch. Lukács was then very much opposed to the bourgeoisie, liberalism, the constitutional state, parliamentarianism, revisionist socialism, the Enlightenment, relativism, and individualism.[87]

Both Honigheim and Marianne Weber's memoirs attest to a cold reception for Dr. Bloch and a warm greeting for Dr. von Lukács; they also indicate that the Weber's new friendship with Lukács aided in the development of a friendship between the Webers and the Simmels. The extremely interesting discussions of Marianne Weber and Gertrud Simmel, recounted in Marianne's memoirs, centered around feminism and the politics of Georg's philosophy. These two female intellectuals must have had much to talk about. Illustrative of their cultural interests was a statement in a letter from Frau Simmel to Frau Weber: "It is the metaphysical essence of a woman to live only through her husband; no, that is only her historical essence!"[88] In addition to several highly philosophical letters from Frau Simmel, Marianne Weber's memoirs contain references to Georg Simmel and his intellectual reputation. She reported: "I studied numerous texts of Georg Simmel, above all those under the title *Philosophical Culture* (1911)."[89] Marianne Weber's memoirs also confirm the existence of a lively debate over feminism not only between Marianne Weber and Georg Simmel but also between Georg and Gertrud. Marianne Weber's memoirs are significant for several reasons. They suggest that Simmel saw himself as a cultural radical and that others also perceived him as such. Marianne Weber, for example, referred several times to the "radical" opinions of Georg and Gertrud Simmel. The memoirs also indicate Simmel's cultural prestige among leading Wilhelmine intellectuals like the Webers. Like his wife, Max Weber was not only familiar with Simmel personally. As though indicating its cultural originality, Simmel's *The Philosophy of Money* was cited in the first footnote of Weber's *The Protestant Ethic and the Spirit of Capitalism.* Finally, the political portrait of Simmel emerging from the memoirs explains why there would have been a stir upon the arrival of two of his students. The Berlin radicals of the Simmel circle had arrived.

PASSIONATE PROTEST AND NEGATIVE FREEDOM

What aspect of Simmel's iconoclastic philosophy of life resonated with Bloch and Lukács? Simmel cultivated passionate protest. Lukács rendered Simmel's philosophy "as nothing other than the protest of life against [traditional] forms. . . . [Simmel] felt and evaluated the great, persistent, and eternal forms as the rape of life—of its riches, its multicoloring, its fullness, and its polyphony."[90] Having moved from Budapest to Berlin in 1909, and thus more directly under Simmel's influence, Lukács quickly followed his drama book with a series of essays that were published under the title *Die Seele und die Formen* (1911). It appeared shortly before he joined the Weber circle and no doubt enhanced his intellectual prestige in Heidelberg. The text was above all a protest of *homo noumena* against the determination of sociological phenomena. As such, it participated in a larger Simmelian culture. *The Soul and the Forms*, Hiller's Expressionist theory, and Bloch's *The Spirit of Utopia* (1918) were part of a constellation of writings that connote a Simmel School.

For the members of this school, Simmel's philosophy contained the affective politics of negative freedom. The central value-feeling of negative freedom was that the soul or spirit—Gertrud Simmel spoke of Georg's philosophy as a soulful-spiritual productivity (*seelische-geistige Produktivität*)[91]—was violated by tradition and uncontainable by fixed institutional or aesthetic forms. Simmel articulated an existentialism of self-creation and formal-overcoming. Essentially, the soul was in protest against institutional (political) and formal (aesthetic) reification in order to experience ethical and behavioral heterogeneity and remain true to its own hard-earned values.

There were two ways in which the negative freedom of Simmel's philosophy was received by his students. First, it was received as a critique of totality. For example, Lukács saw Simmel's critique of totality, as he had Weber's sociology, as a critique of relativism:

> Often Simmel has been called a relativist because of the pluralistic and unsystematic character of his thought. In my view with injustice. . . . In contrast [to relativism], Simmel steadfastly maintains the absoluteness of every individual composition (for example: science and art). He regards every composition as necessary and undetermined. However, he does not believe there could be an a priori interpretation of the world that would actually comprehend the totality of life [*Totalität des Lebens*]. Every interpretation offers only one aspect, an a priori and necessary aspect, but not the totality itself.[92]

Simmel's philosophy, then, was received by Lukács and others as a protest against logocentrism, reification, and hypostatization in the name of perspectival differentiation. Reification was a critical category of Simmel's critique of consumer society and the bourgeois soul in *The Philosophy of Money* and its influence resonates in Lukács's original contribution to Marxism, particularly the social analyses associated with the concept of reification [*Verdinglichung*].[93] Simmel was the intellectual forefather of Lukács's critical denaturalization of the bourgeoisie's ideological, aesthetic, and economic totalizations.

Secondly, Simmel's legacy was an affective politics of *spiritual freedom*. The demand for spiritual freedom was directed toward the alienation [*Verfremdung* and *Entfremdung*] that Simmel had systematically unveiled as the core of Kaiser capitalism. The idea of spiritual freedom, as opposed to the dogmatic freedom of religious law, was an idea that may not resonate with contemporary academicians. For Susman, this lack of resonance speaks to the epochal shift accompanying the First World War. After the war, philosophical critique started from phenomenological *Existenz*. The priority of the noumenal soul, and the concept of the soul itself, was eclipsed by historical materialism or, in Heidegger's case, by metaphysical phenomenology: *Dasein*. Conversely, in early Expressionism, secular spiritualism was derived from Simmel's language of "spiritual activity" (*geistige Aktivität*).[94] The spiritual intensity of Susman, Bloch, and Lukács's works derived from Simmel's search for freedom from the paralyzing inertia of reified cultural institutions. Freedom meant scaling of the prison walls of petrified spiritual traditions, walls which Simmel defined as objective form, reification, and the bourgeois neglect of the soulful dimension of existence.

Lukács's philosophy of forms was more than a brilliant refashioning of Simmel's philosophy of symbolic sociological interiority. It elaborated a new cultural meaning for Simmel's philosophy.

> The critic is one who beholds fate in forms, whose most powerful experience is the *soul-content,* which the forms indirectly and unconsciously conceal within themselves. . . . This form, which has arisen from a symbolic examination of life-symbols, acquires a life for itself from the power of this experience. It becomes a world view, a stand point, a perspective in opposition to the life, out of which it sprang: a possibility to transform life itself and create it anew. The fate-moment of the critic is, therefore, also one where things become forms; the moment when all feelings and experiences, which were above and beyond form, receive a form, are smelted and condensed into form. *It is the mystical moment of the unity of external and internal, of the soul and the form.*[95]

In Lukács's *The Soul and the Forms,* the spiritual meaning of Simmel's sociology was magnified, disseminated, and made accessible. Susman, in her review of *The Soul and the Forms*, stated: "Thus, the forms become at the same time the purest expression of the soul, from redemption to disclosure."[96] Bloch was also drawn to Lukács's philosophy of soulful forms. Concerning Lukács's concepts of "earthly paradise" and "genius" in *Heidelberg Philosophy of Art* (1914), Bloch wrote Lukács in 1915: "It now appears to me all so beautifully clear, effortlessly flowing and illuminating."[97] Later Lukács recalled his methodology at the time as a combination of Simmelian sociology and "mystical subjectivism."[98] Suffice it to say, the vision of moral genius found in the pre–1918 writings of Bloch and Lukács was an intensely spiritual rendition of Simmel's more secular vision of a Nietzschean moral nobility.

BLOCH, LUKÁCS, AND THE ETHICS OF WAR

What must be maintained, however, is that Lukács and Bloch's ethical and activist renunciations of capitalism during the war were not an inevitable element of Simmel's legacy. Previous to the war, Bloch and Lukács had expressed a philosophical and aesthetic critique of capitalism that never attained the ethical sophistication of Simmel's *Introduction to Moral Sci-*

ence. More instructive is the fact that, prior to the war, none of Simmel's intellectual progeny proffered a link between their anticapitalism and socialist party politics. Without the outbreak of the Great War and without the revolutionary culture of war, events which forged these formal links, there may not have been a dramatic eclipse of Simmel's intellectual reputation. It was war culture that produced a new ethical climate and a new civic self-consciousness of tropic proportions.

The ethical intensity of war culture animated Lukács and Bloch to break with two central elements of Simmel's philosophy: the aesthetic individual as the primary locus of ethical philosophy and the assumed and previously viable contention that Simmel's aesthetic philosophy was transferable to the sociological and political realm. Writing in the winter of 1914, Hiller went so far as to blame the prewar primacy of aesthetics for the outbreak of the war:

> Yesterday's prolific spirit of aesthetics [*Schöngeist*] . . . today feels very superfluous—and with absolute justification. If only it, for the sake of decency, had felt itself superfluous yesterday . . . the war would have never broken out between nations, but between *Geist* and *Ungeist*. *Geist* would have triumphed and the war would have been settled.[99]

Although Hiller did not explicitly reference Simmel, others did. Criticizing Simmel's support for the war, Mannheim expressed disdain for Simmel's work, which he claimed was typical of "the exaggerated examinations of details in German academia. These examinations are estranged from that which is essential. The likeness of these detailed examinations is the aesthete."[100] Simmel's thought, which had seized the imagination of so many radical intellectuals before the war, now seemed conservative, inessential, and merely aesthetic. In the culture of war, Simmel's cultural heirs were summoned by the circumstances of total war to seek institutional correlatives for their avant-garde aesthetic/ethical forms. Since Simmel had been the undisputed champion of aesthetic philosophy, his cultural relevance was correspondingly undermined by this activist context. For Simmel's former students who opposed the war (Bloch, Hiller, Lukács, Mannheim, and Stöcker), even Simmel's aesthetic anticapitalism was inadequate to the ethical demands of the war.

Lukács's mental transformation during the war, from a sociological avant-gardist whose focus was aesthetics to a political revolutionary, was typical of a whole generation of young radical intellectuals. Lukács's opposition to the war meant the necessity of a shift from aesthetics, which was already a venue for antibourgeois ruminations, to ethics; "In 1917 I began to interest myself in ethical problems and, thus, I left aesthetic questions by the way side."[101] Antiwar individuals could not simply live "beyond forms," Lukács maintained, since social fate was now in a slave revolt against the hubris of aesthetic philosophies of negative freedom. Mannheim, another radical Simmel student, came to a similar conclusion during the war. In his 1917 review of Simmel's *The War and Spiritual Decisions,* Mannheim intoned: "There is no genuine formlessness for humanity."[102] In essence, the negative freedom of the prewar Simmelian avant-garde was replaced by a new political priority on institutional transformation. This sober radicalism was characteristic of Bloch and Hiller's wartime turn of mind as well. Paradoxically, the generational shift from avant-garde aesthetics to activist politics was actually facilitated by Simmel's own sociological ethics.

The wartime necessity of political and ethical reflection was punctuated by Lukács's interpersonal turmoil with the Simmels and the Webers. While the Simmels and Webers seem to have been drawn together by their support for the war, their support ostracized Lukács and Bloch from their mentors. In a letter to Marianne Weber dated August 14, 1914, a mere two weeks after German mobilization, Simmel wrote to the Webers:

> On the fifth or sixth of November I will hold a lecture in Heidelberg. It will deal with the "Demands of the Day." It is the incomparability of our times that, finally, the demands of our times and the Idea are one and the same. This can obviously only be grasped "intuitively" or, to be more precise, in practical experience. If Lukács does not have this experience, one cannot demonstrate it to him. After all, it is completely logical that he sees "Militarism" in everything; *for us* it is rather precisely the liberation from militarism, because this experience exposes the nature of militarism as an end-in-itself (which it threatens to accept during peace-time); and instead, the experience makes militarism into a form and a means for the collective elevation of life.[103]

This irrational defense of war as a collective elevation of life was so politically repulsive to Simmel's radical students that it scripted the final act of an oedipal saga. The philosophical godfather of the Wilhelmine left avant-garde was dead as a political paragon. On the first page of Lukács's fragmentary autobiography, there is a cryptic reference: "1914 Simmel's letters to Marianne Weber."[104] This surely refers to Simmel's epistolary enthusiasm for war. Simmel's affirmation of war was the defining existential moment in the political maturation of Bloch and Lukács. They were forced by circumstances to go their own way.

Bloch, who was still living in Heidelberg when the war broke out, was also emotionally wrenched by Simmel's public lectures in defense of the war. Previous to the Heidelberg lecture in November 1914, Bloch refused to greet Simmel, but he did attend the lecture. There, Simmel greeted Bloch before addressing those gathered to hear his philosophical interpretation of the war as a "collective elevation of life." For Bloch, it was as though Simmel had written him a final letter. Bloch summarized the meaning of that imaginary letter: "You have avoided the truth your whole life long, because you had seen it. Now you locate the absolute in the trenches. No, not that!"[105] Lukács also referenced Simmel's prowar lecture in his critique of intellectuals and the war.[106] The great critic of social determinism had now relinquished his title as the champion of iconoclastic resistance. The torch of critical resistance to a soulless and unethical fate had been passed to a new generation of activists for whom individual, aesthetic, and philosophical resistance was practically inadequate. A new antibourgeois sociology was necessary.

Until 1917, Lukács remained in Heidelberg and devoted himself to his sociology of aesthetics, a study far more indebted to Simmel than Weber.[107] He still aspired to an academic position in Heidelberg. Bloch, however, relocated to Grünwald shortly after Simmel's lecture. There he wrote *The Spirit of Utopia* from April 1915 to May 1917. In late 1917 he moved to Bern, Switzerland, where he cavorted with a veritable who's who of the antiwar avant-garde. He gravitated toward pacifism and the spiritualism of anarchist socialism.[108] Most importantly, for the first time he began to write about politics in a way that would define his life project: to rediscover and seek to realize anticapitalist utopias.[109] Bloch's politics of armed compassion did constitute a new antibourgeois sociology, but his branch of Marxism drew sustenance from Simmel's intellectual stock.

FROM AESTHETIC AVANT-GARDE TO CULTURAL VANGUARD

Simmel's legacy was never purely methodological. It was always imbricated with the freedoms of nonconformity and the semibohemian values of the avant-garde. His legacy was, as Susman said, the counterimage of bourgeois-capitalist society. Nowhere perhaps is this avant-garde legacy clearer than in the fifth chapter of Lukács's *The Soul and the Forms*, "The Bourgeois Way of Life and Art for Art's Sake." Likewise, in Bloch's prewar letters to Lukács, there are several derisive references to the petite bourgeoisie and the haute bourgeoisie. While my interpretation of Simmel's influence on Lukács and Bloch self-consciously marginalizes their overdetermined influences, in the case of their antibourgeois disposition, its philosophical model was unambiguously Simmel. Again, Simmel should be recognized as the inspirational academic and intellectual origin of the communist politics of Bloch and Lukács, the war and the Russian Revolution being the sociological origin. Bloch's dissertation, for instance, which was written under Oswald Külpe, contains none of the anticapitalist sophistication that stamped his work after studying with Simmel. In the case of Lukács, Simmel, and not Weber, was the model for his anticapitalist aesthetics.

Bloch and Lukács's conversion to Marxism during the Great War was conditioned by Simmel's antibourgeois aristocratic radicalism. Already a socialist, Bloch arrived in Bern in 1917. He joined the antiwar counterculture and became friends with the Dadaist, Hugo Ball. His close association with European modernism distinguished him from Lukács, who was more remote from the politics of Dadaism and early Expressionism. By 1918, Bloch—as though a convert to *Aktivismus*—was proclaiming a new politics based on "the authority of a spiritual aristocracy" and a "spiritual Führer."[110] In *The Spirit of Utopia*, he honored "the colorfully darkened clarity of Expressionistic art with its radical orientation toward objective content as the last stage before the Second Coming."[111] Hiller's "Christ and Activist" (1918) and Bloch's "The Purity of the Soul and the Demonology of the Light" (1917) further indicate the thematic affinities of Bloch and *Aktivismus*.[112] Again, the *Geist-Politik* of the Simmel circle was often a mobilization of secular spirituality (Nietzschean *Geistigkeit*) against the moral hegemony of conservative Christianity (*geistliche* culture) and its institutional siblings.

The philosophical similarities of Bloch and Hiller symbolize a common Simmelian philosophical legacy. This common legacy was antibourgeois but otherwise politically undetermined. Hiller and Bloch, for instance, retained the critical idealism of Simmel but differed in their rhetorical commitment to proletarian revolution. By 1920 Bloch, unlike Hiller, envisioned himself as a spiritual Leninist whose religious calling was service to the proletariat. Hiller had far less commitment to the proletariat than he had to the presupposition that he should be recognized as the philosopher king of a German Platonic Republic. Simply put, Bloch and Lukács were far more supportive of communist politics than the *Aktivisten,* but all were anticapitalist and conceived of themselves as a vanguard of cultural revolution.

For Lukács's part, he came to Communism through an aesthetic interest in form. The realized soul as form was Lukács's translation of Simmel's concept of objective spirit, and it led him to seek an ethical standard outside the individual. Forms, i.e., mental negations born of the countercultural soul, were the source of sociological ethics. Soul-forms arose from, and in opposition to, particular historical circumstances. They were simultaneously determined by social circumstances and free from them. Lukács's philosophy of forms sought to theorize the movement of their "abstract negativity" to *paradiso terreste*; this was a movement of negative ethics to "heaven on earth. If you will: true life."[113] In his essay "Concerning the Poverty of Spirit" (1912), which had a tremendous influence on Bloch, Lukács depicted this movement from negative self-creation to positive deeds in various ways: as transubstantiation, as a necessity of the soul of kindness, as the hunger for the substance of spirit (*Geist*), and as a movement toward a self-created ethical and antitragic form of becoming. Similar to Simmel and the *Aktivisten*, Lukács theorized the path of the moral genius who was, in a refraction of existentialism through Early Christianity, defined as the Gnostic of the deed. He contrasted the spiritual disposition of the moral genius, for whom "virtue is obsession," to "dumb, modern individualism."[114] The moral genius opposed to liberal individualism was a cultural self-conception cultivated by Simmel and retained by his revolutionary heirs. Their aristocratic radicalism envisioned the oceanic pleasure of realized higher values, or as Simmel called it in *Religion*: "a spiritualistic socialization."[115]

SIMMEL'S TRAGIC LEGACY

> *. . . The true Christ-formed purity of the soul is drawn from a dark foundation.*
>
> Ernst Bloch, 1917

> *Simmel rejected the only correct and clear epistemological question concerning the priority of Being or consciousness in the name of a life-philosophical "third way."*
>
> Georg Lukács[116]

We need now to return to the question of tropes, for this can explain the practical unsuitedness of Simmel's aesthetic philosophy for the sociological conditions of war culture. The greatest misinterpretation of Simmel is the view of him as a philosopher of tragedy. He limned in *Schopenhauer and Nietzsche*: "It is clear from the unconditional solidarity of life with his concept of the inner essence of life, that Nietzsche does not appear to feel the immense tragedy that for every other sensibility rests in his [Nietzsche's] conception of life."[117] Or as Nietzsche wrote in the *Twilight of the Idols*: "The tragic artist is not a pessimist—it is precisely he who affirms all that is questionable and terrible in existence."[118] The lives of the most spiritual human beings are structured by tragedy, and they will suffer painful tragedies at the hands of fate. However, this battle is enjoined cheerfully not pessimistically. Paradoxically, Nietzsche's philosophy is tragic, but his sensibilities are not. Simmel's philosophical sensibilities were not tragic either. In 1904, he wrote to Paul Ernst of an aesthetic "fearlessness in the face of fate [*Schicksal*]," and in "The Problem of Fate" (1913), he asserted optimistically that "the conceived world is a product of knowing *Geist*" and that one antitragically can "stand above fate."[119] Nonetheless, the tragic interpretation of Simmel is a leitmotif of his contemporary reception. Scholars of extreme competence—Gertrud Kantorowicz, Andrew Arato and Paul Breines, Michael Löwy, Jürgen Habermas, Regina Mahlmann, Rudolph Weingartner, and David Frisby, to name a few—have characterized Simmel's work with this tropic appellation.[120] Lukács, too, interpreted Simmel as a tragic philosopher in *The Destruction of Reason*.

Two Simmel essays appear to comport with this tragic interpretation: "The Concept and Tragedy of Culture" (1912) and "The Conflict of Modern Culture" (1918). In the former essay, the rendition of tragedy is nearly identical to that found in Lukács's "Metaphysics of Tragedy" in *The Soul and Forms*. However, a differentiation of Lukács's philosophy of tragedy from Simmel's philosophy of tragedy is extremely important for a genealogy of Simmel's legacy. The dialectical narrative goes as follows: First, Simmel's philosophy was the basis for Lukács's tragic struggle of the soul against fate; when Lukács asserted that "the tragic drama must express the timeless-becoming of time," he meant that tragedy must depict the spiritual becoming of the soul as untimely, out of time, and opposed to historical fate.[121] Here, his "Metaphysics of Tragedy" restaged Simmel's conflict of subjective and objective spirit. Secondly, Lukács recast Simmel's philosophical drama as wholly tragic *Lebensphilosophie*; "tragedy is life, an other life, resistant to and excluding ordinary life."[122] Thirdly, Simmel's "The Concept and Tragedy of Culture" (1912), published within a year of the appearance of *The Soul and Forms*, was a response to Lukács's tragic interpretation of his philosophy.

In Simmel's "The Concept and Tragedy of Culture," the soul—through the heroic construction of a higher way of life—anticipates the successful and antitragic overcoming of the subject-object dualism. The soul relinquished its subjectivity, "but not its spirituality," through the creation of the aesthetic object. Because the creative process necessitates "the complete self-forgetful devotion to the objective task," there was a tragic danger that the "inner essence" of the object will be lost to its creator.[123] However, I wish to argue that Simmel, unlike the Lukács of the "Metaphysics of Tragedy," did not see this tragic possibility as a necessity. For Simmel, the goal of creative activity is "synthetic form"; "Therefore, an interest in culture rests with both the pure self-development of subjective *Geist* and its pure germination in things."[124] Simmel, thereby, suggested that the creative genius could indeed create living as opposed to spiritless aesthetic forms and find a synthetic, as opposed to tragic, meaning in them; "Culture is, as it reveals itself, always synthesis."[125] This synthesis was a conscious renunciation of tragedy. As Simmel wrote in "The Problem of the Fate" (1913):

> To stand under fate [*Schicksal*] means to have no life intentions of your own. . . . It means being the pure event itself and to leave things, even when they touch us, alone in their senseless courses. The person who stands above fate possesses a life-intention determined from the inside and which is indivertible and beyond influence.[126]

Simmel's genius figure lived with tragic possibility but was, in fact, living above fate as though peering down at it from a penthouse and discerning people the size of ants. The fact that Lukács, in *The Destruction of Reason*, repeatedly and exclusively interpreted his mentor as a philosopher of tragedy indicates how radically he had elided his own prewar, tragic philosophy and Simmel's cultural legacy.

As a result of the war and his support for it, Simmel's generational reception moved from one of existential freedom and fatelessness to one of historical determinism (tragedy) and political conservatism. For Bloch and Lukács, Simmel's support for the war was a capitulation to a dispirited historical determinism, and, hence, a renunciation of his own existential philosophy. It was an uncritical surrender to conservative culture. Here we can correlate the generational reception of Simmel and Hegel. Like Hegel's view of the Prussian state, Simmel referred to the Great War as the realization of the absolute idea in political form. This indicated to others that his vitalistic philosophy, regardless of its sociological elements, was compatible with a conservative affirmation of the Prussian state. The neo-Simmelians, like the young Hegelians of the nineteenth century, opposed their mentor because of the repugnant nature of his identification of the state and realized spirit. Obviously, the ethical aspirations of the antiwar generation could not be fulfilled by an affirmation of the state. For a generation which perceived the existing state as unethical, capitulation to its laws and norms would mean the acceptance of personal and collective tragedy.

As a result of his support for the war, then, the positive generational perception of Simmel (as soulful genius mocking sociological fate) shifted to a condemnation of his public assent to a conservative and wholly unethical fate. There was a personal correlative to the public reversal of Simmel's reputation. In the culture of war, Simmel became a tragic thinker whose life and work became embroidered by the discourse of fate. For example, he wrote Heinrich Rickert in July 1915 about the "great and beautiful hopes buried in Masuren and Flanders."[127] This pessimism corresponds to a change in the meaning in the discourse of fate in his life and letters. By 1916, there is no more talk of standing above fate, as was typical of his prewar philosophical bent. Now, enveloped by the brutalities of war, he experiences fate as the "rape of all human desires."[128] He wrote to Edmund Husserl in May 1916: "I've learned that your son has become a victim of world fate."[129] Fate and social reality now had shifted from a power that the avant-gardist need not fear to something that had already accomplished the most personal violation of the self. Aesthetic fatelessness had given way to political tragedy. Except polemically, the discourse of fate was neither a significant philosophical nor epistolary presence in Simmel's life and letters prior to the war. However, by the end of the war it had become the reigning tropic ideology governing his personal life. There was also a textual correlative of this new epistolary discourse. In "The Conflict of Modern Culture" (1918) Simmel now described a world that was characterized by the tragedy of social determinism. In stark contrast to his reflections about the liberatory potential of modernity in *The Philosophy of Money*, the individual could no longer find spiritual meaning in extant cultural forms.

By 1917, what separated Simmel from his students was not their perception of social conditions: all were by the end of the war enveloped by a tropic world of cultural decline and spiritual vacuity. The distinction was their attitude toward tragedy. While Simmel believed that "it is senseless to ask about the meaning [of the war]," Bloch and Lukács demanded that fate once again become meaningful.[130] To make fate meaningful, Lukács and Bloch ventured into a realm that was secondary to the Simmel circle prior to the war: the political world of socialist and communist politics. They entered this realm unwillingly, and it brought them to a critique of Simmel's brand of antibourgeois thought which never sought formal links to anticapitalist parties.

Politics, as defined by war culture, became increasingly incompatible with Simmel's philosophy of genius. In his philosophy, the aesthetic genius produced individual moral ideals. Aesthetic critique sought the redemption of these ideals. Prior to the war, Lukács followed Simmel in developing a philosophy based on the "genius of morality"; the moral genius created new, living moral forms, thereby overcoming alienation; this Lukácsian interpretation of Simmel had a tremendous impact on Bloch, who incorporated it into his *The Spirit of Utopia*.[131] In the culture of war and under the influence of Marxism, however, Lukács renounced Simmel's Nietzschean view of ethics. Now the sphere of the individual and state were so condensed that it made no practical sense to conceive of politics as a projection of personalized ethics. What the culture of war demanded was a collective categorical imperative, not an individual law. Lukács located this in the Marxist conception of individual subjectivity: collective being. This may not have differed dramatically from Simmel's notion of the social-individual. Politically, however, the Simmelian and Marxist interpretations of antibourgeois subjectivity were divergent. The popular iconography accompanying the Russian Revolution and the birth of a social democratic German Republic, with its focus on collective as opposed to individual laws, was a central reason for Simmel's intellectual eclipse after 1918.

LUKÁCS: BEYOND THE SIMMELIAN SOUL

As a result of the war, Lukács gravitated to Hegelian Marxism and jettisoned Simmel's view of subjectivity and discourse of the soul as a particularistic and irrational. In "My Path to Marx," he stated: "At this time, Marx was seen no longer through Simmelian, but through Hegelian glasses."[133]

No doubt his Hegelianism originated from his association with the Baden-Baden Hegelians and Windelband in Heidelberg. Hegel radicalized Lukács's political self-consciousness and facilitated a totalizing sociology. In the context of war, Hegel's *Phenomenology of Spirit,* recalled Lukács, "developed a growing meaning" making "ever clearer the imperialistic character of war."[132] Prior to the war, Lukács refused to swallow the cultural syrup of bourgeois life and embraced the avant-garde ideology of individual resistance to convention. War was a different fate. The culture of war was fate as collective (as opposed to individual) tragedy. War culture was social determinism *as tragedy* and, therefore, Lukács—who conceived of himself individualistically as a moral revolutionary prior to becoming a Marxist—came to believe that he could not resist social determinism with an individualist philosophy. To resist the collective fate, one had to develop a collective antitragic philosophy of life. As a means of overcoming the tragic drama of war, Lukács celebrated the Russian Revolution and the Marxist variant of collective consciousness. The collective and rational character of subjectivity—proletarian class consciousness or species being extant in the Russian, German, and Hungarian Revolutions—made possible a philosophy and politics of totality. The universality of communist subjectivity awaited realization, and Lukács wanted to get on with this task. From this perspective, it is easy to understand why, in *The Destruction of Reason,* Lukács reversed his earlier interpretation of Simmel as a critic of relativism (now calling him a relativist) and abandoned Simmel's prewar sociological aesthetics. Simmel's thought rested on a vitalistic and individualistic interpretation of the soul that was ultimately rejected by Hegel and Marx.

With the publication of *The Theory of the Novel* (1915), Lukács began to grapple with the ethics of realism. The reason for Lukács' new found fascination with nineteenth-century realism was its ethical starting point: the social totality of objective institutions. This point of departure induced a complete renunciation of Simmel's ethical point of departure, the individual creative soul. In 1915, however, Lukács had still not broken from his philosophy of the soul, but he was struggling to clarify the role of the soul in political ethics.

> Only the soul possesses a metaphysical reality. That is not a solipsism. The problem rests in finding a way to guide one soul to another soul. Any other way [of interacting] is merely instrumental and individualistic. . . . I see . . . a new form of the old conflict between old ethics (responsibility to institutions) and a second ethics (the imperative of the soul). The question of priority always maintains peculiar dialectical complexities if the soul is focused not on itself but on humanity: namely, in the case of the political person and the revolutionary. Here, in order to save the soul, the soul must be sacrificed; one must be transformed, out of a mystical ethics, into a cruel *Realpolitiker*.[134]

By 1920, Lukács had solved the problem of soulful intersubjectivity by turning to Hegel's rational philosophy. Under the influence of Hegelian Marxism and the Russian Revolution, he would cast aside his and Simmel's discourse of the soul. But his Hegelian Marxism was not only a renunciation of his mentor's philosophy. Rather, his spurning of the discourse of the soul was at the same time a realization of the philosophy of the soul. Like Zarathustra, the communist Lukács came down from the hermetic hill of asocial, if antibourgeois, spiritual polemics. He had decided, or the culture of war decided for him, to dedicate his life to the "old ethics," social responsibility and institutional transformation, and this new dedication was a spiritual decision, a religious need of the first order. In his own mind, he now could not realize the ethical imperative of his antibourgeois soul without abandoning the discourse of the soul itself.

SIMMEL'S DIVERGENT LEGACIES

Simmel's antibourgeois legacy survived in the works of Lukács and Bloch, but in two very different forms. In Lukács, the trope of self-creation became exclusively identified with the collective creation of socialist institutions and with working-class consciousness qua species being. There was, then, a dramatic transmutation of Simmel's legacy in Lukács's case. Whereas Simmel had combined socialist ethics with theoretical skepticism, the revolutionary Lukács renounced the latter antifoundational element of Simmel's sociology. Lukács viewed his anticapitalist philosophy as an entirely objective analysis of sociological totality. This theoretical conception was in direct opposition to Simmel's more humble neo-Kantian assertion that sociological forms could never constitute a totality, but were merely a symbolic interpretation of reality. Simmel never contemplated (in fact he resisted) the pretension that one interpretive form possessed hegemony over all others.

It would be wrong, however, to treat Lukács's communist ontology as mere dogmatism, although this is the tendency in our poststructural milieu. Lukács's communism and critique of Simmel have to be evaluated as a manifestation of war culture.[135] In the culture of war, and perhaps in the life of the proletariat under capitalism, the liberal ideal of a civil life independent from the determination of the state collapsed. While in Heidelberg before the war, Lukács said to Paul Honigsheim: "All this individualism is humbug; Stefan George is allowed to be a personality but the policeman and coachman are not."[136] This is simply another indication that Lukács turn to communist politics was not a radical discontinuity. However, it was the war that induced the political conclusion that Simmel's, and his own, philosophy of the soul—despite antibourgeois pretensions—was homologous with bourgeois individualism. Total war made the philosophy of subjective freedom and individuality appear insincere, impractical, and immoral. The epoch of "perfect sinfulness," as Lukács called the war, demanded of his anticapitalist soul a new collective politics and a new ethics of power, and one that now placed priority on the socially determined nature of the individual as an economic being, as a being stamped by total war.

To respect the ethical integrity and historical validity of Lukács's political vision does not mean that his was the only means to engage energetically the political and ethical demands of war culture. There was more than one way to formulate a philosophy that overcame the liberal dichotomy of private and public. Moreover, while the idea that the-private-is-political facilitated a totalizing communism, this facilitation does not lessen the ethical validity of Lukács antiliberalism. For us, the central issue is: need one renounce the neo-Kantian aporia of *homo noumena* and *homo phenomena* in an attempt to defend an anticapitalist deontology, a deontology that rejects the ethical practicality of the private/public dichotomy? If Simmel is our reference point, then the answer is no. A more historically nuanced answer can be found in an examination of Simmel's generational legacy. Hiller's formation of the *Aktivistenbund,* for instance, provides a very different antiwar reformulation of Simmel's philosophy. Hiller retained the concept of the soul and the Nietzschean component of Simmel's thought, as Lukács did not. Bloch, too, retained the discursive influences of Simmel. As late as 1969, he defined his communist politics with the hyphenated triptych "body-soul-spirit" (*Leib-Seele-Geist*).[137]

Bloch's reformulation of Simmelian philosophy in *The Spirit of Utopia* (1918) shared elements with Hiller and Lukács while differing substantially from both. Like Hiller, he retained the discourse of the soul and, thereby, Simmel's sociological conception of vital subjectivity as social-soul. Like Lukács, he was drawn to Marxist politics. However, there was a fundamental element to Bloch's communist politics that differed markedly from the philosophical premises of Hiller and Lukács: only Bloch retained the antifoundational element of Simmel's philosophical sociology.

PARADISE OR APOCALYPSE?

If Marxism is a sacralization of secular history, then its tropic appellation is paradise on earth. One example of the philosophical discourse of messianic actualization was Lukács's *ontology of social being*.[138] Although Hiller never jettisoned Simmel's vitalistic conception of subjectivity in favor of a rational subjectivity as Lukács did, he, too, developed a trope of totality as a consequence of the war. The central trope of Hiller's "Philosophy of Purpose" (1916) was the trope of *Paradies*. In 1919, he published "Reflections on the

Eschatology and Methodology of Activism (Paradise)," and he would later use the concept of "logocracy" to describe the governmental actualization of a World League of Spirit.[139] In essence, Hiller and Lukács responded to the tragedy of war culture with political philosophies that were logocentric and antitragic. Their unarticulated tropic conclusion was that one can not heroically resist the tragic realities of war culture with tragic tropes. One needs an antitragic tropic politics. Their tropic politics, then, were an exogenous, as opposed to an immanent, critique of a tragic total war.

Bloch, conversely, developed a immanent messianic political philosophy that was stamped by the tragedy of war culture, and that political philosophy adumbrated all of his subsequent work. While he renounced Simmel's optimism that the war was a realization of the absolute idea, in *The Spirit of Utopia* Bloch developed a cultural messianism that retained all the aporetic elements of Simmel's thought. On one hand, his language was intensely personal and passionately religious. Bloch wrote of "the lasting concentration of dream on itself," "the inner becoming of light," "the redemption from malice, emptiness, death, and enigma," "a community with the sanctified," and "the turn of all things toward *Paradies*." But immediately following this discourse of paradisiacal ontology, Bloch placed what he called his system of "practical messianism" and "dark optimism" within a larger tropic metaphysic: "always and everywhere—the apocalypse is the a priori of politics and culture."[140] The apocalypse was the central philosophical interlocutor which Bloch used to express the putrid spirituality and moral vacuity of war culture. The trope of apocalypse signified Bloch's religious intensity, and it was a clarion call for ethical activism in a world devoid of truth, meaning, and God. "Atheism is an immense piety," Bloch concluded, because it is an honest admission of the gulf between God and modernity.[141]

Bloch's apocalyptic politics constitute a resuscitation of religious existentialism within the Marxist tradition. In *The Concept of Dread*, Soren Kierkegaard explained that his understanding of "ethics has nothing to do with the possibility of sin nor with original sin. . . . Ethics has the reality of sin as its province."[142] The war brought Bloch to a similar conclusion. Modern civilization was epochal sinfulness cut off from theological certainty. Therefore, life had no discernible predetermined purpose, and humanity lacked recourse to heaven. In the face of external chaos and spiritual corruption, Bloch turned inward toward the Simmelian soul. The soul was a "true cosmos" situated within the metaphysical category of moral danger.[143] The philosophical concepts of the soul and the apocalypse were so primary to Bloch's project that his text might be better titled *The Soul of Utopia within the Apocalypse*.

Bloch's apocalyptic philosophy, while a rejection of Simmel's war politics, remained remarkably true to his mentor's soulful anti-capitalism and critique of conceptual closure. Despite these continuities, Bloch clearly conceived of his political philosophy as an ethical supersession of Simmelian thought. As he had in his prewar letters to Lukács, Bloch proffered an ambiguous portrait of Simmel in *The Spirit of Utopia*:

> Simmel, the finest mind among his contemporaries, but beyond that one that was totally empty, a purposeless man who wants everything except for the truth, a collector of many standpoints around the truth without at any time wanting or able to possess them, . . . in general thoroughly without will and without a firm position. . . . Conversely, it is undeniable that Simmel, in his flexibility and in his attempted nearness to life and nervous nearness to the soul . . . has lent to thought a malleability and a rise in temperature, which, if taken out of the hands of their inborn corelessness and opposed to Simmel's delicacy, is capable of lending a great and much obliged service to philosophy.[144]

Here, a labyrinthine condemnation of Simmel's "unvirtue" coexists with the suggestion that Simmel's philosophy can aid in resolving some of the ethical and philosophical issues arising from the war. Moreover, Bloch's condemnation of Simmel was marked by the same language used to bleakly depict the spiritual condition of war culture: "we ourselves are in the course of life, which is coreless, yes, which is completely untrue."[145] Bloch repeatedly returns to his thesis that the world is, as a consequence of the war, stale, empty of meaning, and bereft of spiritual dignity. The text reads as though written by a man pinned to the ground by Clio's weighty mail; his movement and breathing restricted by the weight of a war that is emptying the world of spirit.[146] To Bloch, the war confirmed Nietzsche and Kierkegaard's philosophical darkness. There was no way of evading what he called "The Emptiness."[147] To this bleak deontology Bloch fused the ethics of communism.

Similar to Hiller and Lukács, Bloch's opposition to the war compelled him to put forth a public critique of Simmel's wartime conservatism, and embrace a transformative activism. He refined his political ideas through a critique of the Expressionists. Despite their many similarities, Bloch was self-consciously critical of Hiller and the *Aktivisten*. The elitist *Aktivisten*, charged Bloch during the war, were incapable of learning from the "foreign class consciousness of the proletariat, from the secret future of human affairs."[148] This indicates Bloch's discernment of the cultural distance between the elitist—although prosocialist—Aktivisten and Marxists like himself. However, while signing onto the cause of revolution, Bloch was not an orthodox Marxist defender of the proletariat. He interpreted proletarian consciousness not as a subjective ontology but as an objective fantasy. This antifoundational communism was obliged to Simmel. It was Simmel's critical philosophy of the soul that Bloch enlisted during the war to revitalize the empty and seemingly irredeemable spirit of history and humanity. Now, however, the tone of this political idealism is even more intensely antibourgeois, spiritual, communist, and antiauthoritarian: "In human togetherness finally there will be overall no Führer."[149] By 1920 Bloch was seeking to break free from the aristocratic radicalism of the Simmel circle. He was not entirely successful. Like Hiller and Lukács, who both defended an aristocratic vision of political leadership, Bloch continued to conceive of himself as a member of a "spiritual aristocracy" but one that would not provide monetary advantages.[150] Suffice it to say, the language of aristocracy found in *Spirit of Utopie* was quickly abandoned by the communist Bloch. Just as Lukács jettisoned the language of the soul, the communist Bloch came to view the notion of a spiritual aristocracy, so central to the Simmel circle and *Aktivismus*, as a carry-over of bourgeois inegalitarianism. In the 1923 edition of *The Spirit of Utopia*, his reference to a spiritual aristocracy was excised.[151] Bloch's apocalyptic communism retained the Simmelian conception of the social soul but increasingly distanced itself from the cultural elitism of the Simmel circle.

BLOCH, LUKÁCS, AND THE HEGEL DEBATE

There was an extreme divergence of Simmel's legacy, mediated by war culture, in the communist politics of Lukács and Bloch, and it manifests itself in their incommensurable perception of Hegel. Nothing is more telling about Bloch and Lukács's divergent visions of communism than their dispositions toward Hegel. Lukács needed his neo-Hegelian Marx for the same reason that Hegel needed a philosophy of totality: they were both criticizing and seeking to overcome in politics Kant's skeptical and aporetic (a)synthesis of *homo noumena* and *homo phenomena*.[152] For Lukács, Simmel's neo-Kantian thought was inadequate to address positively the problem of shared social institutions, such as the state and economy. In addressing this ethical problem, political economy became Lukács's rendition of the trope of all tropes and the form of all forms.[153] This, above all else, was the basis for his critique of Hiller and Simmel in his famous "Expressionism: Its Basis and its Decline" (1934). (Here, Lukács is alone in recognizing the cultural linkage of Simmel and Expressionism.) An anticapitalist cultural critique, à la Simmel and Hiller, was insufficient without a corresponding proposition of collective political and economic institutions, he asserted.

Lukács put forth a communist philosophy precisely intended to overcome the neo-Kantian antinomies of Simmelian thought. For example, Lukács's *Tactics and Ethics* (1919) relied almost exclusively on a Hegelian interpretation of Marxism. Bloch, on the other hand, remained philosophically indebted to Simmel's neo-Kantian skepticism, and in *The Spirit of Utopia* he identified Hegel as the greatest danger to communism.[154]

"There is in general no better grave digger than the completed content of the concept," Bloch wrote in reference to Hegel who has "closed all Kantian openness."[155] What Hegel suppressed, according to Bloch, was the multiplicity of subjective purposiveness and, thereby, respect for otherness. The Hegelian presumption of a rational and universal subjectivity was a denial of the "Other," and thereby a rejection of spiritual and ethical differentiation.[156] For Bloch, ethical subjectivity was a dionysian *élan vital*. It was a "utopian reality or a not-yet arrived but certainly valid reality of the idea."[157] Conversely, the universal rationality of Hegel was denounced as an instrumental and conservative philosophy.

Most important to our intellectual history is Bloch's tropic interpretation of Hegel. According to Bloch, Hegel (and here by extension, Lukács) was a philosopher of paradise. Conversely, Bloch described his own tropic politics as "negative theology" or "the Fall and the expulsion from paradise."[158] Bloch's disaffinity for Hegel was not merely philosophical. For him, Hegel's claims to philosophical totality contributed to all the ills that humanity suffered in the Great War:

> In the specific organization of Prussian Germany, the most Western, most modern, most rational calculation is unified with . . . Hegel's organic form of thought, with organic traditionalism, with the *Geist* of authority, and with . . . God begotten hierarchy.[159]

His aforementioned reference to Hegel as a grave digger was no mere turn of phrase. An Hegelian state provided authoritarian rationale for Germany's war. Consequently, Bloch feared nothing so much as a neo-Hegelian renaissance because its absence of doubt fortified a Prussian politics lacking compassion and full of authoritarianism.[160]

But how does Bloch combine a radical and groundless subjectivity with a communist ethics? Are these not antipodes? The answer is found in the concluding essay of *The Spirit of Utopia* entitled, "Marx, Death, and the Apocalypse." Here Bloch agreed with Marx's dictum that economic being determined ideas. He referred to communism as the a priori best suited to overcome feudal theology, bourgeois avarice, and capitalistic competition. Communism would end capitalist exploitation, militarism, imperialism, and theological ontology. In this regard, Bloch's communist vision was not unique. What was unique among communist intellectuals was his resistance to undialectical materialism and his compassionate tenor. If communism forgets the primacy of the human soul, then it will become nothing more than a "eudaemonistic heaven on earth without music."[161] Here Bloch resurrected Simmel's philosophy of the sociological soul within the Marxist tradition. It is Bloch, then, and not Lukács, who is the truer heir of Simmelian philosophy.

LOVE, DEATH, AND APOCALYPTIC COMMUNISM

Bloch's exceptional place within the Marxist avant-garde also derives from his retention and expansion of Simmel's philosophy of love. *The Spirit of Utopia* put forward two "tropic essences of purpose": love and the apocalypse.[162] In an essay commemorating Simmel's hundredth birthday, Bloch remarked that Simmel's "vitalistic formalism . . . was completely homeless in the academic philosophy of the time. The phenomenon of love belonged to this situation."[163] Indeed Simmel's philosophy of love is crucial to our analysis of the continuation of his legacy in Bloch. Simmel believed that the central ethical problem of modernity was the "pure negative character of freedom" found in liberal capitalist society.[164] And, in "The Style of Life," the coda of *The Philosophy of Money*, he identified pure negative freedom with all of the ills plaguing Kaiser capitalism: calculating egoism, indifference, and, above all, the death of a compassionate civic consciousness. Furthermore, in contrast to liberal conceptions of freedom, he insisted that there can be "no absolute freedom."[165] Absolute negative freedom of liberal individualism was not only a chimera; it was a harmful ideological buttress of repressive institutions. For Simmel, then, real freedom exists only in the presence of moral restriction. Does not this contradict his neo-Nietzschean philosophy? How can the individual be free if constrained by impersonal moral laws? A philosophy of love was the answer. As a civic morality, love provided individual's with a personal and noninstrumental form of ethical restriction: "Love is the binding of the soul . . . [and this] restriction of freedom is experienced as a higher freedom."[166] Simmel provocatively suggested that a politics of love could answer fundamental questions concerning the "justice and unjustice of our praxis."[167] Bloch consciously retained the civic refrain of what he later called Simmel's "formalistic vitalism and vitalistic formalism."[168]

Bloch's civic doctrine of love also arose from the theological hopes generated by the Russian Revolution: "the Russian Revolution now for the first time has established Christ as king."[169] Bloch's Christ, however, was "not at peace with the world."[170] To establish Christ as king meant that the individual would maintain a constant vigilance of love against instrumentality. Like Simmel before him, Bloch's civic interest in the function of love ensured his homelessness within the German antiwar counrterculture. For instance, in a leading antiwar intellectual journal, *Das Ziel*, Salomo Friedländer (also a Simmel student) and Hiller ridiculed as absurd and undionysian Bloch's hope that the Russian Revolution would be a breakthrough of the power of love.[171] Perhaps this Activist repudiation of Bloch was nothing more than a typical Nietzschean dismissal of love and socialism as an ethics of slave morality. Seen more expansively, however, the Bloch-Hiller debate represents the unresolved tensions between Simmel's neo-Nietzscheanism and civic sociology. Hiller and Friedländer's Activist invectives provide a vista from which to survey the multifaceted inheritance of Simmel's Nietzschean sociology. The *Aktivisten* retained Simmel's model of individual freedom and moral genius and kept their cultural distance from Marxism and the Russian Revolution. At the other extreme, Lukács rejected the Nietzschean element of Simmel's legacy and embraced a Marxist variant of sociology. Bloch was somewhere in between. He was a Marxist whose conception of the dialectic required the preservation of vitalistic subjectivities. However, his political philosophy, while vitalistic, disapproved of dionysian subjectivities that derived pleasure from domination. He denounced what he saw as the vitalistic relativism and anarchistic individualism of Hiller and the *Aktivisten*. To orthodox Marxists like Lukács, Bloch's philosophy appeared too idealistic and to the *Aktivisten* too materialistic.

Bloch espoused the apocalypse as the trope of communism and love as its civic proposition. He interpreted the Christian ethic of love as a critique of hierarchy, spiritual aristocracy, and patriarchy. Love was a doctrine, moreover, that answered profound ethical and political questions. How does one put forth a morality without destroying the validity of the other? The apocalyptic "community of love" was his practical answer. For Bloch—and in this regard he discusses marriage extensively—love can be the basis of personal and cultural mutual recognition. In love, you are *free through restriction*, and in Christ, you have a spiritual leader without domination. Communism was the material imperative and institutional correlative of love as an ethical a priori. Furthermore, love was a moral prescription that, in spite of its categorical nature, affirmed diversity. The law of love possessed a further ethical advantage. It facilitated the celebration of the most liberating element of modernity, diversity, and rejection of its spiritual decadence: economic self-interest, calculating indifference, and moral nihilism. Most importantly, the life of communist love was a profound rejection of the capitalist regime of emotive freedom. Instead of pure negative freedom, the ethic of love was a pure positive freedom of restraint. Love was one of the few examples of a moral law that enhanced freedom and fostered diversity. Parenthetically, we should draw attention to the exceptional nature of Bloch's formulations. Not since Saint-Simon's *New Christianity* (1824) had a socialist thinker developed such a thorough critique of capitalism using the trope of love. (In Bloch's apocalyptic variant of Christian anticapitalism, however, the spirit of utopian socialism was shorn of its previous ontological foundation.) And not since Charles Fourier's passionate philosophy of the human soul had a socialist put forth a more thorough civics of compassion.

In addition to his philosophy of love, there was another element of Bloch's wartime socialism that stood outside the Marxist and inside the Simmelean tradition, namely, his focus on death. In "Towards a Metaphysics of Death" (1911), Simmel had theorized the meaning of death for life. One's image of death, Simmel intoned, was "a positive and a priori" form that shapes "our lives not only in the hour of death, rather it is a formal moment of our life, that colors all of the contents of life."[172] In "Marx, the Apocalypse and Death" (1918), Bloch transformed Simmel's philosophy of death-forms into a new communist politics. His contemplation of death, conditioned by war culture, was a defense of the idea of the soul as a viable anticapitalist and antideterminist conception. More significantly, in this case, the idea of the soul advanced an utopian approach to death, which is an empirical fate that orthodox Marxism was incapable of addressing. In *The Principle of Hope*, Bloch set out to present a "hope-formation against the strongest nonutopia: death."[173] Death, like capitalism and social determinism, was a spiritless materialism. To accept a secular interpretation of death as an end to life was tantamount to capitulating to the physical fate of the body, that is, to spiritless materialism. In essence, Bloch, like the heroic soul against fate, resisted the merely scientific suggestion that death was the fate of our collective bodies. He contended in *The Spirit of Utopia* that only a doctrine of the soul could facilitate a life of resisting "bodily and social fate" and "organic and social pessimism."[174] But Bloch followed Simmel in rejecting the singularity of Christian redemption. There are numerous forms of immortality, and in order to become liberated from what Simmel called "the fate-concept," individuals must choose their own form of death.[175] Bloch's philosophy of death, in contrast to Simmel's, deemphasized that choice as a manifestation of individual freedom. Instead, one's choice of a conceptual form of human immortality was treated as a metaphor for a new collective responsibility to defy capitalist individualism and fashion a positive form of collective freedom.

Bloch alluringly referred to his philosophy of death as a "metempsychosis at a standstill in the apocalypse."[176] The concept of metempsychosis points to theological influences outside of the Judeo-Christian tradition. "All religions except Judaism and Christianity believe in the metempsychosis, in which the soul is united with a new body after death," wrote Bloch.[177] In referring to his wartime political philosophy as "at a standstill," Bloch was not defending a static philosophy of life. Rather, he proposed a dynamic subjectivity tied to the body (communist materialism) and independent of it (soulful antideterminism). He had thereby creatively refashioned the aporetic extremes of Simmel's third way in a communist philosophy of death.

There is a third character of Bloch's communism which illustrates its cultural affinities with Simmelian as opposed to Marxist thought, namely, his respect for and interest in theology. In *Die Religion*, for example, Simmel did not reject religious subjectivities but demanded their "spiritualist socialization," and by that he meant a sociological analysis of the civic legitimacy of religion. This positive view of religious ideals as potentially ethically valid was rejected by the mature Lukács as a manifestation of Simmel's bourgeois individualism and moral relativism.[178] In general, the post–World War I Lukács ridiculed theology and the idea of the soul as irrational. If Lukács (particularly after 1923) sought an ethical standard for communism outside the isolated and therefore irrational self, Bloch conceived of his philosophy as the creation of antifascist and anticapitalist feelings within the self. Rather than reject the vitalist realm of feeling as irrational, Bloch sought to occupy what he called the political terrain of the "Irratio":

> It is time to knock the [spiritual] weapons out of the hands of the reactionaries. It is especially time to mobilize, under socialist leadership, the contradictions of noncontemporaneous classes against capitalism. Here the "Irratio" will not be ridiculed wholesale, but occupied; and precisely from a standpoint which has understood the "Irratio" as something more genuine than the Nazis and their big capitalist allies.[179]

Bloch's unwillingness to equate preemptively all religious traditions with reactionary politics is illustrative of his thought from the *The Spirit of Utopia* to *The Principle of Hope*. This approach to a politics of subjectivity was extremely unusual in the Marxist tradition. Bloch's exceptional brand of Marxist sociology as objective phantasy is a continuation of Simmel's openness to the critical potential of what orthodox Marxists call idealist traditions.

Bloch's vitalistic and antifoundational thought sought to occupy the irratio in order to remove it from the forces of reaction and carry through a revolution of compassion in the realm of value-feelings (*Wertgefühle*), as Simmel called them. It is worth noting that Bloch's encyclopedic search for emancipatory forms of consciousness was much more concrete than Lukács's (and other historical materialists') more abstract and unitary concept of class consciousness. In the *1844 Manuscripts*, young Marx theorized the dialectical emergence of a transformed human body, with new sensibilities and a new politics of feeling. Bloch's Marxism, molded by Simmel's practical idealism, embodies and reincarnates this underappreciated part of Marx's thought.

SIMMEL'S LEGACY IN WESTERN MARXISM

Prior to the war, Simmel was seen as a radical philosopher. He was the closest thing to an academic activist that Wilhelmine Germany possessed. However, his role as a prowar public intellectual irredeemably alienated his radical students and initiated a new chapter in the history of German critical sociology. Traces of his contribution to German critical theory are manifest in Bloch's unorthodox Marxism. In *Introduction to the Science of Morals,* Simmel made a statement relevant to understanding the transformation of his legacy in the culture of war.

> Extreme materialism also needs for its completion precisely a maximum of idealism. . . . And I do not see how one can remove this psychological contradiction from socialism.[180]

Bloch's doctrine of "metempsychosis at a standstill in the apocalypse," does not so much resolve this contradiction—socialist materialism as naturalized idealism—as revise it by retaining and developing the idealist element of socialist philosophy. Simmel asserted that orthodox Marxism was a naturalized eudaemonism paralyzing the need for a concrete, conscious, practical, and countercultural idealism. Bloch's unorthodox Marxism preserved Simmel's defense of practical idealism and critique of conceptual reification within a Marxist tradition that, after the Great War, was becoming increasingly characterized by dialectical dogmatics. The spirit of Simmel's avant-garde sociology was continued in Bloch's open dialectics but now under the imprimatur of an apocalyptic metaphysics. After World War II, Bloch accepted a chair in philosophy at Leipzig University. His comrades in the (East) German Democratic Republic (GDR) attacked him as an idealist enemy of communism, and he became as institutionally isolated by the forces of conservatism in the GDR as Simmel had been in Wilhelmine Germany. With the demonization of Bloch in the Communist bloc, the last hope for avoiding Simmel's dark prophecy of socialism had been lost. Socialism, as Simmel had predicted, became a naturalized eudaemonism paralyzing its need for a critical idealism.[181] In essence, the politics of paradise and absolute truth had silenced the political metaphysics of apocalypse. Dead were Bloch's hopes for a theoretically humble and practically compassionate communism that made no reactionary recourse to absolute truth claims or to "the law of spiritual imperialism," as Albert Camus called Marxism.[182]

Despite all of the criticisms of their mentor, Lukàcs and Bloch retained Simmel's ethical critique of economic liberalism. They also continued his avant-garde repudiation of capitalism in the realm of philosophy and aesthetics. Their sociology transcended Simmel's model of political and cultural agency, heroic individualism, and affirmed proletarian collectivism. This was a cultural transmutation of an antibourgeois avant-garde cultural politics into a communist institutional politics.

By demanding the realization of communism under the a priori of love and apocalypse, Bloch preserved a critical Simmelian subjectivity that was lost in the Marxist sacralization of secular history. This critical and practical idealism was an eschatology at war with religious ontology. Bloch's eschatological antifoundationalism derived from the belief that ontological closure, i.e., Hegel, facilitated conservatism and domination. His antifoundationalism did not mean, however, that he believed subjectivity could remain merely negative. He affirmed the need for a collective economic form, communism, and admitted that this form would come to determine the human spirit. But this defense of a universal form was interpreted as a practical necessity and as an ultimately groundless decision. Communism was a hopeful objective fantasy that should be realized without recourse to the hubris of absolute truth. Bloch's, then, was a communism of zealous humility. Bloch and Lukács's revolutionary hopes developed as a renunciation of their mentor's prowar politics. Nonetheless, their revolutionary hopes continued to versify the antibourgeois "spiritual symbiosis" that they first experienced in the Simmel circle of prewar Berlin.[183]

NOTES

1. Siegfried Kracauer, "Georg Simmel," *Logos* 9 (1920): 307.

2. Georg Lukács, "Georg Simmel," in *Buch des Dankes*, p. 171.

3. Friedrich Nietzsche, *The Birth of Tragedy*, trans. Walter Kaufman (New York: Vintage Books, 1967), p. 17.

4. Oswald Spengler, *Der Untergang des Abendlandes. Umrisse einer Morphologie der Weltgeschichte*, vol. 1, *Gestalt und Wirklichkeit* [1918] (München: Deutscher Taschenbuch Verlag, 1988). The Beck Verlag edition of this first volume had gone through over eighty editions by 1950.

5. The canonical intellectual origin of this distinction is Ferdinand Tönnies, *Gemeinschaft und Gesellschaft* (Leipzig: n.p., 1887).

6. See, for example, Fritz K. Ringer, *The Decline of the German Mandarins*, p. 223.

7. Hayden White, *Metahistory* (Baltimore: Johns Hopkins University Press, 1973), p. xii.

8. Klaus Vondung, "Deutsche Apokalypse 1914," in *Die wilhelminische Bildungsbürgertum*, ed. Klaus Vondung (Göttingen: Vandenhoeck & Ruprecht, 1976), p. 171. Concerning the birth of conservative revolution in the culture of the Great War, see Rolf Peter Sieferle, *Die Konservative Revolution* (Frankfurt a.M.: Suhrkamp, 1995).

9. Ludwig Rubiner, *Kameraden der Menschheit* [1919] (Leipzig: Philipp Reclam, 1971), p. 168.

10. Simmel, "Deutschlands innere Wandlung" [November 1914], in *Der Krieg und die Geistigen Entscheidungen*, p. 20.

11. Max Scheler, *Der Genius des Krieges und der Deutsche Krieg* (Leipzig: Weißen Bücher, 1915), p. 4. Bloch often referred to Scheler in *Geist der Utopie*, and undoubtedly he had this text in mind. He questioned Scheler's purely cultural, i.e., noneconomic, interpretation of the war and vehemently opposed Scheler's spiritualization of war culture: "Er ist von Scheler erhoben worden, der die Wehrhaftigkeit liebt, den Krieg stark und brutal bei seinem Namen nennt und die

Kriegsgewichtigkeit von jeder bloß ökonomischen Bedeutung loslöst. . . . Das alles kommt nun bei Scheler nicht in Frage, weder das Gemeine noch das Geistige, wie sollte sich gerade das Machtpathos cäsarischer Art anders als ökonomisch durchsetzen können." Ernst Bloch, *Geist der Utopie* [1918] (Frankfurt a.M.: Suhrkamp, 1971), pp. 393–94.

The relationship between Scheler and Bloch is interesting, to say the least. They met in a Berlin cafe in 1916 and again in Bern in the summer of 1917. (Whether they had met in Berlin before the war is unknown.) Also in 1917, the now pacifist Bloch published a scathing critique of Scheler's politics, accusing him of philosophical prostitution. The sole surviving correspondence between them is a 1919 letter from Bloch to Scheler recommending his *Geist der Utopie*! The letter did not mention the affronts contained in the text. See Ernst Bloch, "Der Weg Schelers," in *Die "Friedens-Warte,"* 19, no. 9 (1917): 274–76; Ernst Bloch to Max Scheler, 3 September 1919, in Ernst Bloch, *Briefe, 1903–1975*, vol. 1, ed. Uwe Opolka, et al. (Frankfurt a.M.: Suhrkamp, 1985), pp. 253–54.

12. Georg Lukács, *Die Theorie des Romans* [1920] (Frankfurt a.M.: Luchterhand, 1988), p. 12; Letter from Georg Lukács to Paul Ernst, May 1915, in Georg Lukács, *Briefwechsel 1902–1917*, ed. Eva Karadi and Eva Fekete (Stuttgart: Metzler, 1982), p. 352.

13. On Lukács, see "War and Apocalypse" in Lee Congdon, *The Young Lukács* (Chapel Hill: University of North Carolina Press, 1983), pp. 108–11. On the trope of apocalypse in German cultural history, see Klaus Vondung, *Die Apokalypse in Deutschland* (Munich: Deutscher Taschenbuch, 1988). Although the historiography of Benjamin is prodigious and growing, scholars have not understood that his unique Marxist overtures are illustrative of the tropic cords of the Great War. See Walter Benjamin, "Trauerspiel und Tragödie" [1916] and "Die Bedeutung der Sprache in Trauerspiel und Tragödie" [1916], *Gesammlte Schriften* 2.1 (Frankfurt a.M.: Suhrkamp, 1980), pp. 133–40. These essays adumbrate the metaphysical framework of his Fallen communism.

14. Margarete Susman [von Bendemann], *Die geistige Gestalt Georg Simmels*, pp. 36–37.

15. This was the subtitle of Simmel's *Einleitung in die Moralwissenschaft*. Far from a mere "introduction" to the philosophy of ethics, this text was comprised of two volumes and was over 800 pages in length.

16. Michael Landmann, "Bausteine zur Biographie" in *Buch des Dankes*, pp.11–34; Georg Lukács, "Curriculum vitae [1918]," *Text und Kritik* 39, 40 (1973): 5–7.

17. Georg Lukács, *Gelebtes Denken* (Frankfurt a.M.: Suhrkamp, 1981), pp. 39, 241.

18. Quoted in Klaus Christian Köhnke, "Georg Simmel als Jude," *Simmel Newsletter* 5, no. 1 (summer 1995): 53–72; quotation, p. 66. See also Elias Hurwics, "Georg Simmel als Jüdische Denker," *Neue jüdische Monatshefte* 3 (1918–19): 196–98.

19. Michael Landmann, "Ernst Bloch über Simmel," in *Ästhetik und Soziologie um die Jahrhundertwende: Georg Simmel*, ed. H. Böhringer and K. Gründer (Frankfurt a.M.: Vittorio Klosermann, 1976), p. 270.

20. Marianne Weber, *Lebenserinnerungen*, p. 376.

21. On Cohen and Simmel's ethnic affinity see Margarete Susman, "Pole jüdischen Wesens—Hermann Cohen und Georg Simmel," *Die Tat* 15 (1923–1924): 385–89.

22. Hans Simmel, "Auszüge aus den Lebenerinnerungen," in *Ästhetik und Soziologie*, p. 247.

23. See S. Lozinski, "Simmels Briefe zur jüdischen Frage," *Ästhetik und Soziologie*, p. 24–43.

24. Hans Liebeschütz, *Von Georg Simmel zu Franz Rosenzweig: Studien zum jüdischen Denken im deutschen Kulturbereich* (Tübingen: J. C. B. Mohr, 1970), p. 104.

25. Michael Landmann, "Bausteine zur Biographie," in *Buch des Dankes*, p. 12.

26. The most important chronicle of von Bendemann's centrifugal social and intellectual significance is Bloch's *Briefe*. See also Manfred Schlösser, ed., *Für Margarete Susman: Auf gespaltenem Pfad* (Darmstadt: Erato-Presse, 1964), which contains letters from Simmel, Lukács, Buber, Landauer, and Bloch, among others; Margarete Susman, *Das Nah-und Fernsein des Fremden* (Frankfurt a.M.: Jüdischer Verlag, 1992) contains correspondences between von Bendemann, Bloch and Lukács. Most of Simmel's letters and Lukács's letters to von Bendemann were seized by the National Socialists. Buber's *Briefe* and Lukács's *Briefwechsel 1902–1917* also contain references to Susman/von Bendemann.

27. Ingeborg Nordmann, "Wie man sich in der Sprache fremd bewegt," in *Das Nah-und Fernsein des Fremden*, p. 246.

28. "We suggested that it might be plausible to talk of an embourgeoisement of German society"; this chapter is a case study in this plausibility. See David Blackbourn and Geoff Eley, *The Peculiarities of German History* (Oxford: Oxford University Press, 1987), p. 13.

29. Arpad Kadarkay, *Georg Lukács: Life, Thought, and Politics* (Cambridge, Mass.: Basil Blackwell, 1991), pp. 3–8.

30. For a thorough biography of Bloch, see Peter Zudeick, *Der Hintern des Teufels: Ernst Bloch—Leben und Werk* (Moos: Elster Verlag, 1985).

31. Ernst Bloch, *Briefe* I: 48–49.

32. Ernst Bloch to Georg Lukács, 20 February 1913, *Briefe* I: 101–102. Else possessed more than financial and cultural capital. She was described by Bloch as an intelligent person and an accomplished sculptor. However, she also possessed, according to Bloch, corporeal-cultural deficiencies. Bloch reports that "sie hat eine weniger schöne Nase als ich," and this statement appears in the epistolary context of an earlier and otherwise unrelated reference to "die längste, abstrünnigste Judennase."

33. Bloch, *Briefe* I: 75.

34. Bloch, *Briefe* I: 127.

35. "Die Trennung kam 1917," recollected Bloch. See "Erbschaft aus Dekadenz? Ein Gespräch mit Iring Fetscher und Georg Lukács" (1967), in *Gespräche mit Ernst Bloch*, ed. Rainer Traub and Harald Wieser (Frankfurt a.M.: Suhrkamp, 1975), p. 34.

36. François Furet, *Interpreting the French Revolution* (New York: Cambridge University Press, 1990), p. 63.

37. Georg Simmel, *Schopenhauer und Nietzsche*. This was the subtitle of the text's final chapter.

38. Georg Lukács, *Briefwechsel 1902–1917*, p. 349.

39. Lukács, *Gelebtes Denken*, p. 58.

40. Bloch, *Tendenz-Latenz-Utopie* (Frankfurt a.M.: Suhrkamp, 1978), p. 372.

41. The quote is taken from Peter Zudeick, *Der Hintern des Teufels*, p. 38.

42. Bloch, *Briefe*, I: 59, 71. Bloch's hatred of Simmel is expressed in the context of a feud with von Bendemannn. This feud is one of the subtexts of the early Bloch-Lukács correspondence. Apparently, Bloch and von Bendemann patched things up. Bloch eventually dedicated his first overtly revolutionary book, *Thomas Münzer als Theologe der Revolution* (1921), to her.

43. For an interesting discussion of Simmel's radical reputation, see Marianne Weber, *Lebenserinnerungen*, pp. 375–409. This is discussed in more detail below.

44. Susman, *Die geistige Gestalt Georg Simmels*, pp. 9 , 21.

45. The romantic belief in Greek cultural superiority was rejected by Simmel; see Georg Simmel, "Humanistisches Märchen," in *Die Neue Zeit* 10, no. 2 (1891–92): 713–18.

46. Kracauer, "Georg Simmel," *Logos* 9 (1920–1921): 307–38, p. 21. For an interpretation of Simmel's influence on Kracauer, see Frisby's *Fragments of Modernity*.

47. Karl Mannheim, "Simmel als Philosoph," in *Georg Lukács, Karl Mannheim und der Sonntagskreis*, ed. Éva Karádi and Erzsébet Vezér (Frankfurt a.M.: Sender, 1985), pp. 150–53.

48. Susman, *Die geistige Gestalt*, p. 8.

49. For a detailed editorial history of the text, see *Einleitung in der Moralwissenschaft* II: 403–11.

50. Simmel, *Moralwissenschaft* I: 93.

51. Simmel, *Moralwissenschaft* I: 102. For example, in the absence of practical examination we cannot know if the presumably natural doctrine of egoism is a means to altruistic behavior or if liberalism cloaks egoism in the clothing of altruistic behavior. Even more complicated are the cases of the social group. The pursuit of group interests is not in itself altruistic.

52. Simmel, *Moralwissenschaft* I: 102.

53. Simmel, *Moralwissenschaft* II: 289.

54. Ibid., p. 164.

55. Simmel, *Moralwissenschaft* I: 105.

56. Simmel, *Moralwissenschaft* II: 106. See also his reference to "das totalisierungsvermögen der Seele" in *Hauptprobleme der Philosophie* (Berlin: de Gruyter, 1989), p. 12. This latter text, published in 1910, testifies to the continuing significance of *Seelenvermögen* in Simmel's philosophy. Here one can also can find Simmel's philosophical understanding of the "Totalität des Seins"; "Nun ist natürlich die Ganzheit des Daseins im wirklichen Sinne niemandem zugängig und kann auf niemanden wirken. Sie muß erst aus den allein gegebenen Fragmenten der Wirklichkeit zustande gebracht werden—wenn man will: als 'Idee' oder nur als Sehnsucht" (p. 12). As in his *Philosophie des Geldes*, totality is a fragmentary symbol whose existence depends on a value-feeling. For a discussion of Simmel's philosophy in the context of *Lebensphilosophie*, see Martin Jay, "The Discourse of Totality Before Western Marxism," in *Marxism and Totality: The Adventures of a Concept From Lukács to Habermas* (Berkeley: University of California Press,

1984), pp. 21–81. See especially Simmel's reflection on "Geistigkeit" and "Totalität" in *Die Probleme der Geschichtsphilosophie*. The relevant section is entitled "Geistige Principien in der Geschichte."

57. Simmel, *Moralwissenschaft* II: 118.

58. Simmel, *Moralwissenschaft* II: 114.

59. Simmel, *Moralwissenschaft* I: 119, 148.

60. "[Male] trade unions were frequently hostile to female labor and believed that women's work undercut men's wages." Richard J. Evans, *The Feminists*, p. 145.

61. Simmel, *Moralwissenschaft* II: 289.

62. Hayden White, *Metahistory*. Two studies argue that form was the central category of Simmel's sociology and philosophy. Maria Steinhoff, "Die Form als soziologische Grundkategorie Georg Simmel," *Kölner Vierteljahrshefte für Soziologie* vol. 4 (1925): 215–59; Rudolph Weingartner, "Form and Content in Simmel's Philosophy of Life," in *Georg Simmel, 1858–1918: A Collection of Essays*, ed. Kurt H. Woolf (1959), pp.: 33–60.

63. Lukács, "Bemerkungen zur Theorie der Literaturgeschichte," *Text und Kritik* 39/40 (1973): 24–51; quotation from p. 31.

64. Georg Lukács, *Entwicklungsgeschichte des modernen Dramas* [1911], vol. 15, *Georg Lukács Werke*, ed. F. Benseler (Darmstadt: Luchterhand, 1981), pp. 10, 11, 12.

65. See "Lebensform und Lebensinhalt" in Heinrich Rickert, *Die Philosophie des Lebens*. Despite his opposition to *Lebensphilosophie*, Rickert's text is historiographically significant. It places Simmel's language of life, form, and content within the broader discursive context of *Geisteswissenschaften*.

66. Georg Simmel, *Rembrandt: Ein Kunstphilosophischer Versuch* (Leipzig: Kurt Wolff, 1919), pp. 65–76.

67. Simmel, *Schopenhauer und Nietzsche*, p. 296.

68. "Das Problem des klassischen Porträts ist die Form. Das heißt, nachdem das Leben es einmal zu einem bestimmten Phänomen gebracht hat, gewinnt dieses für den Künstler eine ideelle Eigenexistenz, die er nach Normen der linearen, koloristischen, räumlichen Deutlichkeit, Schönheit und Charakteristik vorträgt. Er abstrahiert das Phänomen aus dem Lebensprozeß, der es erzeugt, und damit werden nur die seiner Gestaltung immanenten Gesetzlichkeit für sie gültig—ungefähr wie die abstrakten Begriffe logische Beziehungen untereinander aufweisen, die ganz von denjenigen unterschieden sind, durch die die ihnen zugrundeliegenden Einzeldinge verknüpft sind." This is a good indication of Simmel's distinction between an immanent and/or logical *Gesetzlichkeit* and a "*neue Gesetzlichkeit*." In Classical art, fate produces the law of form. "Bei Rembrandt umgekehrt ist die Form nur der jeweilige Moment des Lebens, in diesem liegt der nie zurücktretende Einheitspunkt ihrer Stimmungen, sie ist nur die—recht verstanden—zufällige Art, in der sein Wesen, d. h. sein Werden, sich nach außen kehrt. . . . Durch ihr verschiedenes Verhältnis zur Zeit und Kraft sind Form and Leben absolut getrennt." Classical art and the portraits of Rembrandt are different constitutions of the "Dynamik von Werden und Schicksal." Simmel, *Rembrandt*, pp. 68–69.

69. Simmel, *Rembrandt*, p. 65; my emphasis.

70. Compare his critique of Classical aesthetic form to his critique of religious forms. "Religious interiority . . . proves to be thoroughly dependent on the socio-

logical possibilities that it finds before itself"; Georg Simmel, *Die Religion* (Frankfurt a.M.: Rüttten & Loening, 1912), p. 75.

71. Simmel, *Rembrandt*, p. 69.

72. Simmel, *Moralwissenschaft* I: 165.

73. Simmel, *Rembrandt*, p. 70.

74. Lukács, "Georg Simmel," p. 175.

75. Lukács, *Entwicklungsgeschichte des modernen Dramas,* vol. 15, *Georg Lukács Werke*, ed. Frank Benseler (Darmstadt: Luchterhand, 1981), pp. 54, 74, 76.

76. Lukács, *Entwicklungsgeschichte des modernen Dramas*, p. 70.

77. Georg Simmel to Georg Lukács, 22 July 1909, in Georg Lukács, *Briefwechsel*, pp. 77–78.

78. Lukács, *Briefwechsel*, p. 77.

79. See Eva Karádi, "Georg Simmel und der Sonntagskreis," *Simmel Newsletter* vol. 5, no. 1 (summer 1995): pp. 45–53.

80. Lukács, *Gelebtes Denken*, p. 58.

81. Ibid., p. 58.

82. Georg Lukács, *Heidelberger Philosophie der Kunst,* vol. 16, *Georg Lukács Werke*, ed. György Márkus and Frank Benseler (Darmstadt: Luchterhand, 1974), p. 9.

83. The degree of Simmel's generational influence and personal influence on Lukács is tremendously underappreciated in the cultural histories of the Wilhelmine period. Heretofore, there has been no systematic interpolation of Lukács's intellectual trajectory that rests upon Simmel's philosophy as an historical a priori. The philosophical homology of Simmel's philosophy of the soul and Lukács's Wilhelmine texts has not been undertaken. Werner Jung's text, *Wandlungen einer ästhetischen Theorie—Georg Lukács Werke 1907 bis 1923* (Köln: Pahl-Rugenstein Verlag, 1981), includes a section on Simmel's *Philosophie des Geldes* as analogous to Lukács's "Romantischen Antikapitalismus," but there is no systematic interpolation of their philosophies; Michael Holzman's *Lukács's Road to God: The Early Criticism Against its Pre-Marxist Background* also includes a section on Simmel. Here there is no understanding of Simmel's intellectual primacy to Lukács and others, like Mannheim, of the Hungarian *Sonntagskreis;* István Hermann's *Georg Lukács: Sein Leben und Wirken* (Wien: Hermann Böhlaus, 1986), Ernst Keller's *Der junge Lukács: Antibürger und wesentliches Leben* (Frankfurt a.M.: Sender, 1984), Jörg Kammler's *Politische Theorie von Georg Lukács: Strucktur und historischer Praxisbezug bis 1929* (Darmstadt: Luchterhand, 1974), Lee Cogdon's *The Young Lukács*, Georg Lichtheim's *Georg Lukács* (New York: Viking Press, 1970), Arpad Kadarkay's *Georg Lukács: Life, Thought, and Politics*, and Andrew Arato and Paul Breines's *The Young Lukács and the Origins of Western Marxism* (New York: Continuum, 1979) all mention Simmel's influence. None of them, however, undertake an integrated analysis of Lukács's early thought from the perspective of Simmel's philosophy of the soul. Moreover, none of them reflect the generational consensus among young intellectuals that Simmel was the most important cultural figure, philosopher, and sociologist of the late Wilhelmine period. The gravity of Lukács's own pronouncements about Simmel, as the greatest and most important thinker in all of modern philosophy, are essentially underdeveloped.

84. The writing of *Entwicklungsgeschichte des modernen Dramas* (the "*Dramabuch*," as he called it) was begun in 1906 and completed by January 1907. Lukács, *Gelebtes Denken*, p. 248.

85. Lukács, "Georg Simmel," p. 175.

86. Georg Lukács, "Mein Weg zu Marx" in *Georg Lukács zum Siebzigsten Geburtstag* (Berlin: Aufbau-Verlag, 1955), p. 226.

87. Paul Honigsheim, *On Max Weber*, trans. Joan Rytina (New York: The Free Press, 1968), p. 24. With the clarity of a Proustian memory, Honigsheim also recollected: "[However, Lukács] was wrong when he went on to say that "Max Weber was the man to get socialism out of . . . [its] miserable relativism.' "

Honigsheim recounts that Julius Ebbinghaus, Hans Ehrenberg and Franz Rozenzweig were Hegelians who participated in monthly seminars on cultural science in Baden-Baden. The seminars were established by younger scholars at Heidelberg and attended by others from Freiburg and Strassbourg. The Hegelian participants in the seminars became known satirically as the "Hegel Club" (pp. 25, 27). In his 1918 obituary of Simmel, Lukács likewise admired Simmel's philosophy for its critique of relativism.

This Hegelian milieu was legitimized by Wilhelm Windelband, a Heidelberg philosophy professor, who was publishing neo-Hegelian essays during this period. Weber and Honigsheim shared a sardonic disposition toward Windelband and the Baden-Baden Hegelians. Their derision of Windelband was, at least in part, political. The socialist Honigsheim, it appears, did not like the conservative Windelband. Weber's politics are contrasted to the far more conservative inclinations of Windelband. Simmel is offered by Honigsheim as a counterpoint to Windelband's relative conservatism.

> And in the matter of trying to get an appointment for Simmel, for which Weber fought and struggled so hard, Windelband did nothing at all. When Weber considered the possibility of allowing a woman, the social welfare politician, Maria Bernays, to be formally qualified, this was just too much for Windelband, and Weber groaned in despair, "To talk to Windelband about either politics or the position of women—it's simply impossible (pp. 16–17).

The role of Windelband's conservatism in Simmel's disrecommendation for a professorship of philosophy at Heidelberg University is unclear. (A second position in philosophy had been open since 1903.) He may have been more conservative than Weber, but there is evidence of his support of Simmel's candidacy. See Windelband's letter to the Bavarian minister of education affirming Simmel's candidacy in Michael Landmann, "Bausteine zur Biographie," in *Buch des Dankes an Georg Simmel*, p. 28. The letter, dated June 11, 1908, praised Simmel's recently published *Soziologie*. In Honigheim's account, Windelband and Weber are presented as cordial, if politically contentious, colleagues.

For an example of Windelband's neo-Hegelianism, see: "Die Erneuerung des Hegelianismus," *Sitzungsberichte der Heidelberger Akademie der Wissenschaften* 9 (1910): 1–15; "Über Gleichheit und Identität," *Sitzungsberichte der Heidelberger Akademie der Wissenschaften* 14 (1910): 1–24; "Über Sinn und

Wert des Phänomenalismus," *Sitzungsberichte der Heidelberger Akademie der Wissenschaften* 9 (1912): 1–26. Also see Paul Honigsheim, "Der Max-Weber-Kreis in Heidelberg," *Kölner Vierteljahrschrift für Soziologie* (1926).

88. Gertrud Simmel to Marianne Weber, *Lebenserinnerungen*, pp. 383–84.

89. Marianne Weber, *Lebenserinnerung*, p. 382.

90. Lukács, "Georg Simmel," p. 173.

91. Letter to Marianne Weber, ca. 1912, in Weber, *Lebenserinnerungen*, p. 382.

92. Lukács, "Georg Simmel," p. 174.

93. Arato and Brienes, *The Young Lukács*, p. 115. Michael Löwy, *Georg Lukács—From Romanticism to Bolshevism*, p. 44.

94. Simmel, *Probleme der Geschichtsphilosophie* (1922), p. 55.

95. von Lukács, *Die Seele und die Formen: Essays* (Berlin: Egon Fleischel, 1911), pp. 17–18, my emphasis.

96. Susman, *Das Nah-und Fernsein des Fremden*, p. 18.

97. Bloch, *Briefe* I: 149.

98. Lukács, "Mein Weg zu Marx," pp. 226–27. He referred to Simmel's *Philosophie des Geldes* and *Soziologie*.

99. Hiller, "Wir," in *Geist werde Herr* (Berlin: Erich Reiss, 1920), pp. 34–35.

100. Mannheim, *Der Krieg*, p. 79.

101. Lukács, *Gelebtes Denken*, p. 77.

102. Karl Mannheim, review of Georg Simmel, *Der Krieg und die geistigen Entscheidungen: Reden und Aufsätze*, in *Huszadik Század* XVIII.XXXVI (1917): 416–18. Trans. from Hungarian by Izabella Fintzsch, rpt. *Simmel Newsletter* 5, no. 1 (summer 1995): 77–80; quotation from p. 78.

103. "Simmels Briefe an Max und Marianne Weber," in *Buch des Dankes,* p. 133.

104. Lukács, *Gelebtes Denken*, p. 239.

105. In Michael Landmann, "Ernst Bloch über Simmel," in *Ästhetic und Soziologie*, p. 271.

106. Lukács, "Die deutschen Intellektuellen und der Krieg," *Text und Kritik* 39, 40 (1973): 65–66.

107. Lukács, *Heidelberger Ästhetik*. On the Simmelian character of this work, see Arato and Briennes, *The Young Lukács and the Origins of Western Marxism*, pp. 57–58; Werner Young, *Wandlungen einer Ästhetischen Theorie–Georg Lukács Werke 1907 bis 1923* (Cologne: Pahl-Rugenstein, 1981), p. 44. Compare "Heidelberg" in Ernst Keller, *Der junge Lukács–Antibürger und wesentliches Leben* (Frankfurt/Main: Sendler, 1984), pp. 155–67; "The Heidelberger Ästhetics" in Congdon, *The Young Lukács*, pp. 111–17.

108. For an account of this period, see Peter Zudeick, *Der Hintern des Teufels*. On Simmel's place in Bloch's intellectual maturation, see Jozef Kosian, *Zukünftigkeit als wesentliche Seinsbeschaffenheit: Ernst Blochs Futurozentrismus* (Wroclaw: Wydawnictwo Uniwersytetu, 1992), pp. 16–18.

109. Bloch, Über einige politische Programme und Utopien in der Schweiz," *Archiv für Sozialwissenschaft und Sozialpolitik* 45, no. 1 (1918): 140–62.

110. Ernst Bloch, *Geist der Utopie* (1918), p. 410; "Über den sittlichen und geistigen Führer oder die doppelte Weise des Menschengesichts" (1920) in

Philosophische Aufsätze zur objektiven Phantasie (Frankfurt a.M.: Suhrkamp, 1969), pp. 204–10.

111. Quoted in Sandor Radnoti, "Bloch and Lukács: Two Radical Critics In a 'God-Forsaken World,'" *Telos* 25 (1975): 155–64. There is no reference to Simmel's mentorship of Bloch and Lukács or to the Simmelean character of Expressionist radicalism.

112. Kurt Hiller, "Christ und Aktivist" (1918) in *Verwirklichung des Geistes im Staat* (Leipzig: Ernst Oldenburg, 1925), pp. 120–35. Hiller's essay begins poignantly: "Der Geist des ursprünglichen Christentums war nicht gegen-, doch außerstaatlich. Eben darum mußte das Problem: wie kommt Geist zu Macht? unter den christlichen Führern als bald akut werden." Ernst Bloch, "Die Güte der Seele und die Dämonie des Lichts" (1917), in *Philosophische Aufsätze*, pp. 119–23. Bloch's text similarly puts forth a Nietzschean interpretation of Christ that contrasts status quo Christianity and its "Sklaven" to "Urchristen . . . ohne allen Sirup des Naturchristentums." These were two classic cases of theological *Geistigkeit* mobilized against the spiritual hegemony of denominational *Geistlichkeit*.

113. Lukács, *Heidelberger Philosophie der Kunst*, p. 45; "Von der Armut am Geiste," *Neue Blätter* 2, nos. 5, 6 (1912): 87, 74.

114. Lukács, "Von der Armut am Geiste," pp. 88–92.

115. Simmel, *Religion*, p. 73. "Das praktische Glaube ist ein Grundverhalten der Seele, das seinem Wesen nach soziologisch ist, d. h. als ein Verhältnis zu einem dem Ich gegenüberstehenden Wesen aktualisiert wird" (p. 47).

116. Ernst Bloch, "Die Güte der Seele und die Dämonie des Lichts" [1917], in *Philosophische Aufsätze*, p. 220; Georg Lukács, *Die Zerstörung der Vernunft*, p. 351.

117. Simmel, *Schopenhauer und Nietzsche*, p. 300.

118. Nietzsche, *Twilight of the Idols* (New York: Penguin Books, 1990), p. 49.

119. Simmel, "Briefe an Paul Ernst," in *Buch des Dankes*, p. 69.

120. See Gertrud Kantorowicz, "Vorwort," in Simmel's *Fragmente und Aufsätze*, pp. v–x; Jürgen Habermas, "Simmel als Zeitdiagnostiker," in Simmel, *Philosophische Kultur* [1923] (Berlin: Wagenbach, 1986), pp. 7–17; Arato and Breines, *The Young Lukács*, pp. 16–17; Michael Löwy, *Georg Lukács*, p. 45; Regina Mahlmann, "Dualität des Individuums," in *Homo Duplex: Die Zweiheit des Menschen bei Georg Simmel*, pp. 39–44; Rudolph Weingartner, "Theory and Tragedy of Culture," in Chapter One of his *Experience and Culture*, pp. 71–85; and David Frisby, "Introduction to the Translation," in *The Philosophy of Money*, pp. 1–49.

121. von Lukács, "Metaphysik der Tragödie," in *Die Seele und die Formen*, p. 340.

122. Ibid., p. 339.

123. Simmel, "Der Begriff und die Tragödie der Kultur," in *Philosophische Kultur*, pp. 204 & 219.

124. Ibid., p. 205.

125. Ibid., pp. 204–205; see also *Fragmente und Aufsätze* where he refers to the "Produkt des Geistes" as a "lebendigen schöpferischen Realität gegenüber etwas Starres" (p. 264).

126. Simmel, "Das Problem des Schicksals," in *Brücke und Tür*, p. 15.

127. Simmel, "Briefe an Heinrich Rickert," in *Buch des Dankes*, p. 113.

128. Simmel, "Briefe an Paul Ernst" in *Buch des Dankes*, pp. 69, 81; "Das Problem des Schicksals," in *Brücke und Tür*, p. 15; see "Anmerkung über den Begriff Schicksals," in *Lebensanschauung*, pp. 122–29.

129. Simmel, "Briefe an Edmund Husserl," *Buch des Dankes*, p. 89.

130. Simmel, "Briefe an Heinrich Rickert," *Buch des Dankes*, p. 113.

131. Bloch, *Geist der Utopie*, p. 347.

132. Lukács, "Mein Weg zu Marx," p. 227.

133. Ibid., p. 227.

134. Georg Lukács to Paul Ernst, 4 May 1915, in Lukács, *Briefwechsel*, p. 352.

135. Lukács, *Die Zerstörung der Vernunft*; see especially "Die Lebensphilosophie in der Vorkriegszeit: Simmel," pp. 350–64.

136. Honigsheim, *On Max Weber*, p. 25.

137. Ernst Bloch, *Tendenz-Latenz-Utopie*, p. 313.

138. Lukács, *The Ontology of Social Being: Hegel,* trans. D. Feinbach (London: Merlin Press, 1978).

139. Hiller, "Überlegungen zur Eschatologie und Methodologie des Aktivismus," *Das Ziel* 3 (1919): 195–218; "Logokratie oder ein Weltbund des Geistes," *Geistige Politik: Fünftes der Ziel-Jahrbücher* (1924): 217–49.

140. Bloch, *Geist der Utopie*, pp. 337, 341, 363.

141. Ibid., p. 341.

142. Soren Kierkegaard, *The Concept of Dread* (Princeton: Princeton Univ. Press, 1970), p. 21.

143. Bloch, *Geist der Utopie*, pp. 294, 332.

144. Ibid., pp. 246–47.

145. Ibid., p. 340.

146. Ibid., p. 340.

147. Ernst Bloch, "Die Leere," in *Durch die Wüste, Kritische Essays* (Berlin: Paul Cassirer, 1923), p. 11.

148. Bloch, "Über den sittlichen und geistigen Führer oder die doppelte Weise des Menschengesichts" [1920] in *Philosophische Aufsätze*. See also "Die Tätigen" [1919] in the same text, p. 190.

149. Bloch, "Über den sittlichen und geistigen Führer," p. 210.

150. Bloch, *Geist der Utopie*, p. 410.

151. Löwy, *Georg Lukács—From Romanticism to Bolshevism*, p. 54.

152. See in particular Lukács's "Kritische Auseinandersetzung mit der Ethik Kants," in *Der junge Hegel und die Probleme der kapitalistischen Gesellschaft* (Berlin: Aufbau Verlag, 1986), pp. 182–207.

153. In *The Differénd: Phrases in Dispute*, trans. Georges Van Den Abbeele (Minneapolis: University of Minnesota Press, 1988), Jean-François Lyotard writes that "There is no genre whose hegemony over others would be just," (p. 158). The hegemony of the economic genre is central to both capitalism and communism. The capitalist and communist narrative occlude the critical dispute between forms of interpretation by claiming to be a history of everything. Lyotard follows Simmel in developing a neo-Kantianism intent on maintaining the critical diversity of forms by rejecting the Marxist and Hegelian demand for a form of all forms; and like Simmel, he is an antiliberal intent on evaluating the discursive force of forms as sociological phenomena. His antiliberalism, moreover, extends to a critical affirmation of

Marxism as a "feeling of the differénd." See especially, "Kant 3," in the chapter, "Genre and Norm," pp. 130–45.

154. Lukács, "Taktik und Ethik," in *Frühschriften II* (Berlin: Luchterhand, 1968), pp. 43–79.

155. Bloch, *Geist der Utopie*, p. 276.

156. Ibid., p. 240.

157. Ibid., p. 276.

158. Ibid., pp. 285–86.

159. Ibid., p. 297.

160. Ibid., p. 248. "Bei Hegel fehlen so die Tat, der Kampf, die den handelnden Menschen aufrufende Sorge und Verzweiflung auch im Ganzen der Geschichte und Kultur," p. 284.

161. Ibid., p. 407.

162. Ibid., p. 433.

163. Bloch, "Weisen des 'Vielleicht' bei Simmel (Zum 100. Geburtstag, 1958)," *Philosophische Aufsätze*, p. 57.

164. Simmel, *Philosophie des Geldes*, p. 722.

165. Simmel, "Über die Liebe," p. 122.

166. Simmel, "Bruchstücke und Aphorismen," *Fragmente und Aufsätze*, p. 115.

167. Simmel, Über die Liebe," p. 49.

168. Bloch, "Weisen des 'Vielleicht' bei Simmel (Zum 100. Geburtstag, 1958)," *Philosophische Aufsätze*, p. 59.

169. Bloch, *Geist der Utopie*, p. 299.

170. Bloch, "Die Güte der Seele," p. 220.

171. Salomo Friedländer, "Der Antichrist und Ernst Bloch," *Das Ziel: Jahrbücher für geistige Politik* 4 (1919): 103–16. See Anson Rabinbach, *In the Shadow of Catastrophe: German Intellectuals Between Apocalypse and Enlightenment* (Berkeley: University of California Press, 1997), pp. 56–57.

172. Simmel, "Zur Metaphysik des Todes," in *Brücke und Tür*, pp. 29–37. The essay was greatly expanded as "Tod und Unsterblichkeit" in *Lebensanschauung,* pp. 99–154. This element of Simmel's existential philosophy has been seen as a precursor to Heidegger's integration of death into a philosophy of life. For an interpretation of Simmel's philosophy of death, see Petra Christian, "Die Todesverflochtenheit des Lebens," in *Einheit und Zweispalt*, pp. 94–106.

173. Ernst Bloch, "Selbst und Grablampe oder Hoffnungsbilder gegen die Macht der Stärksten Nicht-Utopie: den Tod," chapter 52 of *Das Prinzip Hoffnung* (Frankfurt a.M.: Suhrkamp, 1959).

174. Bloch, *Geist der Utopie*, pp. 426, 429.

175. Simmel, "Zur Metaphysik des Todes," p. 30.

176. Bloch, *Geist der Utopie*, p. 425.

177. Ernst Bloch, in Michael Landmann, "Talking with Ernst Bloch: Korcula, 1968," *Telos* 25 (1975): 168.

178. Lukács, *Zerstörung der Vernunft*, pp. 350–64.

179. Bloch, *Erbschaft dieser Zeit* (Frankfurt/Main: Suhrkamp, 1985), pp. 16–17.

180. Simmel, *Moralwissenschaft* II: 399.

181. Johannes Heinz Horn, "Ernst Bloch's Hoffnungsphilosphie—eine anti-

marxistische Welterlösungslehre," in *Ernst Blochs Revision des Marxismus,* ed. Johannes Heinz Horn (Berlin-Ost: Aufbau, 1957). This was the beginning of Bloch's official marginalization within the GDR. See Zudeick, *Der Hintern,* chapter 8.

182. Albert Camus, *The Rebel: An Essay on Man in Revolt* (New York: Vintage, 1956), p. 103.

183. Bloch, "Lebenslauf, Selbstdarstellung," in *Ernst Bloch*, special edition of *Text und Kritik* (Munich: Text + Kritik, 1985), pp. 286–87.

CONCLUSION

SIMMEL'S AFTERLIFE

A Legacy Like Cash

IN 1914, AT THE AGE OF FIFTY-SIX, GEORG SIMMEL FINALLY SECURED A PROFESSORial position at the University of Strassbourg, a provincial city in comparison to Berlin. The timing and location of this appointment was ironic and symbolic. Ironically, his long-awaited academic denouement as a full professor coincided chronologically with the demise of his avant-garde cultural significance. His geographical distance from the heart of German culture, Berlin, was symbolic of his increasingly peripheral status within the Wilhelmine avant-garde after 1914. Simmel's marginalization within German intellectual history was symbolized, moreover, by his final resting place, Strassbourg, which after the Great War was no longer part of the German nation. Perhaps sensing his impending death from liver cancer in 1918, Simmel prophesied his posthumous intellectual legacy in his war diary.

> I know that I will die without intellectual [*geistigen*] heirs (and that is as it should be). My legacy will be like cash which is distributed to many heirs, each transforming his portion into a profit that conforms to his nature: this profit will no longer reveal its derivation from my legacy.[1]

This monetary simile was as prophetic historiographically as it was culturally. His intellectual descent into relative obscurity is evidenced by canonical text of the period, H. Stuart Hughes's *Consciousness and Society: The Reconstruction of European Social Thought, 1890–1930*, which contains no analysis of Simmel's legacy.[2] This omission is particularly noteworthy given Hughes's focus on sociological theory. Simmel's cultural decline meant that, until very recently, we have not fully appreciated his contribution to European intellectual history in general and the German political avant-garde in particular. This study set out to reverse that decline, establish Simmel as the most important intellectual of the Wilhelmine era, and show that his cultural capital has indeed been distributed to a spectrum of nonconformist movements: radical feminism, homosexual rights, literary Expressionism, Activism, and Western Marxism. It is one of the great reversals of German intellectual history that Simmel's countercultural spirit became dominant within avant-garde circles at the same time that his political significance was being eclipsed.

The Great War traditionally has been characterized as a violent caesura that razed the existing cultural architecture of Europe. But a sustained analysis of this historiographical assumption in relation to Simmel had not been undertaken previously. For paradigmatic shifts in culture are rarely pure. They are a question of degrees of continuity and discontinuity, and often reconstruction takes place using foundations that lay in ruins. The Great War was the transition from Wilhelmine culture to Weimar culture. There is no better focus for an analysis of this transition than the legacy of Georg Simmel. During the war, his progeny transformed his philosophy in a decidedly political way. The central component of this revision was an activist critique of academic philosophy akin to that of Marx, but in fact inspired by Simmel's own avant-garde reputation as Germany's greatest "philosopher of the deed."[3] For his reform-minded bourgeois students, Simmel's activist philosophy provided a feeling of cultural rebellion—opposition to both bourgeois culture and historical materialism—while legitimizing their Nietzschean class inclinations toward an aesthetic elitism.[4] His aristocratic radicalism was a model for the literary Expressionists and Activists. After 1914, however, Simmel's blinding reputation as Germany's intellectual supernova was largely blotted out by his support for German militarism. His interpretation of the war as a resolution of the central antinomies of philosophy irrevocably damaged his intellectual prestige.

One obituary reflected upon Simmel's generational significance: "A life has been ended, one which had exerted more influence on the intellectual development of the younger generation than the majority of his colleagues that hold the professorial chairs of philosophy in Germany."[5] That Simmel's generational influence was greatest upon the political avant-garde is not surprising. After all, he was a prominent member of Berlin's avant-garde elite. He personally participated in the Fontane circle and Naturalist subculture and had friendships with such leaders in the arts as Schlenther, Brahm, George, Rilke, and Rodin. This study has argued that Simmel's sociology was an expression of avant-garde culture. Like the Naturalists, Simmel sympathized with the plight of workers and women and feared the cultural annihilation of the individual. True to this cultural milieu, his sociology exerted its greatest influence upon the feminist and socialist avant-garde.

In particular, Hiller, Stöcker, Bloch, and Lukács came to share an activist critique of Simmel and the profession of German philosophy. In the broadest sense, this critique recapitulated the generational crisis of the young Hegelians and, in particular, Marx's activist and socialist critique of German philosophy. This comparison, while instructive, is a historical similarity and not an identity. For Hegel differed from Simmel in at least one fundamental way: Hegel maintained that spirit was not only the subject of history, but also substantially real in the Prussian state. Conversely, due to the influence of Nietzsche and Kant, Simmel's philosophy was premised on the distinction of *homo noumena* and *homo phenomena*, namely, subjective spirit and objective institutions. While he sought to overcome the cultural divide between the individual of character and consumer culture, until the war he had never maintained that this overcoming possessed an existing sociological basis. His Nietzschean-socialist critique of monetary culture was an unrealized "theory of life" and a "great synthesis we still await."[6] As with Nietzsche, Simmel treated the sociological realm polemically; its negation and critique was necessary for the creation of a sublime social-self. Consequently, Simmel's sociology landed more countercultural blows than Hegel's thought. Only in August 1914 did Simmel announce the *Aufhebung* of theory and reality, and even then only as the caesura of mammonist culture.

The culture of war was a generational crucible wherein Simmel's legacy manifested its political ambiguity. The divergent typology of (1) a sociological legacy, and (2) a Nietzschean legacy is one means of tracking this ambiguity. This typology can help explain how Hiller and Lukács came to very different conceptions of socialism in the culture of war. My thesis is that Lukács attempted to realize Simmel's sociological spirit and Hiller to politicize Simmel's Nietzschean spirit. This typology, however, must be deconstructed if it is to prove fruitful for analyzing Simmel's legacy. The essence of Hiller's Activist philosophy was an attempt to provide a sociological basis for Nietzschean philosophy. In *Spirit Becomes Lord*, a collection of his war essays, Hiller described his politics as a "Platonic-Nietzscheanism," and this hyphenation precisely captured his vision of a postwar German Platonic Republic dominated not by the aristocracy of blood, but by socialist Zarathustras like himself—or what he referred to as the aristocracy of *Geist*. For his part, the sociological Lukács gravitated to Hegel and came to the conclusion that the individual could not be the center of ethics.[7] He thereby simultaneously preserved Simmel's sociological critique of liberal individualism and discarded his placement of the individual at the center of ethics and metaphysics. The importance of *Existenz* philosophy after the war—i.e., Lukács's concept of *Ontologie* and Heidegger's concept of *Dasein*—constituted the eclipse of Simmel's avant-garde individualism. As a result of the war, Lukács jettisoned the Nietzschean emphasis on the ethical individual in favor of an institutional and sociological conception of socialist ethics. Ultimately, the distinction between the sociological (Lukács) and Nietzschean (Hiller) reception of Simmel can help to understand the theoretical and political extremes of Simmel's legacy. While Hiller and Stöcker followed Simmel in putting forth a Nietzschean politics of cultural resistance (what Simmel referred to as a personal ethics), Lukács carried on Simmel's sociological and ethical critique of bourgeois negative freedom. These constituted very different interpretations of the antibourgeois individual. Hiller and Stöcker's ethics maintained the centrality of the individual. They drew upon Simmel's philosophy to defend sexual otherness—homosexuality and unwed mothers.

The Russian, German, and Hungarian Revolutions discredited antibourgeois philosophies that were incapable of linking themselves to the politics of working-class organizations. This cultural reality explains the differing fates of Hiller, Simmel, and Lukács in German intellectual history. Lukács contended that Simmel philosophized "in the name of an aristocratic ethics à la Nietzsche, that views the rabble as an ethical consideration of no value."[8] Hiller's reception of Simmel is a clear manifestation of this assertion; Hiller's distance from working-class socialism destined his cultural significance to decline. But an affirmation of working-class politics was not in itself enough to preserve one's intellectual significance after the war. Bloch's relative marginalization, like Benjamin's, stemmed not from opposition to communism; they were both forcefully committed to that goal. Their intellectual marginalization during their lifetimes was a result of their cultural emphasis on religious tropes—negative eschatology as opposed to materialist teleology—and their unwillingness to discard antifoundationalism in the fight against capitalism.[9] Whereas the absence of a political linkage to working class politics doomed Simmel's anticapitalist philosophy of the soul to relative insignificance after the German Revolution, Bloch's maintenance of Simmelian practical idealism likewise ensured his marginalization within the Communist movement and later within the Communist bloc.

The Great war and its subsequent revolutionary atmosphere demanded an end to existing German philosophy and, thus, to the intellectual preeminence of Georg Simmel, and this state of affairs is the best explanation of Simmel's historiographical and cultural fate. For his students, war culture was not only the contextual demand for an end to academic philosophy; it was the origin of their transformation of Simmelian thought into activist political ideologies. Simmel's philosophical claim that the aesthetic individual stood above fate (*Schicksal*), and his public support of the war were substantially rejected by four of his leading students: Hiller, Stöcker, Lukács, and Bloch. Or, stated differently, the war was an empirical phenomenology whereby the cult of individual talent (symbolized by the discourse of genius, the cultural ethic of Stefan George and the philosophy of Simmel) was supplanted by the demand for new collective forms—ideological and institutional. The antiwar sensibility of a new countercultural generation of social critics renounced and refined the antibourgeois disposition of Simmel in favor of a transformative activity critical of capitalist, patriarchal, and heterosexist culture. What remained of Simmel's modernist philosophy was a soulful intensity bent on resisting bourgeois fate.

The dynamic narrative of Simmel's avant-garde legacy has a close parallel in Sartre's intellectual development. With both, an existential philosophy that conceives of freedom as the individual's opposition to sociological fate—i.e., prostration to sociological determinism as bad faith—gives way to an existential socialism that treats the sociological realm positively and immanently, if critically and dialectically. But just as Marx did not simply cast Hegel aside in the process of developing an activist critique of dialectical contemplation, in their antibourgeois philosophies of the future, Hiller, Stöcker, Lukács, and Bloch transcended and preserved the critical thought of their mentor.

NOTES

1. Simmel, "Aus dem Nachlassenen Tagebuche," in *Fragmente und Aufsätze*, p. 1.

2. H. Stuart Hughes, *Consciousness and Society*. The text contains merely two references to Simmel and this despite the fact that Simmel's thought clearly participates in most of the themes of the text: the revolt against positivism, the critique of Marxism, the recovery of the unconscious, neo-idealism, and the transcendence of positivism and idealism.

3. Theodor Lessing, *Philosophie als Tat* I: 303.

4. One of his earliest essays is entitled "Sociological Aesthetics." See Simmel, *Aufsätze und Abhandlungen*, pp. 197–214.

5. Paul Fletcher, "Georg Simmel," *Norddeutsche Allgemeine Zeitung,* 28 September 1918, in *Buch des Dankes,* p. 157.

6. Simmel , "Tendencies," p. 182.

7. Hiller, *Geist Werde Herr*, p. 11.

8. Lukács, *Die Zerstörung der Vernunft*, p. 362.

9. Walter Benjamin's intellectual trajectory, which falls outside of the scope of this work, has not been sufficiently analyzed in light of the tropic culture of war. His essays, "Trauerspiel und Tragödie," [1916] and "Die Bedeutung der Sprache in Trauerspiel und Tragödie," [1916], both in *Gesammelte Schriften*, signal the war's tropic impact on his subsequent work. Benjamin attended Simmel's seminars in Berlin and subsequently published in the first edition of Hiller's journal, *Das Ziel*, in 1915. His philosophy can not be understood without reference to the *Aktivisten*, among whom was counted his mentor, Gustav Wyneken. His language theory is the metaphysical foundation of what I call his "fallen communism." Indeed, it is no accident that Simmel's *The Philosophy of Money* was the theoretical basis of his most mature work, *Das Passagen-Werk*. His fallen communism, expressed here with concept of the "dialectic at a standstill," recalls Simmel's aporetic socialism, and was very similar to Bloch's "metempsychosis at a standstill in the apocalypse."

BIBLIOGRAPHY

Adler, Max. *Georg Simmels Beduetung für die Geistesgeschichte*. Leipzig: Anzengruber-Verlag, 1919.

Adorno, Theodor. *Negative Dialektik*. Frankfurt a.M.: Suhrkamp, 1975.

Allen, Ann Taylor. *Feminism and Motherhood in Germany, 1800–1914*. New Brunswick, N.J.: Rutgers University Press, 1991.

———. "German Radical Feminism and Eugenics, 1900–1908." *German Studies Review* 11 (1988): 31–56.

———. "Mothers of the New Generation: Adele Schreiber, Helene Stöcker and the Evolution of the German Idea of Motherhood, 1900–1915." *Signs* 10, no. 3 (1985): 418–38.

Allen, Roy F. *Literary Life in German Expressionism and the Berlin Circles*. Ann Arbor: UMI Research Press, 1983.

Arato, Andrew, and Paul Brienes. *The Young Lukács and the Origins of Western Marxism*. New York: Seabury Press, 1979.

Arnold, Heinz Ludwig, ed. *Ernst Bloch*. München: Text und Kritik, 1985.

Aschheim, Steven. *The Nietzsche Legacy in Germany 1890–1990*. Berkeley: University of California Press, 1992.

Aulinger, Barbara. *Die Gesellschaft als Kunstwerk: Fiktion und Methode bei Georg Simmel*. Vienna: Passagen Verlag, 1999.

Bab, Julius. *Die Chronik des deutschen Dramas, Erster Teil 1900–1906*. Berlin: Oesterheld, 1922.

Bahr, Ehrhard. *Ernst Bloch*. Berlin: Colloquium Verlag, 1974.

Beauvoir, Simone de. *The Ethics of Ambiguity*. Translated by B. Frechtman. New York: Citadel, 1976.

Benjamin, Walter. *Charles Baudelaire: A Lyric Poet in the Era of High Capitalism*. Translated by Harry Zohn. London: Verso, 1973.

———. *Gesammelte Schriften*. Frankfurt a.M.: Suhrkamp,1980.

———. "Das Leben der Studenten." *Das Ziel. Aufrufe zu tätigem Geist* 1 (1916): 141–55.

Bernhardi, Friedrich von. *Germany and the Next War*. New York: Longman's, Green & Co., 1914.

Bessel, Richard. "German Society during the First World War." In *Germany after the First World War*. Oxford: Claredon Press, 1993.

Bevers, A. M. *Dynamik der Formen bei Georg Simmel*. Berlin: Duncker & Humblot, 1985.

Biesenbach, Klaus Peter. *Subjektivität ohne Substanz: Georg Simmels Individualitätsbegriff als produktive Wendung einer theoretischen Ernüchterung*. Frankfurt a.M.: Lang, 1988.

Blackbourn, David and Geoff Eley. *The Peculiarities of German History*. New York: Oxford University Press, 1987.

Blass, Ernst. "The Old Café des Westens," in *The Era of German Expressionism*. Edited by Paul Raabe. Woodstock, New York: Overlook Press, 1974.

Bloch, Ernst. *Briefe, 1903–1975*. 2 vols. Frankfurt a.M.: Suhrkamp, 1985.

———. *Durch die Wüste: Frühe kritische Aufsätze*. Munich: Duncker & Humblot, 1923.

———. *Erbschaft dieser Zeit*. Frankfurt a.M.: Suhrkamp, 1962.

———. *Geist der Utopie* [1918]. Frankfurt a.M.: Suhrkamp, 1971.

———. *Gespräche mit Ernst Bloch*. Edited by Rainer Traub and Harald Wieser. Frankfurt a.M.: Suhrkamp, 1975.

———. "Die Tätigen [1919]," in *Philosophische Äufsatze zur objectiven Phantasie*. Frankfurt a.M.: Suhrkamp, 1985.

———. *Tendenz–Latenz–Utopie*. Frankfurt a.M.: Suhrkamp, 1978.

———. *Thomas Münzer als Theologe der Revolution* [1921]. Frankfurt a.M.: Suhrkamp, 1969.

———. "Über das Problem Nietzsches." *Das Freie Wort* 14 (1906): 566–70.

———. "Über den sittlichen und geistigen Führer oder die doppelte Weise des Menschengesichts [1920]," in *Philosophische Äufsatze zur objectiven Phantasie*. Frankfurt a.M.: Suhrkamp, 1985.

———. "Wie ist Sozialismus möglich?" *Die Weissen Blätter* (1918): 193–201.

———. "Der Weg Schelers," in *Die "Friedens-Warte*." 19, no. 9 (1917): 274–76.

———. "Weisen des 'Vielleicht' bei Simmel (Zum 100. Geburtstag, 1958)," in *Philosophische Äufsatze zur objectiven Phantasie*. Frankfurt a.M.: Suhrkamp, 1985.

———. "Zur Rettung von Georg Lukács." *Die Weissen Blätter* (1919): 529–30.

Blüher, Hans. "Die Untaten des bürgerlichen Typus." *Das Ziel. Aufrufe zu tätigem Geist* 1 (1916): 9–31.

———. "Der Bund der Geistigen." *Tätiger Geist! Zweites der Ziel-Jahrbücher* 1 (1918): 12–51.

Böhringer, Hanns, and Karlfried Gründer, eds. *Ästhetik & Soziologie um die Jahrhundertwende: Georg Simmel*. Frankfurt a.M.: Vittorio Klostermann, 1976.

Bourdieu, Pierre. " 'Vulgar' Critique of 'Pure' Critiques." In *Distinction: A Social Critique of the Judgement of Taste*. Translated by Richard Nice. Cambridge: Harvard University Press, 1984.

Brahm, Otto. "Ibsen in Berlin." In *Kritiken und Essays*. Stuttgart: Artemis Verlag, 1964.

Brakeman, Gunter. *Protestantische Kriegstheologie im Ersten Weltkrieg*. Bielefeld: Luther-Verlag, 1974.

Buchon, Max. "An Introduction to the *Stonebreakers* and the *Funeral at Ornans*." Translated by Petra Chu. In *Courbet in Perspective*. Englewood Cliffs, N.J.: Prentice-Hall, 1977.

Bürger, Peter. *Theory of the Avant-Garde*. Translated by M. Shaw. Minneapolis: University of Minnesota Press, 1984.

Canning, Kathleen. "Feminist History after the Linguistic Turn: Historicizing Discourse and Experience." *Signs* 12, no. 2 (1994): 368–404.

Cassirer, Ernst. *The Philosophy of Symbolic Forms: Language*. New Haven: Yale University Press, 1955.

Chartier, Roger. *The Cultural Origins of the French Revolution*. Durham: Duke University Press, 1991.

Chickering, Roger. "Imperial Germany at War, 1914–1918." In *Imperial Germany: A Historical Companion*. London: Greenwood Press, 1996, pp. 489–512.

Chu, Petra, ed. and trans. *The Letters of Gustave Courbet*. Chicago: University of Chicago Press, 1992.

Clark, T. J. *Image of the People: Gustave Courbet and the Second French Republic 1848–1851*. Greenwich, Conn.: New York Graphic Society, 1973.

Congdon, Lee. *The Young Lukacs*. Chapel Hill: University of North Carolina Press, 1983.

Coser, Lewis, ed. *Georg Simmel*. Englewood Cliffs, N.J.: Prentice-Hall, 1965.

———. "Georg Simmel's Contribution to the Sociology of Women." *Signs* 2, no. 4 (1977): 869–76.

Cotkin, George. *William James Public Philosopher*. Baltimore: Johns Hopkins University Press, 1990.

Dahme, Heinz-Jürgen. "Frauen- und Geschlechterfrage bei Herbert Spencer und Georg Simmel." *Kölner Zeitschrift für Soziologie und Sozialpsychologie* 38 (1986): 490–509.

———. "Georg Simmel und Gustav Schmoller: Berührung zwischen Kathedersozialismus und Soziologie um 1890." *Simmel Newsletter* 3, no. 1 (summer 1993): 39–52.

Dahme, Heinz-Jürgen, and Otthein Rammstedt. "Die zeitlose Modernität der soziologischen Klassiker. Überlegungen zur Theoriekonstruktion von Emile Durkheim, Ferdinand Tönnies, Max Weber und besonders Georg Simmel." In *Georg Simmel und die Moderne*. Frankfurt a.M.: Suhrkamp, 1984, pp. 449–78.

Dahme, Heinz-Jürgen, and Otthein Rammstedt, eds. *Georg Simmel und die Moderne*. Frankfurt a.M.: Suhrkamp, 1984.

Damas, Renate. *Ernst Bloch: Hoffnung als Prinzip, Prinzip ohne Hoffnung*. Meisenheim: Anton Hain, 1971.

Daniel, Ute. *The War from within: German Working-Class Women in the First World War.* Oxford: Berg, 1997.

Danner, Stefan. *Georg Simmels Beitrag zur Pädagogik*. Bad Heilbrunn: Klinkhardt, 1991.

Derrida, Jaques. *The Truth of Painting*. Translated by G. Bennington and I. McLeod. Chicago: University of Chicago Press, 1987.

———. *Specters of Marx*. Translated by Peggy Kamuf. New York: Routledge, 1994.

Detwiler, Bruce. *Nietzsche and the Politics of Aristocratic Radicalism*. Chicago: University of Chicago Press, 1990.

Dilthey, Wilhelm. *Die Einbildungskraft des Dichters: Bausteine für eine Poetik*. Vol. 6 of *Wilhelm Dilthey. Gesammelte Schriften*. Leipzig: B.G. Teubner, 1924.

———. *Einleitung in die Geisteswissenschaften: Versuch einer Grundlegung für das Studium der Geselleschaft und der Geschichte* [1883]. Leipzig: B.G. Teubner, 1923.

———. *Das Erlebnis und die Dichtung*. Leipzig: Reclam, 1991.

———. *Die geisteige Welt: Einleitung in die Philosophie des Lebens*. Leipzig: B.G. Teubner, 1924.

———. "Die Kultur der Gegenwart und die Philosophie." In *Philosophie des Lebens*.

———. *Die Philosophie des Lebens*. Stuttgart: B.G. Teubner, 1961.

———. "Praktische Philosophie," in *System der Ethik*. Stuttgart: B.G. Teubner, 1958.

———. *System der Ethik*. Stuttgart: B.G. Teubner, 1958.

———. *Weltanschauungslehre: Abhandlungen zur Philosophie der Philosophie*. Leipzig: B.G. Teubner, 1931.

Edschmid, Kasimir. *Lebendiger Expressionismus: Auseinandersetzung, Gestaltung, Erinnerung*. Wien: Kurt Desch, 1961.

Eisler, Michael Josef. *Der Elfenbeinturm*. Berlin: Otto von Holten, 1910.

Eksteins, Modris. *The Rights of Spring: The Great War and the Birth of the Modern Age*. Boston: Houghton Mifflin, 1989.

Eley, Geoff. *Reshaping the German Right. Radical Nationalism and Political Change after Bismarck*. New Haven: Yale University Press, 1980.

Emmel, Felix. "Eros als Träger des Ethos." *Das Ziel* 2 (1920): 67–70.

Enckendorff, Marie-Louise. *Realität und Gesetzlichkeit im Geschlechtsleben*. Leipig: Duncker & Humblot, 1910.

———. *Über Religiöse*. Leipzig: Duncker & Humblot, 1919.

———. *Von Sein und vom Haben der Seele*. Leipzig: Duncker & Humblot, 1906.

Ernst Blochs Wirkung: Ein Arbeitsbuch zum 90. Geburtstag. Frankfurt a.M.: Suhrkamp, 1975.

Evans, Richard. *The Feminist Movement in Germany, 1894–1933*. London: Sage, 1976.

Falk, Walter. *Der kollektive Traum von Krieg: Epochale Strukturen der deutschen Literatur zwischen Naturalismus und Expressionismus*. Heidelberg: Carl Winter, 1977.

Felski, Rita. *The Gender of Modernity*. Cambridge, Mass.: Harvard University Press, 1995.

Finney, Gail. "Ibsen and Feminism." In *The Cambridge Companion to Ibsen*. New York: Cambridge University Press, 1994, pp. 89–105.

Fletcher, Paul. "Georg Simmel," in *Buch des Dankes an Georg Simmel*. Edited by Kurt Gassen and Michael Landmann. Berlin: Duncker & Humblot, 1958.

Foucault, Michel. *The History of Sexuality*. Vol. 1. Translated by Robert Hurley. New York: Vintage, 1980.

Fout, John C. "Sexual Politics in Wilhelmine Germany: The Male Gender Crisis, Moral Purity, and Homophobia." *Journal of the History of Sexuality* 2, no. 3 (1992): 388–421.

Friedlaender, Salomo. "Dionysisches Christentum." *Die Weissen Blätter* 4 (1913): 317–327.

———. "Der Antichrist und Ernst Bloch." *Das Ziel* 2 (1920): 103–18.

———. *Friedrich Nietzsche: Eine intellektuale Biographie*. Leipzig: G.J. Göschen'sche, 1911.

———. "Individuum." *Tätiger Geist! Zweites der Ziel-Jahrbücher* (1918): 145–50.

———. *Psychologie (Der Lehre von der Seele)*. 1907.

———. *Schöpferische Indifferenz*. Munich: Georg Müller, 1918.

Frisby, David. "Afterword." In *The Philosophy of Money*. Translated by Tom Bottomore and David Frisby. London: Routledge, 1990.

———. *Fragments of Modernity: Theories of Modernity in the Work of Simmel, Kracauer, and Benjamin*. Cambridge, Mass.: MIT Press, 1988.

———. *Georg Simmel*. New York: Travistock, 1984.

———. "Preface to the Second Edition." In *The Philosophy of Money*. Translated by Tom Bottomore and David Frisby. London: Routledge, 1990.

———. *Sociological Impressionism: A Reassessment of Georg Simmel's Social Theory*. London: Routledge, 1992.

Furet, François. *Interpreting the French Revolution*. New York: Cambridge University Press, 1990.

Fussel, Paul. *The Great War and Modern Memory*. New York: Oxford University Press, 1975.

Gadamer, Hans-Georg. *Truth and Method*. New York: Continuum, 1982.

Gassen, Kurt, and Michael Landmann, eds. *Buch des Dankes an Georg Simmel: Briefe, Erinnerungen, Bibliographie*. Berlin: Duncker & Humblot, 1958.

Genovese, Eugene. *Roll, Jordan, Roll: The World the Slaves Made*. New York: Vintage, 1976.

Gluck, Mary. *Georg Lukács and His Generation 1900–1918*. Cambridge: Harvard University Press, 1985.

Greven-Aschoff, Barbara. *Die bürgerliche Frauenbewegung in Deutschland, 1894–1933*. Göttingen: Vandenhoeck & Ruprecht, 1981.

Grossman, Atina. *Reforming Sex: The German Movement for Birth Control and Abortion Reform, 1920–1950*. New York: Oxford University Press, 1995.

Günther, Katharina. *Literarische Gruppenbildung im Berliner Naturalismus*. Bonn: Bovier, 1972.

Habereder, Julianne. *Kurt Hiller und literarische Aktivismus*. Frankfurt a.M.: Lang, 1981.

Habermas, Jürgen. "Simmel als Zeitdiagnostiker." In Simmel, *Philosophische Kultur*, pp. 7–17.

Hackett, Amy. "Helene Stocker: Left-wing Intellectual and Sex Reformer," in *When Biology Became Destiny: Women in Weimar and Nazi Germany*. Edited by Renate Bridenthal, Atina Grossman, and Marion Kaplan. New York: Monthly Review Press, 1984.

Hammann, Richard, and Jost Hermand. *Gründerzeit. Deutsche Kunst und Kultur von der Gründerzeit bis zum Expressionismus.* Munich: Nymphenburger, 1972.

Hammer, Karl. *Deutsche Kriegstheologien 1870–1918*. Munich: Kosel-Verlag, 1971.

Hanna, Martha. "The *Kultur* War." In Hanna, *The Mobilization of the Intellect.* Cambridge: Harvard University Press, 1996.

Hauptmann, Gerhardt. *The Weavers*. In *Social Dramas*, vol. 1 of *The Dramatics Works of Gerhart Hauptmann.* New York: Huebsch, 1912.

Hegel, Georg Wilhelm Friedrich. *Phenomenology of the Spirit.* Oxford: Oxford University Press, 1977.

———. *The Philosophy of History*. New York: Dover, 1956.

———. *Philosophy of the Right*. Translated by T. M. Knox. New York: Oxford University Press, 1967.

Heinemann, Fritz. *Neue Wege der Philosophie: Geist / Leben / Existenz*. Leipzig: Quelle & Meyer, 1929.

Heller, Agnes. *A Theory of Feelings*. Translated by M. Fenyö. Assen: Van Gorcum, 1979.

Heller, Agnes, et al. *Die Seele und das Leben: Studien zum frühen Lukács.* Frankfurt a.M.: Suhrkamp, 1977.

Heller, Eric. *Thomas Mann: The Ironic German*. Cleveland: Meridian, 1961.

Hense, Paul. "Eine Philosophie des Geldes." *Der Lotse* 48 (1901): 722–29.

Herf, Jeffrey. *Reactionary Modernism*. London: Cambridge University Press, 1984.

Hermann, István. *Georg Lukács: Sein Leben und Wirken*. Wien: Hermann Böhlaus, 1986.

Herzog, Wilhelm. "An die geistige Internationale." *Das Forum* (October 1918): 1–5.

Heubner, Friedrich Markus. "Der Expressionismus in Deutschland." In *Expressionismus: Der Kampf um eine literarische Bewegung*. Edited by Paul Raabe. Zürich: Arche Verlag, 1987.

Heym, Georg. *Dichtungen und Schriften*. Edited by Karl Ludwig Schneider. Darmstadt: Wissenschaftliche Buchgesellschaft, 1960.

Hiller, Kurt. "Aus einem Brief." In *Georg Heym: Dokumente zu seinem Leben und Werk*. Edited by Karl Ludwig Schneider and Gerhard Burkhardt. Darmstadt: Wissenschaftliche Buch-Gesellschaft, 1968.

———. "Begegnungen mit Expressionisten." In *Expressionismus: Aufzeichungen und Erinnerungen der Zeitgenossen*. Edited by Paul Raabe. Olten: Walter-Verlag, 1965.

———. "Christ und Aktivist" (1918). In *Verwirklichung des Geistes im Staat.* Leipzig: Ernst Oldenburg, 1925, pp. 120–35.

———. "Ein Deutsches Herrenhaus." *Tätiger Geist! Zweites der Ziel-Jahrbücher* (1918): 379–425.

———. "Erinnerung an Simmel." In *Buch des Dankes*, pp. 257–67.

———. "Haager Friedenkongreß." *Die Neue Rundschau* 1 (1923): 157–68.

———. "Herkunft und Kindheit." In *Leben gegen die Zeit. Logos*, pp. 11–24.

———. "Homosexualismus und Deutscher Vorentwurf." In *Die Weisheit*, vol. 2, pp. 24–45.

———. "Logokratie oder Ein Weltbund des Geistes." *Das Ziel* 4 (1920): 217–47.

———. "Kameradin im Kampf: Helene Stöcker." In *Köpfe und Tröpfe: Profile aus einem Vierteljahrhundert*. Hamburg: Rowohlt, 1950.

———. "Kongreßbericht." *Das Ziel* 2 (1920): 207–16.
———. *Köpfe und Tröpfe: Profile aus einem Vierteljahrhundert*. Hamburg: Rowohlt, 1950.
———. *Leben gegen die Zeit. Eros*. Hamburg: Rowohlt, 1973.
———. *Leben gegen die Zeit. Logos*. Hamburg: Rowohlt, 1969.
———. "Litteraturpolitik." *Die Aktion* 2 (1911): 138–39.
———. "Logokratie oder ein Weltbund des Geistes." *Geistige Politik: Fünftes der Ziel-Jahrbücher* (1924): 217–48.
———. "Die neue Partei; oder, Politik der Synthese." *Geistige Politik! Fünftes der Ziel-Jahrbücher* (1924): 115–66.
———. "Öffener Brief an Dr. Georg Zepler." *Die Aktion* 1 (1911): 10–12.
———. "Philosophie des Ziels." *Das Ziel. Aufrufe zu tätigem Geist* (1916): 187–218.
———. *Das Recht über sich selbst: Eine Strafrechtsphilosophie*. Heidelberg: Carl Winter, 1908.
———. "Der Sinn eines Lebens (Magnus Hirschfeld)," in *Köpfe und Tröpfe: Profile aus einem Vierteljahrhundert*. Hamburg: Rowohlt, 1950.
———. "Über Kultur." *Der Sturm* 1 (1910): 187–88, 196–97, 203–204.
———. "Überlegungen zur Eschatologie und Methologie des Aktivismus." *Das Ziel* 3 (1919): 195–218.
———. *Die Weisheit der Langenweile. Eine Streit- und Zeitschrift*. 2 vols. Leipzig: Kurt Wolff, 1913.
———. "Wir." In *Geist werde Herr*. Berlin: Erich Reiss, 1920, pp. 34–35.
———. "Zentralstelle Völkerrecht." *Tätiger Geist! Zweites der Ziel-Jahrbücher* (1918): 145–50.
Hiller, Kurt, ed. *Der Kondor*. Heidelberg: Richard Weissbach, 1912.
———, ed. "Politischer Rat geistiger Arbeiter." *Das Ziel* 4 (1920): 218–23.
Hirschfeld, Magnus. *Zur Reform des Sexualstrafrechts*. Leipzig: Ernst Birscher, 1926.
Holzman, Michael. *Lukács's Road to God: The Early Criticism Against Its Pre-Marxist Backround*. Lanham, Maryland: University Press of America, 1985.
Honigsheim, Paul. "Der Max-Weber-Kreis in Heidelberg." *Kölner Vierteljahrschrift für Soziologie* (1926)
———. *On Max Weber*. Translated by Joan Rytina. New York: The Free Press, 1968.
Hoover, Arlie. *God, Germany, Britain in the Great War: A Study of Clerical Nationalism*. New York: Praeger, 1989.
Horn, Johannes Heinz. "Ernst Blochs Hoffnungsphilosophie—eine anti-marxistische Welterlösungslehre," in *Ernst Blochs Revision des Marxismus*. Edited by J. H. Horn. Berlin-Ost: Aufbau, 1957.
Hughes, H. Stuart. *Consciousness and Society: The Reconstruction of European Thought, 1890–1930*. New York: Vintage Books, 1958.
Hurwicz, Elias. "Simmel als jüdischer Denker." *Neue jüdische Monatshefte* 3 (1919): 196–98.
Ibsen, Henrik. *Sämtliche Werke*. Edited by P. Schlenther. Berlin: Fischer, 1921.
———. *Speeches and New Letters*. Translated by A. Kildal. Boston: Gorham Press, 1910.

Jay, Martin. *Adorno*. Berkeley: University of California Press, 1984.

———. *The Dialectical Imagination: A History of the Frankfurt School and the Institute for Social Research, 1923–1950.* Boston: Little, Brown and Co., 1973.

———. "The Discourse of Totality before Western Marxism." In Jay *Marxism and Totality: The Adventures of a Concept from Lukács to Habermas*. Berkeley: University of California Press, 1984.

Joël, Karl. "Kameradschaft (ein Brief)." *Das Ziel. Aufrufe zu tätigem Geist* 1 (1916): 156–66.

———. *Neitzsche und die Romantik*. Jena: Eugen Dietrichs, 1905.

———. *Seele und Welt*. Jena: Eugen Dietrichs, 1912.

———. "Eine Zeitphilosophie." *Neue deutsche Rundschau* 12 (1901): 812–26.

Jung, Werner. *Wandelungen einer ästhetischen Theorie—Georg Lukács Werke 1907 bis 1923*. Köln: Pahl-Rugenstein, 1981.

Kadarkay, Arpad. *Georg Lukács: Life, Thought, and Politics*. Cambridge, Mass.: Basil Blackwell, 1991.

Kammler, Jörg. *Politische Theorie von Georg Lukács: Struktur und historischer Praxisbezug bis 1929*. Darmstadt: Luchterhand, 1974.

Kandinsky, Wassily. *Concerning the Spiritual in Art.* Translated by M.T.H. Sadler. New York: Dover, 1977.

Kant, Immanuel. *Critique of Pure Reason.* Translated by N. K. Smith. New York: St. Martin's Press, 1965.

———. *Critique of Judgment*. Translated by W. S. Pluhar. Indianapolis: Hackett Publishing, 1987.

———. *Kritik der Urteilskraft*. Frankfurt a.M.: Suhrkamp, 1974.

———. *Prolegomena to Any Future Metaphysics*. New York: Liberal Arts Press, 1950.

Karádi, Éve, and Ersébet Vezér, eds. *Georg Lukács, Karl Mannheim und der Sonntagskreis*. Frankfurt a.M.: Sender, 1985.

Kayser, Rudolf. "Krieg und Geist." *Das Ziel. Aufrufe zu tätigem Geist* 1 (1916): 31–36.

Keller, Ernst. *Der junge Lukács: Antibürger und wesentliches Leben. Literatur- und Kulturkritik 1902–1915*. Frankfurt a.M.: Sender, 1984.

Kevles, Daniel J. *In the Name of Eugenics*. New York: Knopf, 1985.

Kierkegaard, Soren. *The Concept of Dread.* Princeton: Princeton University Press, 1970.

Kintzelé, Jeff, and Peter Schneider, eds. *Georg Simmels Philosophie des Geldes*. Frankfurt a.M.: Hain, 1993.

Kocka, Juegen. *Klassengesellschaft im Krieg: Deutsche Sozialgeschichte, 1914–1918*. Göttingen: Vanderhoeck & Ruprecht, 1978.

Köhnke, Klaus Christian. *Entstehung und Aufstieg des Neukantianismus: Die deutsche Universitätsphilosophie zwischen Idealismus und Positivismus*. Frankfurt a.M.: Suhrkamp, 1986.

———. "Georg Simmel als Jude." *Simmel Newsletter* 5, no. 1 (summer 1995): 53–72.

———. *Der junge Simmel in Theoriebeziehungen und sozialen Bewegungen*. Frankfurt a.M.: Suhrkamp, 1996.

Koonz, Claudia. *Mothers in the Fatherland: Women, the Family, and Nazi Politics*. New York: St. Martin's Press, 1981.

Körner, Stephan. *Kant*. Göttingen: Vandenhoeck & Ruprecht, 1980.

Kosian, Jozef. *Zukünftigkeit als wesentliche Seinsbeschaffenheit: Ernst Blochs Futurozentrismus.* Wroclaw: Wydawnictwo Uniwersytetu, 1992.

Kracauer, Siegfried. *Aufsätze 1915–1926*. Edited by Inka Mülder-Bach. Frankfurt a.M.: 1990.

———. "Georg Simmel." *Logos* 9 (1920–21): 307–38.

Laible, Wilhelm, ed. *Die deutschen Theologen über den Krieg*. Leipzig: Dorffling & Franke, 1915.

Landmann, Edith. "Erinnerungen an Simmel." In *Buch des Dankes an Georg Simmel: Briefe, Erinnerung, Bibliographie*. Edited by Kurt Gassen and Michael Landmann. Berlin: Duncker & Humblot, 1958.

Landmann, Michael. "Bausteine zur Biographie." In *Buch des Dankes an Georg Simmel: Briefe, Erinnerung, Bibliographie*. Edited by Kurt Gassen and Michael Landmann. Berlin: Duncker & Humblot, 1958.

———. "Ernst Bloch über Simmel." In *Ästhetik und Soziologie um die Jahrhundertwende: Georg Simmel*. Edited by H. Böhringer and K. Gründer. Frankfurt a.M.: Vittorio Klostermann, 1976.

———. "Georg Simmel und Stefan George." In *Georg Simmel und die Moderne*, pp. 147–73.

———. "Konflikt und Tragödie." *Zeitschrift für Philosophische Forschung* 6 (1951): 115–33.

Lange, Annemarie. *Das Wilhelminische Berlin. Zwischen Jahrhundertwende und Novemberrevolution*. Berlin: Dietz, 1976.

Lawrence, Peter, ed. *Georg Simmel: Sociologist and European*. New York: Barnes & Noble, 1976.

Leck, Ralph. "Conservative Empowerment and the Gender of Nazism." *Journal of Women's History* 12, no. 2 (2000) (forthcoming).

Lederer, Emil. "Zur Soziologie des Weltkrieges." *Archiv für Sozialwissenschaft und Sozialpolitik* 39(1915): 347–84.

Leonhard, Rudolf. "Das Problem der Gewalt und der bürgerlichen Pazifismus." *Das Ziel* 3 (1920): 175–78.

Lepsius, Sabine. *Ein Berliner Künstlerleben um die Jahrhundertwende*. Munich: Gotthold Müller, 1972.

———. "Erinnerungen an Georg Simmel." In Gassen and Landmann.

Lessing, Theodore. *Philosophie als Tat*. 2 vols. Göttingen: Otto Hapke Verlag, 1914.

Levine, Donald, ed. *Georg Simmel. On Individuality and Social Forms*. Chicago: University of Chicago Press, 1971.

Lichtblau, Klaus. "Eros and Culture: Gender Theory in Simmel, Tönnies and Weber." *Telos* 82 (1989): 89–110.

———. *Kulturkrise und Soziologie um die Jahrhundertwende: Zur Geneologie der Kultursoziologie in Deutschland*. Frankfurt a.M.: Suhrkamp, 1996.

Lichtheim, George. *George Lukács*. New York: Viking Press, 1970.

Liebeschütz, Hans. *Von Georg Simmel zu Franz Rosenzweig: Studien zum jüdischen Denken im deutschen Kulturbereich*. Tübingen: J.C.B. Mohr, 1970.

Lieber, Hans-Joachim. *Kulturkritik und Lebensphilosophie: Studien zur deutschen Philosophie der Jahrhundertwende*. Darmstadt: Wissenschaftliche Buchgesellschaft, 1974.

Liebersohn, Harry. *Fate and Utopia in German Sociology, 1870–1923*. Cambridge, Mass.: MIT Press, 1988.

Löwy, Michael. *Georg Lukács—From Romanticism to Bolshevism*. Translated by Patrick Camilller. London: New Left Books, 1979.

Lozinski, S. "Simmels Briefe zur jüdischen Frage." *Ästhetik und Soziologie*, pp. 24–43.

Lübbe, Hermann. *Politische Philosophie in Deutschland*. Basel: Benno & Co., 1963.

Ludwig, Emil. "Geschenke des Lebens. Ein Rückblick." In *Buch des Dankes an Georg Simmel*. Edited by Kurt Gassen and Michael Landmann. Berlin: Duncker & Humblot, 1958.

Luhman, Niklas. *Soziale Systeme*. Frankfurt a.M.: Suhrkamp, 1987.

Lukács, Georg. "Bemerkungen zur Theorie der Literaturgeschichte." *Text + Kritik* 39/40 (1973): 24–51.

———. *Georg Lukács: Briefwechsel I, 1897–1918*. Edited by Éva Fekete and Éva Karádi. Stuttgart: J.B. Metzlersche, 1982.

———. "Curriculum vitae." *Text und Kritik* 39, 40 (1973): 5–7.

———. *Entwicklungsgeschichte des modernen Dramas* [1911]. Vol. 15, *Georg Lukacs Werke*. Edited F. Benseler. Darmstadt: Luchterhand, 1981.

———. "Die deutschen Intellektuellen und der Krieg." *Text und Kritik* 39, 40 (1973): 65–69.

———. *Entwicklungsgeschichte des modernen Dramas*. Vol. 15, *Georg Lukács Werke*. Edited by Frank Benseler. Darmstadt: Luchterhand, 1981.

———. "Expressionism: Its Significance and Decline." In Lukács, *Essays on Realism*. Translated D. Fernbach. Cambridge: MIT Press, 1981.

———. *Gelebtes Denken*. Frankfurt a.M.: Suhrkamp, 1981.

———. "Georg Simmel." In *Buch des Dankes an Georg Simmel*. Edited by Kurt Gassen and Michael Landmann. Berlin: Duncker & Humblot, 1958.

———. *Heidelberger Ästhetik (1916–1918)*. Vol. 17, *Georg Lukács Werke*. Edited by György Márkus and Frank Benseler. Darmstadt: Luchterhand, 1974.

———. *Heidelberger Philosopie der Kunst (1912–1914)*. Vol. 16, *Georg Lukács Werke*. Edited by György Márkus and Frank Benseler. Darmstadt: Luchterhand, 1974.

———. *Der junge Hegel und die Probleme der kapitalistischen Gesellschaft*. Berlin: Aufbau Verlag, 1986.

———. "Mein Weg zu Marx." In *Georg Lukacs zum siebzigsten Geburtstag*. Berlin: Aufbau-Verlag, 1955.

———. *The Ontology of Social Being. Hegel*. Translated by David Feinbach. London: Merlin Press, 1978.

———. *Die Seele und die Formen: Essays*. Berlin: Egon Fleischel, 1911.

———. "Taktik und Ethik" [1919]. In *Geschichte und Klassenbewußtsein*. Vol. 2, *Georg Lukács Werke*. Neuwied: Luchterhand, 1968.

———. *Theorie des Romans* [1920]. Frankfurt a.M.: Luchterhand, 1988.

———. "Von der Armut am Geiste." *Neue Blätter* II/5–6 (1912): 67–92.

———. *Die Zerstörung der Vernunft: Der Weg des Irrationalismus von Schelling zu Hitler* [1955]. Berlin: Aufbau Verlag, 1988.

Lunn, Eugene. *Marxism and Modernism*. Berkeley: University of California Press, 1982.

———. *Prophet of Community. The Romantic Socialism of Gustav Landauer*. Berkeley: University of California Press, 1973.

Lyotard, Jean-François. *The Differend: Phrases in Dispute*. Translated by Georges Van Den Abbeele. Minneapolis: University of Minnesota Press, 1988.

Mah, Harold. *The End of Philosophy, the Origin of "Ideology": Karl Marx and the Crisis of the Young Hegelians*. Berkeley: University California Press, 1987.

Mahlmann, Regina. *Homo Duplex: Die Zweiheit des Menschen bei Georg Simmel*. Würzburg: Königshausen & Neumann, 1983.

Mann, Heinrich. "Geist und Tat. " *Das Ziel. Aufrufe zu tätigem Geist* (1916): 1–9.

Mann, Thomas. *Betrachtungen eines Unpolitischen*. Frankfurt a.M.: Fischer, 1991.

———. *Essays II: Politische Reden und Schriften*. Edited by Hermann Kurzke. Frankfurt a.M.: Fischer, 1977.

———. *Reflections of an Unpolitical Man*. Translated by Walter Morris. New York: Ungar, 1987.

Mannheim, Karl. *Wissenssoziologie*. Edited by Kurt Wolff. Berlin: Luchterhand, 1964.

———. Review of Simmel, *Der Krieg und die geistigen Entscheidungen*. In *Huszadik Század* XVIII.XXXVI (1917): 416–18. Translated from Hungarian by Izabella Fintzsch, rpt. *Simmel Newsletter* 5, no. 1 (summer 1995): 77–80.

———. "Simmel als Philosoph." In *Georg Lukács, Karl Mannheim und der Sonntagskreis*. Edited by Éve Karádi and Ersébet Vezér. Frankfurt a.M.: Sender, 1985.

Marks, Elaine, and Isabelle de Courtivron. *The New French Feminism: An Anthology*. New York: Schocken, 1981.

Marx, Karl. *Das Kapital: Kritik der politischen Ökonomie*. Berlin: Dietz, 1974.

Maurer, Charles. *Call to Revolution: The Mystical Anarchism of Gustav Landauer*. Detroit: Wayne State Press, 1971.

Mauthner, Fritz. "Georg Simmel." *Vossische Zeitung*, 18 October 1918.

Mestrovic, Stjepan. "Simmel and Durkheim as the First Sociologists of Modernity." In *The Coming Fin De Siecle: An Application of Durkheim's Sociology to Modernity and Postmodernism*. London: Routledge, 1992.

Meyer, Thomas, et al. *Lexikon des Sozialismus*. Köln: Bund, 1986.

Meyer-Renschhausen, Elizabeth. *Weibliche Kultur und soziale Arbeit: eine Geschichte der Frauenbewegung am Beispiel Bremens 1810–1927*. Cologne: Böhlau, 1989.

Michels, Robert. *Political Parties: A Sociological Study of the Oligarchical Tendencies of Modern Democracy*. Translated by Eden and Cedar Paul. New York: Free Press, 1962.

Moeller, Robert. *Protecting Motherhood: Women and the Family in the Politics of Postwar West Germany*. Berkeley: University of California Press, 1993.

Moi, Toril. *Sexual/Textual Politics: Feminist Literary Theory*. New York: Methuen, 1985.

Mommsen, Wolfgang J. "Der Geist von 1914: Das Programm eines politischen *Son-*

derwegs der Deutschen." In *Nation und Geschichte: Über die Deutschen und die deutsche Frage.* Munich: Piper, 1990, pp. 87–105.

Morris, William. *News from Nowhere*. New York: Penguin Books, 1986.

Mosse, Georg. *Germans and Jews: The Right, the Left, and the Search for a Third Force in Pre-Nazi Politics*. New York: H. Fertig, 1970.

Müller, Hoerst H. W. "Nachwort. Zielcourage in Person: Kurt Hiller." In *Leben gegen die Zeit. Eros*, pp. 177–78.

Müller, Horst. *Lebensphilosophie und Religion bei Georg Simmel*. Berlin: Duncker & Humblot, 1960.

Muller, Gerry. *The Other God that Failed: Hans Freyer and the Deradicalization of German Conservatism.* Princeton: Princeton University Press, 1987.

Müster, Arno, et al. *Verdinglichung und Utopie: Ernst Bloch und Georg Lukács zum 100. Geburtstag*. Frankfurt a.M.: Sender, 1987.

Nicholls, Roger. *Nietzsche in the Early Works of Thomas Mann*. New York: Russell & Russell, 1976.

Nietzsche, Friedrich. *The Birth of Tragedy*. Translated by Walter Kaufman. New York: Vintage, 1967.

———. *Ecco Homo*, in *The Basic Writiings of Nietzsche*. Translated and edited by Walter Kaufman. New York: Modern Library, 1968.

———. *Twilight of the Idols*. London: Penguin Books, 1990.

Oakes, Guy, ed. and trans. *Georg Simmel: On Women, Sexuality, and Love*. New Haven: Yale University Press, 1984.

———. *Weber and Rickert*. Cambridge, Mass.: MIT Press, 1988.

Osborne, John. *The Naturalist Drama in Germany*. Manchester: Manchester University Press, 1971.

Ott, Hugo. *Martin Heidegger. Unterwegs zu seiner Biographie*. Frankfurt a.M.: Reihe Campus, 1992.

Pascal, Roy. From *Naturalism to Expressionism: German Literature and Society, 1880–1918*. New York: Basic Books, 1973.

Paulsen, Wolfgang. *Deutsche Literatur des Expressionismus.* Bern: Peter Lang, 1983.

———. *Expressionismus und Aktivismus: Eine typologische Untersuchung.* Stassburg: Heinz & Co., 1935.

Pfemfert, Alexandra. "The Birth of *Die Aktion*." In Raabe, *The Era of German Expressionism*, pp. 35–37.

Pinthus, Kurt, ed. *Menschenheitsdämmerung. Symphonie jungster Dichtung.* Berlin: Rowohlt, 1920.

Plenge, Johann. *1789 und 1914: Die symbolischen Jahre in der Geschichte des politischen Geistes.* Berlin: Springer, 1916.

Poggi, Giofranco. *Money and the Modern Mind: Georg Simmel's Philosophy of Money*. Berkeley: University of California Press, 1994.

Poggioli, Renato. *The Theory of the Avant-Garde*. Translated by Gerald Fitzgerald. Cambridge, Mass.: Belknap Press, 1968.

"Politischer Rat geistiger Arbeiter." *Das Ziel* 4 (1920): 218–23.

Pressel, Wilhelm. *Die Kriegspredigt 1914–1918 in der Evangelischen Kirche Deutschlands*. Göttingen: Vandenhoeck & Ruprecht, 1967.

Preyer, David C. *The Art of the Berlin Galleries*. Boston: L.C. Page, 1912.

Przywara, Erich. *Gott.* Köln: Oratoriums Verlag, 1926.

Quartaert, Jean. *Reluctant Feminists in German Social Democracy, 1885–1917.* Princeton: Princeton University Press, 1979.

Raabe, Paul. "Das literarische Leben in Expressionismus." In *Die Zeitschriften und Sammlungen des literarisches Expressionismus 1910–1921*. Edited by Paul Raabe. Stuttgart: J.B. Metzlersche, 1964.

———. "Verzeichnis der Mitarbeiter." In reissue of *Die Aktion*. 1961.

Raabe, Paul, ed. *Die Zeitschriften und Sammlungen des literarisches Expressionismus 1910–1921*. Stuttgart: J.B. Metzlersche, 1964.

———. *Expressionismus: Der Kampf um eine literarische Bewegung*. Zürich: Arche Verlag, 1987.

Rabinbach, Anson. *In the Shadow of Catastrophe: German Intellectuals Between Apocalypse and Enlightenment.* Berkeley: Universty of California Press, 1997.

Radnoti, Sandor. "Bloch and Lukács: Two Radical Critics In a 'God-Forsaken World'," *Telos* 25 (1975): 155–64.

Rammstedt, Angela. "Getrud Kinel/Simmel–Malerin." *Simmel Newsletter* 4, no. 2 (winter 1994): 140–62.

———. "Stefan George und Georg Simmel." *Simmel Newsletter* 9, no. 1 (summer 1999): 101–103.

Rammstedt, Otthein, ed. *Georg Simmel. Gesamtausgabe*. Frankfurt a.M.: Suhrkamp,

———. *Simmel und die frühen Soziologen: Nähe und Distanz zu Kurheim, Tönnies und Max Weber*. Frankfurt a.M.: Suhrkamp, 1988.

Rantzsch, Petra. *Helene Stöcker (1869–1943): Zwischen Pazifismus und Revolution*. Berlin: Der Morgen, 1984.

Ratz, Ursula. *Sozialreform und Arbeiterschaft. Die "Gesellschaft für Sozialreform" und die sozialdemokratische Arbeiterbewegung von der Jahrhundertwende bis zum Ausbruch des Ersten Weltkrieges*. Berlin: Colloquium, 1980.

Reagin, Nancy R. *A German Women's Movement: Class and Gender in Hanover, 1880–1933.* Chapel Hill: University of North Carolina Press, 1995.

Rickert, Heinrich. *Die Philosophie des Lebens: Darstellung und Kritik, der Philosophischen Modeströmungen unserer Zeit.* Tübingen: Mohr, 1920.

Ringer, Fritz. *The Decline of the German Mandarins*. Cambridge: Harvard University Press, 1969.

Rothe, Wolfgang, ed. *Der Aktivismus 1915–1920*. Munich: Deutscher Taschenbuch Verlag, 1969.

Rubin, James Henry. *Realism and Social Vision in Courbet and Proudhon.* Princeton: Princeton University Press, 1980.

Rubiner, Ludwig. "Die Änderung der Welt." *Das Ziel. Aufrufe zu tätigem Geist* 1(1916): 99–121.

———. *Kameraden der Menscheit: Dichtungen zur Weltrevolution* [1920]. Leipzig: Reclam, 1971.

———. "Mitmensch." *Tätiger Geist! Zweites der Ziel-Jahrbücher* (1918): 344.

Rüden, Peter von. *Sozialdemokratisches Arbeitertheater (1848–1914): ein Beitrag zur Geschichte des politischen Theaters*. Frankfurt a.M.: Athenäum, 1973.

Scheible, Hartmut. "Georg Simmel und die 'Tragödie der Kultur.'" *Die Neue Rundschau* 91 (1980): 133–64.

Scheler, Max. *Der Genius des Krieges und der deutsche Krieg*. Leipzig: Weißen Bücher, 1915.

Schlenther, Paul. *Wozu der Lärm? Genesis der Freien Bühne*. Berlin: S. Fischer, 1890.

Schlösser, Manfred, ed. *Für Margarete Susman: Auf gespaltenem Pfad*. Darmstadt: Erato-Presse, 1964.

Schmidt, Burghart. *Ernst Bloch*. Stuttgart: J.B. Metzler, 1985.

Schmidt, Conrad. "Eine Philosophie des Geldes." *Sozialistische Monatshefte* 5 (1901): 180–85.

Schmitt, Carl. *Der Begriff des Politischen*. Berlin: Duncker & Humblot, 1991.

———. *The Crisis of Parliamentary Democracy*. Translated by Ellen Kennedy. Cambridge: MIT Press, 1988.

———. *Politische Romantik*. Berlin: Duncker & Humblot, 1991.

———. *Politische Theologie*. Berlin: Duncker & Humblot, 1990.

Scholem, Gershom. *Walter Benjamin: The Story of a Friendship*. Translated by Harry Zohn. Philadelphia: Jewish Publication Society of America, 1981.

Schorske, Carl. *German Social Democracy, 1905–1917: The Development of the Great Schism*. Cambridge: Harvard University Press, 1983.

Schulte-Sasse, Jochen. "Foreword." In Peter Sloterdijk, *Thinker on Stage: Nietzsche's Materialism*. Minneapolis: University of Minnesota Press, 1989.

Schwabe, Klaus. *Wissenschaft und Kriegsmoral: Die deutschen Hochschullehrer und die politischen Grundfragen des Ersten Weltkrieges*. Göttingen: Musterschmidt-Verlag, 1969.

Simmel, Georg. "Aus dem Nachgelassenen Tagebuche." In *Fragmente und Aufsätze*. Munich: Drei Masken, 1923.

———. "Anfang einer unvollendeten Selbststellung." In *Buch des Dankes an Georg Simmel: Briefe, Erinnerung, Bibliographie*. Edited by Kurt Gassen and Michael Landmann. Berlin: Duncker & Humblot, 1958.

———. "Anhang über sexuelle Aufklärung." In *Schulpädagogik*. Osterwieck: Zickfeldt, 1922.

———. *Aufsätze 1887–1890. Über sociale Differenzierung. Die Probleme der Geschichtsphilosophie (1892)*. Edited by Heinz-Jürgen Dahme. Vol. 2 of *Georg Simmel. Gesamtausgabe*. Edited by Otthein Rammstedt. Frankfurt a/M: Suhrkamp, 1989.

———. *Aufsätze und Abhandlungen 1894–1900*. Edited by Heinz-Jürgen Dahme and David Frisby. Vol. 5 of *Georg Simmel. Gesamtausgabe*. Frankfurt a/M: Suhrkamp, 1992.

———. *Aufsätze und Abhandlungen 1901–1908*. 2 Vols. Edited by R. Kramme, A. Rammstedt, and O. Rammstedt. Vol. 7 of *Georg Simmel. Gesamtausgabe*. Edited by Otthein Rammstedt. Frankfurt a/M: Suhrkamp, 1995.

———. *Aufsätze und Abhandlungen 1901–1908*. Vol. 2. Edited by A. Cavalli and V. Krech. Vol. 8 of *Georg Simmel. Gesamtausgabe*. Edited by Otthein Rammstedt. Frankfurt a.M.: Suhrkamp, 1993.

———. "Aus dem nachgelassenen Tagebuche." In *Fragmente und Aufsätze*. Munich: Drei Masken, 1923.

———. "Die Bedeutung des Geldes für das Tempo des Lebens." In *Aufsätze und Abhandlungen 1894–1900.*

———. "Die beiden Formen des Individualismus." *Das freie Wort* 1 (1902): 397–403.

———. "Briefe Georg Simmels an Stefan George und Friedrich Gundolf." In *Georg Simmel und die Moderne*. Edited by Heinz-Jürgen Dahme and Otthein Rammstedt. Frankfurt a.M.: Suhrkamp, 1984.

———. "Briefe an Susa [Margarete Susman]." In *Für Margarete Susman*. Edited by M. Schlösser. Darmstadt: Erato-Presse, 1964.

———. *Brücke und Tür: Essays des Philosophen zur Geschichte, Religion, Kunst und Gesellschaft*. Edited by Michael Landmann. Stuttgart: K. F. Koehler, 1957.

———. "Deutschlands innere Wandlung." In *Der Krieg und die geistigen Entscheidungen*. Munich: Duncker & Humblot, 1917.

———. "Einiges über die Prostitution in Gegenwart und Zukunft." In *Schriften zur Philosophie und Soziologie der Geschlechter*. Edited by Heinz-Jürgen Dahme and Klaus Christian Köhnke. Frankfurt a.M.: Suhrkamp, 1985.

———. *Einleitung in die Moralwissenschaft: Eine Kritik der ethischen Grundbegriffe*. 2 vols. Edited by K. C. Köhnke. Vols. 3 and 4 of *Georg Simmel. Gesamtausgabe*. Frankfurt a.M.: Suhrkamp, 1989, 1991.

———. "Europa und Amerika. Eine weltgeschichtliche Betrachtung." *Berliner Tageblatt*. 4 July 1915.

———. "Exkurs über die Negativität kollektiver Verhaltungsweisen." In *Soziologie*.

———. *Fragmente und Aufsätze*. Munich: Drei Masken, 1923.

———. "Der Fragmentcharacter des Lebens." *Logos* 7 (1916–17): 40.

———. "Frauenstudium an der Berliner Universität" [1899]. In *Schriften zur Philosophie und Soziologie der Geschlechter*, pp. 157–58.

———. "Friedrich Nietzsche: eine moralphilosophische Silhouette" (1896), in Simmel, *Vom Wesen der Moderne*.

———. "Der Frauenkongreß und die Sozialdemokratie." In *Schriften zur Philosophie und Soziologie der Geschlechter.* Edited by Heinz-Jürgen Dahme and K.C. Köhnke. Frankfurt a.M.: Suhrkamp, 1985.

———. "Die Gegensätze des Lebens und die Religion." In *Aufsätze und Abhandlungen 1901–1908.* Vol. 1. Frankfurt a.M.: Suhrkamp, 1995.

———. "Das Geld in der modernen Cultur." *Aufsätze und Abhandlungen 1894–1900.* Frankfurt a/M.: Suhrkamp, 1992.

———. "Geld und Nahrung." *Der Tag*. Berlin, 25 March 1915.

———. "Gerhardt Hauptmann's 'Webers.' " In *Vom Wesen der Moderne: Essays zur Philosophie und Aesthetik, 1892–93.*

———. *Goethe*. Leipzig: Klinkhardt & Biermann, 1923.

———. "Goethes Liebe." *Die Neue Generation* 12 (1916): 101–103.

———. "Die Großstädte und das Geistesleben." In *Brücke und Tor*.

———. *Grundfragen der Soziologie (Individuum und Gesellschaft)*. Berlin: G. J. Göschen'sche, 1917.

———. *Hauptprobleme der Philosophie* [1910]. Berlin: Walter de Gruyter, 1989.

———. *Das individuelle Gesetz*. Frankfurt a.M.: Suhrkamp, 1987.

———. "Individuum und Gesellschaft in Lebensanschauungen des 18. und 19.

Jahrhunderts." In *Grundfragen der Soziologie*. Berlin: G.J. Göschen'sche Verlagshandlung, 1917.

———. "Das Individuum und die Freiheit." In *Das Individuum und die Freiheit*. Frankfurt a.M.: Fischer Verlag, 1993.

———. "Ein Jubiläum der Frauenbewegung." In *Schriften zur Philosophie und Soziologie der Geschlechter*. Edited by Heinz-Jürgen Dahme and Klaus Christian Köhnke. Frankfurt a.M.: Suhrkamp, 1985.

———. *Kant und Goethe*. Leipzig: Kurt Wolff, 1916.

———. *Der Konflikt der modernen Kultur*. Munich: Duncker & Humblot, 1918.

———. *Der Krieg und die geistigen Entscheidungen*. Munich: Duncker & Humblot, 1917.

———. "L'art pour l'art." In *Zur Philosophie der Kunst*. Potsdam: Gustav Kiepenheuer, 1922.

———. "Der Militarismus und die Stellung der Frau" [1894]. In *Schriften zur Philosophie und Soziologie der Geschlechter*.

———. "Nietzsche und Kant." *Aufsätze und Abhandlungen, 1901–1908*, II.

———. "Parerga zur Socialphilosophie." In *Einleitung in die Moralwissenschaft*. Vol. 2. Edited by K. C. Köhnke. Vol. 3 of *Georg Simmel. Gesamtausgabe*. Frankfurt a.M.: Suhrkamp, 1989.

———. *Philosophie des Geldes*. Frankfurt a.M.: Suhrkamp, 1989.

———. *Philosphische Kultur: Gesammelte Essais*. Berlin: Klaus Wagenbach, 1986.

———. *The Philosophy of Money*. Translated by Tom Bottomore and David Frisby. New York: Routledge, 1990.

———. "Der platonische und der moderne Eros." In *Fragmente und Aufsätze*. Munich: Drei Masken, 1923.

———. *Die Probleme der Geschichtsphilosophie*. Leipzig: Duncker & Humblot, 1892.

———. *Die Probleme der Geschichtsphilosophie*. Leipzig: Duncker & Humblot, 1905.

———. "Psychologie der Koketterie." In *Schriften zur Philosophie und Soziologie der Geschlechter*, pp. 187–99.

———. "Das Relative und das Absolute im Geschlechter-Problem." In *Philosophische Kultur*

———. *Die Religion* [1912]. Frankfurt a.M.: Rütten & Loening, 1922.

———. *Rembrandt: Ein kunstphilosophischer Versuch*. Leipzig: Kurt Wolff, 1919.

———. "Rodins Plastik und die Geistesrichtung der Gegenwart." In *Vom Wesen der Moderne*, pp. 263–76.

———. *Schopenhauer und Nietzsche*. Hamburg: Junius, 1990.

———. *Schulpädagogik*. Osterwieck: Zickfeldt, 1922.

———. "Simmels Briefe." In *Buch des Dankes an Georg Simmel: Briefe, Erinnerung, Bibliographie*. Edited by Kurt Gassen and Michael Landmann. Berlin: Duncker & Humblot, 1958.

———. "Socialismus und Pessimismus." In *Aufsätze und Abhandlungen 1901–1908*. Vol. 1. Frankfurt a.M.: Suhrkamp, 1995.

———. *Soziologie*. Frankfurt a.M.: Suhrkamp, 1992.

———. *Schriften zur Philosophie und Soziologie der Geschlechter*. Edited Heinz-Jürgen Dahme and Klaus Christian Köhnke. Frankfurt a.M.: Suhrkamp, 1985.

———. "Stefan George. Eine Kunst Philosophische Betrachtung" [1898]. In *Vom Wesen der Moderne*.

———. "Stefan George. Eine kunstphilosophische Studie" [1901]. In *Vom Wesen der Moderne*

———. "The Stranger." In Kurt Wolff, *The Sociology of Georg Simmel*.

———. "Tendencies in German Life and Thought Since 1870." Translated by W. D. Briggs. *International Monthly* 5 (1902): 93–111, and 166–84.

———. "Tendenzen im Deutschen Leben und Denken seit 1870." In *Schopenhauer und Nietzsche*. Hamburg: Junius, 1990.

———. Review of Ferdinand Tönnies. *Der Nietzsche-Kultus: Ein Kritik*. In *Deutsche Literatur-Zeitung* 47 (1897): 1645—51.

———. *Über sociale Differenzierung*. In *Gesamtausgabe*. Vol. 2. Frankfurt a.M.: Suhrkamp,1989.

———. "Über Geiz, Verschwendung und Armut." In Rammstein, *Gesamtausgabe*. Vol. 5. Frankfurt a.M.: Suhrkamp, 1992.

———. "Über die Liebe." In *Fragmente und Aufsätze*. München: Drei Masken, 1923.

———. "Ueber den Underschied der Wahrnehmungs- und der Erfahrungsurteile." *Kantstudien* I (1897): 416–25.

———. "Über räumliche Projektionen socialer Formen." *Zeitschrift für Sozialwissenschaft* 6 (1903): 287–302.

———. "Über den Unterschied der Wahrnehmnungs- und der Erfahrungsurteile. Ein Deutungsversuch [Kants]," *Kantstudien* 1 (1897): 424–25.

———. "Die Umwertung der Werte. Ein Wort an die Wohlhabenden." *Frankfurter Zeitung*, 5 March 1915.

———. *Vom Wesen der Moderne: Essays zur Philosophie und Ästhetik*. Edited by Werner Jung. Hamburg: Junius, 1990.

———. "Was ist uns Kant?" In *Aufsätze und Abhandlungen 1894–1900*. Edited by Heinz-Jürgen Dahme and David Frisby. Vol. 5 of *Georg Simmel. Gesamtausgabe*. Frankfurt a.M.: Suhrkamp, 1992.

———. "Weibliche Kultur." In *Schriften zur Philosophie und Soziologie der Geschlechter*. Edited by Heinz-Jürgen Dahme and K. C. Köhnke. Frankfurt a.M.: Suhrkamp, 1985.

——— [H. M. pseud.]. "Weltpolitik." *Die Neue Zeit* 12 (1893): 165–70.

———. "Werde was du bist." In *Zur Philosophie der Kunst*. Potsdam: Gustav Kiepenheuer, 1922.

———. "Ein Wort über soziale Freiheit." *Sozialpolitisches Zentralblatt* 1 (1892): 334.

———. "Zum Problem des Naturalismus." In Simmel, *Fragmente und Aufsätze*.

———. *Zur Philosophie der Kunst*. Potsdam: Gustav Kiepenheuer, 1922.

———. "Zur Psychologie der Frauen." In *Schriften zur Philosophie und Soziologie der Geschlechter*. Edited by Heinz-Jürgen Dahme and K. C. Köhnke. Frankfurt a.M.: Suhrkamp, 1985.

———. "Zur Psychologie des Geldes." In *Aufsätze 1887–1890*.

———. "Zur Soziologie der Familie." In *Schriften zur Philosophie und Sociologie der Geschlechter*, pp. 119–32.

Simmel, Hans. "Auszüge aus den Lebenserinnerungen." In *Ästhetik & Soziologie um die Jahrhundertwende: Georg Simmel*. Edited by Hanns Böhringer and Karlfried Gründer. Frankfurt a.M.: Vittorio Klostermann, 1976.

Sokel, Walter. *The Writer in Extremis: Expressionism in Twentieth-Century German Literatur*. Stanford: Stanford University Press, 1959.

Sombart, Werner. *Händler und Helden: Patriotische Besinnungen*. Munich: Duncker & Humblot, 1915.

Sowerwine, Charles. "The Socialist Women's Movement from 1850–1940." In *Becoming Visible: Women in European History*. Edited by Renate Bridenthal, et. al. Boston: Houghton Mifflin, 1987, pp. 399–428.

Snyder, Louis, ed. *Documents of German History*. New Brunswick, N.J.: Rutgers University Press, 1958.

Spengler, Oswald. *Der Untergang des Abendlands* [1918]. Munich: Deutscher Taschenbuch, 1988.

———. *Preussentum und Sozialismus*. Munich: n.p., 1920.

Spykman, Nicholas. *The Social Theory of Georg Simmel*. New York: Russel & Russel, 1964.

Steakley, James D. *The Homosexual Emancipation Movement in Germany*. Salem, N.H.: Ayer Co., 1975.

Steinhoff, Maria. "Die Form als soziologische Grundkategorie bei Georg Simmel." *Kölner Vierteljahrshefte für Soziologie* 3 (1923): 215–59.

Stöcker, Helene. "Frauengedanken." In *Die Liebe und die Frauen*. Minden: Bruns' Verlag, 1906.

———. *Die Liebe und die Frauen*. Minden: Bruns' Verlag, 1906.

———. *Lieben oder Hassen. Kriegshefte des Bundes der Mutterschutz*. Berlin: Oesterheld, 1914.

———. *Menschlichkeit. Kriegshefte des Bundes der Mutterschutz*. Berlin: Oesterheld, 1916.

———. "Militarisierung der Jugend und Mütterlichkeit." *Tätiger Geist! Zweites der Ziel-Jahrbücher* 1 (1918): 150–66.

———. "Moderne Bevölkerungspolitik." *Die Neue Generation* 12 (1916): 79.

———. "Die moderne Frau." In *Die Liebe und die Frauen*. Minden: Bruns' Verlag, 1906.

———. "Mutterschaft und geistge Arbeit." In *Die Liebe und die Frauen*. Minden: Bruns' Verlag, 1906.

———. "Die Neue Mutter." In *Die Liebe und die Frauen*. Minden: Bruns' Verlag, 1906.

———. "Das Recht über sich selbst." *Der Neue Generation* 4 (1908): 270–73.

Stoehr, Irene. "'Organisierte Mütterlichkeit.' Zur Politik der deutschen Frauenbewegung um 1900." In *Frauen suchen ihre Geschichte: Historische Studien zum 19. und 20. Jahrhundert*. Edited by Karin Hausen. Munich: Beck, 1983, pp. 221–49.

Stromberg, Roland. *Redemption by War: Intellectuals and 1914*. Lawrence: Kansas University Press, 1982.

Susman, Margarete. "Erinnerung an Simmel." In *Buch des Dankes*, pp. 278–91.

———. *Die Geistige Gestalt Georg Simmels.* Tübingen: J. C. B. Mohr, 1959.

———. *Ich habe viele Leben gelebt. Erinnerungen.* Stuttgart: Deutsche Verlags-Anstalt, 1958.

———. *Das Nah- und Fernsein des Fremden.* Edited by Ingeborg Nordmann. Frankfurt a.M.: Jüdischer Verlag, 1992.

———. "Pole jüdischen Wesens—Hermann Cohen und Georg Simmel." *Die Tat* 15 (1923–24): 385–89.

Thomas, H. Hinton. *Nietzsche in German Politics and Society 1890–1918.* La Salle, Ill.: Open Court, 1983.

Thompson, E. P. *William Morris: Romantic to Revolutionary.* New York: Pantheon, 1976.

Thönnessen, Werner. *The Emanicpation of Women: The Rise and Decline of the Women's Movement in German Social Democracy 1863–1933.* Translated by Joris de Bres. London: Pluto Press, 1973.

Tönnies, Ferdinand. *Fundamental Concepts of Sociology (Gemeinschaft und Gesellschaft).* Translated by C. Loomis. New York: American Book Co., 1940.

———. *Gemeinschaft und Gesellschaft.* Leipzig: n.p., 1887.

———. *Die Nietzsche-Kultur: Ein Kritik.* Edited by Günther Rudolph. Berlin: Akademie-Verlag, 1990.

———. "Simmel as Sociologist." In *Georg Simmel.* Edited by Lewis Coser. Englewood Cliffs, N.J.: Prentice Hall, 1965, pp. 50–52.

Troeltsch, Ernst. *Der Historismus und seine Probleme.* Tübingen: J.C.B. Mohr, 1922.

———. "Die Ideen von 1914." In *Deutsche Geist und Westeuropa.* Tübingen: Mohr Verlag, 1925.

Über Ernst Bloch. Frankfurt a.M.: Suhrkamp, 1968.

Unseld, Siegfried, ed. *Ernst Bloch zu ehren.* Frankfurt a.M.: Suhrkamp, 1965.

Vondung, Klaus. *Die Apokalypse in Deutschland.* Munich: Deutscher Taschenbuch, 1988.

———. "Deutsche Apokalypse 1914." In *Die Wilhelminische Bildungsbürgertum.* Edited by Klaus Vondung. Göttingen: Vandenhoeck & Ruprecht, 1976, pp. 153–71.

Vromen, Suzanne. "Georg Simmel and the Cultural Dilemma of Women." *History of European Ideas* 8, nos. 4, 5 (1987): 563–79.

Watier, Patrick. "The War Writings of Georg Simmel." In *Theory, Culture, and Society* 8 (1991): 219–33.

Weber, Marianne. "Beruf und Ehe" [1905]. In *Frauenfrage und Frauengedanken,* pp. 20–37.

———. "Die Frau und die objektive Kultur" [1913]. In *Frauenfrage,* pp. 95–133.

———. *Frauenfrage und Frauengedanken: Gesammelte Aufsätze.* Tübingen: J.C.B. Mohr, 1919.

———. *Lebenserinnerungen.* Bremen: Strom Verlag, 1948.

Weber, Max. *Der Sozialismus.* Munich: Dunker & Humblot, 1918.

———. *Politik als Beruf.* Munich: Dunker & Humblot, 1919.

———. *Wissenschaft als Beruf.* Munich: Dunker & Humblot, 1919.

Weingartner, Rudolf. *Experience and Culture: The Philosophy of Georg Simmel.* Middletown Conn.: Wesleyan Press, 1962.

———. "Form and Content in Simmel's Philosophy of Life." In *Georg Simmel, 1858–1918*. Edited by Kurt Wolff. Columbus: Ohio State University Press, 1959.

White, Hayden. *Metahistory: The Historical Imagination in Nineteenth-Century Europe*. Baltimore: Johns Hopkins University Press, 1973.

Wickert, Christl. *Helene Stöcker 1869–1943: Frauenrechtlerin, Sexualreformerin und Pazifistin*. Bonn: Dietz, 1991.

Winter, Jay. *Sites of Memory, Sites of Mourning: The Great War in European Cultural History*. New York: Cambridge University Press, 1995.

Windelband, Wilhelm. "Die Erinnerung des Hegelianismus." *Sitzungsberichte der Heidelberg Akademie der Wissenschaften* 14 (1910): 1–24.

———. "Über Begriff und Geschichte der Philosophie." *Präludien* (1884): 29.

———. "Über Sinn und Wert des Phänomenalismus." *Sitzungsberichte der Heidelberg Akademie der Wissenschaften* 9 (1912): 1–26.

Wolff, Kurt H, trans. and ed. *The Sociology of Georg Simmel*. New York: The Free Press, 1964.

Wurgaft, Lewis. *The Activists: Kurt Hiller and the Politics of Action on the Left 1914–1933*. Philadelphia: The American Philosophical Society, 1977.

Wylie, Thomas. *Back to Kant*. Detroit: Wayne State University Press, 1978.

Wyneken, Gustav. *Eros*. Lauenburg: Adolf Saal, 1921.

———. *Der Europäische Geist*. Leipzig: Neue Geist, 1926.

———. "Jugendliche Erotik." *Die Neue Generation* 12 (1916): 191–98.

———. *Die Neue Jugend: Ihr Kampf um Freiheit und Wahrheit in Schule und Elternhaus in Religion und Erotik*. Munich: Georg Steinicke, 1919.

———. *Revolution und Schule*. Leipzig: Dr. Werner Klinkhardt, 1918.

———. "Schöferische Erziehung." *Das Ziel. Aufrufe zu tätigem Geist* I (1916): 121–34.

Young, Werner. *Wandlungen einer ästhetischen Theorie–Georg Lukács Werke 1907 bis 1923*. Cologne: Pahl-Rugenstein, 1981.

Zöckler, Christopher. *Dilthey und die Hermeneutik*. Stuttgart: J.B. Metzler, 1975.

Zudeick, Peter. *Der Hintern des Teufels: Ernst Bloch—Leben und Werk*. Moos: Elster Verlag, 1985.

Zweig, Stefan. "Das neue Pathos." *Das literarische Echo* 11 (1909): 1701–1709.

———. *The World of Yesterday*. Lincoln: University of Nebraska Press, 1964.

INDEX